<u>**MADRAS DISTRICT GAZETTEERS**</u>

GODAVARI DISTRICT GAZETTEER

MADRAS DISTRICT GAZETTEERS

GODAVARI
DISTRICT GAZETTEER

F. R. HEMINGWAY

IN TWO VOLUMES

VOL. I

ISBN : 978-93-5324-407-1 (Set)

ISBN : 978-93-5324-408-8 (HB)

First Published, Madras, 1915

Published, 2020

Published by

Facsimile Publisher
12 Pragati Market
Ashok Vihar, Ph-2
Delhi-110052
E-mail: books@facsimilepublisher.com

Printed at: G. Print Process, Delhi.

Godavari District Gazetteer

Author: F. R. HEMINGWAY

MADRAS DISTRICT GAZETTEERS.

GÓDÁVARI.

VOLUME I.

[PRICE, 2 *rupees.*] [3 *shillings.*]

MADRAS DISTRICT GAZETTEERS

GÓDÁVARI

BY

F. R. HEMINGWAY,

INDIAN CIVIL SERVICE,

MADRAS:

REPRINTED BY THE SUPERINTENDENT, GOVERNMENT PRESS.

1915.

PREFACE.

THIS Gazetteer has been prepared on the plan prescribed by Government according to which statistics have been relegated as far as possible to a separate Appendix which is to be revised decennially. The original 'District Manual' was written by Mr. H. Morris of the Madras Civil Service in 1878.

I have gratefully to return thanks for help from many quarters. The account of the early history has been almost entirely based on information supplied by Rai Bahádur V. Venkayya, M.A., the Government Epigraphist, whose kindness in reading and correcting my drafts and answering my questions I cannot too warmly acknowledge. The District officials have all given me their ready and cordial assistance, and so have many non-official residents of the district. I wish particularly to express my obligations to the Revs. J. H. Harper, J. Cain and A. Gangloff, to Messrs. E. B. Elwin, I.C.S., H. Laflamme, C. Mildred, G. F. F. Foulkes, M. G. K. Waite, J. F. Marshall, M. Woodhouse, W. J. M. Inkster, L. D. Buchanan, H. J. Allen, F. Armitage, A. C. Pranatartihara Aiyar, R. Venkata Rao and V. Parthasaradhi Chetti and to Capt. M. N. Chaudhuri, I.M.S. All these gentlemen have helped me with the records at their disposal or with their personal experience; and they have supplied a large portion of the material found in this Gazetteer. I have also to thank Mr. J. A. Cumming, I.C.S., for reading through the proofs and for many valuable suggestions.

F. R. H.

PLAN OF CONTENTS.

TABLE OF CONTENTS.

CHAPTER I.

PHYSICAL DESCRIPTION.

PAGE

CHAPTER II.

POLITICAL HISTORY.

CHAPTER III.

THE PEOPLE.

CHAPTER IV.

AGRICULTURE AND IRRIGATION.

CHAPTER V.

FORESTS.

CHAPTER VI.

OCCUPATIONS AND TRADE.

CHAPTER VII.

MEANS OF COMMUNICATION.

CHAPTER VIII.

RAINFALL AND SEASONS

CHAPTER IX.

PUBLIC HEALTH.

CHAPTER X.

EDUCATION.

CHAPTER XI.

LAND REVENUE ADMINISTRATION.

CHAPTER XII.

SALT, ABKÁRI AND MISCELLANEOUS REVENUE.

CHAPTER XIII.

ADMINISTRATION OF JUSTICE.

CHAPTER XIV.

LOCAL SELF-GOVERNMENT.

CHAPTER XV.

GAZETTEER.

GAZETTEER

OF THE

GÓDÁVARI DISTRICT.

CHAPTER I.

PHYSICAL DESCRIPTION.

GENERAL DESCRIPTION—Chief towns—Etymology of the name—Natural divisions. HILLS—The Gháts. RIVERS—The Gódávari—Its sanctity—Its islands and encroachments—The season of its floods—Its tributaries—The Yeléru. SOILS. GEOLOGY—Physical changes now in progress. MINERALS—Coal—The Gauridévipéta field—Bedadanúru—Gold—Iron—Graphite—Mica - Building stone—Rock-crystals, garnets, sapphires. CLIMATE—Rainfall—Temperature—Wind and weather. FLORA. FAUNA—Cattle—Buffaloes—Sheep and goats—Cattle-breeding—Feeding methods—Cattle diseases—Cattle fairs—Game—Fish—Native sportsmen.

CHAP. I.
GENERAL DESCRIPTION.

THE Gódávari district lies on the north-east coast of the Madras Presidency. It has an area of 5,634 square miles and extends from 16° 20′ to 18° 4′ N. and from 80° 52′ to 82° 36′ E. It is bounded on the north-east by Vizagapatam, on the north by the same district and the Bastar State of the Central Provinces, and on the west and south-west by the Gódávari river, which separates it from the Nizam's Dominions and Kistna. The district, however, extends across this river at one point to include the Pólavaram division. Gódávari is roughly triangular in shape, its base being formed by the line of the coast from the western mouth of the Gódávari river to the Vizagapatam border, one side by the Gódávari river itself, and the other by the irregular frontier of Vizagapatam and the Central Provinces.

The district is made up of ten taluks and two deputy tahsildars' divisions; namely, the taluks of Nagaram,[1] Amalápuram, Rámachandrapuram and Cocanada, which make up the fertile delta of the Gódávari river; the upland taluks of

[1] Nagaram taluk is also commonly known as the Tátipáka *síma* ('country') from the village of that name within it, and Amalápuram taluk as the *Kóna síma* ('the end country').

CHAP. I. GENERAL DESCRIPTION.

Rajahmundry and Peddápuram;[1] the hilly divisions of Yellavaram, Chódavaram and Pólavaram; the taluk of Bhadráchalam beyond the Eastern Ghâts; and the two zamindari deputy tahsildars' divisions of Pithápuram and Tuni in the north-eastern corner of the district, the former of which resembles in character the upland taluks and the latter the three hilly divisions. Statistical particulars of each of these areas will be found in the separate Appendix to this volume, and some account of each and of its chief towns and villages is given in Chapter XV below. Yellavaram, Chódavaram, Pólavaram and Bhadráchalam are tracts covered with hill and jungle and inhabited by uncivilized tribes to whom it is inexpedient to apply the whole of the ordinary law of the land. Under the Scheduled Districts Act of 1874, these have been formed (see p. 190) into an Agency in which civil justice is administered under special rules and the Collector has special powers in his capacity of 'Government Agent.' They are consequently always known as 'the Agency' or 'the Agency tracts.'

Chief towns.

The capital of the district is the busy seaport and municipality of Cocanada, and with the exception of Nagaram taluk and Yellavaram division, the head-quarters of the various taluks and divisions are the towns or villages from which they are named. The head-quarters of Nagaram taluk is Rájavólu (Rázóle); and of Yellavaram, Addatígela. Besides the tahsildars' stations, both Samalkot in the Cocanada taluk and Dowlaishweram near Rajahmundry are towns of importance and interest.

Many places in the delta, such as Coringa, Georgepet, Nílapalli, and Injaram in the Cocanada taluk and Bendamúrlanka in Amalápuram, were notable ports or settlements of the East India Company at the beginning of the nineteenth century. All these have now sunk into insignificance. The little village of Chandurti in the Pithápuram division has given its name, under the distorted form of Condore,[2] to the decisive battle by which the sovereignty of the whole of the Northern Circars was wrested by the British from the French. Yanam in the Cocanada taluk is one of the few French settlements in India.

Etymology of the name.

Gódávari takes its name from the great river which forms its western boundary and the delta of which is its richest and most fertile portion. Rai Bahádur V. Venkayya, M.A., the

[1] The parts of Cocanada and Peddápuram taluks and of the Pithápuram division which are watered by the Yeléru river are often spoken of as Porlunádu. *Cf.* Chapter XV, p. 221.

[2] See below Chapter II, p. 31 and Chapter XV, p. 227.

Government Epigraphist, considers that the word means literally either 'streams giving water' (sometimes in old writings abbreviated to Gódá or 'giving water') or 'streams giving kine.' Another Sanskrit authority[1] interprets the word in a somewhat similar way as meaning 'the best *(vari)* [of those that] give water'; and adds the alternative 'the chief [of those that] give heaven' with reference to the sanctifying power of the river. The local and popular etymology of the name says that it means 'the expiation for killing a cow,' and a well-known story relates how the rishi Gautama brought the Gódávari to the district to expiate the sin of having killed a cow in a moment of anger. Kovvúr in Yernagúdem taluk, Kistna district, the name of which is said to mean 'the village of the cow,' is pointed out as the place where the cow was slain and the water was first made to flow.

Natural divisions.

The district consists of four very dissimilar natural divisions; namely (beginning in the north-west), the undulating taluk of Bhadráchalam above the Eastern Gháts; the hilly agency divisions which really form a part of that range; the upland taluks which divide the agency hills from the low lands of the delta; and the delta of the Gódávari itself.

The delta presents a vast expanse of rice fields dotted with gardens of plantains, betel and cocoanut and with innumerable palmyras; the uplands form a gently undulating and fairly wooded plain; the Agency consists of broken, forest-clad hills; and the Bhadráchalam taluk above the gháts resembles the uplands except that its undulations are sharper and its woods much more dense. It is broken up by the clusters of the Bodugúdem and Rékapalle hills, which are not unlike the gháts themselves.

HILLS.

The Gháts.

The only hills in the district are the Eastern Gháts, which rise by gentle gradations from the level of the coast. The scenery of these mountains, particularly in the neighbourhood of the Gódávari river, is exceedingly picturesque. Their sides are clothed with luxuriant forests, interspersed with bamboo and a thick undergrowth of forest shrubs. Their highest point is Dumkonda, 4,478 feet, and another prominent peak stands to the south of the fine gorge through which the Gódávari passes them, and is called Pápikonda or Bison Hill. A hill in the range which runs from that peak across the river into the Pólavaram division is locally known as Bíraiya Konda, and is regarded as the haunt of a demon called Bíraiya who is worshipped by the native navigators of the Gódávari.[2]

[1] The *Sabdakalpadruma* by Sir Rájah Rádha Kántha Déva (Calcutta, 1886).

[2] See below p. 5.

CHAP. I.
RIVERS.

The Gódávari.

Among the great rivers of India the Gódávari takes rank next after the Ganges and Indus. It runs nearly across the peninsula, its course is 900 miles long, and it receives the drainage from 115,000 square miles, an area greater than that of England and Scotland combined. Its maximum discharge is calculated to be one and a half million cubic feet per second, more than 200 times that of the Thames at Staines and about three times that of the Nile at Cairo.[1]

It rises at Trimbak, a village about seventy miles north-east of Bombay and only fifty miles from the Arabian Sea. The place traditionally regarded as the source of the river is a reservoir on a hill behind the village. This is approached by a flight of 690 stone steps, and the water trickles into it drop by drop from the lips of a carven image, shrouded by a canopy of stone.[2] From thence the river flows in a south-easterly direction until, after it has completed a course of 650 miles, it receives from the north at Siróncha the waters of the Wardha, the Painganga and the Wainganga united in the single noble stream of the Pránhíta. From this point the river has some 200 miles to run to the Bay of Bengal. It is soon joined by the Indrávati, also from the north, and before long skirts the Bhadráchalam taluk of this district. A few miles below the Bhadráchalam border is the Dummagúdem anicut, almost the sole relic of the great scheme conceived by Sir Arthur Cotton (see p. 80) for the navigation of the upper waters of the river. Next the beautiful Saveri (or Sabari) flows in from the north, skirting the edge of the forest-clad Rékapalle hills. From there the Eastern Gháts come into view, some 2,500 feet in average height, bounding the whole horizon and towering above the lesser and detached hills that flank the river.

The Gódávari has by this time assumed imposing proportions, being generally a mile, and sometimes two and a half miles, broad. After its junction with the Saveri, however, its bed is suddenly contracted by spurs of the gháts till at length it forces a passage between them, penetrating by an almost precipitous gorge to the very heart of the range. The scenery of this gorge is famous for its beauty. The steep wooded slopes of the mountains which overhang it approach at one place to within 200 yards of each other; and they constantly recede and advance and form a succession of beautiful little lakes from which there is apparently no outlet. Here and there a faint line of smoke indicates the

[1] *The Engineering Works of the Gódávari Delta*, by Mr. G. T. Walch (Madras, 1896), p. 1.

[2] Hunter's *Imperial Gazetteer*.

existence of a Kóya or Reddi village, but the hills are very sparsely inhabited.

In flood time the water flows with terrific force. 'Through the gorge,' writes Dr. King, 'the pent-up waters tear their way with, I have been told, a surface so strangely concave on the cross section that adventurous boatmen glide along the bottom of a trough whose sides rise up to a good height and hide away the immediate banks; and out of this gorge away towards the open country of the Gódávari district the river has such a fall that the sensation produced on the mind of the traveller is said to be that of sliding down an inclined plane.'[1] Native boatmen are much afraid of navigating the river at such times; and none of them, of whatever creed, omit to break a number of cocoanuts at the mouth of the gorge to appease the dangerous demon Bíraiya already mentioned, who will dash on a rock or drown in a whirlpool the navigator who omits this homage. So great is the action of the stream during floods that the rocky bed has been scoured out to depths popularly supposed to be unfathomable, but which really vary normally from 100 to nearly 200 feet. High floods rise quite 50 feet above the normal level, so that the gorge then encloses a torrent of waters from 150 to 250 feet in depth.[2]

After passing this point and entering the open country, the river widens out and flows by the old zamindari strongholds of Pólavaram and Gútála and the picturesque and sacred islands of Mahánandísvaram and Pattisam.[3] At Rajahmundry it is nearly two miles wide, and some five miles further down, at Dowlaishweram, at the head of the delta, it is crossed by the celebrated anicut which renders its waters at last available for irrigation. At this point the river is nearly four miles broad, though about a third of this width is taken up by three islands, and the spot is more fully described in Chapter IV. At Dowlaishweram the Gódávari divides into two main streams--the eastern or Gautami Gódávari flowing past Injaram, the little French settlement of Yanam, and Nílapalli, and entering the sea near Point Gódávari, and the western or Vasishta Gódávari flowing nearly due south and entering the sea at Point Narasapur. A few miles above this latter mouth another large branch, the Vainatéyam, breaks off to the east of the Vasishta Gódávari (forming the island of Nagaram between itself and the latter river) and reaches the

[1] *Memoirs*, Geol. Surv., India, xviii, pt. 3, 5.

[2] Mr. G. T. Walch in *The Engineering Works of the Gódávari Delta* (Madras, 1896), p. 1.

[3] See Chapter XV, p. 279.

CHAP. I. RIVERS.

sea near Bendamúrlanka. The three factories of the old East India Company at Injaram, Bendamúrlanka and Madapollam were situated near these three principal mouths of the Gódávari. Part of Madapollam village has been swept away by the river.

Its sanctity.

Seven traditional mouths are recognized as sacred by Hindus. The holy waters of the Gódávari are said to have been brought from the head of Siva[1] by the saint Gautama, and the seven branches by which it is traditionally supposed to have reached the sea are said to have been made by seven great *rishis*. The mouths of these are considered especially holy, and to bathe in the sea at any one of them is considered an act of great religious efficacy. It is customary for the pious (especially childless persons desirous of offspring) to make a pilgrimage to each in turn and bathe there, thus performing the *sapta-ságara-yátrá* or 'pilgrimage of the seven confluences.' The Vainatéyam is not one of these traditional mouths, but is supposed to have been created afterwards by a rishi of that name who stole a part of the Vasishta for the purpose.[2] The traditional seven are the Kasyapa or Tulya (the Tulya Bhága drain), the Atri (the Coringa river), the Gautami, the Bháradvája, the Visvámitra or Kausika, the Jamadagni and the Vasishta. The Bháradvája, Visvámitra and Jamadagni no longer exist; but pilgrims bathe in the sea at the spots where they are supposed to have been.[3] Several other sacred bathing-places in the delta are noticed in Chapter XV. The most important of them is Kótipalli in the Rámachandrapuram taluk. But a bath in the river anywhere along its course has great sanctifying virtue. Every thirteenth year this virtue is supposed to be much increased, and the *pushkaram* festival which then takes place is performed all along the stream in recognition of the fact.

Its islands and encroachments.

Several islands of a permanent character stand in various parts of the Gódávari; but the river constantly forms new temporary islands and modifies old ones. Islands liable to these changes are called *lankas*. They are rendered extraordinarily fertile by the silt deposited upon them by the river, and the rich tobacco grown on them is known as *lanka* tobacco. Other physical changes are produced by the force of the stream. Its encroachments upon the banks are noticeable in

[1] Another account says they were brought from the Ganges. The Gódávari is frequently spoken of by the name of the Ganges in ancient writings.

[2] See Chapter XV, p. 202.

[3] The traditional Bháradvája mouth is located at Tírtálamondi, a hamlet of Guttinádévi, and the Kausika mouth in Rámésvaram, a hamlet of Sámantakurru, both in the Amalápuram taluk.

more than one place. At Tállapúdi above Rajahmundry it presses hard against the right bank, which is in many places cut down precipitously by the action of the stream, and Tállapúdi and other villages, which used to be some distance from the river, now stand on its bank. In 1679 the encroachments of the river at Narasapur on the Vasishta Gódávari forced many of the English merchants to leave their houses.[1]

The season of its floods.

The greater portion of the area drained by the Gódávari receives more rain in the south-west than in the north-east monsoon, and it is during the former, therefore, that the river brings down most water. It begins to rise at Dowlaishweram some ten days after the south-west rains set in at Bombay—usually about the middle of June—and it is almost always high till October. The season for floods is then over; but during the next two months or so occasional freshes are caused by the north-east monsoon rains. When these have ceased the river gets lower and lower, till about the middle of May (its lowest stage) its discharge is at times as little as 1,500 cubic feet per second.

The navigation on the river and on the delta canals is referred to in Chapter VII.

Its tributaries.

Two tributaries of the Gódávari flow through this district. The Saveri rises in the hills in the Vizagapatam Agency, and afterwards runs in a south-westerly course, forming for some distance the boundary between that tract and the Bastar State. It receives several tributaries on the way, and, at the point where Bastar, Vizagapatam and Gódávari meet, is joined by the Siléru river from the hills of Jeypore. The latter forms for many miles the boundary between the Rampa country of this district and the Jeypore zamindari. The united waters of these two rivers are much used for floating timber from the Rékapalle hills, which are enclosed between the Saveri and the Gódávari.

The Yeléru.

One or two insignificant streams run down from the north into the Gódávari, and from the Tuni hills into the sea; but the only other noteworthy river in the district is the Yeléru. This is formed by the union of three streams which take their rise in the hills of Rampa, Golgonda and Jaddangi respectively and unite a little to the north-east of Yellavaram. It flows through Peddápuram taluk to a point a little above Víravaram, where it again separates into several streams. The westernmost of these continues its course, still under the name of the parent stream, along the boundary of Pithápuram division into Cocanada taluk; passes under the Samalkot canal, which

[1] Journal of the tour of the Agent of Fort St. George to Madapollam in 1679.

CHAP. I. RIVERS.

crosses it by an aqueduct near that town, and finally drops into the Bikkavólu drain and the Cocanada tidal creek, and so into the Cocanada bay. Meanwhile the two other branches have both flowed into the Pithápuram division, where, united again under the name of the Górikanadi, they distribute their waters to numerous works of irrigation, and finally reach the sea near Uppáda.

SOILS.

The following table gives the clsssification of the soils in the Government land in the district excluding the taluk of Bhadráchalam, which has not yet been settled by the Madras Government:—

Taluk or division.	Total area (in sq. miles).	Area classified (in sq. miles).	Percentage of area classified which is				
			Alluvial.	Permanently improved.	Black regar.	Red ferruginous.	Arenaceous.
Plains.							
Amalápuram	506	235	86·78	...	...	...	13·22
Cocanada	294	84	86·45	...	5·93	7·41	0·21
Nagaram	137	120	60·64	...	...	...	39·36
Peddápuram	504	203	6·19	0·21	11·53	82·07	...
Rajahmundry	350	230	0·20	0·23	28·36	71·21	...
Rámachandrapuram ...	296	194	91·08	0·02	0·22	8·68	...
Total, Plains ...	2,087	1,066	50·56	0·09	8·82	33·17	7·36
Agency (excluding Bhadráchalam).							
Chódavaram	715	2	...	...	...	100·00	...
Pólavaram	564	67	...	...	0·19	99·81	...
Yellavaram	950	25	...	...	4·33	95·67	...
Total, Agency ...	2,229	94	...	...	1·26	98·74	...
Grand total ...	4,316	1,160	46·48	0·09	8·21	38·46	6·76

It will be seen that the delta taluks are mainly covered with alluvial soil, though there are sandy areas along their coasts, while the uplands are chiefly made up of red ferruginous earths varied by small areas of the black regar.

GEOLOGY.

The ultimate foundation of the country above the gháts,[1] as of most of peninsular India, is gneiss. Various other kinds of rock of less but varying antiquity have been superimposed upon different parts of the district. The gneiss is usually

[1] The geological formation of the country above the gháts is described in some detail by Dr. W King in the *Memoirs* of the Geological Survey of India, xviii, pt. 3, and that of the area below the hills in *Memoirs*, xvi, pt. 3.

uppermost throughout Bhadráchalam, Chódavaram and the eastern portion of Pólavaram, and, in the form of what is called Bezwáda gneiss, throughout Yellavaram and much of Tuni as well as in the north of Rajahmundry and Peddápuram taluks.

After the gneiss, the next most ancient formation is three groups of the Lower Gondwána rocks. The Tálchir group is found in very small and scattered tracts in the Nizam's Dominions and also near Dummagúdem, between Dummagúdem and Bhadráchalam, and between Bhadráchalam and Rékapalle; the Kámthi group stretches all along the river on the Hyderabad side, but only reaches into this district at the south-western corner of the Pólavaram division; and the Barákar group occurs in small and scattered areas in two places in the district, namely Bedadanúru in the south-west corner of Pólavaram, and Gauridévipéta sixteen miles down the river from Bhadráchalam. This group is of particular interest, because coal is found in it.[1]

Among still more recent geological formations, a few small outcrops of the older Tirupati sandstones occur between the gneiss and the alluvium of Peddápuram and Tuni. A broad belt of the Cuddalore sandstone also stretches, like an island in the middle of the alluvium, from Rajahmundry to Samalkot with a narrow strip of Deccan trap and some isolated patches of gneiss on its north-western edge. The whole of the rest of the district is formed of fluviatile alluvium. This occupies nearly the whole of the delta, and above the gháts stretches in some places a long way from the river on either side.

Physical changes now in progress.

At some remote period the great plain which is now covered with alluvial soils must have been occupied by the sea, the sandstone 'island' between Rajahmundry and Samalkot must have been an island in fact, and the salt water must have stretched to the edge of the northern hills. This plain was gradually raised above tidal level by the deltaic deposits of the Gódávari and the minor streams in the north-east of the district, and the process still continues. It is particularly noticeable in the constant extension of the shore round Point Gódávari and the gradual silting up of Coringa bay. In Pliny's time the village of Coringa, now miles inland, stood apparently upon a cape, and even within the memory of man great changes have taken place. The map of 1842 had to be much modified in 1891 and already needs further alteration. A spit of land is extending to the north from the old Point Gódávari at an estimated rate of one

[1] See below p. 10.

CHAP. I. GEOLOGY. mile in 20 years and is gradually enclosing the Coringa bay; and the anchorage in the bay is said to be shallowing at the rate of a foot every ten years. But a compensating process of erosion is taking place elsewhere. At Uppáda on the Pithápuram coast the land has been much encroached upon by the sea. Since 1900 over fifty yards have been swept away and the process must have been going on for many years. A ruin about half a mile out at sea still catches the fishermen's nets, and children hunt the beach at spring tides for coins which are occasionally washed up from what must be a submerged town.

MINERALS. Coal. As above remarked, there are two places in the district where the coal-bearing Barákar strata are found, viz., near Bedadanúru in Pólavaram division, and at Gauridévipéta in the Bhadráchalam taluk.

The Gauridévipéta field. The Gauridévipéta field was first reported on in 1871 by Mr. W. T. Blanford, who summarized the position as follows:[1] 'Just below Bhadráchalam the Gódávari traverses a small field of Barákar rocks about seven miles across from east to west and five miles, where broadest, from north to south. The whole area is about 24 square miles, the greater portion of which lies on the right bank of the river in the Nizam's territory. The portion of this field on the north (left) bank of the river has been thoroughly explored by boring and some coal has been found, but the quality is altogether inferior and the quantity small, the seams being thin and much mixed with shale.' An attempt to work this field was made by the Gódávari Coal Company, Limited, in 1891. The operations were not successful, as coal was not found in paying quantities, and soon after the commencement of the work a fault was encountered which made it impossible to recover the seam. The seam, moreover, was of poor quality and contained a quantity of shale.[2] It is thought possible that better and more plentiful supplies might be found on the southern bank of the river.

Bedadanúru. The Bedadanúru field[3] is the most southerly outcrop of Barákar rocks known in the Madras Presidency. It was once hoped that good coal would be found there, and extensive borings were undertaken under the superintendence of the Executive Engineer at Dummagúdem in 1874; but these resulted only in the discovery of some thin seams of very poor coaly shales, and the exploration was abandoned. The field

[1] *Records*, Geol. Surv., India, iv, 59 foll.

[2] Information kindly supplied by Messrs. Binny & Co., Madras, the agents of the Company.

[3] See *Memoirs*, Geol. Surv., India, xviii, pt. 3, 29, 45.

is about five and a quarter square miles in extent and is situated near the head waters of a large feeder of the Yerra Kálwa with the small village of Bedadanúru in its midst. Further prospecting was undertaken about six years ago. Some eight square miles near the village were thoroughly explored by borings, but the only discovery was a one-inch seam.

Gold.

The existence of gold in the bed of the Gódávari is mentioned in several works published about the beginning of the last century. The *Gazetteer* of the Central Provinces[1] says that the metal used to be washed at the point where the Kinarsáni river falls into the Gódávari just below Bhadráchalam. Local enquiries at Bhadráchalam vaguely substantiate the former existence of the industry there.

Iron.

Iron is smelted from scattered ore in several villages in the Bhadráchalam taluk.

Graphite.

Graphite or plumbago is distributed in small quantities among the gneissic rocks in the north-west of the district, notably near Velagapalli and Yerrametla in the Chódavaram division and at Gullapúdi in Pólavaram. The South Indian Export Company has been prospecting recently at the last-named place. The Gódávari Coal Company possesses a graphite mine at Pedakonda in Bhadráchalam taluk, and has prospected for the mineral in several parts of the surrounding country. Outcrops are said to be plentiful and the samples obtained to be of fair quality but not so good as those from Ceylon. A good average quality fetches from £13 to £15 per ton in the London market at present.[2]

Mica.

Mica is said to exist in parts of the Agency and is being prospected for near Pólavaram by the South Indian Export Company.

Building stone.

Good building stone is obtained from the different sandstone and trap groups in the alluvial plains of the Gódávari. A locality particularly mentioned by Dr. King is Peddápuram. A little cutstone is also obtained in the Chódavaram division.

Rock crystals, garnets, sapphires.

Very pure rock-crystal, inferior garnets and some sapphires occur in the neighbourhood of Bhadráchalam. The crystals are kept as curiosities or used in native medicines. The garnets are said to be found in the beds of the Gódávari and Kinarsáni rivers, especially near Gauridévipéta.

CLIMATE. Rainfall.

Detailed statistics of the rainfall in Gódávari are given in Chapter VIII below. The average annual fall for the district is 40·26 inches.

[1] Nagpur, 1870, 506.

[2] Information furnished by Messrs. Binny & Co., Madras.

CHAP. I. CLIMATE.

Temperature.

The only station in the district at which systematic meteorological observations (other than the registration of rainfall) are made is Cocanada. There a daily record of the temperature is kept, and the results are telegraphed to the Meteorological Reporter at Madras. The marginal statement gives the average maxima and minima and the mean for each month in degrees Fahrenheit deduced from the figures of a series of years. It will be seen that the weather is very hot from April to June and that the mean temperature does not fall below 80 degrees till after October. The climate in December and January is cool, the average maximum temperature not exceeding 81 degrees and the average minimum being as low as 65. Along the coast the effect of the heat is much enhanced by the dampness of the air. The hill tracts and the country above the gháts are both cooler and drier than Cocanada.

Month.	Temperature.		
	Average maximum.	Average maximum.	Mean.
	°	°	°
January ...	81·0	65·3	73·2
February ...	85·8	69·6	77·7
March	91·7	73·5	82·6
April	95·6	78·3	86·9
May	100·7	82·8	91·8
June	95·2	81·0	88·1
July	91·7	79·3	85·5
August	89·7	78·5	84·1
September ...	89·2	78·1	83·7
October ...	87·9	75·8	81·9
November ...	83·5	70·5	77·0
December ...	80·7	65·7	73·2
The year ...	89·4	74·9	82·1

Wind and weather.

Light north-easterly breezes in January and February, the driest months of the year, are followed in March and April by light south and south-east winds which blow during the day but die down at sunset. This south breeze is called by the natives *payiru gáli*, or the 'crop wind.' By May the wind, which is still light, has veered round to the south-west, but north-westerly squalls frequently occur, generally in the early part of the night, and sometimes blow with great violence. The south-west monsoon arrives in June and continues for some three months. In September and October land and sea breezes alternate, and the weather becomes calm and sultry as the north-east monsoon approaches. The latter sets in with light or moderate currents of air about the beginning of November, and brings bright and cool weather with it. Cyclones (see Chapter VIII) are apt to occur in this month. In December the wind blows from the east during the day and from the north during the night. The latter is called the hill *(konda)* wind.

FLORA.

The botany of Gódávari is interesting from several points of view. The physical geography of the district permits the

CHAP. I. FLORA.

existence of several distinct floras, while the residence of the great Indian botanist, Roxburgh, at Samalkot has caused the native plants to be more carefully studied than elsewhere. The irrigated delta teems with weeds of cultivation, the uplands yield the plants of the dry scrub forest, while the hill tracts of Rampa present an entirely different series. The latter are most easily studied where the Gódávari pierces the backbone of the Eastern Gháts, and the deep ravines near Bison Hill afford the nearest approach to a moist evergreen forest to be met with in this part of India. Among the interesting plants of the Gódávari gorges may be noted the beautiful blue *Barleria strigosa, Oldenlandia nudicaulis, Sauropus quadrangularis, Bauhinia Vahlii, Euphorbia elegans* and *Payllanthus suberosus.* Bordering the stream and in the rapids *Euphorbia 'Lawii* appears to be at home, while on the banks such exotic ferns as *Luffa echinata* and *Melilotus parviflora* may be found. Many Gódávari plants are illustrated and described in the magnificent *Coromandel Plants* prepared by Roxburgh while he was Carnatic Botanist to the Hon. East India Company.[1]

FAUNA. Cattle.

Five kinds of cattle are locally recognized ; viz., the *désaváli* (or country), the *paramati* (western), the *turpu* (eastern), the Kóya and the Sugáli. The *désaváli* are found both in the plains and in the Agency ; in the latter they are called also *gommu* (riverside) cattle and are generally stronger than in the plains. The western cattle are easily recognized by their peculiar and plentiful branding and by the shortness of their horns. They are not found in the Agency and are imported in small numbers from Nellore and Guntúr. The cows give better milk than the country animals. The eastern cattle come from Vizagapatam, but are apparently merely animals bought as calves from Guntúr and Nellore and reared in that district. The Kóya cattle are inferior animals raised by the hill tribe of that name. The Sugáli breed are brought by Sugális (Lambádis) of the Nizam's Dominions to this district and are especially common in the Rajahmundry and Rámachandrapuram taluks. These Sugális are wandering traders and use the cattle to transport forest produce from the upper reaches of the river and to carry grain for the ryots.

Buffaloes.

Four kinds of buffaloes occur in the district. In the plains 'country buffaloes' and 'eastern buffaloes' from Vizagapatam district are the usual breeds. They are much alike in appearance. A larger kind, called the Bobbili or *Gauvada* buffalo, is less common. In Bhadráchalam a fine animal

[1] This paragraph was written by Mr. C. A. Barber (the Government Botanist) for the *Imperial Gazetteer.*

CHAP. I. FAUNA.

called the northern *(uttaráddi)* buffalo is used. It generally has white patches on the forehead and just above the hoofs.

Sheep and goats.

There are three kinds of sheep; namely, the country sheep, which give milk, manure and meat, but bear no wool; the *kulam* sheep, which are valued for their wool but are rare; and the *síma* (foreign) sheep, which have long tails, give no wool, and seem only to occur in Tuni.

Of goats the 'large' or 'country' kind and the 'small' or '*Kánchi*' breed are distinguished. The latter are also called the 'Calcutta' breed. They yield richer and more wholesome milk and are more prolific than the former. Some care is taken about the breeding of both sheep and goats. Most of the males are sold for meat, and only one or two superior animals are kept for breeding purposes.

Cattle-breeding.

Two local practices are of considerable importance to the improvement of the cattle. In almost every village a really good bull or two is set free to roam among the herds, and in the Agency the owners of cattle often set apart a superior animal, called the *vittanam* (seed) bull, to be used exclusively for crossing purposes. In many parts of the district, also, people castrate the inferior bulls.

Feeding methods.

Cattle are usually fed on paddy straw in the plains and cholam straw in the Agency. In the central delta and in Rajahmundry taluk they are also given sunn hemp *(janumu)*, which is much grown there. In Amalápuram, where grazing is especially scarce, they are fed on rice husk, horse-gram and gingelly oil-cake. When the crops are on the ground and there is no particular work for the cattle, *i.e.*, from August to December, they are sent from the plains to graze in the forests in the Yellavaram and Chódavaram hills. The Pithápuram ryots drive theirs to Tuni. The Amalápuram and Nagaram ryots do not as a rule send their animals away owing to the trouble of getting them across the rivers. The Bhadráchalam ryots drive theirs in the hot weather to Bastar and the Jeypore zamindari, where the grazing is better. The Pólavaram forests are resorted to by the cattle of the Kistna district.

Cattl diseases.

Cattle mortality is said to be heavy in the delta (especially in the central delta and Rámachandrapuram), where fodder is scarce, the animals are crowded and the ground is saturated with moisture. 'They suffer from the absence of grazing and deficient food at one time and from feeding on rank, quickly-grown herbage at others.'[1]

[1] Mr Benson in G.O. No. 28, Revenue, dated 11th January 1884, p. 15. See also p. 13 of the same G.O.

The chief diseases in the district are foot and mouth disease *(góllu)*, anthrax *(domma)*, rinderpest *(peddajádyam)*, fever *(kurama)* and *sugalirógam* or malignant sore throat. Eruptions all over the body, an occasional symptom of rinderpest, are called by the natives *kinka*. Cattle are said to be not infrequently poisoned by Mádigas, who then eat their flesh and take their hides.

Cattle fairs.

Generally speaking, the cattle are bought by merchants and ryots at the large weekly fairs at Tummapála (in Vizagapatam district), Pithápuram, Drákshárámam (in Rámachandrapuram), Ambájipéta (in Amalápuram) and Palokollu in the Kistna district. Merchants go the round of these markets with their herds until they are all sold. The Pithápuram and Drákshárámam cattle fairs are famous. Sometimes drovers take their cattle round the country and sell them to the ryots in their own villages. This is what is usually done by the Sugális, who seem never to frequent the markets.

Game.

Big game is plentiful in the hills of the Agency and less so in the uplands of Tuni and Peddápuram. Tigers and panthers are numerous; bears are fairly common; bison (gaur) occur; nílgai have been shot in the Bhadráchalam taluk; sambur, spotted deer, jungle sheep, black-buck and pig are all common. Dholes (wild dogs) are found in Bhadráchalam and Pólavaram. Small game exists in great abundance. Good snipe-shooting is to be had in the neighbourhood of Rajahmundry and in many other spots. Wild geese, duck and teal are common on the river and its lankas, and the two latter swarm on many jhils and tanks and on the sea at the mouth of the creeks between Cocanada and Coringa, whence they fly inland to feed at night. Partridge, peafowl, jungle-fowl and the smaller quail are all fairly common. The larger quail, florican and sand-grouse are more rarely met with. Other uncommon birds found in the district are the imperial pigeon, pied mina, and *bhímaráj*. Hares and partridges are captured in quantities by native shikáris, the former with nets, the latter with the help of decoy birds. Crocodiles are found in the upper Gódávari in large numbers and people are afraid to enter the deep parts of the river even as far down as Rajahmundry.

Fish.

Mahseer occur in the Gódávari, Saveri and Panniléru rivers. The large sable fish (*clupea palasah* or hilsa) are netted in very large quantities near the Dowlaishweram anicut, when they come up the river to spawn. Fine carp and labeo are caught near Pólavaram and in the tanks, as the villagers will not allow the drinking-water tanks to be netted. The fishing in the tidal water near Cocanada and Coringa is

CHAP. I. FAUNA.

said to be particularly good. A fine fish which the natives call *pundikuppa* and which runs up to 100 lb. comes up the creeks. The mango fish and the mullet may also be caught in large quantities near the sea.

Native sportsmen.

Yerukalas are the commonest shikári caste. Ídigas, Kápus, Rázus, Musalmans and Málas also shoot. Nakkalas hunt jackals and foxes for food. In Bhadráchalam and Pólavaram the Kóyas, Reddis and Mutráchas are keen sportsmen. Some of the methods employed are interesting, if the accounts given by the natives are to be credited. Jackals and foxes are killed with assegais of split bamboo; antelope are caught by sending out a tame buck with nooses on his horns which entangle, the wild ones when they try to eject him; some animals are shot from behind a trained cow which conceals the sportsman and provides a rest for his gun; and spring guns are sometimes placed in the tracks of game. Birds are caught in nooses placed near the cage of a decoy; and by limed twigs baited with worms. Waterfowl are driven, by a man concealed behind a trained cow, over a net spread under water.

CHAPTER II.

POLITICAL HISTORY.

EARLY HISTORY—Asóka's conquest, 260 B.C.—The Andhras, down to 200 A.D.—The Pallavas, about 200-615 A.D.—The Chálukyas—Their conquest of Vengi, about 615—Separation of the Eastern and Western Chalukyas, about 630—Hiuen Tsiang's description of the former—Eastern Chálukya rule, 630-999—Chóla conquest, 999—Kulóttunga Chóla I—He obtains the Chóla and Vengi thrones, 1070—His viceroys in Vengi—His death in 1119 and the decline of the Chólas—The Vélanándu chieftains, twelfth century—The Kóna chiefs of the delta—Local chiefs of Ellore, Nadendla, etc.—The Kákatíyas of Warangal conquer Kistna about 1200—And Gódávari about 1300—Pratápa Rudra's viceroys—Temporary Musalman conquest of the district, 1323—The Kórukonda Reddis, 1325-95—The Reddis of Kondavíd, 1344-1422—The Rajahmundry Reddis, 1422-50—The Gajapatis of Orissa take the district, 1450—But cede part of it to the Muhammadans, 1470—The latter ousted, 1489—Conquest by Vijayanagar, 1515—Musalman conquest of Kistna, 1540—And of Gódávari, 1571. MUHAMMADAN PERIOD—Weakness of their rule—Aurangzeb establishes his authority, 1687—The Subadar of the Deccan becomes independent, 1724—The Northern Circars ceded to the French, 1753—Their difficulties there—Bussy at length obtains possession, 1757—Forde's expedition against the French, 1758—His victory at Condore—The country cleared of the French—Cession of the Northern Círcars to the English, 1765. ENGLISH PERIOD—Early administration—Disturbances of the peace—In 1785-90—In 1790-1800—Quieter times thereafter—Subba Reddi's rebellion, 1858—Outbreaks in Rampa.

CHAP. II. EARLY HISTORY.

Asóka's conquest, 260 B.C.

THE earliest historical mention of the Gódávari district occurs in the inscriptions of Asóka, the Buddhist ruler of the great Mauryan empire, the capital of which was at Pátaliputra, the modern Patna. In 260 B.C.[1] this monarch conquered the kingdom of Kalinga (a tract of varying extent which may be taken to have comprised the country between the Mahánadi river on the north and the Gódávari on the south) and he claims also to have subdued the Andhras, a dynasty whose sway apparently extended as far north as the Gódávari river. Asóka was the great apostle of the Buddhist religion, which he extended far and wide in India, and the magnificent Buddhist remains at Amarávati on the Kistna river are proof that the faith he espoused obtained a strong hold in country even further south than the Gódávari. They contain an inscription in the Mauryan character.

[1] *Indian Antiquary*, xx, 247.

CHAP. II. EARLY HISTORY.

The Andhras, down to 200 A.D.

But his conquest of the Andhras by no means terminated the existence of that dynasty. For long after his reign they retained, and probably increased, their power in this district. Pliny mentions them as a strong people with 30 fortified cities, 100,000 infantry, 2,000 cavalry and 1,000 elephants. Their conquests extended far to the north, and even to the western coast of the peninsula, for one of their earlier kings, Simuka, covered the walls of a large cave at Nánághát (50 miles north-west of Poona) with inscriptions recording his sacrifices; and his successors have left evidence by their coins and in their inscriptions in the cave temples at Násik, Kárlé and Kánheri that they extended their power to Málwa and the borders of Gujarát. Towards the south their dominions included parts of Mysore. Their capital was at first at Sríkákulam on the Kistna, nineteen miles west of Masulipatam, but was afterwards removed to Dharanikóta, near Amarávati. From coins, inscriptions and other material have been ascertained the names and dates of kings of the line who ruled from about 110 to 220 A.D.

The Pallavas, about 200–615 A.D.

The next power to appear upon the scene were the Pallavas. This race, like others of the invaders of the south, perhaps passed into central India from the north-west during the second century A.D. In an inscription, the Andhra king Gótamiputra (172–202 A.D.) boasts that he defeated them, but they shortly afterwards subdued the Andhras and extended their empire as far south as Conjeeveram and the borders of the Tanjore country, and as far to the north-east as the frontiers of Orissa. Records of them are few and far between; but the absence of inscriptions of the Andhras after about the year 218 and the discovery at Mayidavólu and Kondamudi (in the Guntúr district) of two Pallava records which on palæographical grounds may be assigned to the end of the second century, go to show that their conquest of the Andhras occurred about that period. Moreover inscriptions of two kings named Attivarman and Prithivimúla, who were also apparently Pallava rulers, have been found in the Gódávari district and seem to belong to a slightly later period. In the fourth century, the Allahabad inscription mentioned on p. 233 refers to a chief of Pithápuram who was apparently a Pallava. Whether these Pallavas were independent monarchs or merely local feudatories of the main Pallava empire, the capital of which was at Conjeeveram, cannot be stated with certainty.

The Chálukyas.

About the beginning of the seventh century, the Chálukyas, who were also invaders from the north-west and who possessed a large empire in central and western India the capital of which was Bádámi in the Bombay Presidency, came into prominence. An unusually distinct picture of them is drawn by the Chinese pilgrim Hiuen Tsiang, who visited India between the years 629 and 644 A.D.: CHAP. II. EARLY HISTORY.

'This disposition of the people is honest and simple; they are tall of stature and of a stern, vindictive character. To their benefactors they are grateful, to their enemies relentless. If they are insulted, they will risk their lives to avenge themselves. If they are asked to help one in distress, they will forget themselves in their haste to render assistance. If they are going to seek revenge they first give their enemy warning; then, each being armed, they attack each other with spears. When one turns to flee, the other pursues him, but they do not kill a man who submits. If a general losses a battle, they do not inflict punishment, but present him with woman's clothes, and so he is driven to seek death for himself. The country provides for a band of champions to the number of several hundred. When about to engage in conflict they intoxicate themselves with wine, and then one man with lance in hand will meet ten thousand and challenge them to fight. If one of these champions meets a man and kills him, the laws of the country do not punish him. Every time they go forth they beat drums before them. Moreover they make drunk many hundred head of elephants; and, taking them out to fight, and after themselves drinking wine, they rush forward in mass and trample everything down so that no enemy can stand before them. The king in consequence of his possessing these men and elephants treats his neighbours with contempt. He is of the Kshatriya caste and his name is Pulakêsi.'[1]

The monarch here referred to (Pulakésin II, 609–42) extended his conquests throughout the Gódávari district and into Vizagapatam, drove the Pallavas to the walls of Conjeeveram and threatened the country of the Chólas of Tanjore.

Their conquest of Vengi, about 615.

His conquest of Gódávari is detailed in a stone inscription at Aihole (in the Bombay Presidency) in which he mentions the reduction of Pithápuram and Ellore.[2] It took place about 615 A.D.

Separation of the Eastern and Western Chálukyas, about 630.

During his absence on this campaign, Pulakésin had made his younger brother Vishnuvardhana I his regent at his capital of Bádámi, and on his return he deputed him to govern the country he had recently conquered. By 632 Vishnuvardhana had established himself in these new territories as an independent sovereign of the kingdom of 'Vengi,' the capital of which was at Pedda Végi near Ellore and which included the Gódávari district, and there he founded the Eastern Chálukya dynasty, which held that country for at least five centuries

[1] *Bombay Gazetteer* (1896), i, pt. 2, 353.
[2] *Indian Antiquary*, xx, 94.

CHAP. II. EARLY HISTORY.

and remained throughout distinct from, and independent of, the Western Chálukyas.

Hiuen Tsiang's description of the former.

Hiuen Tsiang visited this kingdom also. He describes it as being nearly 1,000 miles in circuit and its capital as some seven miles round, but the country was thinly populated—possibly owing to its recent conquest. The once numerous Buddhist convents were in ruins and deserted, for, though the Andhras and Pallavas had been Buddhists or Jains, the Eastern Chálukyas were Vaishnavites by creed.

Eastern Chálukya rule, 630-999.

The genealogy and some of the acts of the Eastern Chálukya kings of Vengi are given with great chronological distinctness in the various grants of the dynasty that have come down to us.[1] In the early part of the eighth century Udayachandra, the general of the Pallava king Nandivarman, claims that he subdued the Eastern Chálukya king Vishnuvardhana III (709-46);[2] but this reconquest by the ancient owners of the country seems to have been short-lived. Vijayáditya II (799-843) had to defend himself against his neighbours on the west, the Ráshtrakútas of Málkhéd (90 miles west by south of Hyderabad), who had subdued and taken the place of the Western Chálukyas. What was the result of the fighting is not clear. Vijayáditya II relates how 'during twelve years by day and by night he fought a hundred and eight battles with the armies of the Gangas (probably the Mysore Gangas) and the Rattas' (*i.e.*, the Ráshtrakútas); but his Ráshtrakúta contemporary, Góvinda III, boasts that he ordered the king of Vengi into his presence and made him assist in building and fortifying a city.

Chóla conquest, 999.

At the end of the tenth century, the mighty Rájarája I, who had laid the foundations of a great Chóla empire with its capital at Tanjore, conquered the Eastern Chálukya country. He seems to have appointed a prince of the fallen line (Saktivarman, 999-1011) as king (or perhaps feudatory) in Vengi.[3] This man's brother and successor, Vimaláditya (1011-22),[4] though he had married a Chóla princess, apparently attempted to throw off his allegiance, for Rájarája's son Rájéndra Chóla (1011-14) again invaded the Vengi country and advanced as far as the hill called Mahéndragiri in Ganjám, where he planted a pillar of victory. Vimaláditya was not deposed, however, and was succeeded by his son

[1] *Indian Antiqury*, xx, 93 ff. and 266 ff.

[2] *South Indian Inscriptions*, ii, 364.

[3] *Epigraphia Indica*, vi, 349.

[4] There is some doubt about the duration of his reign, for though the dates of his and his successor's accession are given as in the text, his reign is generally represented as having only lasted seven years.

Rájarája (1022-62), who also married a princess of the Chóla royal house. This king fixed his capital at Rajahmundry, and it was during his reign that the Mahábhárata was translated into Telugu.[1]

Kulóttunga Chóla I.

His son Kulóttunga was afterwards the famous Kulóttunga Chóla I, who, though belonging on his father's side to the ancient line of Vengi, claimed to succeed to the Chóla throne at Tanjore through his mother and his grandmother, and ultimately founded a new Chóla dynasty in the south. While heir-apparent to the Vengi throne he distinguished himself by capturing elephants and defeating a king, but when his father Rájarája died he was ousted from the succession by his paternal uncle Vijayáditya VII.

The latter's rule appears to have been disturbed by invasion. The Western Chálukya kingdom had revived after the fall of the Ráshtrakútas, and its great monarch Vikramáditya VI (whose capital was at Kalyáni, north-west of Hyderabad) was by this time harassing both the Chóla and the Vengi countries. He twice invaded the latter,[2] but was, however, defeated by the Chóla king, who re-established his authority in Vengi and restored Vijayáditya VII to his throne there.[3] 'His elephants drank the water of the Gódávari. He crossed even Kalingam, and beyond it despatched for battle his invincible army as far as the further end of Chakrakótta. He reconquered the good country of Véngai and bestowed it on Vijayáditya, whose broad hands held weapons of war and who had taken refuge at his lotus feet.'[4]

He obtains the Chóla and Vengi thrones, 1070.

About 1069 the then Chóla king died, and his son secured the throne with the help of the Western Chálukya king Vikramáditya VI. The Kulóttunga already mentioned claimed, however, to succeed as both grandson and adopted son of a former Chóla ruler. He took up arms, slew the new king, and entered on a fierce conflict with Vikramáditya VI. The accounts given by the two monarchs of the events which followed are widely different; but victory finally rested with Kulóttunga, who made himself king of the Chóla country and overlord of Vengi, and ruled till 1118 with the title of Kulóttunga Chóla I.

His viceroys in Vengi.

He magnanimously allowed his uncle Vijayáditya VII, who had before supplanted him, to continue in charge of

1 *Ep. Ind.*, v, 31. He is well known to local tradition to this day under the name Rájarája Naréndra. *Cf.* Mackenzie MSS., Local Records, ii, 231; xix, 75; and lx, 24.

2 *S. Ind. Inscr.*, iii, 37.

3 Dr. Hultzsch in *S. Ind. Inscr.*, iii, 128.

4 His inscription quoted in the Government Epigraphist's report for 1898.

CHAP. II. EARLY HISTORY.

Vengi, and appears to have treated him with cordiality. When this man died in 1077, Kulóttunga appointed his own second son, Rájarája II, as viceroy of Vengi. The latter seems to have been uncomfortable and insecure in his position. An inscription of this date says that finding 'a kingdom not such a pleasure as the worship of the illustrious feet of the elders, he returned to his parents, after having ruled over Vengi for one year.'[1] He was replaced (1078) by his younger brother Víra Chóda, 'the brave prince, the incarnation of valour,' who 'joyfully put on the tiara of the world.' This prince was superseded in 1084 by Kulóttunga's eldest son Rájarája Chóda Ganga, but was reinstated in 1088-89 and continued to rule till at least 1092-93. He was then succeeded by another and better known brother, Vikrama Chóla, who ruled the Vengi country till about 1118. The reasons for these constant changes are nowhere stated; but it would appear that Kulóttunga placed no great reliance on his sons' loyalty to himself.

The only event of importance in this period is the conquest of Kalinga which was achieved by Kulóttunga some time before 1095-96. Kalinga was feudatory to Vengi and had withheld tribute for two years. Vikrama Chóla also claims to have effected this victory, and it was perhaps achieved during his viceroyalty. He governed the Vengi country for some 20 years, and in 1118 he was called to the south to become co-regent with, and shortly afterwards the successor of, Kulóttunga, who seems to have died in that or the following year. On his departure a certain Chóda, the son of Gonka, was appointed as viceroy of Vengi, and was even honoured with adoption into Kulóttunga's family. His descendants (see below) long played a prominent part in the history of the district.

His death in 1119 and the decline of the Chólas.

The Chóla supremacy in Vengi was at this point disturbed for a few years by the aged Western Chálukya king Vikramáditya VI, who took advantage of the departure of Vikrama Chóla and the death of his old enemy Kulóttunga to invade this northern province of theirs. Their viceroy Chóda submitted to him, and from 1120 to 1124 Vikramáditya was undisputed king of Vengi. His rule cannot have lasted long, as inscriptions of Vikrama Chóla, dated 1127 and 1135 respectively, occur in Kistna. After the latter of these years, however, neither he nor his successors took an active part in the government of Vengi. Occupied with their own troubles in the south, the Chólas gradually lost their influence in that province, and, though they were recognized as overlords by

[1] *S. Ind. Inscr.*, i., 60.

the various petty rulers who now divided the country, even down to a time when their power in Tanjore was shattered, they had little, if any, real influence in Vengi after the death of Vikrama Chóla.

The Vélanándu chieftains, twelfth century.

Of these petty rulers, the most important (and apparently the admitted suzerains over the others) were the Vélanándu family, to which belonged that Chóda who was adopted into Kulóttunga's family and left as viceroy of Vengi when Vikrama Chóla went in 1118 to join his father in the south. Vélanándu is said [1] to be 'an old name for the Chandhavólu country' (*i.e.*, the western part of the Kistna delta), where the family appear to have been long established and to have ruled as feudatories of the Eastern Chálukyas. Chóda's father, Gonka I, seems to have ruled 'the Andhra country' under Kulóttunga I, and is mentioned in an inscription at Chebrólu in the Kistna district dated 1076. A cousin of his named Vedura was a minister of Kulóttunga's son Víra Chóda when viceroy of Vengi; and, in recognition of his services against 'a Pándyan king,' was given by his master the overlordship of the country between the Kistna and the Gódávari. It was however under Chóda that the Vélanándu family first attained the position of viceroys of the Vengi country. He and his successors wielded considerable power. Chóda, as has been seen, bowed the neck to Vikramáditya VI, but his son Gonka II (*alias* Kulóttunga Chóda Gonka) claims to have ruled from Kálahasti in North Arcot to Ganjám. The queen of the latter's grandson, Gonka III (1137-56), covered with gold the idol at Simháchalam near Vizagapatam. The family seems to have been suppressed by the Kákatíyas of Warangal, in what is now the Nizam's Dominions, who forced their way into the country south of the Gódávari at the beginning of the thirteenth century. The last of them who is known to history was Prithísvara, the son of Gonka III, who ruled from 1163 to at least 1186.

The Kóna chiefs of the delta.

Meanwhile another family, the Haihiya chiefs of 'the Kóna country,' were in power in the delta of the Gódávari. The delta taluk of Amalápuram is still known as the Kóna country. These people were apparently hereditary chieftains subordinate to the Vengi viceroys and the Vélanándu family. Their inscriptions in this district range from 1128 to 1206.

Local chiefs of Ellore, Nadendla, etc.

Other local rulers were the chiefs of Nadendla in the Kistna district, who seem to have recognized the authority of the Vélanándu line and have left inscriptions ranging from

[1] *Ep. Ind.*, iv, 33. and *Manual of the Kistna district*, 214. The Velinádu Smárta Telugu Bráhmans have a tradition that Vélanándu is a name for the country near Kondavíd. See Chapter III, p. 52.

CHAP. II. EARLY HISTORY.

1130 to 1232; the chieftains of Ellore, whose records date from 1139–40 to 1211–12; a family whose inscriptions are found in several places in the delta, who claim descent from the Eastern Chálukya king Amma I (918–25) and the best known of whom is Mallapa III who seems to have ruled from 1173 to at least 1223; and Annala Reddi of Kórukonda (in Rajahmundry taluk), who is stated in one of the Mackenzie MSS. to have ruled over the greater part of the lowlands of district 'for a long time' till he was 'succeeded' (*i.e.*, ousted) by king Pratápa Rudra of the Kákatíya line of Warangal.

The Kákatíyas of Warangal conquer Kistna about 1200.

These Kákatíya kings had by now begun to lay the foundations of their empire on the ruins of the western Chálukya kingdom. As early as 1162 their king Rudra Déva boasted [1] that he had conquered the whole country as far as Srísailam (in Kurnool) in the south, and up to the salt sea on the east. The first indubitable inscription of the dynasty found in the Vengi country is one of Rudra Déva's son Ganapati at Chebrólu (in the Kistna district) dated 1213–14; [2] and that this king overcame the Vélanándu chieftains is indicated by the existence of an inscription of his at Chandhavólu, their capital.

And Gódávari about 1300.

When the Kákatíyas first crossed the Gódávari is doubtful. An inscription at Drákshárámam mentions king Ganapati (1213–53), but it is fragmentary and undated, and may belong to the time of his successor; and the first record in this district which can be unhesitatingly ascribed to the dynasty is one of Pratápa Rudra, dated 1317, at Palivela in the Amalápuram taluk. Ferishta moreover speaks of the king of Rajahmundry as an independent prince in 1295.[3] It would thus seem that the Kákatíyas did not cross the Gódávari till some time after their conquest of Vengi proper, and that this district did not fall under their dominion until the end of the thirteenth century.

Pratápa Rudra's viceroys.

One of the Mackenzie MSS.[4] which (where it can be checked) agrees in its facts and dates with local inscriptions and is thus presumably trustworthy, throws an interesting side-light on Pratápa Rudra's rule of the district. His local viceroys were two brothers named Pedda Malla Rázu and Chinna Malla Rázu, who held their court with great pomp and luxury at Bendapúdi in the Tuni division. They were most oppressive in their rule, and a long list is given of the enormities they perpetrated. Finally, in 1322–23, Pratápa

[1] *Ind. Antiq.*, xi, 9 ff.
[2] *Ep. Ind.*, v, 143.
[3] Scott's *Ferishta* Introduction, p. xii.
[4] Wilson's Catalogue, p. 396, 8, 3.

Rudra had himself to interfere, since 'the cultivators refused to follow their occupation and fled the country.' The MS. describes at length the rules he then laid down for the revenue administration of the province. The two viceroys eventually fell foul of the 'Rája of Cuttack' (the Ganga king of Kalinga), Pedda Malla Rázu having kidnapped the bride of one of that potentate's relatives as she was passing through the district. The Ganga king sent an expedition to revenge the affront; and, after a long siege, Bendapúdi was taken and the two brothers were captured and beheaded.

CHAP. II. EARLY HISTORY.

Temporary Musalman conquest of the district, 1323.

The Mughal emperor of Delhi had long been jealous of the growing power of the Kákatíyas. In 1303 he had unsuccessfully attempted to crush their kingdom; in 1310 his general Malik Káfur captured Warangal, but Pratápa Rudra soon recovered his independence; but in 1323 the Delhi heir-apparent, Muhammad Tughlak, took the town again and carried off its king to Delhi.

Muhammad Tughlak seems to have penetrated as far as Rajahmundry itself, for an inscription, dated 1324, on a mosque there describes its erection by him in that year. The tide of Muhammadan invasion receded almost at once, but from this point the influence of the kings of Warangal in the Telugu country disappears, and Vengi was ruled by the Reddi chiefs of Kórukonda, Kondavíd and Rajahmundry.

The Kórukonda Reddis, 1325-95.

A history of the Kórukonda Reddis is given in the Mackenzie MS. already quoted. The founder of the line was Kóna or Kúna Reddi, 'a good Súdra,' who built the fort at Kórukonda and made the place into a big town. His son Mummidi Reddi succeeded him, and (along with his two brothers) is said to have ruled as far as Tátipáka (either the village of that name in Nagaram island or its namesake in Tuni division) and to have founded one of the Kórukonda temples in 1353. Mummidi Reddi was followed by his son Kúna Reddi, and he by his two brothers Anna Reddi and Kátama Reddi, one after the other. Their reigns are said to have lasted 40 years. The latter was succeeded by his son Mummidi Náyak, by whom another of the Kórukonda temples was repaired in 1394-95.

The Reddis of Kondavíd, 1344-1422.

The Reddis of Kondavíd were Súdra cultivators; but the family seems to have been in the service of the kings of Warangal and no doubt derived the beginnings of its power from this circumstance. They apparently ruled side by side with the Kórukonda Reddis, for the inscriptions of the two overlap. Their earliest extant record is dated in 1344. Their original capital was at Addanki in Guntúr, but they subsequently moved to Kondavíd. The founder of the dynasty was Véma, the son of Próla, who boasts that he conquered Raichúr and defeated certain kings, calls himself 'the lion to the elephant which was the Pándyan king' (whatever that may mean), and was a great patron of Telugu and Tamil literature. Of his successors, two are stated to have fought against the Musalmans and three were men of letters. His grandson Kumáragiri placed his minister and brother-in-law, Kátaya Véma, in charge of the eastern portion of his dominions and made Rajahmundry the capital thereof. Kátaya Véma's dates range from 1385 to 1422 and an inscription of his occurs in the Simháchalam temple in Vizagapatam.

The Rajahmundry Reddis, 1422–50.

On the death of Kátaya Véma, one Allåda the son of Dodda Reddi obtained (it is not clear how) the throne of Rajahmundry, and founded a new, though short-lived, dynasty. His inscriptions appear as early as 1415–17 in the delta (at Pálakollu, Palivela, and Drákshárámam) and he is represented therein as being the friend or servant of Kátaya Véma, whose enemies he claims to have 'uprooted.' His military operations were extensive. He says that he 'befriended' the Gajapati of Orissa and the king of Karnáta (*i.e.*, the king of Vijayanagar, in the Bellary district) who was allied with the Gajapati, and defeated a Musalman general called Alpa Khán. He also claims to have defeated the Reddis of Kondavíd. His sons Allaya Véma and Vírabhadra ruled jointly; and members of the family are mentioned in the Drákshárámam inscriptions until as late as 1447.

The Gajapatis of Orissa take the district, 1450.

In 1434 the Gajapati dynasty of Orissa was founded by Kapilésvara, the minister of the last Ganga king of that country.[1] Kapilésvara had shortly before been in alliance with the Rajahmundry Reddis and the Vijayanagar king against the Muhammadans, but he none the less obtained the assistance of the Báhmani king of Kulbarga, then the most powerful Musalman chief in the Deccan, in establishing himself in his new position. By 1454 he was recognized as suzerain as far south as Kondavíd, and a minister of his was ruling at Rajahmundry in 1458; so, though the details of the conquest are unknown, he had apparently seized the whole of this district.

But cede part of it to the Muhammadans, 1470.

In 1470, however, his successor Purushóttama applied to the Báhmani king of Kulbarga, for help against a rival claimant, and was forced to cede to that ruler, as the price of his assistance, the districts of Rajahmundry and Kondapalle in Kistna. The Hindu inhabitants of Kondapalle, however, soon afterwards revolted, murdered the Muhammadan governor,

[1] Babu Man Mohan Chakravarti's paper in J.A.S.B., lxix, pt. 1, No. 2.

and called for help from Purushóttama, who accordingly came and besieged Rajahmundry. A Musalman army relieved that place, and about 1478 the Kulbarga king Muhammad took terrible vengeance on the Orissa country and forced Purushóttama to purchase his withdrawal by a present of valuable elephants. Kondapalle was retaken, its temple destroyed (the Bráhman priests being massacred), and a mosque erected on the site. The Kulbarga king remained three years at Rajahmundry, expelling or reducing refractory zamindars and establishing military posts. He appointed one Málik Ahmed as his viceroy, and at the end of 1480 left the district to prosecute his conquests in the south.

The latter ousted, 1489.

A few years afterwards, however, the Kulbarga kingdom was dismembered by revolutions which resulted in the formation of the three Muhammadan kingdoms of Bijápur, Ahmadnagar and Golconda in the years 1489, 1490 and 1512 respectively; and the kings of Orissa recovered this district.

Conquest by Vijayanagar, 1515.

In 1515, Krishna Déva, the greatest of the kings of the Hindu empire of Vijayanagar, the capital of which was at Hampe in the Bellary district, and which was now at the zenith of its power, marched northwards in great strength. He took the strong fort of Udayagiri in Nellore after a siege of a year and a half, and then invested Kondavíd. The king of Orissa, Pratápa Rudra, came south to relieve the latter place, and Krishna Déva quitted the siege and advanced to meet him. The two armies came face to face at 'a large river of salt water crossed by a ford' (presumably the Kistna), and Krishna Déva offered to retire six miles so that his adversary might cross the river unmolested and they might then fight on equal terms. Receiving no reply, he forded the river himself in the face of the Orissan army, losing heavily in the operation; engaged the enemy on the other side; and won a complete victory. He took Kondapalle after a siege of three months, escaladed Kondavíd (capturing there the wife and son of the Orissan king and many of his nobles) and then advanced as far north as Potnúru in the Vizagapatam district, where he set up a pillar of victory. From this place he despatched several challenges to Pratápa Rudra, daring him to come and fight, and when these met with no response he eventually returned south to his own capital. He subsequently sent back Pratápa Rudra's queen and married his daughter.

Musalman conquest of Kistna, 1540.

Before many years had passed the Muhammadans again attacked the country. The invader this time was the first king of the new dynasty of Golconda, Qutb Shah (1512–43), and the cause of the war was the assistance given by the house

CHAP. II. EARLY HISTORY.

of Orissa to a rebellious feudatory of Golconda. The large forces of the Hindus were routed by the fanatical courage of the Musalmans, who took Kondapalle and won a battle in the neighbourhood of Rajahmundry. The king of Orissa sued for peace, and consented to surrender to Golconda the whole of the territory between the Kistna and Gódávari rivers.

And of Gódávari, 1571.

Meanwhile domestic revolutions had weakened the kingdom of Orissa. Two sons of Pratápa Rudra succeeded him one after the other, and ruled for a year or two till they were both murdered in 1541–42 by a minister named Góvinda Déva, who took the kingdom for himself.[1] He and his sons ruled till 1559-60, when a Telugu named Harichandana raised a revolt, killed two of the sons of the usurper, and himself ruled till 1571, when the kingdom fell finally into the hands of the Muhammadan kings of Golconda.

This conquest had not been effected without severe fighting. The Hindu Rája of Kondavíd attacked the Musalman garrison of Kondapalle, and the chief of Rajahmundry, one Vidiádri, who was apparently [2] a prince of the house of Orissa, laid siege to Ellore, which was also held by the Muhammadans. The latter was signally defeated and fled to Rajahmundry. The Golconda troops laid waste the country round that town and were then called away (1564) to assist the other Musalman kings of the Deccan in the joint attack on Vijayanagar which resulted in the overthrow of that empire in the great battle of Talikóta, north of the Kistna river, in 1565. That decisive campaign won, Golconda's conquest of Gódávari soon recommenced. The forts of Peddápuram and Rájánagaram (from which reinforcements and provisions were being sent to Rajahmundry) were first taken, the latter with difficulty because of the narrowness of the paths and the thickness of the jungles which had to be traversed. Rajahmundry was then attacked. The Hindus were defeated in a desperate battle outside the walls (though they broke the left wing of the invader's army) and the fort was then invested for four months, when it surrendered. This took place in 1571–72. The Muhammadans then marched north, reducing the fortified places on the way, and finally conquered all the country of Orissa as far as Chicacole in Ganjám.

MUHAMMADAN PERIOD. Weakness of their rule.

Their control of their new possessions was apparently far from firm, and disorders and outbreaks were continual. The Reddis of the hills, for example, plundered Ellore and

[1] Mr. Chakravarti's paper already quoted.

[2] Grant's *Political Survey of the Northern Circars*, appended to the *Fifth Report on the affairs of the East India Co.* (1812), Madras reprint of 1883. p. 142.

Nidadavólu, and for some time kept up a desultory resistance against the forces sent to suppress them. When attacked, they dispersed, only to reassemble in difficult passes and ravines, and it was with difficulty that tranquillity was restored. A standing militia appears to have been maintained; but its efforts to keep order were not always successful, and its exactions from the inhabitants increased the miseries of the country.

It was during the Golconda rule that the earliest English settlements on this coast were made. Masulipatam was first visited in 1611 and the factory at Madapollam near Narasapur (also in Kistna) was founded about 1678. Of the settlements in this district, that at Injaram near Yanam was established in 1708, and that at Bendamúrlanka in 1751. The Dutch had several important outposts in the neighbourhood, but the only one in this district was Jagannáthapuram, now a part of Cocanada. The French started a factory at Yanam about 1750. None of these outposts had at this time any influence worth mentioning on the history of the district, and it is sufficient for the present to chronicle the fact of their existence.

Aurangzeb establishes his authority, 1687.

Meanwhile, in 1686, Aurangzeb, emperor of Delhi, marched to reduce the south of India to his authority. In the next year he overthrew (among others) the kingdom of Golconda, and the country passed under the direct rule of Delhi. He appointed to rule his new territories a viceroy who was known as the Subadar of the Deccan (and later as the Nizam of Hyderabad) and resided first at Aurangabad and afterwards at Hyderabad. The subadari consisted of 22 provinces, of which Rajahmundry and Chicacole were two. With the provinces of Kondapalle, Ellore and Guntúr they formed what were known as 'the Northern Circars,' a name which still survives. The system (or want of system) of administration remained unchanged, and disorders continued as freely as before.

The Subadar of the Deccan becomes independent, 1724.

In 1724 the Subadar of the Deccan (Nizam), who had long been virtually independent of Delhi, became so in fact, and appointed his own nominees as Nawábs of the provinces under him. Rustum Khán was appointed to Rajahmundry and is still known to local tradition as Háji Hussain.

The country was in great disorder. Zamindars, or farmers of the revenue, had generally availed themselves of the late political disturbances to usurp the rights and feeble authority of their Muhammadan superintendents. They defrauded the public treasury and squeezed with an iron hand the husbandman and manufacturer. The new ruler set himself to suppress

CHAP. II. MUHAMMADAN PERIOD.

them. 'Those who escaped the sword were proclaimed as traitors; and, a reward being offered for their own with their adherents' heads, a sufficient number was soon collected to erect two shocking pyramidical monuments, called *kulla-minár*, near each of the provincial capitals.'[1] Temporary *áméns* were for a time appointed in place of the refractory zamindars to collect the revenue; but the indolence and depravity of the ruling nation soon made it necessary to revert to the ancient system, and new zamindars were appointed. These quickly became guilty of the same outrages as their predecessors; and in later years their descendants caused constant disorders throughout the Northern Circars.

The Northern Circars ceded to the French, 1753.

In 1748 the Subadar of the Deccan died; and a great struggle followed for his place. The events of this contest relate less to the history of Gódávari than to that of the southern districts, and it is sufficient to note here that the French and English (who were now powers of importance) each took different sides, and that after many vicissitudes Salábat Jang became Subadar in 1751 through the influence and aid of the former. In his gratitude for their help, Salábat Jang ceded the Kondavíd country to them in 1752 and four of the Northern Circars (not Guntúr) in 1753. They had already (in 1750) been granted Masulipatam and the adjacent country; and Bussy, the French general, sent M. Moracin, the officer in charge at Masulipatam, instructions to take over the newly ceded territory.

Their difficulties there.

Jafar Ali, governor of Chicacole, was however in no way disposed to surrender his position quietly to the French, and conspired with the Rája of Vizianagram, the most powerful of the renter-chiefs who had come into existence during the Musalman rule, to oppose M. Moracin's entry. The latter seduced the Rája from the compact by offering to lease him the Rajahmundry and Chicacole circars at a rate much below their value, and Jafar Ali then called in the aid of the Maráthas of Nagpore, who crossed the gháts with a large force, devastated both circars from end to end, and regained their own country by way of Ellore with an immense booty.

In July 1754 Bussy went in person to Masulipatam and Rajahmundry and restored order there. Some of the troublesome zamindars were dismissed; efforts were made to ascertain the real revenue collections made by these renters and on this datum to found an adequate assessment; and they were required to maintain a sibbandi, or militia, of 12,000 men to keep the public peace, collect the rents, and, when called upon, to repel invasion.

[1] Grant's *Political Survey, etc.*, 143.

Soon afterwards, however, relations between Bussy and the Nizam became strained, at last an open breach occurred, and for six weeks in 1756 the former had to entrench himself near Hyderabad against the latter's troops.

Bussy at length obtains possession, 1757.

He was eventually relieved by reinforcements from Masulipatam and taken back into favour, and at the end of 1756 he went to Rajahmundry with a strong force to re-establish his fallen authority in the Circars. Aided by the Rája of Vizianagram, he soon reduced the country to obedience; and a force from Rajahmundry took the three English factories at Madapollam, Bendamúrlanka and Injaram. Except for twenty men at the last-named, these places had no garrisons, and resistance was out of the question.

Forde's expedition against the French, 1758.

In January 1758 Bussy returned to Hyderabad, and in July he was summoned by Lally, the new Governor of Pondicherry, to proceed south, with all the troops that could be spared, to assist in the operations against Madras. His departure was a fatal blow to the fortunes of the French, who within ten months were driven out of the Circars.

Almost as soon as he had gone, the new Rája of Vizianagram, who was dissatisfied with the arrangements made by the French at the time of his predecessor's decease, seized Vizagapatam, hoisted the English flag there and made overtures to the English in Calcutta and Madras, offering to render them every assistance in his power if they would send an expedition to invade the Northern Circars.[1] Clive, who was then at Calcutta, determined, despite the unanimous opposition of his Council, to fall in with the Rája's proposals; an expedition was at once arranged; and the command of it was conferred on Colonel Forde. His force consisted of 500 Europeans, including artillerymen, 2,000 sepoys and 100 lascars. It reached Vizagapatam in October 1758, marched thence in November, effected a junction with the levies of the Rája of Vizianagram, and then proceeded southwards into this district.

His victory at Condore.

The French had assembled in force at Rajahmundry and moved thence to Gollaprólu, a few miles north-east of Pithápuram. Their force consisted of 500 Europeans, 6,000 sepoys and a great many local troops, of whom 500 were cavalry. The whole was under the command of the Marquis de Conflans, Bussy's successor. The opposing forces came in sight of each other at Gollaprólu on December 3rd. Nearly a week elapsed before they joined battle; but at length on the 9th a most

[1] Orme's history (Madras, 1861), ii, 355.

CHAP. II. MUHAMMADAN PERIOD.

decisive action was fought near the little village of Condore (Chandurti) a few miles north of Gollaprólu. The result was a complete victory for the English, the French losing all their baggage and ammunition and nearly all their artillery and retreating in confusion to Rajahmundry. The battle is described in more detail in Chapter XV.

Forde at once sent forward a force of 1,500 sepoys to occupy Rajahmundry; and the garrison there, imagining that the whole of the English force was upon them, abandoned the fort on 10th December and retired to the south. Forde again advanced on January 28th and reached Ellore on February 6th. Thence he detached a force to occupy the French factory at Narasapur, which was abandoned on its approach.

De Conflans had retired to Masulipatam, and at his earnest request the Subadar of the Deccan, Salábat Jang, marched to assist him down the valley of the Kistna. On the 6th March Forde appeared before Masulipatam and, after a month's siege, carried that fort by a brilliant assault. On the 14th May 1759 he concluded a treaty with Salábat Jang (who was so awed by his successes and harassed by disputes with a brother that he made no attempt to assist the French) by which the country round Masulipatam and Nizampatam was ceded as 'inam' to the English, and the Subadar promised to renounce all friendship with the French and prohibit them from ever again settling in the Circars.[1] By this treaty the whole of the country north of the Gódávari returned again to the dominions of the Subadar of the Deccan.

The country cleared of the French.

The district was not at once cleared of the French. A small force of about 250 Europeans and 2,000 sepoys had remained between Masulipatam and Rajahmundry to cut off the supplies of the English troops from that direction. This proceeded to Rajahmundry, where only a very small garrison had been left, and compelled the place to surrender. Soon afterwards, however, it left the district with the object of joining Salábat Jang.

M. Moracin, who had been sent from the south with reinforcements for Masulipatam before its fall was known, landed on November 11th at Cocanada (which was still in the possession of the Dutch) and endeavoured to foment disturbance by intriguing with Jagapati Rázu, a cousin of the Vizianagram Rája, who had assisted the French in the recent campaign and was still under arms. His efforts were unsuccessful, and he soon re-embarked and sailed for Pondicherry.

[1] Aitchison's *Treaties, etc.* (1892), viii, 278.

In December of the same year a small French force of 50 Europeans and 100 sepoys landed at Cocanada with the object of entering into negotiations with this same Jagapati Rázu. By this time the English army at Masulipatam, now under the command of Captain Fischer, had commenced its return march. Learning on his arrival at Rajahmundry of the presence of the French at Cocanada, Fischer proceeded thither at once and found the enemy posted in a village two miles from the Dutch fort. They fled at once inside the fort and eventually surrendered, and thenceforth no French forces set foot in the district.

The country north of the Gódávari was now nominally subject to the Nizam, but he was too busy with other affairs to attend to its administration, and the consequence was that 'for seven succeeding years, the completest anarchy recorded in the history of Hindustan prevailed over all the Northern Circars. The forms, nay even the remembrance, of civil government seemed to be wholly lost.'[1] The provinces had been leased to one Hussain Ali Khán, but his authority was little more than nominal, and an English force despatched to establish it was interrupted by the invasion of the Carnatic by the Subadar. A small body of 200 sepoys and twelve artillerymen under Lieutenant (afterwards Sir Henry) Cosby did, however, reach Rajahmundry, was instrumental in saving Hussain Ali from a conspiracy formed by a disappointed rival to seize the town, and remained there till the Northern Circars were eventually ceded to the English.

Cession of the Northern Circars to the English, 1765.

This event occurred in 1765. Lord Clive, who had returned to India, entered into negotiations regarding the cession, and on August 12, 1765, received a grant of the Circars from the emperor of Delhi. The Madras Government hesitated to avail themselves at once of this grant of country which the Subadar of the Deccan considered to be his own property, alleging that there was no immediate necessity for taking possession, since Hussain Ali Khán had already collected the revenues and but little more could be obtained that year. In the following March, however, they published the emperor's firman and sent General Calliaud to take possession. The Nizam threatened to retaliate by invading the Carnatic; and Calliaud was ordered to meet him at Hyderabad and negotiate a cession from him. The result was a treaty dated November 12, 1766, whereby the whole of the Northern Circars with the exception of Guntúr (which was not ceded till 1788) was handed over to the English. The

[1] Grant's *Political Survey, etc.*, 146.

CHAP. II. MUHAMMADAN PERIOD.

latter on their side engaged to pay the Subadar a tribute of nine lakhs of rupees per annum, and to furnish him with military assistance whenever required. The treaty made no mention of the previous free grant of the country by the emperor.

Almost immediately afterwards the Subadar faithlessly joined Haidar Ali of Mysore against the British; but the success of the latter nation in the south and an invasion of his country from Bengal brought him to his senses; and, by a second treaty dated February 23, 1768, the tribute was reduced and the imperial grant was acknowledged. Tribute continued to be paid until as late as 1823, when it was capitalized by the payment of a lump sum of Rs. 1,66,66,666.[1]

ENGLISH PERIOD. Early administration.

The country was not at once administered directly by the English, but was leased out to native renters. The Gódávari district continued to be under Hussain Ali Khán. His lease expired in 1769, and then the system of Provincial Chiefs and Councils described in Chapter XI was introduced, this district being placed under the Chief and Council of Masulipatam.

Disturbances of the peace.

It only remains to refer to the various disturbances of the peace by the rebellions of zamindars or the outbreaks (*fitúris*, as they are locally called) of hill tribes which have occurred since the English occupation. The powerful zamindars of Pithápuram, Pólavaram and Peddápuram occupied most of the centre and north of the district, while beyond them ruled the untamed mansabdars of Rampa, Tótapalli and Jaddangi. At first, the latter recognized no authority whatever; while the former maintained large bodies of troops and did much as they liked. Constant attempts were made to reduce the power of both, but for a long time in vain. 'It has been the object,' wrote the Board of Revenue in 1794, 'of every new settlement with the zamindars to endeavour to reduce their military force, and a clause has been inserted in their cabooliats binding them to keep up only such sibbendy (militia) as may be indispensably necessary for the purpose of collection and (in some situations near the hills) for protection; but a clause so vague and indefinite, it may easily be supposed, has never met the smallest attention from the zamindars.' Considerable difficulty was consequently experienced in keeping the hill men and the zamindars from breaking the peace.

In 1785–90.

The first disturbance appears to have occurred in 1785, and was due to disputes about the division and management of the property belonging to three brothers who owned,

[1] Aitchison's *Treaties, etc.* (1892), viii, 269.

respectively, the zamindaris of Gútála, Pólavaram and Kottapalli: A hill zamindar of Nágavaram took a part in the quarrel and opened hostilities by capturing Gútála in 1785. Troops had to be moved up to restore order, and some fighting took place. Somewhat similar disorders occurred in 1786, 1787 and 1790, and are described in more detail in the account of Pólavaram in Chapter XV.

In 1790-1800.

These troubles were really in the nature of a family quarrel, and only incidentally involved resistance to Government. In 1794 Collectors replaced the Chiefs in Council, and since a famine had depopulated the country, the revenue due by the zamindars had been raised, and Government had resolved to be more stringent in the collection of its dues than hitherto, these new officers met with considerable opposition in the discharge of their duties. Difficulties in Peddápuram and Pithápuram were solved without bloodshed; but the renters of Mogalturru estate (near Narasapur in Kistna district) raised a serious outbreak.

This property had been administered by Government since 1787, and a petty insurrection occurred there in 1791. At the end of that year it had been resumed by Government and leased out to renters. These people would not pay their dues, and were imprisoned and sent to Conjeeveram. They escaped thence and made their way to Hyderabad territory, their families also flying from Mogalturru to Bhadráchalam. The zamindar of that place and the amildar at Kammamet in Hyderabad assisted the fugitives, who succeeded in collecting a force of 2,000 peons and making an incursion into the district in July 1795. They marched by way of Yernagúdem to Mogalturru. The Collector was nearly surprised in his house; and was unable to attempt an armed resistance. The party, however, behaved with great moderation, committed no excesses whatever, and, on being assured by the Collector that a memorial of what they considered their wrongs would be forwarded to the Board of Revenue, returned to Bhadráchalam. Little further came of this disturbance; the memorial was dismissed, and the malcontents (who continued at Bhadráchalam) made no further incursion. In September of the same year some of their peons attacked Chagallu, on the other side of the river facing Rajahmundry, but were easily dispersed. A petty disturbance was also created in 1798 by a revenue defaulter who had fled the country along with the Mogalturru renters. He proceeded with 200 or 300 pikemen as far as Undi (near Bhímavaram), where he brutally murdered the tánáhdár; but he retreated into Hyderabad territory on the arrival of troops.

CHAP. II. ENGLISH PERIOD.

The most serious outbreak of this period occurred in the Gútála and Pólavaram estates, and involved something in the nature of a campaign. It is described in the account of Pólavaram in Chapter XV.

Quieter times thereafter.

After the permanent settlement, things quieted down, and there have been few important outbreaks since. The pressure of that settlement and the enforcement of decrees against defaulting zamindars occasionally caused disturbances. It is to these that Munro refers in his minute of 1822 quoted in Chapter XI. 'We are every day liable,' he wrote, 'to be dragged into a petty warfare among unhealthy hills, where an enemy is hardly ever seen, where numbers of valuable lives are lost by the climate, and where we often lose but never gain reputation.' He deplored the want of respect and loyalty to Government in the province, which he ascribed to the prevalence of the zamindari system. It was no doubt largely due to the gradual downfall of that system that the increased peace and order of the country were due.

Subba Reddi's rebellion, 1858.

A petty disturbance took place in 1858 among the hills north of Yernagúdem, which is of interest as having been indirectly connected with the Mutiny. It originated in a private dispute among some hill chiefs about a woman; but the leader of the affair, Subba Reddi, pleaded that he had heard that Nána Sáhib was advancing with his victorious army and that 'whoever did most against the English would be rewarded most.' At the head of a large body of Kóyas he killed the village magistrate of Buttayagúdem, who kept as his mistress a rich widow whom Subba Reddi wanted to marry to his son, plundered some villages, and successfully resisted a body of 60 or 70 peons led against him by the Head Assistant Magistrate. Two companies of Sappers and Miners were sent to Yernagúdem and thence marched against the rebels. The only place where they made a stand was Jílugumilli (Pólavaram taluk) but their resistance was brief and they dispersed into the jungle. They were pursued by a force of armed peons embodied for the purpose, and Subba Reddi and seven other ringleaders were ultimately captured and hanged.

Outbreaks in Rampa.

The Rampa country was a continual source of trouble. The disturbances there were not generally in the nature of a revolt against supposed oppression, since no revenue was collected in the country till towards the end of the century. They were either plundering raids or internal feuds. Government became involved in the latter by championing the mansabdar against his muttadars, and it was his abuse of this support which ultimately led to the Rampa rebellion of

1879 and the removal of the mansabdar. The chief disturbances which occurred were the mansabdar's incursion of 1813 into the plains; the trouble consequent on his expulsion in 1840; the resistance to him in 1858 and 1862, and the 'Rampa rebellion' of 1879. These are briefly described in the account of Rampa in Chapter XV.

CHAPTER III.

THE PEOPLE.

GENERAL CHARACTERISTICS—Density of the population—Its growth—Parent-tongue—Religions. THE JAINS. THE MUSALMANS. THE CHRISTIANS—American Evangelical Lutheran Mission—The Canadian Baptist Mission—The Church Missionary Society—The Roman Catholic Mission. THE HINDUS—Villages — Houses — Dress—Food—Amusements—Superstitions—Village, caste, and family gods—Marriage rules and ceremonies—Funerals. PRINCIPAL CASTES—Telugu Bráhmans—Rázus—Kómatis—Kápus—Kammas—Perikes—Ídigas—Gamallas—Karnabattus—Sánis—Málas—Mádigas—Kóyas—Hill Reddis.

CHAP. III. GENERAL CHARACTERISTICS. — Density of the population.

THE Gódávari district contained, in 1901, 1,445,961 inhabitants, or 257 to the square mile. The density of the population in the various taluks and divisions varies greatly. In the Agency as a whole it averages only 51 persons to the square mile, while in the rest of the district it is as high as 516. In the Chódavaram and Yellavaram divisions of the Agency the figure is less than 35, but in Pólavaram it rises to 103. Outside the Agency, the rich delta taluks of Nagaram, Cocanada and Rámachandrapuram are the most thickly populated, while Peddápuram and Tuni come at the bottom of the list.

Its growth.

The population increased by ten per cent. in the decade 1891–1901, against an average of seven per cent. in the Presidency as a whole. Much of this was due to the extraordinary amount of emigration from Vizagapatam which has occurred. The greatest proportional increase was in Cocanada, where it was as high as 16·5 per cent., in Bhadráchalam, 15 per cent. and in Rajahmundry, 14 per cent. The relative advance was smallest in Pitháburam, Tuni and Peddápuram.

Parent-tongue.

The prevailing language of the district is Telugu, which is spoken by 96 per cent. of the people. Hindustáni is the homespeech of 1·4 per cent. of them, and the small remainder talk Uriya, Yerukala, Maráthi, and Kóya, the vernacular of the hill tribe of that name.

Religions.

The large majority of the people (1,411,573) are Hindus or Animists. Only 24,646 of them are Musalmans and only 5,497 Christians. There are hardly any Jains. Musalmans are found in the largest numbers in Rajahmundry, Cocanada and Amalápuram, and are fewest in Tuni and the Agency. Christians are commonest in Rajahmundry and Cocanada, the head-quarters of the chief missionary bodies.

THE JAINS.

As already noted in Chapter II, the district was once ruled by the Buddhist emperor Asóka and perhaps remained

THE JAINS.

Buddhist in religion until the middle of the seventh century. A number of Buddhist or Jain remains survive in it. The village of Áriyavattam in Cocanada taluk is sometimes called Jain-pádu ('the Jain ruins') and contains several large but rude images of figures sitting cross-legged in the traditional attitude of contemplation. These are not now worshipped, but images of a similar nature in the streets of Pithápuram are still worshipped by Hindus there under the name of *sanyási dévulu* ('ascetic gods'), and are honoured with a festival in times of drought. At Nédunúru in the Amalápuram taluk are other images of this king which are said to be the largest in the district, and yet other similar relics are found at Kazulúru, Yendamúru and Síla in Cocanada taluk, Jallúru in Pithápuram division, Atréyapuram in Amalápuram, Tátipáka in Nagaram, and Drákshárámam in Rámachandrapuram taluk. There are also many large revetted wells in the Nagaram and Amalápuram taluks which for some obscure reason are called 'Jain wells.'

THE MUSALMANS.

The relations of the Musalmans with their Hindu neighbours are on the whole friendly; though petty disputes sometimes arise at festival times, when the processions or observances of the one offend the other. Followers of the faith are generally engaged in menial work or petty trade, and few of them are wealthy. They have no local places of pilgrimage, though the Muhammadans of Drákshárámam in Rámachandrapuram taluk say that the *darga* of their local saint was once regularly visited by the pious of the district. A few of the mixed class called Dúdékus occur. They are said to be the descendants of converts from Hinduism, and, though they profess the Muhammadan religion, most of them speak only Telugu, wear the Hindu cloth and not the trousers or the kilt *(lunji)* of the Muhammadans, and adopt Hindu names. They cannot intermarry with other Musalmans and are looked down upon because they are musicians and cotton-cleaners.

THE CHRISTIANS.

There are four Christian missions in the district; namely, the Roman Catholics and the Canadian Baptist Mission with their head-quarters at Cocanada, the American Evangelical Lutheran Mission of Rajahmundry, and the Church Missionary Society, which works a small 'district' from Dummagúdem in Bhadráchalam taluk.

American Evangelical Lutheran Mission.

The American Evangelical Lutheran Mission was founded by the North German Mission Society in 1844. The first missionary sent out was the Rev. L. M. Valette. He selected Rajahmundry as his head-quarters and took up his residence there in 1844. Soon afterwards, in consequence of the

CHAP. III. THE CHRISTIANS.

unsettled condition of things in Germany and financial embarrassment in the church, the North German Mission Society found itself unable to support the mission; and in 1851 transferred the care of it to the General Synod of the American Lutheran Church, which was working in the Kistna district with head-quarters at Guntúr.

Owing to the difficulties regarding both men and means occasioned by the American Civil War, the General Synod found it impossible to carry on the work at all its stations; and in 1870 the mission was transferred to the General Council of the American Lutheran Church, by whom it is now managed.

Six European missionaries and six ladies are now working in this district. The 'field' visited by them includes large portions of all the low country taluks except Nagaram, Cocanada and Tuni, and also the northern portion of Kistna, whence come the majority of the converts. Statistics of the work in this district alone are not available, but altogether the mission has now some 250 congregations and a baptized membership of nearly 12,000, manages a number of schools, and is educating some 5,800 boys in primary classes. Of its schools, the girls' and boys' central schools at Rajahmundry (the latter of which contains 150 pupils) are considerable institutions with substantial buildings, and the high schools at Rajahmundry and Peddápuram contain 350 and 540 boys respectively on their rolls. The mission is now erecting buildings for a new central boys' school and seminary at Rajahmundry and a hostel for the accommodation of 200 boys the estimated cost of which is Rs. 60,000, and has also decided to put up new accommodation for the Peddápuram high school. The mission also supports a large dispensary [1] and a small hospital at Rajahmundry, and the erection of a new hospital building there, at a cost of Rs. 60,000 has been sanctioned by the American Board which controls its affairs. The mission has nine churches in the district, ten bungalows and 154 school houses. Its total expenditure on education in 1904 was over Rs. 20,000, and on medical institutions nearly Rs. 5,000. The mission is in charge of the Rev. J. H. Harper, who has kindly furnished the above information.

The Canadian Baptist Mission.

The Canadian Baptist Mission owes its origin to the Revs. Thomas Gabriel and John McLaurin, D.D., who started work in Cocanada in 1869. The present mission premises in that town were acquired in 1876. A station was established at Tuni in 1878, a seminary for training school-masters and

[1] See Chapter IX, p. 151.

CHAP. III. THE CHRISTIANS.

preachers at Samalkot in 1882, and stations at Peddápuram in 1891 and Rámachandrapuram in 1893.

The mission's 'field' in this district includes the whole of Cocanada and Tuni divisions and parts of the Pithápuram division and the Rámachandrapuram, Rajahmundry and Peddápuram taluks. Its European staff includes six missionaries, all of whom are ordained and five of whom are assisted by their wives, and nine unmarried lady missionaries. One of the missionaries possesses full medical qualifications and two of the ladies are trained nurses. The mission possesses 2,400 adherents and 24 churches, five of the latter being substantial buildings.

It also undertakes educational and philanthropic work. Its educational institutions include 35 day schools with an average attendance of 450 boys and 425 girls, 88 Sunday schools with 2,000 pupils, free primary boarding schools for boys at Rámachandrapuram and Tuni (preparatory for the Samalkot seminary), a free lower secondary boarding school for girls at Cocanada, the Timpany Memorial high school at Cocanada and the Samalkot seminary. The high school was founded in memory of the Rev. A. V. Timpany, who was in charge of the mission from 1879 till 1885, when he died of cholera, and receives European boys and girls (the latter as boarders) and a few native girls. The Samalkot seminary comprises a theological school, a training school for primary teachers, a lower secondary school and a primary school, and its pupils number about a hundred. The mission has also a small industrial school with some twenty pupils at Cocanada. The total expenditure of the mission on education in 1903, including the salaries of the missionaries engaged solely in that work, amounted to Rs. 25,580.

The philanthropic institutions of the mission include the Kellock Leper Home, the Phillips Memorial Home, and the hospital and dispensary at Rámachandrapuram ; and a hospital is being built at Pithápuram. The two Homes are referred to in Chapter IX. The mission publishes a weekly newspaper in Telugu and maintains a public reading room at Cocanada. The Rev. H. F. Laflamme has been good enough to furnish this information regarding its work.

The Church Society.

The mission at Dummagúdem was started through the influence of Sir Arthur Cotton, and work was first begun there by his brother-in-law, the late Major-General Haig, R.E.,[1] when in charge of the Upper Gódávari navigation works (see p. 128), and at the cost of the engineers on that project. The mission is now under the Church Missionary Society. No

[1] The builder of the Gannavaram aqueduct; see p. 86.

CHAP. III. THE CHRISTIANS.

European missionaries resided regularly at Dummagúdem till 1874, but since then, with an interval from 1879 to 1882, the Rev. J. Cain has been stationed there. The field of the mission is practically confined to the Bhadráchalam taluk, and the work lies mainly among the Kóyas and Málas. The converts number 900, and the mission maintains at Dummagúdem a dispensary, a lower secondary boys' school, a girls' day school and boys' and girls' boarding schools, besides seventeen day schools in other parts of the district. The lace-work done by the converts at Dummagúdem is referred to in Chapter VI.

The Roman Catholic Mission.

The Roman Catholic Mission was started about 50 years ago by French priests of Savoy belonging to the mission of St. Francis of Sales. It is included in the Diocese of Vizagapatam. The convent in Yanam was built by Bishop Neyret in 1850, the church at Cocanada in 1854 by Bishop Tissot, and the church at Yanam in 1859. Chapels have been erected at Samalkot, Dowlaishweram and Rajahmundry. Two European priests are working in the district at Cocanada and Rajahmundry. The Roman Catholic congregation numbers some 900, of whom about one-third are Europeans and Eurasians and most of the others Tamils. Want of funds has hampered attempts to convert the Telugus.

The mission owns a handsome convent at Cocanada which is in charge of seven European Sisters, is used as a lower secondary school, and gives instruction to some eighty or ninety European and Eurasian girls, about half of whom are boarders. The convent at Yanam is used as a Hindu girls' school and teaches some 150 pupils ; and the mission manages a boys' lower primary school at Cocanada and a small dispensary at the same town.

THE HINDUS.

The very large majority of the population of the district are Hindus or Animists, and these require more lengthy treatment. The Animists, those who reverence animistic deities and not the gods of the Hindu pantheon, are almost all found in the Agency. An attempt will first be made to describe the salient features of the religious and social life of the Hindus of the low country (customs in the Agency are referred to in the accounts below of the Kóyas and hill Reddis) and then to give some description of the castes which are characteristic of the district or occur in it in unusual numbers.

Villages.

The villages of the district, unlike those in the Deccan, were seldom fortified, and consequently (except in the delta) the houses are not closely crowded together, but are built with plenty of room between them, like those in southern villages.

CHAP. III. THE HINDUS.

The lowest castes are required to live in separate quarters; but the Bráhmans, unlike those of the south, do not mind dwelling side by side with Súdras and do not always have their own distinct streets.

Houses.

The houses seldom have terraced roofs, and are generally thatched with palmyra leaves. Tiles are common in towns, but much less so outside them. Under the roof a terrace or ceiling of mud is often made with the double object of serving as a loft or store-house, and of protecting the house itself if the roof gets on fire. The walls of houses are generally of mud. Brick and stone are comparatively rare. In the Agency the walls are generally of split bamboo, sometimes smeared with mud. Outside the big towns, houses of two storeys are rare.

Among all but the lowest classes, houses are very usually built on one of two type plans, called respectively the *chávadi illu* or 'hall house,' and the *manduva illu* or 'courtyard house,' also called the 'fourroom plan.' The two figures below will give an idea of how each is arranged:—

Manduva house.

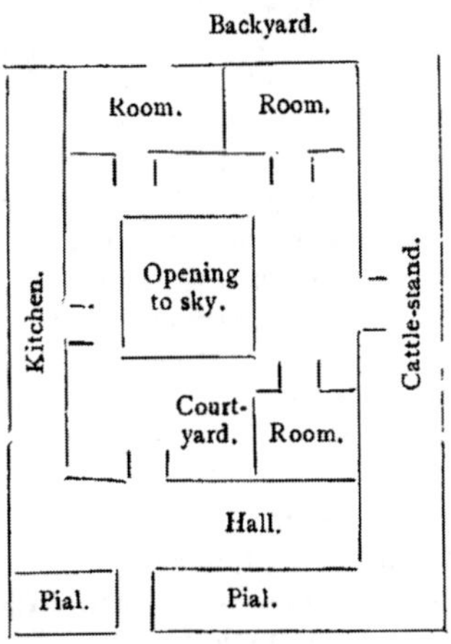

Chávadi house.

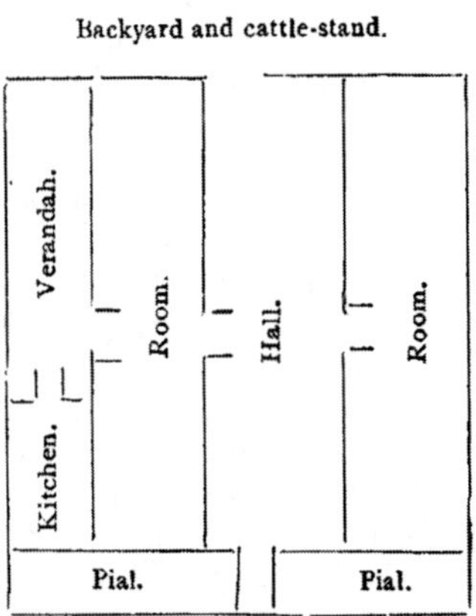

Both have narrow pials in front. The essential difference is that in the *chávadi illu* the door leads into a long broad hall *(chávadi)* which stretches from the front of the house to the back, with rooms at the sides; whereas in the other the hall is a narrow passage running from one side of the house to the other, from which a door leads into a courtyard, open in the centre but surrounded by verandahs out of which the rooms open. The latter kind is most commonly used by the higher

CHAP. III. THE HINDUS.

or richer classes, and resembles the typical house of the southern country in having an opening *(manduva)* in the middle of the courtyard to let in light. The kitchen is usually located if possible in the western part of the house, but even if it is not, it is still called the 'west room' *(padamati illu)*. The front steps of the houses are usually decorated with lines of powdered chunam, the lower parts of the doorposts with the usual saffron and kunkumam in honour of Lakshmi, and the sides of the pials and walls with white spots made with chunam and water.

Dress.

The dress of the Hindus presents no very special peculiarities. Little boys of the higher castes usually wear short breeches or drawers as their only garments, and those of the poorer classes nothing but the langúti or piece-cloth. Little girls of the two classes wear respectively a petticoat and bodice, and a bit of cloth wound round their waists. Orthodox married Bráhman men tie their waist-cloths in the usual complicated manner called *panchakachcham*. Others of the upper classes tie them, as elsewhere, once or twice round the waist and then pass the upper front fold between their legs and tuck it in at the back. The favourite colour for the cloth is red. Málas and Mádigas ordinarily wear only a langúti. The women usually dress in white cloths. Dancing-girls wear petticoats and bodices, and bodices are common among other castes also. The women's cloths are nearly always of cotton; silk is a rarity. Bráhman women, as elsewhere, pass between their legs the outer front fold of the part which goes round their waists, and tuck it into their waists behind. Women working in the fields tuck their garments between their legs and then pull them up as high as they can. The women of most subdivisions of the Bráhmans, and also those of the Kómatis, Kamsalas and Perikes, wear the cloth over the left shoulder instead of the right.

The men do not usually shave the whole of their heads except one top-knot, as in the south, but often cut their hair like Europeans. Telugu Bráhmans differ from their Tamil caste-fellows in frequently wearing moustaches.

Tattooing is very common as an adornment among the women, and two or three straight lines are sometimes tattooed across painful swellings, to act as a blister. The *ponna chettu* (the favourite tree of Krishna) is a popular ornamental pattern, and Ráma's feet and the chank and *chakram* of Vishnu are also common.

Food.

The ordinary food-grain of the district is rice. Even outside the delta, in such upland parts as Tuni and Pithápuram, rice is commonly eaten, though it is often mixed with cambu *(ganti)* and ragi *(tsódi)*. In the Agency, cholam *(jonna)* is the commonest food. Bráhmans, Kamsalas, and the Gavara and Lingadhári Kómatis are apparently the only castes which do not eat meat. Málas and Mádigas will eat beef and carrion, and Nakkalas are fond of jackal. A good many castes will eat hare, which elsewhere is often considered unclean.

The labouring classes have three meals a day, at 8 A.M., midday, and 8 P.M.; orthodox Bráhmans two meals, at about 11 A.M., and 8 P.M.; while officials and the richer people eat at 10 A.M., 3 P.M., and 8 P.M., and often have early coffee as well at about 7 A.M. But coffee is much less drunk in this district than in the south. Smoking, on the contrary, is a habit with all except the orthodox Bráhmans. Even the women of many castes smoke, and little boys and girls may also often be seen with cheroots in their mouths. Opium is freely eaten by most classes, especially, it is said, as a prophylactic against fever. It is also considered an excellent tonic for children and the aged.[1]

Amusements.

The boys of the district play much the same kinds of games as in the south. They fly kites and play at marbles, tipcat *(gónibilla)*, a kind of rounders *(banthulu)*, a sort of blind man's buff and many other games. Girls and women of the higher castes have quieter indoor pastimes, such as tossing up and catching tamarind seeds, and various games with cowries on a board. Men have no outdoor sports, but play cards and chess. A popular local card-game is called *dasâvatári*. This is played with a pack of 120 cards, containing ten suits of twelve cards each. Each suit consists of a king, a vizier and ten plain cards and is called after, and marked with the image of, one of the ten incarnations *(avatárs)* of Vishnu. In half the suits the higher plain cards take the lower, as in English cards, and in the other half the opposite is the case. A trump card is turned up and the tricks are won in much the same way as at Bridge. All except the higher classes are devoted to cock-fighting. Boatmen going down the river often take their cocks with them to pit them against the birds of the villages on the way. Puppet shows are very common. The puppets are concealed from the audience by a sheet on to which their shadows are thrown by a light behind them.

[1] The two common medicines of the district are *nalla mandu* ('black medicine,' *i.e.*, opium) and *tella madu* ('white medicine,' *i.e.*, a preparation of mercury). These are everywhere known and frequently used. The latter is a laxative. The former has a contrary effect.

CHAP. III. THE HINDUS. — Superstition.

The superstitions of the people are legion. A few typical examples may be given. If an owl perches on a house, it brings ill luck to the inmates. A crow cawing on the roof of a house indicates the arrival of a guest. Bad omens include being questioned regarding business on which one is setting out, or, directly after leaving the house, catching sight of one Bráhman, two Súdras, a widow, oil, a snake, a shikári, or a sanyási. Good omens are hearing a bell ring, a cannon go off, the braying of an ass, the cry of a Bráhmani kite, or, on first leaving the house, seeing a married woman, a corpse, flowers, water or a toddy pot. Talismans are commonly worn. A usual kind is a flat piece of metal with a figure of Hanumán on it. Another, made of leather with the skin of a lizard got from a Mádiga stitched into it, is hung round the shoulders of weak and sickly children. Women and houses are supposed often to be possessed of devils, whom only a professional sorcerer can exorcise. Yerukala women are in great request as exorcists. In cases of illness supposed to be due to the ill will of a god or spirit, three handfuls of rice are carried round the invalid, and are then placed in a winnowing fan, which is held by both the patient and the sorceress. The latter then scans the former's face, professes to be able to read there the name of the offended spirit, and advises as to the propitiation to be made. In the Agency, belief in witchcraft is exceptionally strong, and almost every ill is thought to be due to the person's being bewitched. The old rája of Cherla, just across the border, was especially afraid of witches and wizards, and before the British occupation of the taluk an easy method of ridding oneself of an enemy there was to accuse him of practising the black art. The rája immediately seized and hanged him.[1]

Childbirth is surrounded by a number of superstitions. A pregnant woman should not see an eclipse, or her child will be born deformed. The pains of childbirth are relieved by turning the face of the bull god in a Saivite temple away from the emblem of Siva, or by the woman's touching a ring made of a mixture of gold, silver, copper, lead and iron by a fasting blacksmith on the day of an eclipse. A child whose first tooth comes in the upper jaw is supposed to foreshadow evil to its maternal uncle; and may not be seen by that relative till he has neutralized the omen by seeing the reflection of the child in a bowl of oil and broken a cocoanut. Similarly, as elsewhere, a girl who has attained maturity in an inauspicious hour may not be looked at by her husband until they have seen each other's reflections in a bowl of oil. Some

[1] Rev. Mr. Cain in the *Indian Antiquary*, v. 303.

dreams are supposed to foretell events. Thus it is a good thing to dream of being bitten by a cobra, especially if the bite drew blood.

It is believed that a barren tree will bear if a naked man cuts a piece off it on the day of an eclipse; that the nesting of a clay-building fly in a house foretells the birth of a child; that the appearance of a swarm of ants or a blood-sucker in the house foreshadows some benefit; that a child which sneezes on a winnowing fan or on the door-frame will meet with misfortune unless balls of boiled rice-flour are thrown over it; and that a man who sneezes during his meals, especially at night, will also be unlucky unless water is sprinkled over his face and he is made to pronounce his own name and that of his birth-place and his patron deity. People who have lost two children and expect to have a third generally beg small pieces of gold from their neighbours with which they make a gold ornament to put in the nose of the new-born baby. The child is called, if a boy, Pullayya or Pentayya, and if a girl, either Pullamma or Pentamma, meaning respectively 'used up leaf-plates' or 'refuse.' The idea is to propitiate by due humility the nemesis of the power whose enmity has caused the death of the previous children, and is common in other districts.

Scarcity of rain is dealt with in various ways. It is considered very efficacious if the Bráhmans take in procession round the village an image of Varuna (the god of rain) made of mud from the bank of a river or tank. Another method is to pour 1,000 pots of water over the lingam in the Siva temple. Málas tie a live frog to a mortar and put on the top of the latter a mud figure representing Gontiyálamma, the mother of the Pándava brothers. They then take these objects in procession, singing 'Mother frog, playing in water, pour rain by pots full.' The villagers of other castes then come and pour water over the Málas.

Village, caste, and family gods.

Besides the orthodox gods of the Hindu pantheon, three other classes of supernatural beings are commonly worshipped. These are the village goddesses referred to below, who are essentially local in character; the caste deities, who are objects of special reverence among special castes; and the family deities, namely the *virudu*, or soul of some dead bachelor of the family, and the *pérantam* or spirit of some woman outlived by her husband, who have been accorded apotheosis because they appeared in a dream to some member of the family and announced that they had been made immortal.

CHAP. III. THE HINDUS.

The village deities are always female, and usually can only be propitiated by the shedding of blood. They are not, however, merely malevolent, but will confer benefits on those whom they favour. Some of the most common of them are Núkálamma, Paradésamma, Néralamma, Mallamma, Pólérammа, Muthyálamma, Peddintamma, Sómalamma, Bangárammа, Mávullamma, and Talupulamma. Wherever one of them is established, her brother, who always goes by the name of Póturázu, is also worshipped. Some of them have a reputation far beyond the local limits of their villages, and are visited by pilgrims from distant places. Núkálamma of Kándrakóta in Peddápuram taluk, Mávullamma of Márédipáka in Rámachandrapuram and Sómalamma of Rajahmundry are famous almost throughout the district. These village goddesses are ordinarily worshipped only on the occasion of their annual festival. A buffalo and a number of sheep and fowls are then sacrificed to them. The fowls are killed at the four corners of the village; the buffalo is slain at about midnight on the last day of the festival, its blood is collected in a pot, and grain of various kinds is put into it. The blood is left in the temple in front of the goddess, and a day or two later the prospects of the harvest are foretold from the degree to which the various kinds of grain have sprouted.

Among the deities who are worshipped by special castes are Kanyakamma, the goddess of the Kómatis, referred to later, the Káttumai (who is also sometimes called Káttumáhésvarudu) of the Gamallas and Idigas, the Gontiyálamma (the mother of the Pándava brothers) of the Málas, the Kamsalas' Kámákshi-amma, the Karnabattus' Sómésvara, and the Mádigas' Mátangiralu. Bráhman families also often have some favourite deity whom they worship in preference to all others.

Maridamma, who in many respects corresponds to the Máriamma of the south, is purely malevolent in character and is not in the habit of conferring benefits. She brings disease upon the villages, but can be induced by becoming worship to hold her hand. She is offered animal sacrifices whenever serious sickness visits a village. Sometimes a small car is made to which pigs and fowls are tied and which is then dragged through the village. Every household pours offerings of rice, etc., upon it and it is at last left outside the village limits to symbolise the departure of the goddess. The animals are taken away by the Málas and Mádigas.[1]

[1] A somewhat similar ceremony is mentioned in the *Bellary Gazetteer*, 60.

CHAP. III. THE HINDUS.

Marriage rules and ceremonies.

Before proceeding to refer to the principal castes of the district it will be convenient to refer to some general aspects of the rules and ceremonies which prevail at marriages and funerals among the non-Bráhman castes of the low country.

Most of these castes are split into endogamous subdivisions, marriage outside of which is forbidden, and some have also exogamous sections of these subdivisions, marriage outside which is compulsory. The latter are known as *inti pérulu*, or 'house-names.' The most suitable bride for a man is usually thought to be his maternal uncle's daughter, and in some castes he is compelled to marry her unless she be deformed or mentally deficient. This rule is called *ménarikam*. Divorce and the re-marriage of widows and divorcées are not allowed by Bráhmans or the castes which copy Bráhman ways. The same may be said of the practice of paying a bride-price.

There are three stages in the ordinary marriage. First a formal betrothal, secondly the wedding which makes the couple man and wife, and lastly a nuptial ceremony when they begin to live together.

The betrothal usually takes place in the bride's house, and is a formal ceremony at which *pánsupári* is exchanged, the bridegroom is given new clothing *(sápu)*, or some other token of the undertaking is granted.

The wedding sometimes takes place in the bride's house and sometimes in the bridegroom's. It generally occurs after dark and usually occupies only one day, but among the Bráhmans and some higher castes it lasts for three or five days. In the latter cases the marriage-badge *(táli* or *satamánam)* referred to below is tied round the bride's neck on the first day, and the saffron threads removed from the wrists of the happy pair on the last. On the day previous to the wedding the bridegroom's party goes to the bride's house with presents of fruit, etc., and a new cloth for her. Some married woman of the party then ties a saffron-coloured thread *(bondu)* round the neck of the bride, the ceremony being called *pradánam*. Sometimes this is done on the night of the wedding. On this night the couple are seated side by side, their toe-nails are solemnly cut by a barber man and woman, the bridegroom's front hair is clipped, and they both put on new clothes. Next the bride worships a rice mortar representing Gauri, the wife of Siva, and her parents make obeisance to the bridegroom. The pair then tie saffron threads *(kankanam)* round each others' wrists, put a little cummin on each others' heads, and do reverence to the *táli*, which the bridegroom ties round the bride's neck. They next pour rice mixed with ghee and milk on each others' heads (a ceremony

CHAP. III. THE HINDUS.

called *talambrálu* and signifying a solemn vow of fidelity) and the bridegroom places his foot on the bride's. This and the tying of the *kankanam* are the binding parts of the ceremony. The star Arundhati (popularly called Aranjóti) is pointed out to the bride as typical of chastity, and the couple do worship to some coloured pots *(avirédi)* representing the gods. The relatives give presents of money *(katnam)* to the bride, which are not supposed to be retained, but are returned to the givers on the first convenient occasion. The final rites are performed next morning, or in some castes on the third or fifth day. The bridegroom ties a string of black glass beads round the bride's neck, and the saffron threads are removed from the couple's wrists. They then are given a pot of water coloured with chunam and saffron in which a ring and some other ornaments have been placed, and they scramble for the ornaments, like children hunting in a bran pie.

The nuptial rites, which are simple, are performed on a separate occasion, since days auspicious for weddings are not suitable for them.

The ceremonies at the re-marriage of a widow are, as elsewhere, much shorter. The bridegroom merely goes to her house, ties the *táli*, and takes her to his house the same night.

Funerals.

The dead are usually burnt, but children are buried and some simple rite is performed, such as the pouring of milk, either alone or mixed with rice or oil and ghee, on the grave. The ceremonies at the funerals of adults are much the same in all non-Bráhman castes. The body is bathed and is borne to the burning-ground on a bier. The Málas and Mádigas carry it in their arms in a sitting posture. The corpse is set down three times on the road while rice is placed at the four corners of the bier. When it has been placed on the pyre, the son of the deceased walks thrice round it with a pot of water in which three holes have been made, and lights the pyre with face averted. The relatives then go home and worship a lamp. Further ceremonies are performed on the eleventh day afterwards (called the *pèdda dinam* or 'great day') and on some day between the second and fifth after it, which is called the *chinna dinam* or 'small day.' On the latter the bones and ashes are collected and are offered a ball of cooked rice. The party then returns home and feasts.

PRINCIPAL CASTES.

Statistics of the numerous castes which occur in the Gódávari district will be found in the separate Appendix to this volume. Space prevents reference to the whole of them, and most of them, indeed, are common to the whole of the Telugu country and their ways do not differ in this district from those of their caste-fellows elsewhere.

PRINCIPAL CASTES.

The six most numerous communities (taking them in the order of their strength) are the Kápus, the landowning class; the Málas, outcaste agricultural labourers; the Ídigas, who draw toddy; the Mádigas, outcaste workers in leather; the Kammas, who are closely connected with the Kápus and resemble them in their social customs; and the Telugu-speaking Bráhmans.

All these are shortly referred to below, and, in addition, some notes are given regarding a few communities which occur in greater strength in this district than in any other; namely, the Rázus, who claim to be Kshatriyas; the Kómatis, traders and money-lenders; the Perikes, who are cultivators; the Gamallas, an offshoot from the Ídigas; the Karnabattu, weavers; the Sánis, many of whose women are dancing-girls; and the two hill tribes of the Kóyas and the hill Reddis.

Of all of these castes the Bráhmans take the highest social position, and they may be first referred to.

Telugu Bráhmans.

Telugu-speaking Bráhmans are unusually numerous in Gódávari. Some of them, though their home-speech is Telugu, appear to have a Tamil or Canarese origin. Among the former are the Kónasíma Bráhmans of Amalápuram taluk, who have a tradition (see p. 204) that they came from near Kúmbakónam in Tanjore district; the Áramas, who are few and scattered; and the Divilis, who are to be found chiefly in Pithápuram taluk. The Telugu Bráhmans proper, also called Ándhras, are a linguistic division of the Drávidas, one of the two great classes (Drávida and Gauda) into which all Bráhmans in this Presidency are divided. They are popularly subdivided into the following sectarian, territorial and occupational groups:—

- Ándhra Bráhmans.
  - Vaishnavites.
    - Tengalais.
    - Nambis.
    - Golconda Vyápáris.
  - Smártas ...
    - Velinádu ... ...
      - Vaidíki.
      - Niyógi or Áruvéla Niyógi.
      - Pújári.
    - Véginádu ...
    - Telagánya ...
      - Vaidíki.
      - Niyógi.
    - Kásiléya.
    - Murikinádu.
    - Kákumánu.
    - Kalinga.
    - Tambala Pújári.
    - Karnakamma.
      - Vyápári.
      - Vaidíki.
    - Prathamasákha.

CHAP. III. PRINCIPAL CASTES.

It will be seen that the primary division is sectarian, into Vaishnavites and Smártas. Among the former there are none of the Vadagalais, the rival sect to the Tengalais; Nambis are priests in the temples; and the origin of the name Golconda Vyápáris ('traders') is not clear.

Among the Smártas, the Velinádus say they came from 'the Vidarbha country near Kondavídu'; the Véginádus claim to have come from the Vengi country in the neighbourhood of Ellore; the Telagányas give their original home as the Trilingam country, which they locate between Srísailam in Kurnool, Kálahasti in North Arcot, and Drákshárámam in this district; the Kásiléyas state that they belong to the Kósala country, or Orissa; the Murikinádus say that they come from 'the Máladamo country in the north'; the Kákumánus are perhaps connected with the village of that name in the Kistna district; and the Kalingas are evidently connected with the ancient country of that name referred to in the last chapter. The Tambala Pújáris are an occupational subdivision, who officiate as priests in the Saivite temples and correspond to the Tamil Gurukkals. The Karnakammas say their real name is Karna Rukkumus and is derived from their adherence to the Rig Véda. The Prathamasákhas ('people of the first division') profess to owe their name to the fact that they follow that division of the Yajur Véda. They also go by the name of the 'mid-day Paraiyans,' the story being that they labour under a curse which makes them Paraiyans for an hour at midday. The Velinádus and Telagányas are further subdivided into the well-known occupational groups of Vaidíkis (or priests) and Niyógis (or secularists), and the former have also a third group, namely, the Pújáris. Karnakammas are split into Vaidíkis and Vyápáris, or traders. The name Áruvéla Niyógi by which the Velinádu Niyógis are known is said to be due to the fact that this section numbered just 6,000 persons when it split off from the Vaidíkis. Its members have three sectarian subdivisions; namely Smártas, Lingadháris (who favour Lingáyat practices) and Golconda Vyápáris, who have gone over to the Vaishnavite creed. Some of these Smártas have taken to Vaidíki occupations, though Niyógis by descent, and are called Paddatis. With a few unimportant exceptions these numerous subdivisions of the Telugu Bráhmans will eat together but will not intermarry.

Though in the study of the Védas and the observance of the more important ceremonies of the caste the Telugu Bráhmans are not inferior to their castemen in the southern districts, they are less scrupulous in several minor matters. They will smoke, for example, and eat opium. They perhaps, also, have less influence in religious and social matters over other castes than in the south. The lower classes do not make them the ready *namaskáram* obeisance which is usual in Tanjore, for example, nor is there the same anxiety to follow their social and domestic ceremonies. Nor do the Telugu Bráhmans hold themselves as severely aloof from the upper non-Bráhman castes as in the south. It has already been mentioned that they seldom live in separate quarters in the villages, and they will give a respectable non-Bráhman food in any part of their houses except the kitchen, a piece of latitude which would be most unusual in Tanjore.

Attached to the caste is the beggar community called Vipravinódis ('amusers of Bráhmans'), who are professional sorcerers and jugglers who decline to perform unless some Bráhman is present, and subsist chiefly on alms begged from the members of that caste. Several unconvincing tales are told to account for this odd connection between two such widely differing classes but, as will be seen immediately, several other castes in this district have beggar communities attached particularly to them and in some cases these are declared to consist of their illegitimate descendants.

Rázus.

The Rázus also stand high in the social scale. They are numerous in the Amalápuram and Rámachandrapuram taluks, and there is a large colony of them in Tuni town. They say they are Kshatriyas, wear the sacred thread, keep their womenkind strictly gósha, have Bráhmanical gótras, decline to eat with other non-Bráhmans, and are divided into the three clans of Súrya (sun), Chandra (moon), and Machi (fish) Rázus, of whom the first claim to be descended from the kings of Oudh, of the same lineage as Ráma; the second, from the kings of Hastinápura, of the same line as the Pándavas; and the third from Hanumán and a mermaid. These subdivisions may eat together, and among the zamindars the first two intermarry. The solar line is the commonest in this district. Written contracts of marriage are exchanged; the wedding is performed in the bride's house; at the *pradánam* ceremony no *bondu* (saffron thread) is tied round the bride's neck; the bridegroom has to wear a sword throughout the marriage ceremonies, and he is paraded round the village with it before they begin; and the saffron thread *(kankanam)* which is tied round the wrists of the couple is of wool and cotton instead of cotton alone.

The Rázus are chiefly employed in cultivation. Their turbans are made to bunch out at the left side above the ear, and one end of them hangs down behind. They do not shave

CHAP. III. PRINCIPAL CASTES.

any part of their heads and allow long locks to hang down in front of their ears.

The beggar community attached to them are the Bhatrázus, who were originally their court bards and panegyrists, but now beg from other castes as well and have less special claim upon them than formerly. These people are notorious for their importunity and their gift for lampooning those who refuse them alms, and they trade upon the fact.

Kómatis.

The Kómatis are the great trading and money-lending caste of the Telugu country, and are not popular. They call themselves Vaisyas, wear the sacred thread, claim to have 102 'gótras,' and of late years some of them have adopted Védic rites at their marriages and funerals in place of the Puránic rites which are traditional with them. But on the other hand their gótras are not Bráhmanical and they follow the Dravidian rule of *ménarikam* in their marriages. In this district they are subdivided into the Gavaras, Kalingas, and Traivarnikas ('third-caste-men'), who neither intermarry nor dine together, and the last of whom differ from the others in the strictness of their observance of Bráhmanical ways. The Gavaras are by far the most numerous.

Their caste goddess, Kanyakamma or Kanyaká Paramésvari already mentioned, is said to be a deification of a beautiful Kómati girl named Vasavamma who belonged to Penugonda in Kistna. The Eastern Chálukya king Vishnuvardhana wanted to marry her, her caste-people objected and were persecuted accordingly, and at last she burnt herself alive to end the trouble. The headmen of 102 families, the ancestors of the present 'gótras,' sacrificed themselves with her. She has many temples, but the chief is at her native village of Penugonda. The fines collected at caste pancháyats are even now sent to this.

Of the 102 'gótras' some at least are totemistic, which is another argument against the twice-born origin of the caste. They are derived from the names of plants, and to this day the members of these gótras may not touch their eponymous plants, and even involuntary contact with them involves ceremonial pollution which must be removed by a bath. Some of these are given in the report on the Madras census of 1901, p. 162. The same volume gives authorities for the custom among Kómatis (which is strenuously denied by them) requiring them to give betel and nut to a Mádiga before a wedding is performed in the caste. The practice is said to be dying out or to be usually veiled by the Kómati giving the Mádiga some cobbling work to do and handing him the betel and nut with the amount of his bill. Members of the caste who admit an obscure connection with these Mádigas explain it by saying that the latter protected them during their trouble with Vishnuvardhana. Some of the Velamas somewhat similarly arrange that a Mála couple shall be married just before a wedding in their own houses, and even find the funds. The Rev. J. Cain says that with the Bhadráchalam Velamas it is a Palli couple that is thus first married. Velamas explain the story by saying that a Mála once allowed a Velama to sacrifice him to propitiate the goddess who guards hidden treasure, and that the custom is kept up out of gratitude for the discovery of the treasure which resulted. Among some classes of Kómatis the women do the cooking while in a state of nudity. Those who admit the practice say that it is done for cleanliness' sake, lest the touch of an impure garment should defile the food.

Attached to the Kómatis are two begging castes called Víramushtis and Mailáris. They are said by the Kómatis to have been the messengers in their dealings with Vishnuvardhana, and, at the last, to have delayed the advent of the king till the holocaust was over. The Víramushtis are wrestlers and bards, and the Mailáris carry round an image of Kanyakamma and sing songs in her praise.

Kápus.

The Kápus or Reddis, by far the most numerous of the castes of the district, are landowners by occupation and are among the most respected of the non-Bráhman bodies. Closely connected with them are the Velamas, the Telagas, the Vantarlu and the Kammas referred to below; and all four of these are probably offshoots of the great Kápu clan. They will usually eat with Kápus even now, but they do not intermarry with them or with one another, and in several instances peculiarities of dress or customs have arisen. The Vantarlus, for example, arrange their top-knot further forward, and more to the left, than the others; tie their cloths differently; dress their women in petticoats and keep them gósha.

It is said that in some districts the Kápus have totemistic subdivisions, but these do not appear to exist in Gódávari. Their marriages are usually celebrated in the bride's house; the women of the bridegroom's family do not attend; and on the last day of the ceremony the couple pretend to plough and sow, a custom which exists among some of the Telugu castes who have emigrated to the Tanjore and Trichinopoly districts.

Kammas.

The Kammas are a cultivating caste closely akin to, and probably a subdivision of, the Kápus. Some of them say they were originally Kshatriyas, but were persecuted by a king because one of them called him a bastard, and therefore

CHAP. III. PRINCIPAL CASTES.

sought refuge with the Kápus and adopted the customs of their protectors. Others of them say that they are descended from the same ancestor as the Velamas and some of the Kápus and that the subdivisions in these castes are the same as in their own. Like the Kápus, they are generally cultivators, and their social position and characteristics are similar.

In this district, Kammas are subdivided into the Kávitis, Erédis, Gampas or Gúdas, Uggams and Ráchas, who eat in each others' houses and intermarry. The names have a totemistic flavour, but according to local accounts are derived from curious household customs, generally from traditional methods of carrying water. Thus the Kávitis ordinarily will not carry water except in pots on a *kávidi;* the Erédis except on a pack-bullock; the Uggams except in pots held in the hand and not borne on their hips or heads; and the Ráchas except in pot carried by two persons. The Gampa women, when they first go to their husbands' houses, take the customary presents in baskets, *gampa* or *gúda.* It is said that these practices are generally observed to the present day. The Káviti and Uggam women are said to wear their cloths over the right shoulder and the Erédi and Gampa women over the left. The Erédi and Uggam women are said to be strictly gósha. The Kammas, support a special beggar caste, namely the Pichchiguntas. These beg only of Kammas, Velamas and certain Kápus.

Perikes.

The Perikes are a small cultivating caste who are particularly numerous in Gódávari. The name means a gunny-bag, and the caste were originally gunny-bag weavers. Those in this district are now mostly cultivators (the Písu Perikes, who still weave gunny, are said not to belong to the caste proper, who call themselves Rácha Perikes) but the gunny-bag plays a part in their traditions and ceremonies. They are perhaps commonest in the Prattipádu subdivision of Peddápuram taluk and the southern villages of Tuni. Their social position is similar to that of the Kápus and Kammas, whom they resemble generally in character and customs. Like some of the Kammas, they claim to be of Kshatriya stock, and say they are of the lineage of Parasu Ráma but were driven out by him for kidnapping his sister while pretending to be gunny-weavers. They say they were brought into this country by the king Nala mentioned in the Mahábhárata in gratitude for their having taken care of his wife Damayanti when he quitted her during his misfortunes. Perikes support the begging caste of the Varugu Bhattas, who, they say, helped them in their exile, and to whom they gave a *sanad* authorizing them to demand alms. These people go round the Perike houses for their dues every year.

The Perike marriage ceremonies are peculiar. On the day of the wedding the bride and groom are made to fast, as are three male relatives whom they call *suribhaktas*. At the marriage the couple sit on a gunny-bag, and another gunny, on which a representation of the god Mailar is drawn or painted, is spread before them. A figure of the same god is drawn on two pots, and these, and also a third pot, are filled with rice and dholl which are then cooked by two married women of the party. The food is then offered to Mailar. Next the three *suribhaktas* take 101 cotton threads, fasten them together, and tie seven knots in them. Bride and bridegroom are then given cloths which have been partly immersed in water coloured with saffron and chunam, and they and the *suribhaktas* are fed with the rice and dholl cooked in the three pots. The couple are then taken round the village in procession, and on their return the knotted cotton threads are tied round the bride's neck instead of a *táli*.

Ídigas.

The Ídigas or Índras are very numerous in Gódávari. They are the Telugu toddy-drawing caste. They are commonly called Chettis *(Chettigándlu)* in this district, but the name Índra is used in the north-east divisions and Ídiga in the central delta. They claim to be descended from Vyása, the traditional compiler of the Mahábhárata. They are still largely employed in toddy-drawing (though some are cultivators) and consequently occupy a low position in the social scale. In some districts, it is said, they bury their dead, prohibit the consumption of alcohol and have endogamous subdivisions, but these things are not so in this district. Some are Saivites and some Vaishnavites, but these are allowed to intermarry.

Two of their marriage ceremonies are peculiar. The couple walk three times round four upright sticks placed so as to make a small square and connected with each other by cotton threads, and then the bridegroom cuts the cotton with a knife. They also make two cakes of rice flour, ghee and sugar, one of which is eaten by themselves and the other by their relatives.

The Ídigas' special god is Káttumai, to whom they annually sacrifice fowls on New Year's Day, and daily offer a few drops of toddy from the first pot taken from the tree.

Gamallas.

The Gamallas are ordinarily supposed to be Ídigas who have bettered themselves and separated from that caste. The more wealthy of them are toddy and arrack shop-keepers, but the poorer members of the caste draw toddy like the Ídigas. Both classes worship the Ídiga deity Káttumai. They support a begging caste called Yenútis or Gavuda Jettis,

CHAP. III. PRINCIPAL CASTES. Karnabattus. The Karnabattus are almost entirely confined to the Gódávari district, and are weavers by occupation. They forbid the re-marriage of widows, but eat even pork. They bury their dead in a sitting posture. Their caste headman is called *sénápati* 'leader of an army.' Their special deity is Sómésvara, whom they unite to worship on the new-moon day of Pushyam (January-February). The god is represented by a mud idol made for the occasion. The *pújári* throws flowers over it in token of adoration and then sits before it with his hands outstretched and his mouth closed until one of the flowers falls into his hands.

Sánis. The Sánis are a small caste of dancing-girls and prostitutes. In this district this class of women is made up of six perfectly distinct castes which are in danger of being confused; namely, the Sánis proper, the Bógams, the Dommara Sánis, the Turaka Sánis, the Mangala Bógams, and the Mádiga Bógams. Of these, the Bógams claim to be superior and will not dance in the presence of, or after a performance by, any of the others. The Sánis do not admit this claim, but they do not mind dancing after the Bógams or in their presence. All the other classes are admittedly inferior to the Sánis and the Bógams. The Mádiga Bógams only dance before, and consort with, Mádigas and Málas. The Dommara Sánis, Turaka Sánis and Mangala Bógams will consort with any of the non-polluting castes.

The Sáni women are not exclusively devoted to their traditional profession. Some of them marry the men of the caste and live respectably at home with them. The men moreover do not, as in the dancing castes of the south, assist in the dancing (as by playing the accompaniments or forming a chorus), but are cultivators and petty traders. Bógam men, however, follow the southern custom. The Sánis, like the dancing-girl castes of the south, keep up their numbers by the adoption and even purchase of girls of other castes, such as Kápus, Kammas and Ídigas. They do service in the temples, but they are not required to be formally dedicated or married to the god, as in the Tamil country. Those of them who are to become prostitutes are usually married to a sword on attaining maturity.

Málas. The Málas are the great agricultural labourer class and are very numerous in the district. They are split into four endogamous subdivisions, the Kantes, the Bóyas or Sadur Bóyas, the Páyikis and the Mála Dásaris. Kúpe, Arava (Tamil) and Bruda ('marsh') are also given as subdivisions. The Mála Dásaris are the caste priests and the Páyikis are sweepers by occupation. The former are admittedly superior to the rest of the caste and the latter are generally regarded as inferior.

None of the subdivisions intermarry or eat in each others' houses. Málas eat beef and are consequently almost at the bottom of the social scale. They are not allowed to enter the Hindu temples; no other caste (not even excluding the Mádigas) will eat in their houses; and they pollute all Súdra castes by touching them or entering their houses, and a Bráhman by even approaching him. Even the Mádigas pretend to be polluted if a Mála enters their houses; but the Málas return the compliment. The ordinary barbers will not work for Málas and they either shave each other or have their own barbers. The ordinary washermen will wash their clothes if these have first been given a preliminary soaking. A peculiar ceremony at their weddings (which is also observed by the Mádigas) consists in burying handfuls of different kinds of grain, and sacrificing a fowl over the spot.

They have their own beggar castes, namely the Máshtigas, who are gymnasts, the Pambalas, who are musicians, and the Kátikápus, who are jugglers. Round Tuni the jungle tribe there called Chentzus are also included among the Mála beggars.

Their special caste deity is Gontiyálamma, the mother of the five Pándava brethern. They say (it is not an edifying story) that Bhíma, one of the five, threatened to kill his mother, who accordingly took refuge under an *avirédi* pot (the painted pot used at weddings) in a Mála house. For this, she was solemnly cursed by her sons, who said she should remain a Mála woman for ever. In commemoration of this story, a handful of growing paddy is pulled up every year at the Dasara, and eight days later the earth adhering to its roots is mixed with saffron and milk, made into an image of the goddess, and hidden under an *avirédi* pot. For the next six months this image is worshipped every Sunday by all the villagers in turn, and on the Sivarátri night it is taken in procession round the village, accompanied by all the Málas bearing pots of rice and other food carried in a *kávidi*, and is finally thrown with much ceremony into a river or tank. This rite is supposed to mean that the goddess is the daughter of the caste, that she has lived with them six months, and that they are now solemnly sending her back with suitable gifts (the rice, etc.) to her husband. A common form of religious vow among Málas is to promise to send a cloth and a cow with the goddess on the last day of the rite, the gifts being afterwards presented to a married daughter. The part played by the image of Gontiyálamma in the Málas' rain-making ceremonies has already (p. 47) been described. Both Málas and Mádigas hold a feast in honour of their ancestors at Pongal—an uncommon rite.

CHAP. III. PRINCIPAL CASTES.

Mádigas. The Mádigas are a numerous caste whose traditional occupations are tanning and shoe-making. Some of them say they are the descendants of a saint or demi-god called Jámbha-muni and a woman called Puramási who disturbed the saint in his contemplation and became his wife.

They are subdivided into the occupational classes of Mádiga Dásaris (priests), Mádiga Páyikis (sweepers), the Kommalas (who blow horns) and the ordinary Mádigas who follow the traditional callings of tanning and shoe-making. These will not dine together or intermarry. The last of them is by far the most numerous. The Dásaris are considered socially the highest, and the Páyikis the lowest, of the subdivisions.

Mádigas are much despised by other castes because they are leather-workers and eat beef and even carrion, and they take much the same low social position as the Málas. Their curious connection with the Kómatis has been mentioned in the account of that caste above. Their marriage and other ceremonies are very similar to those of the Málas. Their special caste goddess is Mátangi, who they say was defeated by Parasu Ráma and concealed herself from him under the tanning-pot in a Mádiga's house. At Pongal they worship their tanning-pots, as representing the goddess, with offerings of fowls and liquor.

The begging castes specially attached to the Mádigas are the Dekkalas, Mástidis and Tappitas or Bágavatas. Of these the Dekkalas are musicians who sing the praises of their patron's ancestors, the Mástidis are gymnasts, and the Tappitas are the same as the Mádiga Bógams, and are the dancers and prostitutes of the caste.

Kóyas. The Kóyas are a caste of jungle men found in the country on either side of the Gódávari from the point where the Indrávati joins it down to the apex of the delta. They occur as far south as Kammamet in the Nizam's Dominions, and on the north they stretch far into the Bastar State. The Rev. J. Cain of Dummagúdem, who has lived among them for thirty years and published several accounts of their ways, and who has been kind enough to supply information embodied below, estimates that they form one-fourth of the inhabitants of Bhadráchalam taluk, but only a small portion of the population of Chódavaram. They are also common in Bastar and the Malkanagiri taluk of Vizagapatam. In the case of a tribe spread over such a large extent of such wild country it is difficult to be sure that statements regarding customs are universally applicable. What follows applies primarily to the Kóyas of Pólavaram and Bhadráchalam taluks and the south of Bastar State.[1] It has been stated[2] that the Kóyas are a section of the great Gond tribe, but in this district they have no theory of their origin except that they are descended from Bhíma, one of the five Pándava brothers. By the people of the plains they are called Kóya Doralu, or 'Kóya lords.' Their language, called Kóya, is Dravidian and bears anologies to Tamil and Telugu. Most of the men, however, can speak Telugu, though the women know little but their own vernacular. The highland, or *kutta*, Kóyas, who live in the uplands of Bastar, are distinct from the riverside, or *gommu*, Kóyas with whom we are concerned. The latter say they were driven down from the Bastar plateau some two hundred years ago by the former. They are rather despised by the highlanders, who call them rascals *(máyalótilu)* and they acknowledge their inferiority by sending the *kutta* Kóyas gifts on festal occasions. The tribe is also split up into occupational endogamous subdivisions, among whom are the Kammaras (blacksmiths), Musaras (brass-workers), Dólis (professional beggars), Pattidis (cultivators and beggars), Oddis (superior priests), Káka and the Matta Kóyas, and the Rácha or Dora Kóyas. These last are by far the most numerous subdivision and consider themselves superior to all the others except the Oddis. Some of the others are apparently not true Kóyas at all. The Dólis are Málas from the plains, and definite traditions regarding the reception into the tribe, many generations ago, of the Kákas (who were Kápus) and the Mattas (who were Gollas) have been published by Mr. Cain. A contrary process is exemplified by the Bása Gollas, who were once Kóyas.

Exogamous divisions called *gattas* occur in the tribe. Among them are Múdó ('third'), Náló ('fourth') or Párédi, Aidó ('fifth') or Ráyibanda, Áró ('sixth'), Nútamuppayó ('130th'), and Perambóya. In some places the members of the *Múdó, Náló*, and *Aidó gattas* are said to be recognizable by the difference in the marks they occasionally wear on their foreheads, a spot, a horizontal line and a perpendicular line respectively being used by them. The *Áró gatta*, however, also uses the perpendicular line.

The Kóyas are looked upon with a certain respect by the Hindus of the plains, but are held to pollute a Bráhman by

[1] Information regarding the caste will be found in the Rev. J. Cain's articles in *Indian Antiquary*, v, 301, 357; viii, 33, 219; and x, 259; the *Christian College Magazine*, v (old series), 352–9 and vi (old series), 274–80; the Census Reports of 1871 and 1891 (paragraph 406 and page 227 respectively); Taylor's *Catalogue Raisonné of Oriental MSS.*, iii, 464; and the Rev. Stephen Hislop's *Aboriginal Tribes of the Central Provinces* (Nagpore, 1866), 4.

[2] *Aboriginal Tribes of the Central Provinces*, 4.

CHAP. III.

PRINCIPAL CASTES.

touch and the better non-Bráhmans by entering their kitchens. But the Kóyas, like other hill tribes, have no respect at all for Bráhmans or other Hindus merely on account of their caste.

The Kóyas proper are chiefly engaged in agriculture. Their character is a curious medley. They excite admiration by their truthfulness; pity by their love of strong drink, listlessness and want of thrift; surprise by their simplicity, and their combination of timidity and self-importance; and aversion by their uncanny superstitions. Their truthfulness is proverbial, though it is said to be less characteristic than of yore, and they never break their word. Their intemperate ways are largely due to the commonness of the *ippa (Bassia latifolia)* tree, from the flowers of which strong spirit is easily distilled, and are most noticeable when this is in blossom. Their listlessness has often been remarked. "To the officer enquiring after *khabar* of game the reply is invariably *lédu* ('nothing'); while if approached on the subject of the utilization of their labour, they passively obstruct all progress by their exasperating reply of *répu* ('to-morrow')." Their reckless and primitive modes of agriculture will be described in Chapters IV and V. Their ignorance and simplicity are attested by numerous stories. One, vouched for by Mr. Cain, relates how some of them, being despatched with a basket of fruit and a note describing its contents, and being warned that the note would betray any pilfering, first buried the note 'so that it could not see,' then abstracted some of the fruit, afterwards disinterred the note and delivered it and the basket, and were quite at a loss, when charged with the theft, to know how the note could have learnt about it. They are terribly victimized by traders and money-lenders from the low country, who take advantage of their guilelessness to cheat them in every conceivable way. Their timidity has on occasion driven them to seek refuge in the jungle on the appearance of a stranger in clean clothes, but, on the other hand, they expect (and receive) a considerable measure of respect from lowlanders whom they encounter. They are perfectly aware that their title 'Dora' means 'lord,' and they insist on being given it. They tolerate the address 'uncle' (mámá) from their neighbours of other castes; but they do not like being called Kóyas. When so addressed they have sometimes replied 'whose throat have I cut?' playing on the word *kóya,* which means to 'slice' or 'cut the throat.' When driven to extremes they are capable of much courage. Blood feuds have only recently become uncommon in British territory and in 1876 flourished greatly in the Bastar State.

Of the Hindu religion the Kóyas know nothing. They worship deities of their own. Some of them have adopted the village goddesses of the plains, such as Kondalamma and Bairamma (near Pólavaram), Maisamma and Póléramma (near Bhadráchalam) and Muthyálamma and her brother Póturázu. Mr. Cain says that Muthyálamma is specially reverenced as the goddess of disease, and as equivalent to the Maridamma of the plains. Other Kóyas adhere to the worship of the animistic deities of the hills and forests, the *konda dévatulu*. Pálamuni, Nílamuni and Korrarázu, the god of tigers, are three of these. Mr. Cain also mentions Kommalamma and a fearsome female devil called Pida, who is propitiated in December with curious rites. The Pándava brothers (especially Bhíma), and the wild-dogs who are supposed to be their messengers, are also worshipped. Human sacrifices, made sometimes to a dread deity called Mamili, were not unknown in former days. Writing in 1876, Mr. Cain said that there was strong reason to believe that two men had been sacrificed that year not far from Dummagúdem, and that there was no doubt that in Bastar strangers were kidnapped and secretly offered up every year. During the Rampa outbreak of 1879-80 several constables and others were openly sacrificed by the rebels.[1] Mr. Cain says that a *langúr* (white-faced monkey) was ordinarily substituted for the human victim, under the name of *kurommapotu* ('a male with small beasts'), as an offering to appease the deity.

Most peculiar objects of reverence are the *vélpus*, a name which Mr. Cain says is the Kóya for 'god.' They consist of small pieces of metal, generally iron and less than a foot in length, which are kept in a hollow bamboo deposited in some wild and unfrequented spot. They are guarded with great secrecy by those in charge of them and are only shown to the principal worshippers on the rare occasions when they are taken out to be adored. The Kóyas are very reticent about them. Mr. Cain says there is one supreme *vélpu* which is recognized as the highest by the whole Kóya tribe and kept hidden in the depths of Bastar. There are also *vélpus* for each *gatta* and for each family. The former are considered superior to the latter and are less frequently brought out of their retreats. One of them called Lakkála (or Lakka) Rámu, which belongs either to the Áró or Perambóya *gatta*, is considered more potent than the others. It is ornamented with eyes of gold and silver and is kept in a cave near Sítánagaram, not far from Parnasála in Bhadráchalam taluk. The

1 For a description by an eye-witness, see G.O. No. 2275, Judicial, dated 4th September 1879.

CHAP. III. PRINCIPAL CASTES.

others are deposited in different places in the Bastar State. They all have names of their own, but are also known by the generic term Ádama Rázu.

Both the *gatta* and family *vélpus* are worshipped only by members of the sept or family to which they appertain. They are taken round the country at intervals to receive the reverence and gifts of their adherents. The former are brought out once in every three or four years, especially during widespread sickness, failure of crops or cattle-disease. The *vélpu* is washed, and a flag is then planted beside it. An animal (generally a young bullock) is stabbed under the left shoulder, the blood is sprinkled over the deity, and the animal is next killed, and its liver is cut out and offered to the deity. A feast, which sometimes lasts for two days, takes place and the *vélpu* is then put back in its hiding-place. The flag is taken round the villages where members of the *gatta* or family reside, and these make a feast and offer gifts. The flag of a family *vélpu* is a large three-cornered red cloth on which are stitched a number of figures roughly cut out of bits of cloth of other colours to represent various ancestors. Whenever any important male member of the family dies, a new figure is added to commemorate his services.

Like other hill tribes, the Kóyas are firm believers in the black art and the power of wizards. In some parts whenever any one falls ill the professional sorcerer *(vezzugádu)* is consulted, and he reads both the cause and the remedy in a leaf-platter of rice which he carries thrice round the invalid. Whenever a man dies he is supposed to have been the victim of some sorcerer instigated by an enemy. An enquiry is then held as to who is guilty. Some male member of the family, generally the nephew of the deceased, throws coloured rice over the corpse as it lies stretched on the bed, pronouncing as he does so the names of all the known sorcerers who live in the neighbourhood. It is even now solemnly asserted that when the name of the wizard responsible is pronounced the bed gets up and moves towards the house or village where he resides. Suspected wizards have to clear themselves by undergoing the ordeal of dipping their hands in boiling oil or water. Sometimes they flee in terror rather than attempt this Reputed wizards and witches are held in the greatest abhorrence; and one of the old complaints against British rule was that it prevented these people from being put to death. Mr. Cain mentions a case in which a Kóya was compelled (in 1876) to murder a woman of his family because she was thought to be a witch.

The Kóyas appear to have few festivals now. Formerly those who lived near Dummagúdem used to celebrate one whenever any crop was ripening. They still keep a feast for *jonna kotta*, 'the new cholam' harvest. The rites seem to vary. Mr. Cain says that a fowl is killed and its blood sprinkled on a stone. In some places the victim is a sheep, and it and the first fruits are offered to the local gods and to ancestors. The *mango kotta* and *sámai kotta* are also important. Once a year is celebrated a feast similar to the well-known Chaitra Saturnalia in the Vizagapatam Agency, whereat all the men go out and beat for game and those who return empty-handed are pelted with mud and filth by the women and not allowed to enter the village that night. This is called the Bhúdévi Pandigai, or festival of the earth goddess. In times of drought a festival to Bhíma, which lasts five days, is held. When rain appears, the Kóyas sacrifice a cow or pig to their patron. Dancing plays an important part at all these feasts and also at marriages. The men put on head-dresses of straw into which buffalo-horns are stuck, and accompany themselves with a kind of chant.

In Pólavaram and Bhadráchalam, Kóya villages are divided into groups, sometimes called *samutús*, over each of which is an hereditary head called the *samutú dora* or *yetimani*.

If a Kóya youth is refused by the maiden of his choice he generally carries her off by force. But a boy can reserve a girl baby for himself by giving the mother a pot and a cloth for the baby to lie upon, and then she may not be carried off. Widows and divorced women may remarry. The wedding takes place in the bridegroom's house and lasts five days. A *táli* and a saffron-coloured thread are tied round the neck of the girl. If the marriage was effected by capture, matters are much simplified. The girl is made to kneel, the boy stoops over her, and water is poured over both of them. The boy then ties a saffron-coloured thread round her neck and the ceremony is over. Girls who consort with a man of low caste are purified by having their tongues branded with a hot golden needle and by being made to pass through seven arches of palmyra leaves, which are afterwards burnt.

The Kóyas generally burn their dead, but infants are buried. Mr. Cain says babies less than a month old are buried close to the house, so that the rain dropping from the eaves may fall upon the grave and cause fertility in the parents. When a Kóya dies, a cow or bullock is slaughtered and the tail is cut off and put in the dead person's hand. The liver is said to be sometimes put in his mouth. His widow's *táli* is always placed there, and when a married woman dies her *táli* is put in her mouth. The pyre of a man is lighted by

CHAP. III. PRINCIPAL CASTES.

his nephew, and of a woman by her son. After the body is burnt, the ashes are made into balls and deposited in a hole at the side of the road, which is covered with a slab. Many Kóyas place a perpendicular stone about three feet high, like the head-stone of a tomb, over the slab. No pollution is observed by those attending the funeral. The beef of the animal slain at the beginning of the rites provides a feast, and the whole party returns home and makes merry. On the eighth day a pot full of water is placed in the dead man's nouse for him to drink, and is watched by his nephew. Next morning another cow is slaughtered and the tail and a ball of cooked rice are offered to the soul at the burning-ground. Mr. Cain says that when a man passes an old friend's tombstone he will often place a little tobacco on it, remarking that the deceased liked the herb when alive and will probably be glad of it now.

The same authority states that the only conception of a future state among the Kóyas is that the dead wander about the jungle in the form of *pisáchas* or ghosts. The Rev. F. W. N. Alexander however says that some of them believe that there is a heaven, a great fort full of good things to eat, and a hell in which an iron crow continually gnaws the flesh of the wicked. People who are neither good enough for heaven nor bad enough for hell are born again in their former family. Children with hare-lips, moles, etc., are often identified as reincarnations of deceased relations.

Kóya villages are small and are usually inhabited solely by people of the tribe. Any outsiders live in a separate quarter. The houses are made of bamboo with a thatch of grass or palmyra. The Kóyas are very restless; and families change frequently from one village to another. Before moving, they consult the omens to see whether the change will be auspicious or not. Sometimes the hatching of a clutch of eggs provides the answer; or four grains of four kinds of seed (representing the prosperity of men, cattle, sheep and land) are put on a heap of ashes under a man's bed, any movement among them during the night being a bad omen.

Tattooing is common. It is considered very important for the soul in the next world that the body should have been adequately tattooed.

Hill Reddis.

The hill Reddis (or Konda Reddis) are a caste of jungle men having some characteristics in common with the Kóyas. They appear to be found only in the Rékapalle country, the hills in the north of the Pólavaram division and in Rampa, and still further north. They usually talk a rough Telugu, clipping their words so that it is often difficult to understand them; but it is said that some of them speak Kóya. They are of slighter build than the Kóyas and their villages are even smaller. They will not eat in the house of a Kóya.

They call themselves by various high-sounding titles, such as Pándava Reddis, Rája Reddis and Reddis of the solar race *(súrya vamsa)*, and do not like the simple name Konda Reddi. They recognize no endogamous subdivisions, but have exogamous septs. In character they resemble the Kóyas, but are less simple and stupid and in former years were much given to crime. They live by shifting *(podu)* cultivation. They do not eat beef, but will partake of pork.

They profess to be both Saivites and Vaishnavites and occasionally employ Bráhman priests at their funerals; and yet they worship the Pándavas, the spirits of the hills (or, as they call them, 'the sons of Rácha'), their ancestors (including women who have died before their husbands) and the deities Muthyálamma and her brother Póturázu, Sáralamma and Unamalamma. The last three are found in almost every village. Other deities are Doddiganga, who is the protector of cattle and is worshipped when the herds are driven into the forests to graze, and Désaganga (or Paraganga), who takes the place of the Maridamma of the plains and the Muthyálamma of the Kóyas as goddess of cholera and small-pox. The shrine of Sáralamma of Pedakonda (eight miles east of Rékapalle) is a place of pilgrimage, and so is Bison Hill (Pápikonda), where an important Reddi festival is held every seven or eight years in honour of the Pándava brothers, and a huge pig fattened for the occasion is killed and eaten. The Reddis, like the Kóyas, also observe the harvest festivals. They are very superstitious, believing firmly in sorcery and calling in wizards in time of illness. Their villages are formed into groups like those of the Kóyas and the hereditary headmen over these are called by different names, such as *dora*, *muttadár*, *varnapedda* and *kulapátradu*. Headmen of villages are known as *Pettamdars*. They recognize, though they do not frequently practise, marriage by capture. If a parent wishes to show his dislike for a match, he absents himself when the suitor's party calls and sends a bundle of cold rice after them when they have departed.

Children are buried. Vaishnavite Reddis burn their adult dead, while the Saivites bury them. Sátánis officiate as priests to the former and Jangams to the latter. The pyre is kindled by the eldest male of the family and a feast is held on the fifth day after the funeral. The dead are believed to be born again into their former families.

CHAPTER IV.

AGRICULTURE AND IRRIGATION.

WET CULTIVATION—Paddy ; its seasons—Its varieties—Rain-fed paddy—Sowing *versus* transplantation—Methods of raising seedlings—Preparation of fields—Transplantation and care of the crop—Second-crop cultivation—Third crops—Agricultural maxims—Wet crops other than paddy—Rotations—Cultivation of sugar-cane—Jaggery-making—Ratooning—Varieties of sugar-cane—Recent sugar-cane disease and the Samalkot experimental farm. DRY CULTIVATION—Seasons, etc.—Cultivation—Cholam—Tobacco—Improvement of the leaf—Shifting cultivation in the Agency—Storage of grain. IRRIGATION—Protected area. THE GÓDÁVARI ANICUT—Origin of the idea—First estimates—The site and design—Progress of construction—Subsequent difficulties—Alterations since effected—Distributary works—The Gannavaram aqueduct—Completion of distributaries—Financial results of the scheme—Possible extensions of it—Its administration. OTHER IRRIGATION SOURCES—Minór channels and tanks—Wells—Artesian wells. ECONOMIC CONDITION OF AGRICULTURISTS.

CHAP. IV. WET CULTIVATION. Paddy, its seasons.

THE immense area irrigated from the Gódávari anicut has naturally resulted in paddy being the most important crop in the district. The seasons for growing it in Bhadráchalam (where, however, very little is raised) differ from those elsewhere. In Bhadráchalam a short crop *(pinna vari)* is raised between May and August and a longer one *(pedda vari)* between August and January; while in the rest of the district the first (and chief) crop is grown between June and December and the second (if any) between January or February and April or May. The first crop season is called either the *sárava* ('white') season, from the fact that white paddy is grown in it, or the *tolakari* ('early') season; and the second is known as the *dálava* ('black') season, because black paddy is grown then, the *sítakattu* ('cold') season, since the crop is sown in January, or the *vásangi* ('hot') season, because it is reaped in May.

Except in the delta and Bhadráchalam, two wet crops are seldom raised on the same land, but a dry crop is raised when the paddy has been harvested. This dry crop season is called the *payiru* or *aparálu* season.

Its varieties.

Many varieties of paddy are grown in the district. The ryots divide them according to two main principles of classification; namely, the time a variety takes to mature—whether it is long *(pedda)* or short *(pinna* or *punasa)*—and its colour—whether 'white' or 'black.' The varieties raised in the delta taluks, with their unfailing irrigation, naturally differ from those grown in the uplands of Peddápuram and Tuni, and both differ again from the favourite species in the different climate of Bhadráchalam. Apparently none of the white kinds are ever grown without irrigation; but on the other hand many varieties of black paddy are raised on wet lands. The most valuable and most popular species of all are called *atrakadalu* and *akkullu*, both of which are long white varieties. They are grown all over the district and have several sub-species. They require more water than the rest, but resist floods better. The kind known as *prayága* (again long and white) is also very hardy, resisting droughts and floods equally well. The least valuable is the short white *rasangi* paddy, which is worth Rs. 10 less per garce than the *atrakadalu* and *akkullu*. Though most prolific, it is very indigestible. A kind of intoxicating liquor is extracted from it.

Rain-fed paddy.

Rain-fed paddy is raised on lankas, superior dry land or high-level wet land. Only certain kinds of paddy will flourish in this way, and the outturn is naturally smaller than on irrigated land. The seed is sown broadcast without preliminary soaking when the early showers fall in June. Weeds are removed twice with a weeder *(tollika)* some two or three weeks after sowing and again a fortnight or a month later. In the upland taluks the ryots weed with what is called a *gorru*, a log of wood provided with iron or wooden teeth and drawn by cattle. The crop is ordinarily harvested in September or October, but the shorter Bhadráchalam crop is reaped in August.

Sowing *versus* transplantation.

Except in the case of this rain-fed crop, paddy is seldom sown broadcast, but is transplanted from seed-beds. In Rajahmundry, Pólavaram, Pithápuram and Tuni sowing is of necessity resorted to in the case of the very deep wet fields in which, owing to their low level, it is impossible to control the depth of the water in the manner necessary with transplanted seedlings. In these fields a special kind of paddy, called *kásari*, is sown (unsoaked) in May before the rains or floods are received, the field having been ploughed when dry. This variety does not mind being submerged. Broadcast sowing is also sometimes adopted by ryots who cannot afford the expense of transplantation, but this is generally looked upon as bad farming.

Methods of raising seedlings.

There appear to be four recognized methods of raising paddy in seed-beds, which are known as *karéddku, mettapadunu, mokkáku* and *dúkáku*. In the case of the two former, the beds are ploughed when quite dry, before water comes down the

CHAP. IV. WET CULTIVATION.

channels; while with the two latter they are not cultivated until they have been well soaked. The two former methods are very similar, the only noteworthy difference between them apparently being that in the *karédáku* system an inch of water is let in directly the grain is sown and is drained off an hour later, while in the *mettapadunu* method the seed is sown after rain and the land allowed to get quite dry again before any water is let on to it. Similarly the *mokkáku* and *dúkáku* systems closely resemble one another except that with the former the seed is soaked and allowed to sprout before being sown. The cultivation of the seed-beds when dry is far more popular than the rival method, and the *dúkáku* system seems to be confined to Cocanada taluk and the *mokkáku* chiefly to Nagaram and Amalápuram.

Preparation of fields.

The fields are first levelled with a crowbar *(geddapára)* or a pickaxe *(guddali)*, various kinds of manure (chiefly the dung of sheep and cattle penned on the field, village sweepings, ashes, and oil-cake—green manuring is rare) are next applied, and then the field is irrigated and ploughed. On heavy soils (as near Rámachandrapuram) the ploughing is done after rain and before flooding, lest the plough-cattle should sink too deeply into the soil. Ploughing is always done at intervals, so that the soil gets thoroughly aërated, but as it does not begin until floods come down the river, the intervals are short. The parts of the fields near the ridges, which the plough cannot get at properly, are dug up with *mamuttis*. The field is levelled with a plank called the *patti*, drawn by hand or by bullocks. In Bhadráchalam a log of wood with iron teeth *(buruda gorru)* is used.

Transplantation and care of the crop.

The seedlings are transplanted in July or August. The usual rule governing the irrigation of them is to give them a span's depth of water until the ears are formed and then to allow the field to dry up. The water is changed periodically in order to obtain a fresh supply of silt and to wash away alkaline matter. In Amalápuram, however, as much as a foot of water is let in after the first fortnight, while in the middle of September the field is drained and left dry for the fortnight known as the *uttara kárti* because it is believed that worms which eat the stalks are generated in the water during that period.

Weeding is done one or two months after transplantation. In Amalápuram taluk manures of various kinds, such as gingelly, cocoanut and castor cake and a kind of fish called *chengudi royyi* are powdered and thrown broadcast over the fields three weeks after transplantation.

Second crop cultivation.

The second wet crop does not follow as close on the first as in Tanjore. In the latter district the ryots get seedlings ready for transplantation in the seed-bed before the harvest of the first crop is over, whereas in Gódávari it is believed that seedlings will not thrive until the warm 'corn wind' *(payiru gáli)*, which is expected in December, sets in from the south. The first crop is harvested in November or December, and seedlings for the second crop are sown in December or January and are ready for transplantation in February and March. The preparation of the field for the second crop is a somewhat perfunctory operation. Levelling is generally omitted; and, in Amalápuram, manuring is generally omitted also. The kinds of paddy most commonly used (outside Bhadráchalam) are called *garika sannam* and *dálava.*

Where the second crop is a dry crop, it is generally green, black, Bengal, or horse-gram, gingelly, or sunn hemp. Beans *(anumulu)*, ragi and onions are also raised. Except Bengal gram, gingelly, ragi and onions, these are generally sown a week before the harvest of the wet crop and left to take care of themselves. For Bengal gram and gingelly, the field is ploughed and the seed is covered by dragging a green, leafy branch *(kampa)* across it, or, in sandy soil by ploughing it in. Ragi and onions are transplanted into plots about two yards square, made after the field has been ploughed without water five or six times in the course of a week, and are watered a week after transplanting and thereafter once a month.

Third crops.

Both cambu and gingelly are not infrequently grown as a third crop, sometimes called the *punása* crop. In Tuni (perhaps elsewhere also) they are put down at the beginning of the first wet-crop season on the chance of the rains being late or insufficient and it being therefore impossible to grow a wet crop at the proper time, if at all. If the rains come while the crop is on the ground, it is either ploughed up to make room for the paddy, or, if nearly ripe, is left to mature, the paddy transplantation being delayed accordingly.

In Rajahmundry and Rámachandrapuram third crops are sometimes secured by growing a short wet crop between June and September, followed by a dry crop harvested by January, and then by a short paddy crop of the *garika sannam, dálava* or *rájabhógala* varieties, which is harvested in May.

Agricultural maxims.

The Gódávari ryots divide the six months from June to December into twelve *kártis* of about a fortnight each, called by the names of various stars. To each of these periods some agricultural operation or other is considered particularly appropriate. Even the Kóyas and hill Reddis, for example, believe that the best time for sowing paddy is the *mrigasira, kárti*, which begins about the end of the first week in June; the *anúrádhá kárti* (the latter part of December) is a name of happy augury, suggesting the harvest and the fulfilment of ryot's hopes; thunder on the first day of the *magha kárti* is the happiest possible omen for the future, and 'will make even a pole on a fort wall grow'; and so on. On the day before harvest the ryots run round their fields thrice repeating the name of the village goddess and crying out that she has given them a good crop. They then cut three handfuls of ears to represent the goddess and sacrifice fowls to them. When measuring the first heap of paddy of the first harvest of the year, they pour boiled rice-flour over it to propitiate the belly-god.

Wet crops other than paddy. Next to paddy, the irrigated crops chiefly grown are sugar-cane, betel, turmeric and plantains. Cocoanut and areca palms are also largely raised in Amalápuram and Nagaram taluks, and are occasionally irrigated. Sugar-cane is grown everywhere except in the Agency and the Tuni division, but is commonest in Peddápuram, Rámachandrapuram, Cocanada, Nagaram and Rajahmundry taluks. Betel on wet lands appears to be almost confined to Rámachandrapuram and Nagaram taluks and turmeric to Peddápuram, Rajahmundry and Amalápuram, in which last it is raised without irrigation. Plantains are found chiefly in Rámachandrapuram, Amalápuram and Nagaram. In Rajahmundry and elsewhere a kind of sweet potato *(mádapalam dumpa)* is much cultivated.

Rotations. As elsewhere, paddy is frequently grown year after year on the same land. When other crops are cultivated, a definite rotation is observed, but this differs widely in different parts. The ryots of Peddápuram and Pithápuram, for example, consider that an interval of two years is sufficient between two crops of sugar-cane, while those of Cocanada, Rajahmundry and Amalápuram say that four years is necessary, and those of Rámachandrapuram and Nagaram from six to eight years.

Cultivation of sugar-cane. In the cultivation of sugar-cane, the ground is sometimes broken up with a plough and sometimes with a crowbar. When a plough is used, the field is first well manured (in December or January) and then ploughed (without being flooded) from five to ten times. The ryots say the soil should be brought into such a soft and powdery condition that the footprints of the birds should be easily seen in it, and that a chatty full of water should neither spill nor break when dropped on to it. The field, still unirrigated, is next divided into small plots (spaces being left for the channels which are to be dug later on) either with a hoe or a plough.

The crowbar method of preparing the ground is partly adopted for the sake of economy, and so in this system manuring is also generally dispensed with. The jaggery which results is inferior, but the difference in the cost of cultivation is said to more than counterbalance this drawback. The land is dug up with the crowbar in January, and the clods are left to weather for ten days, when they are broken up and roughly powdered. The soil is not rendered sufficiently fine to be formed into plots without water, and the field has to be flooded.

Before planting the cuttings of sugar-cane the field is watered till it attains 'the consistency of cooked ragi' *(ambali padunu)* and then (in February or March) the cuttings are thrown on the ground and one end of them is pressed gently in with the foot. The tops are usually considered to make the best cuttings, but the rest of the cane is often used. The cuttings are kept in the shade for a fortnight before planting.

Regarding the irrigation of the crop, practice varies. In Peddápuram, for example, the field is flooded once a fortnight and then drained immediately. In Rámachandrapuram and Cocanada it is watered once a week, without draining off the water for six months; and then allowed to dry up as the rainy season approaches. The Peddápuram system is the better, since stagnant water injures the roots of the cane.[1] Two months after being planted, the crop is manured round the roots with castor cake, green gram husk, bats' dung, or mud from the village site.[2] In some places green gram is sown in the field and dug in as a green manure. Three weedings are made with a hoe *(tolika)* at intervals of a fortnight. When the crop has been about two months on the ground the plots are broken up and the irrigation trenches are dug, the soil from them being thrown round the roots of the cane. About four months after planting, the leaves are twisted round the canes to prevent them from cracking or being dried up by the sun, and to check the growth of weakening lateral shoots. In the fifth month the canes are supported by bamboos. The crop is cut in February with a bill-hook *(póta katti)* and made into jaggery the same day.

The canes are crushed in iron mills, and the juice is boiled for about two and a half or three hours with chunam (a piece

[1] Papers printed with G.O. No. 1193, Revenue, dated 30th December 1901, p. 24. *Cf.* G.O. No. 1020, Revenue, dated 14th September 1904, p. 31.

[2] The 'saltpetre earth' of Mr. Benson's report, G.O. No. 28, Revenue, dated 11th January 1884, pp. 7, 14.

CHAP. IV
WET CULTIVATION.

Jaggery-making.

of chunam the size of a tennis ball is added to every pan of eight pots, or 168 seers, of juice), until it reaches such a consistency that it will no longer drip from the finger. It is then put into a pot and well stirred, and afterwards poured on to a bamboo mat to set. Some of the ryots say that an acre of land generally yields 15 candies of jaggery worth Rs. 300, and that the cultivator makes a clear profit of Rs. 100.

Ratooning.

Ratooning is usual. The ratooned crop is ready to cut in ten months. It is inferior to the first, but the saving in the cost of cultivation is considerable.[1] Sometimes a third crop is cut.

Varieties of sugar-cane.[2]

Previous to the building of the Dowlaishweram anicut the cane grown in Gódávari was a thin, white, reed-like variety, similar to, if not identical with, the canes of Ganjám, South Arcot, Trichinopoly and other districts, which was called the *dêsaváli* or 'country' cane. Its hard rind enabled it to resist the attacks of jackals, so that it was possible to grow it at a distance from the villages; it did not require much water; and the jaggery it gave was small in quantity, though very sweet and white. When the anicut was made, softer, larger and more juicy canes were introduced. The *síma* variety, a stout dark kind sometimes called the Mauritius cane, was introduced about 1870 by Messrs. Cotton and Rundall for their factory near Rájavólu (Rázóle), but the history of the other species is obscure.

At the present time the kinds grown are *dêsaváli* or 'country,' *bonthakarri* or Bombay, *erra* or *sannakarri*, *kéli*, *bontha* or *bontha námalu*, *námalu* or *sára*, *mogili* and *pálabontha* (which seem to be only found in Rámachandrapuram taluk), and *válu*, confined to Peddápuram. The Bombay or *bonthakarri* is very similar to, and possibly identical with, the *síma*; its jaggery is poor and of a purple colour. The *erra*, or *sannakarri* variety is a thin, dark cane producing similar jaggery. The *kéli* is a white cane with a cracked bark giving watery juice which wants more boiling than usual. The *bontha* or *bontha námalu* is a stout, striped cane, but the jaggery it gives is said to be very inferior. The *námalu* is a thin, striped variety, also producing a bad jaggery. The *mogili* is a very thick kind with knots at short intervals; its jaggery is

[1] The advantages of ratooning are still the subject of careful experiment at the Samalkot experimental farm. G.O. No. 1020, Revenue, dated 14th September 1904, p. 29.

[2] Much of what follows has been taken from the report of Mr. C. A. Barber, the Government Botanist, in G.O. No. 1193, Revenue, dated 30th December 1901, pp. 21 foll.

again like that of the Bombay cane, but it gives much juice and has hitherto shown a considerable immunity from disease. The *pálabontha* is a soft cane which is sold for chewing. The *válu* is like the 'country' cane, but a little thinner; and the juice is a little more watery and requires longer boiling. The *mogili*, 'country' and *pálabontha* canes grow only about six or seven feet high. The rest run up to nine feet.

Recent sugar-cane disease and the Samalkot experimental farm.

About the end of the last century an obscure disease decimated the sugar-cane in the district. In March 1900 Government introduced cuttings from Hospet in Bellary, where disease was rare, but this did little good. The Government Botanist, Mr. C. A. Barber, was accordingly deputed to make a thorough investigation of the crops and the disease, and his report, dated 24th April 1901, threw much light on the subject and suggested the starting of a Government agricultural station at which the matter might be further studied. The station was opened in 1902 at Samalkot. It has been recently decided that it shall be a permanent institution.

The diseases of the sugar-cane in the district are described in Mr. Barber's first report. The moth borer, the ravages of which do such an infinity of harm in the West Indies and no small damage in Ganjám, is responsible for very little of the evil; perhaps owing to the scattered cultivation of the cane, or the system of tying the leaves round the stem, or the existence of its antagonist the *Isaria Barberi* fungus. The 'small borer,' or scolytid beetle, and the 'red smut,' or *Colletotrichum falcatum* fungus, are the greatest enemies of the Gódávari canes. These two pests go hand in hand, and it cannot as yet be said which prepares the cane for the ravages of the other. The fungus manifests itself inside the cane in 'well marked blotches with a characteristic white centre.' It can attach itself to any abrasion on the surface of the cane, even to the scar left by a fallen leaf, and thence makes its entry into the tissues of the plant. It is very slow in its progress. The *conidia* of the fungus are found at the base of the black tufts of hair in the holes left by old dead roots, and as an incrustation on the surface of the dead and dried up canes below the origin of the leaf. If a cane infested with the 'small borer' is opened, the surface is found to be covered with a mass of small dark beetles about one-twelfth of an inch in length, which are seen busily emerging from and re-entering their small burrows. A strong vinous odour of fermented juice fills the air, and the infested canes are entirely useless for sugar. The evil acts very quickly. In the West Indian islands whole fields have been completely destroyed by it.

CHAP. IV. WET CULTIVATION.

The infection of the fungus can be carried by the air; but it seems likely that water, either flowing from infected fields or into which diseased canes and refuse have been thrown, is the chief agent for its diffusion. The water-logged condition of the ground, the lack of rotation, and the consequent exhaustion of the soil, are among other contributing causes.

A number of interesting results bearing upon defects in the present methods of sugar-cane cultivation have been obtained at the Samalkot farm by employing different manures, growing different varieties and raising selected canes under different systems. These are detailed in G.O. No. 1020, Revenue, dated 14th September 1904, pp. 20 ff. The chief conclusions arrived at are briefly: (1) that it is important to tread in the cuttings properly, (2) that they should be planted in rows so as to facilitate weeding, supervision and irrigation, (3) that they are best put out in trenches, (4) that the use of a rake to supplement two thorough weedings with the *tolika* would be easier and much less expensive than the use of the *tolika* throughout, (5) that green dressing is good, but that the plants usually employed by the ryots are leguminous and suffer from insect and other pests, and (6) that the use of cane trash as a mulch in the first instance and its burial in the fields after the canals are reopened has several advantages.

Other matters are under investigation; among them the best number of cuttings per acre, the quantityof water required, the abolition of the expensive bamboo supports, the advantages of ratooning, and the improvement of the methods of making jaggery.

DRY CULTIVATION.

The commonest dry crops are gingelly *(núgu* or *nuvvu)*, cholam *(jonna)*, horse-gram *(ulava)*, ragi *(tsódi)*, green gram *(pesara)*, sunn hemp *(janumu)*, castor *(ámuda)*, cambu *(gante)*, black gram *(minumu)*, tobacco *(pogáku)*, and Bengal gram *(salaga* or *sanaga)*. Gingelly, horse-gram and ragi are most widely grown in Peddápuram and Rajahmundry. Cholam is chiefly raised in Bhadráchalam in the Agency, in all the upland taluks and in Amalápuram in the delta. Castor is popular in Pólavaram; cambu in Peddápuram; Bengal gram in Amalápuram, Peddápuram and Rámachandrapuram; and sunn hemp in Amalápuram, Nagaram and Cocanada. Tobacco grows best in the Gódávari lankas and in Yellavaram.

Seasons, etc.

The two seasons of dry cultivation are known respectively as the *tolakari* or *pundsa panta* and the *sítakattu* or *payiru panta*. The former begins any time between May and July inclusive, and the latter between the beginning of September and the middle of December. With local exceptions, ragi, gingelly and cambu are grown in the first season; and horse-gram, cholam, castor, and black, green and Bengal gram in the second. No regular rotations are observed. In Bhadráchalam the ryots say vaguely that they vary the crop when it begins to fail for want of a change. In Peddápuram, Tuni, Amalápuram and Pólavaram they profess to change the crop every year and say that castor and Bengal gram require intervals of three and seven years respectively before they are repeated on the same land.

The place of rotation is to some extent taken by mixing the crops, a system which is usual everywhere. Typical and common combinations are horse-gram or black gram with ragi; dhall with ragi, sámai or gingelly; black gram and beans *(anumulu)* with cholam; and cambu with sámai or korra. The principal advantage of the system is that it economises space, a small or slow-growing crop being raised in the intervals between spreading or quickly-maturing plants.

Cultivation.

In the delta and the Agency, manuring is rare; but it is frequent elsewhere. Ragi, tobacco and gingelly are thought to require it more than other crops. Fields are ploughed from four to six times, but twice is considered enough for horse-gram. Tobacco and onions seem to be always transplanted and cambu and ragi generally so. The seedlings are laid in a furrow and covered by ploughing another furrow alongside the first. Most of the other dry crops are sown broadcast, but castor and Bengal gram are sown seed by seed in a furrow, and in places a drill is used. The seed is covered by dragging a leafy branch across the field or ploughing again. Weeding of any kind appears to be the exception.

Cholam.

There appear to be four kinds of cholam in this district, namely two varieties (the *mudda* and the *ralla)* of yellow *(pacha)* cholam, white cholam *(tella jonna* or *man jonna)*, and 'hill cholam' *(konda jonna)*. The white variety is peculiar to Bhadráchalam and the 'hill cholam' to *pódu* cultivation. Yellow cholam is generally sown mixed with green gram. The seed is covered as usual. Six or eight weeks afterwards the field is lightly ploughed, which is believed to strengthen the young plants. In Pólavaram the ryots first weed the crop and loosen the soil with a *gorru*, a log of wood provided with iron or wooden teeth, which is drawn by bullocks. The crop is sown in October or November and is on the ground for three or four months.

Tobacco.

There are two varieties of tobacco—lanka and pati. The former, which is much the superior, is grown on the alluvial soils of the lankas and banks of the Gódávari, which require no manure owing to their being covered with silt by the river

CHAP. IV. DRY CULTIVATION.

every year. The latter is raised in fields near the villages. The crop is always transplanted. The seed is sown in seed-beds in the *pubba kárti* (first half of September) and transplantation takes place after the *uttara kárti* (at the end of that month), when the floods in the river have subsided, and sometimes as late as December. Great care is taken in the preparation of the seed-beds, the land being ploughed many times and plantifully manured with cattle-dung and ashes. Sheep-dung is usually considered hot and injurious, but is employed in Nagaram. Before sowing, the seed is mixed in the proportion of one to sixteen with sand, so as to enable it to be thinly scattered. It is sometimes soaked and kept for four or five days (like paddy) in a damp place until it germinates. The seed-bed is kept moist by daily (or even more frequent) sprinklings of water, and is also weeded almost daily. When the seedlings are from one and a half to two and a half months old they are transplanted at intervals from half a yard to a yard apart. They are frequently watered for three or four weeks, but not after that. The plants blossom in some six or eight weeks, and then their buds and tops are cut off to strengthen the eight or ten leaves which remain. All lateral shoots are also cut off from time to time and so, at length, are the bottom two or three of the eight or ten leaves.

The crop is on the ground for five and a half months from the time it is sown. It is harvested at midday; and the leaves are left in the sun for two hours and then hung from strings in the shade for a fortnight. They are next pressed under weights for a month, after which water is sprinkled on them and they are fit for use.

Improvement of the leaf.

Attempts are being made to improve the quality of the tobacco grown in the district. Messrs. T. H. Barry & Co. of Cocanada have established a tobacco factory in that town and foreign seed has been imported by Government for experimental cultivation in the lankas leased to Mr. T. H. Barry. The chief defect of the existing tobacco is the excessive thickness and dark colour of the leaf. It is sold in other parts of India and Burma and, to a limited extent, in Mauritius, Bourbon and London.

Shifting cultivation in the Agency.

The majority of the hill Reddis and the Kóyas in the Agency carry on shifting cultivation, called *pódu*, by burning clearings in the forests. The conflict between their interests and those of forest reservation are referred to in Chapter V. Two methods prevail: the ordinary (or *chalaka*) *pódu*, and the hill (or *konda*) *pódu*. The former consists in cultivating certain recognized clearings for a year or two at a time, allowing the forest to grow again for a few years, and then again burning and cultivating them; while under the latter the clearing is not returned to for a much longer period and is sometimes deserted for ever. The latter is in fashion in the more hilly and wilder parts, while the former is a step towards civilization.

CHAP. IV. DRY CULTIVATION.

In February or March the jungle trees and bushes are cut down and spread evenly over the portion to be cultivated; and, when the hot weather comes on, they are burnt. The ashes act as a manure, and the cultivators also think that the mere heat of the burning makes the ground productive. The land is ploughed once or twice in *chalaka pódus* before and after sowing, but not at all in *konda pódus.* The seed is sown in June in the *mrigasíra kárti.* Hill cholam and sámai are the commonest crops. The former is dibbled into the ground.

Storage of grain.

Grain is usually stored in regular granaries *(kottu)* or in thatched bamboo receptacles built on a raised foundation and called *gádi.* These are not found in Bhadráchalam or the central delta, where the *puri* (a high, round receptacle made of twisted straw) is used. Grain is also stored, as elsewhere, in pits.

IRRIGATION. Protected area.

The chief irrigation source of the district is the Gódávari, the channels from which protect 240,800 acres in all seasons. Some 4,600 acres of this are in Rajahmundry, and the rest in the delta taluks of Rámachandrapuram, Cocanada, Amalápuram and Nagaram. Tanks and channels from smaller rivers safeguard 31,800 acres in all seasons and 53,800 acres in ordinary seasons. Wells irrigate a very small area. Only in Amalápuram taluk does the extent protected by them rise above 100 acres.

THE GODÁVARI ANICUT.

The Gódávari water is rendered available by the great anicut at Dowlaishweram and the immense system of canals and channels leading off from it. Those in this district are shown in the accompanying map, and there are yet others in Kistna.

This anicut was the first of any real magnitude to be built by Europeans in this Presidency (the Cauvery system was an elaboration of native enterprize) and is one of the greatest triumphs of engineering skill in all India. Its history is of the greatest interest. Not only were the physical difficulties encountered in damming up so huge a river enormous, but the opposition of those who doubted the possibility and financial prospects of the work had to be overcome. Both were met by the engineers in charge of the project with indomitable perseverance and fortitude.

CHAP. IV. THE GÓDÁVARI ANICUT.

Origin of the idea.

The project consists of a dam across the Gódávari at Dowlaishweram (where the river is nearly four miles wide) and a net work of canals covering almost every part of the delta.[1] Some of these canals are navigable, and the traffic along them is referred to in Chapter VII. The conception of the scheme was due to the genius of Sir Arthur Cotton. The idea of an anicut across the river originated[2] as far back as 1789 with Mr. Topping, an astronomer in the service of the Madras Government who was appointed to survey the coast of the district in that year. It was revived in 1844 by Sir Henry Montgomery,[3] who had been appointed (see p. 167) Special Commissioner to report on the best means of improving the then unhappy condition of the district. As a result of his recommendations, Sir Arthur (then Captain) Cotton of the Madras Engineers was ordered in 1845 to report professionally on the possibility of building an anicut on the river. He pronounced in favour of the idea; his representations were earnestly backed by the then Governor of Madras, the Marquis of Tweeddale; and the Court of Directors, in a despatch dated December 23rd, 1846, sanctioned the project.

First estimates.

Sir Arthur Cotton's first idea had been to build a dam above Rajahmundry similar to the two anicuts on the Coleroon which had been recently constructed under his supervision. But he eventually recommended that the work should be constructed just below Dowlaishweram, at the head of the delta. The breadth of the river was much greater there than above Rajahmundry, but a great portion of the width was occupied by islands, and the site had the great advantage of being close to a hill of coarse, strong sandstone 'of a degree of hardness exactly suited to the case; neither too hard to be expensive in working nor yet soft enough to be unfit for the purpose.' Round this hill, also, lay several hundred thousand tons of broken stone, the accumulations of years of native quarryings, which would be of great value for rubble work. The cost of constructing the anicut itself Sir Arthur estimated at only 4¾ lakhs, and that of the subsidiary works as 7¼ lakhs, or only twelve lakhs in all. At the same time he indulged in the most sanguine hopes of increased irrigation and revenue, and of a rich return upon this 'absurdly small' sum. It will be seen immediately that he very greatly under-estimated the cost of both dam and project.

[1] The following brief sketch has been for the most part abstracted from the graphic account, in *The Engineering works of the Gódávari delta*, by Mr. G. T. Walch, late Chief Engineer for Irrigation, Madras, published by the Government Press in 1896.

[2] First report of the Public Works Commission at Madras, 1852, p. 100.

[3] His report dated 18th March 1844, para. 40.

CHAP. IV. THE GODAVARI ANICUT.

The site and design.

The breadth of the Gódávari at the point selected for the dam is rather over $3\frac{3}{4}$ miles; but of this more than a third is occupied by three islands and the head of the central delta, which separate the river into four channels. About a mile from the Dowlaishweram (or eastern) bank of the river is the island known as the Pichika-lanka, nearly 800 yards broad, the branches flowing on either side of which are known as the Dowlaishweram and Ráli branches respectively. Next beyond the Ráli branch comes the head of the central delta, known as the Bobbarlanka, which is about 470 yards wide. Then comes a narrow channel called the Maddúr branch; next the Maddúr lanka, about 630 yards broad; and, lastly, the fourth, or Vijésvaram, branch of the river. The lengths of the sections of the dam over each of the four branches, exclusive of under-sluices and wings, were as given in the margin. It will be seen that the total length of the work was about 4,000 yards. It was intended to be 12 feet high and connected with embankments on the different islands 2,455 yards in length.

	Yards.
Dowlaishweram branch ...	1,646
Ráli branch	953
Maddúr branch	516
Vijésvaram branch	866

The river bed was of pure sand and the islands were thin alluvial deposits thereon, while floods upwards of 25 feet in depth swept one and a half millions of cubic feet of water past the place every second. The problem how to bring the river under the necessary control at such a site was thus no easy one.

The actual design of the dam was modified more than once; and none of the sections across the various branches is precisely similar to any other. The original plans provided for a narrow crest with a vertical drop for the water on to a cut-stone floor behind, the section being very similar to that of the Upper Anicut on the Coleroon. Before work began, however, Sir Arthur adopted a very different design with a broad crest and a long sloping apron behind it of rubble masonry covered with cut-stone. The great advantage of this was that it required much less cut-stone work, for skilled masons were exceedingly scarce. It was not adhered to universally, different modifications being introduced in each of the four sections, but the general principle of a long rough-stone apron was retained in all. This had a very serious drawback, the full effect of which its designer did not first appreciate. Water rushing down such a sloping apron sets up reverse under-currents which tend to scour holes in the river bed and so undermine the foundation of the work. It was soon found that a further extension of the apron by a long

CHAP. IV. THE GODAVARI ANICUT.

rough-stone talus was necessary, and at the present time it is from three to six times as wide as it originally was, and its thickness has been greatly increased by the enormous quantities of stone thrown in to make good the sinkage which has from time to time taken place. In the first twenty years of the anicut's existence over 500,000 tons of stone were used for this purpose, and vast quantities more have been used since. Nowadays very little is required, and that only at certain places.

Another considerable change in the original design was the adoption of the plan of founding the anicut on the sand confined between its face wall and the retaining wall at the toe of the apron, instead of upon a mass of loosely deposited stone. The Ráli branch alone was constructed on the latter method and its foundations were the only ones which gave any trouble. They allowed the water to pass through in great quantities.

Three sets of under-sluices of fifteen vents each were built, one near the head-sluice of each of the main canals of the three sections of the delta. Three locks were also built, one at the head of each of those canals. Three head-sluices were also ultimately necessary.

Progress of construction.

The sanction of the Court of Directors to the execution of the work was received early in 1847. In April of that year operations were vigorously commenced. A detachment of Sappers and Miners was posted to Dowlaishweram, and a Sub-Collector (Mr. H. Forbes) was appointed to superintend the recruitment and payment of labourers and to procure the necessary supplies. His exertions (it may here be noted) were more than once acknowledged to have contributed largely to the success of the work (Sir Arthur said 'his vigorous and active measures have roused this district to a degree that could not have been expected') and he was specially thanked in the Government order reviewing the completion of the project. Before July had arrived, as many as 10,200 labourers, 500 carpenters and the same number of smiths had been collected to put in hand preliminary preparations. Boats were built, railway waggons constructed, the quarry opened and two double lines of rail ran from it to different points on the river banks, and the embankments on the islands put in hand.

In the working season of 1848 the actual construction of the dam was begun, and the Dowlaishweram and Maddúr sections were both built to the height of nine feet, and good deal of work was also done to the Dowlaishweram and Vijésvaram sluices. In the middle of 1848 Sir Arthur Cotton

THE GODÁVARI ANICUT.

had to go Home on leave 'exhausted by unremitting work and anxiety'; and for the next two years his place was taken by Captain (afterwards General) C. A. Orr, R.E., who had from the first been his most successful lieutenant and to whom much of the credit for the completion of the undertaking is due.

Next year (1849) the whole of the Vijésvaram section was built to a height of nine feet under circumstances of great difficulty. The work could not be begun until February 10th owing to want of funds. During its progress a sudden rise in the river breached it, and extensive temporary dams had to be erected to turn the river away from it. It was completed by the end of May. The season's operations also included the repair of 80 yards of the Maddúr section, the raising of the whole section by one and a half feet, the completion of the head and under-sluices and locks both at Dowlaishweram and Vijésvaram, of the under-sluice and wing walls of the Ráli section and of about 50 yards at each end of this section, and the lengthening of the Dowlaishweram section by some 250 yards.

At the beginning of the following year (1850) the only outlet for the whole stream of the Gódávari was down the Ráli branch, the section across which alone remained to be completed. A temporary dam of loose stone had been made across this in 1848 and strengthened in 1849 to prevent the stream from cutting too deep a channel in the bed of the river; but the water escaped both through and over this, and it became necessary to make it water-tight and high enough to turn the stream down the Dowlaishweram and Vijésvaram branches, and through the head and under-sluices in them. This would have been no easy matter at any time, but now considerably more water than usual was passing down owing to heavy rain in Hyderabad and Nagpore.

An exciting struggle with the river ensued. In February about 50 yards of the temporary dam was swept away, and no sooner was the damage repaired than 80 yards more was washed down stream. This branch was nearly closed when the river asserted itself and widened it to 80 yards again, surging through the narrow opening between 20 and 30 feet deep. With immense difficulty this breach was at length closed and the river turned aside on the 23rd April, and before the end of the next month the Ráli section was completed to a height of 10½ feet. The head-sluice and lock on this section were built the same year, and the great anicut was thus at last an accomplished fact.

Subsequent difficulties.

Though the battle was now won, the difficulties were far from over. On the 9th June 1850 the river began to rise

CHAP. IV. THE GÓDÁVARI ANICUT.

steadily. It was passed through the Dowlaishweram and Ráli under-sluices, but the apron behind the latter was only 25 feet wide, and on the 17th June it began to sink. The sluices were closed and an attempt was made to replace the apron; when suddenly the great head of water forced the sand from beneath the foundation of the sluices into the hollow formed by the sinking of the apron, and a portion of the sluices fell in. Seven out of fourteen piers collapsed; but fortunately the massive masonry formed a dam preventing any great rush of water and gave time for measures to be taken to check the extension of the damage.

In the working season of 1851 and the early part of 1852 these under-sluices were rebuilt and the finishing touches were put to the anicut and head-works. Their virtual completion may be considered to have been achieved by March 31st, 1852.

Alterations since effected.

Large repairs and alterations in the dam have been carried out since its first construction. The constant additions to the rough-stone aprons have already been alluded to, and another important improvement has been the raising of the crest of the work. Even before it was finished in 1852, its height was found insufficient to secure an adequate supply of water to the canals at all seasons; and cast-iron grooved posts, fitted with horizontal planks to hold up when necessary an additional two feet of water, were fixed along its crest. This was still insufficient; and between 1862 and 1867 the masonry itself was raised two feet at a cost of nearly three lakhs, and the iron posts and planks were replaced on the top of the new work. In 1897–99 the crest was raised an additional nine inches with Portland cement concrete, and on this were fitted self-acting cast-iron shutters, two feet high, which fall automatically when the water rises to six inches above their tops.

The only serious accident to the anicut itself happened in 1857. On the 14th November of that year, when the season for floods was over and the water was comparatively low, the eastern end of the Maddúr branch suddenly subsided into a deep scour-hole below it, and a breach was formed through which the river poured with such depth and volume that it was impossible to stop it. The disaster was met by damming up the river (with great difficulty) some way above the anicut and then rebuilding the fallen portion. The operation cost half a lakh.

The three sets of head-locks, head-sluices and under-sluices, have all been altered or replaced at various times, and of the original constructions only one head-sluice and the three sets of under-sluices now survive. The original Vijésvaram head-lock was destroyed in the floods of 1852. It was rebuilt next year, but was eventually converted into sluices; and the present head-lock was built in 1891. The original Vijésvaram head-sluices fell in 1853; were rebuilt in 1854; and are still in use. The central delta head-sluices fell in 1878 in a high flood, and great difficulty was experienced in preventing damage to the canal below. The head-lock beside them became so shaky that in 1889-90 it was replaced by a new one. Of the eastern delta works, the head-lock toppled over in 1886, when there was 14½ feet of water on the anicut. It carried the lock gates with it and left a gap into the canal fifteen feet wide, through which the water poured. The river continued to rise, and in two days reached the then unprecedented height of 17 feet above the anicut, so that the breach was only stopped with great difficulty. A new lock in a rather better position was built next year and opened on Jubilee day.

A gradually increasing shoal which has been forming on the left side of the Gódâvari river above the Dowlaishweram branch of the anicut has been for some time past a source of anxiety and of inconvenience to navigation. The old Dowlaishweram under-sluices not being sufficiently powerful to arrest the progress of this shoal towards the head-sluice, it was considered necessary to build more powerful substitutes for them. An estimate was sanctioned in 1903 and the work is now in progress. The new under-sluices are to consist of ten vents 20 feet wide and 10 feet high, regulated by iron lift shutters and with their sill four feet below that of the head-sluice. The shutters are to be in two tiers—the upper measuring 20 feet by 6 feet and the lower 20 feet by 4 feet—are to be constructed of half inch plates stiffened with rolled steel beams 12 feet by 6 feet, and are to be worked by chain gearing arrangements.

Distributary works.

Simultaneously with the construction of the head-works, arrangements were made for carrying to the various parts of the delta the water they rendered available. Even before the building of the anicut, certain portions of the delta had been irrigated. Sir Henry Montgomery's report of 1846 already mentioned deplored the neglect with which the then existing channels had been treated, and Sir Arthur Cotton described them as partial works of small extent not kept in an effective state. They were merely inundation channels, the heads of which were 12 or 15 feet above the deep bed of the river, and they received a supply only during floods, or for about 50 days in the year. Some of them lay on the western side of the river in the present Kistna district; the central delta contained none worth mention; but on the eastern side of the river four

CHAP. IV. THE GÓDÁVARI ANICUT.

considerable channels were in existence. One of these, called the Tulya Bhága, led off from near the site of the anicut and ran in a fairly straight line to Cocanada, terminating in the salt creek there. In 1846 a branch was taken from it to Samalkot from near Dowlaishweram. These two channels were connected with the head-works of the eastern delta.

At the end of 1849 a start was made with the new distributary works, sanction being obtained to the cutting of the main canals in the eastern and central deltas, the first of which (see the map) leads along the river bank nearly as far as Yanam and the second runs past Ráli. In April 1851 the western delta main canal (now in the Kistna district) was sanctioned, and in February 1852 considerable extensions of the eastern main canal and large distributary works in the central delta, including the great Gannavaram aqueduct, were agreed to.

The Gannavaram aqueduct.

This aqueduct carries a large canal across a branch of the Gódávari to the Nagaram island, which is surrounded by the sea and two arms of the river and to which water can only be taken in this way. The aqueduct may be roughly described as an arched bridge of brick thrown across the branch of the river, upon which, in the place where the roadway of an ordinary bridge is laid, runs a channel from 22 to 24 feet broad and some four feet deep. Its total length between abutments is 2,248 feet, and it consists of 49 arches with 40 feet waterway and 48 piers 6 feet thick. Ordinarily, the water of the branch of the river across which it is thrown flows through the arches of the aqueduct, but in times of high flood it completely submerges the whole work and pours over the top of it. It was impossible to make the aqueduct higher, because of the expense and danger involved in raising the embankments of the channels connected with it to a corresponding height above the level of the surrounding country. The work had therefore to be made of sufficient strength to resist floods sweeping over it.

The most noteworthy fact about the work is the wonderfully short period within which it was built. The estimate was submitted by Sir Arthur Cotton in August 1851 but was not sanctioned till February 14th 1852. It was considered of paramount importance to finish the work before the floods of that year came down, and, to effect this, extraordinary efforts were necessary. Between the first preparation of the materials for the work and the completion of all its 49 arches only four months elapsed, and in another four it was ready for its work. 'In any part of the world,' says Mr. Walch in his book already cited, 'this would have been a noteworthy achievement; in an

THE GÓDÁVARI ANICUT.

out-of-the-way part of the Madras Presidency, where machinery was almost unobtainable and most of the skilled labour had to be trained as the work went on, it was an extraordinary feat.' The construction was under the charge of Lieutenant (afterwards General) G. T. Haig, R.E., and his energy and skill are commended in the highest terms by Sir Arthur Cotton: 'That a single officer with two or three overseers should have managed about 5,000 workmen, and with the help of only one or two efficient workmen, is one of the most surprising things I have met with. Every time I visited the work I was astonished at the energy and admirable arrangement of this young officer. I cannot say less than that I think him the most effective officer I have ever had attached to me. I have never yet seen such energy displayed by any other man.' It is, in truth, difficult to realize, as one views this imposing work, that it was actually completed in one working season.

Completion of distributaries.

Money for further extensions of the distributary works was at first grudged by Government, who were sceptical of the prospects of the scheme and aghast at the enormous excess over the original estimates of expenditure which had been incurred. 'The records teem with remonstrances from Colonel Cotton and with 'minutes,' 'notes' and letters by Governors, Members of Council, Boards and Secretaries, now wrathful and now penned more in sorrow than in anger, on the subject of the surprises which Colonel Cotton was springing on them in his demands for what they considered unexpected developments of the original scheme, or to cover expenditure incurred on work which had not been sanctioned or had been much altered or largely exceeded in execution. . . . On the one hand was the enthusiast whose genius and special knowledge enabled him to see clearly that what he proposed to do was in the best interests of Government as well as of the people, and who was impatient of delay; on the other hand were the controlling powers who held the purse strings and whose duty it was to check too hurried an advance along a path the issue from which to them was obscure.'[1] It was not till 1853 that the success of the project became so apparent that funds were granted readily for its development. From that time onwards the canals and channels were rapidly pushed forward. At the present time there are in the Gódávari district (not counting the works in Kistna, on the western bank of the river) 287 miles of canal (nearly all of which are navigable) and 1,047 miles of distributaries.

[1] Mr. Walch, *op. cit.*, p. 89.

CHAP. IV. THE GÓDÁVARI ANICUT.

Financial results of the scheme.

The total capital outlay on the whole scheme up to the end of 1904-05 is returned as Rs. 1,36,93,000, the gross receipts of that year at Rs. 35,58,000, the annual working expenses at Rs. 9,10,000, and the net revenue at Rs. 26,48,000 or 19·34 per cent. on the capital outlay. The benefits and increase of wealth which the project has conferred upon the people of the district are incalculable. The misery it has prevented may be gauged from a perusal of Chapter VIII below, where the ghastly sufferings from famine which the people endured before its construction are faintly indicated.

Possible extensions of it.

Mr. Walch considers that 'it may be assumed that there is land available for an extension of irrigation of at least 100,000 acres; exclusive of the considerable areas in the Coringa and Pólaram islands, to both of which anicut water could be taken without any very serious engineering difficulty; to the former by a tunnel or articulated pipes and to the latter by an aqueduct across the Vriddha Gautami.' Whether, however, sufficient water can be rendered available for any such extension is another matter. For some three months in every year vastly more water comes down the river than is required for the area at present irrigated, and this excess pours uselessly over the anicut and down to the sea. But in almost every season the period of superabundance is followed by one of scarcity, the water barely sufficing for the present area of wet crops. Either therefore the 'duty' of the water must be increased (no easy matter) or some method of storage must be resorted to. It has been suggested [1] that reservoirs might perhaps be formed on the Saveri or one of its larger tributaries.

Its administration.

The administration of the irrigation works of the central and eastern deltas in this district involves the maintenance of a large establishment. An Executive Engineer and two Assistant Engineers are in charge of them exclusively, the rest of the district being administered by another Executive Engineer with an Assistant Engineer subordinate to him; and under their orders are the anicut superintendent and sub-overseers, who supervise the distribution of the water, the conservancy establishment in charge of the locks and river embankments, and the navigation establishment referred to in Chapter VII. A new division for the conservancy of the river bed is being organized.

The embankments give much trouble in times of high freshes, and the country is not yet adequately protected from the effects of abnormal floods. In 1886, 1892 and 1900 the

[1] Mr. H. E. Clerk's *Preliminary Report for the Irrigation Commission* (1902), 3, 50.

CHAP. IV. OTHER IRRIGATION SOURCES.

embankments breached and serious inundations were caused. Most of them have been raised since 1900. Drainage, though not so burning a question as in the Tanjore delta, is a matter of great difficulty near the coast, where the fall of the land is very gradual. Large tracts there are liable to be flooded by a heavy north-east monsoon.

Mionr channels and tanks.

As above remarked, the district contains 31,800 acres protected in all seasons by minor channels and tanks, and 53,800 acres safeguarded in ordinary seasons. Of this extent, the greater part lies in Rajahmundry (20,300 and 27,300 acres respectively) and Peddápuram (18,400 acres in ordinary seasons). In Pólavaram, Cocanada and Bhadráchalam only 2,800 acres, 1,300 acres and 100 acres respectively are protected by these sources in all seasons, and in ordinary seasons 2,800 acres in Yellavaram, 100 acres in Chódavaram and an additional 1,700 acres in Pólavaram. Tanks occur in all these tracts. The largest in the district is at Lingamparti in Peddápuram taluk, which irrigates 4,686 acres. Other considerable reservoirs are the Kottapalli tank (970 acres), the Kápavaram tank (823 acres), and the Ganapavaram tank (686 acres), all in Rajahmundry. The only considerable minor channels are those from the Yeléru, which irrigate some 8,000 acres in Peddápuram taluk and a further extent in the PitHápuram zamindari. A small area in Peddápuram is also irrigated from the Ravutulapúdi stream.

Wells.

Irrigation from wells is very rare in the uplands and the Agency, and the only taluk in the district in which over 100 acres is so watered is Amalápuram. Cheap temporary wells are sunk in small numbers in parts of Peddápuram, Tuni, Cocanada and Rámachandrapuram. In the two latter they are only used for about two months in each year, average 12 feet in depth, and hold some six feet of water. In Cocanada they are called *doruvu* wells. In Tuni they last much longer and more labour is expended on them. On the Yalésvaram river shallow wells are dug which last for five or six years. It is only in Nagaram and Amalápuram taluks that permanent revetted wells are found. They are very large, from 18 to 24 feet deep, hold from six to twelve feet of water, are revetted with bricks and are said to be very ancient. They are sometimes called 'Jain' wells, and are supposed to date from the days when the Jain faith prevailed in the country;[1] in Amalápuram they are sometimes called 'Reddis' wells.' They are largely used for the irrigation of areca and cocoanut palm plantations, and the supply in them is said to be practically perennial. The ordinary water-lift employed in the

[1] See Chapter III, p. 39.

CHAP. IV. OTHER IRRIGATION SOURCES.

central delta is the *kapila* or *mótu* worked by bullocks, but the picottah (called *tokkudu yétham)* is usual elsewhere.

Artesian wells.

A peculiarity of the district is its artesian wells. The existence of an artesian supply was accidentally discovered while digging an ordinary well in the railway-station compound at Samalkot in 1892-93, the water being encountered at a depth of about eighty feet. Since then several other artesian wells have been sunk; namely, a second in the station compound, two in 1904 in the sugar refinery at the same place (water being reached at some 110 feet), and a fifth in the railway-station yard at Cocanada Port, where the water was nearly 300 feet below ground level. Artesian water has also been found on the Pólavaram and Yernagúdem border during the recent explorations for coal in that neighbourhood but borings at Pithápuram have been unsuccessful.

ECONOMIC CONDITION OF AGRICULTURISTS.

In the zamindaris the ryots have usually no admitted occupancy right. They pay money rents fixed each year. In the Agency, the tenants of the muttadars are apparently protected from rack-renting and eviction by the scarcity of cultivators and the consequent desire of each landholder to keep those he has.

In Government land, fields are frequently sub-let by the pattadars, the consideration being either a share of the actual crop *(samgóru)* or, much more commonly, a fixed payment in money or grain called sist.

The sharing system seems to be chiefly restricted to inferior wet land, and under it the crop is everywhere divided equally between the landholder and the tenant. The latter usually finds the seed, the cattle and the labour, but in Bhadráchalam a landholder will often let his permanent farm-servants cultivate a piece of his land with his cattle and seed on condition of receiving half the crop resulting.

Fixed rents are only paid in grain in the case of wet land. Grain rents are usually rather lower than money rents, as there is less chance of evading payment of them. The tenant, as before, finds seed, cattle and labour; but in Pithápuram a variant called the backyard *(peradu)* system prevails under which the landholder lends the cattle. Agricultural labourers are either farm-servants engaged by the year *(pálikápu)* or coolies hired by the day or job. The former usually engage themselves for the whole year to some landholder, who then has the exclusive right to their services. Accounts are settled, and fresh engagements made, on the eleventh day of the bright fortnight of the month Áshádha (July-August), which is well known throughout the district under the name of 'the initial ékádasi' (*toli ékádasi*). Then, as the proverb significantly says, 'the *pálikápus* are companions to their master's sons-in-law,' they remind him of his petty tyrannies during the past year and haggle over the renewal of their agreements.

The rates of wages for *pálikápus,* which are always fixed by the year and (except in Bhadráchalam) in paddy, vary, when commuted into money at the usual rate of 10 kunchams per rupee, from Rs. 24 (or one anna a day) in Pólavaram to Rs. 60 (two annas, eight pies a day) in Peddápuram, Pithápuram, Rajahmundry and Rámachandrapuram. These labourers are also given a small varying quantity of straw and unthreshed paddy at the end of the year, a new cloth, some tobacco and a palmyra tree, or, if the master has no palmyras, a gift of one rupee. They also get advances of their wages free of interest. In Amalápuram various different customs prevail. These rates of wages are said to have increased by one-third or one-half in the last ten or fifteen years. Payment is usually made at the end of the year.

The day labourer is paid from two to four annas a day, women getting half these rates. The rates of wages were only about half these sums a few years ago. Labour, however, is not really scarce. The great immigration from Vizagapatam (p. 38) has done much to supplement it, and there is no 'labour problem' as in some places, the Tanjore delta, for example. The rates of interest on loans are much the same as usual, 12 to 24 per cent. being common. Loans are often made on the security of standing crops on the condition that they shall be sold to the sowcar at less than the market price, an arrangement which is known as the *jatti* system.

CHAPTER V.

FORESTS.

EARLY OPERATIONS—Progress of reservation. SETTLEMENT—Proprietary rights—Susceptibilities of the jungle tribes—*Podu* cultivation. ADMINISTRATION—In Rampa—In the rest of the Agency—River transit rules—Fire-protection—Artificial reproduction; casuarina—Mangrove—Introduction of exotics, etc. GENERAL CHARACTER OF THE FORESTS—On the coast—In the uplands—In Pólavaram and Yellavaram—In Rampa—In Bhadráchalam—Timber and the market for it—Minor forest produce—Forest revenue.

CHAP. V. EARLY OPERATIONS.

THE best forests in the district are those in the Agency, and trade in their timber, facilitated as it is by the waterway provided by the Gódávari river, has flourished from the earliest times. The Committee of Circuit (see p. 162) refer to it as far back as 1786 and it was still in existence when the Government recently began forest conservancy. The Bhadráchalam and Rékapalle country was the chief centre. Dealers from the plains employed the Kóyas and hill Reddis to cut timber at so much a log, or bamboos at so much a thousand, and to drag them to the riverside, where they were made into rafts and floated down stream [1] to the markets nearer the coast.

Progress of reservation.

Forest conservancy was first begun in the Bhadráchalam taluk, which was transferred to the district from the Central Provinces in 1874. Soon after the transfer, the Madras Government threw open its forests to exploitation on the permit system, and annually netted a very fair revenue from them.[2] In 1876-77 reserves amounting to 138 square miles (subsequently reduced to 68 square miles) were selected in the taluk by Mr. Boileau, the Deputy Conservator of Forests who had been sent to the district for the purpose; but the hill tribes were permitted to cut whatever wood they chose for their own use, and complaints were frequently made that they sold timber and other produce to outside dealers. Although only four guards were sanctioned for the protection of these reserves, yet the average annual revenue between 1874 and 1882 was Rs. 21,000, while the expenditure averaged only Rs. 3,800. In the latter of these two years Mr. Boileau reported very unfavourably on the condition of the forests; and Dr. (afterwards Sir Dietrich) Brandis, who was then

[1] B.P. No. 1992 (Forest No. 372), dated 7th July 1885, p. 11.

[2] B.P. Forest No. 222, dated 30th July 1902.

CHAP. V. EARLY OPERATIONS.

in Madras advising the Government regarding its future forest policy, recommended that conservancy in this taluk should be abandoned unless Government was prepared to introduce the Forest Act and to sanction the reservation of large compact blocks, capable of subsequent extension, and stated that it was the unanimous opinion of the local officers that grazing, fires, indiscriminate cutting and the clearings made by the hill men for their shifting cultivation were ruining the forests.

The Government accordingly directed Mr. J. S. Gamble, the Conservator of the Northern Division, to inspect the taluk and report on Sir Dietrich Brandis' proposals, and his detailed account of the forests [1] finally dispelled any doubt as to their importance. Mr. Gamble rearranged Mr. Boileau's reserves and proposed new ones which brought up the forest area to 530 square miles. Most of this tract was notified under the Forest Act between 1889 and 1891; but the large Rékapalle hills reserve of 93,500 acres was not notified till 1896.

Reservation was soon begun in other taluks also. By 1893 large areas had been notified in the Peddápuram taluk and Yellavaram division, but the major portion of the large Pólavaram forests were not reserved till 1899, and it was not until 1901 that the forests of the district as a whole attained their present proportions.

Amalápuram	13
Bhadráchalam	460
Cocanada	86
Peddápuram	72
Pólavaram	111
Rajahmundry	34
Yellavaram	166
Gódávari district ...	942

The marginal figures show in square miles the area of the reserves and reserved land in each taluk or division and in the district as a whole. They do not include Rampa, which though containing large areas of jungle, has for political reasons been excluded from the operations, and yet it will be noticed that 737 square miles of the total of 942 square miles is situated in the agency divisions.

SETTLEMENT. Proprietary rights.

The rights of Government over the forests in the Agency have been established in different ways in different tracts. In Rampa, the muttadars at one time claimed the right to lease out the forests, and large quantities of timber were removed by the lessees they appointed. But it was eventually ruled that Government stood in the exact place of the former mansabdar of Rampa and that consequently neither the muttadars nor the mokhásadars had any right to lease out the jungle or fell timber for sale, and that the Rampa forests were

[1] Printed in B.P. No. 1992 (Forest No. 372), dated 7th July 1885.

CHAP. V. SETTLEMENT.

the property of the State.[1] As however these subordinate proprietors had hitherto been enjoying a considerable forest revenue of which it seemed harsh to deprive them absolutely, it was resolved in December 1892 to pay them an annual allowance amounting to half the net average of this revenue during the previous three years, on the understanding that they would assist Government in the future administration of the forest. In the Yellavaram and Pólavaram divisions, no such difficulty occurred in settling the rights of proprietors.

In the Bhadráchalam taluk the Government of the Central Provinces had adopted, in their permanent settlement with the zamindars, a policy regarding forests which differs from that traditional in this Presidency. The forests and waste lands in zamindari estates were not handed over to the zamindars, but, after a liberal deduction from them (called the *dupati* land) had been made round each village to allow for the possible extension of cultivation, were declared to be State property.[2]

Susceptibilities of the jungle tribes.

Reservation was complicated not only by claims to the proprietary ownership of the forests, but also by the unusual habits and susceptibilities of the hill tribes who dwelt among them. These people, though possessing few sustainable rights over the jungle, had from time immemorial enjoyed and abused a general freedom to fell or burn whatever growth they chose. The Kóyas and hill Reddis lived in villages situated on the borders of, and even within, the proposed reserves, and for political reasons great care was considered necessary in dealing with them. Dissatisfaction with the new forest rules in Rékapalle was apparently the reason which had led the Kóyas of that taluk to join in the Rampa rebellion of 1879.

Pódu cultivation.

Both the Kóyas and the Reddis lived by the shifting *(pódu)* cultivation described in the last chapter (p. 78), making clearings in the heart of the forest by felling and burning the trees, cultivating them for a year or two until their first fertility was exhausted, and then moving on to new ground. Not only were acres of valuable forest thus felled, but the fires lit for burning these patches spread over enormous areas. On the other hand, reservation, to be thorough, necessitated the exclusion of this class of cultivation from the reserved blocks and meant a considerable curtailment of the old privileges of the hill men, who had been accustomed to wander and burn wherever they liked.

[1] See B.P., Forest No. 128, dated 6th March 1890 and G.O. No. 1280, Revenue, dated 21st December 1892.

[2] See Chapter XI, p. 176.

SETTLEMENT.

In the earlier stages of the forest settlement in Pólavaram and Yellavaram the officers in charge of the Agency held that reservation had been too wholesale and that the allowance of jungle left in the neighbourhood of villages to provide for the extension or rotation of cultivation and for the supply of timber for implements and other domestic purposes was inadequate. Mr. (now Sir A. T.) Arundel, then a Member of the Board of Revenue, consequently visited the district in October 1893 and enquired into the matter on the spot. He came to the conclusion that the habits of the hill men had not received adequate consideration, and it was accordingly ordered that the Assistant Agent and the District Forest Officer should personally investigate the complaints and see that equitable claims were satisfied. Without laying down hard-and-fast rules it was indicated that *pódus* which had long been abandoned and were covered with jungle need not necessarily be excluded from reservation, but that well-recognized *pódus* should be excluded and handed over to the cultivators; and that for the rotation and extension of cultivation a sufficient extent (eight times the existing area annually under cultivation as a maximum) should be set aside.

In Bhadráchalam the settlement was completed without controversy. The hill men of that taluk had long been accustomed to the idea of reservation, and considerable leniency was shown in the provision of areas for cultivation. It is however only in the last few years that *pódu* cultivation in the reserves there has been completely stopped.

In Rampa, the scene of a violent rebellion as recently as 1879, it was considered better not to run any risk of arousing discontent by attempts at reservation, and the forests there were never demarcated at all. They are still administered on a system different from that followed in the rest of the district.

ADMINISTRATION. In Rampa.

The susceptibilities of the hill men led to cautious systems of forest administration throughout the Agency, all orders being issued through the Agent or his Special Assistant, but in Rampa the methods adopted were quite distinct. The country was exempted from the operation of all but section 26 of Chapter III, and Chapters V, VII, IX and X of the Forest Act. These rendered it possible to regulate the cutting and transit of timber, and special rules were drawn up regarding those matters. The people were allowed to cut timber for their own use except tamarind, jack, *ippa*, soap-nut, gall-nut and mango trees; but any one desirous of exporting any wood had to take out a permit before doing so, to pay certain fees, and to cart it by one or other of certain prescribed routes,

CHAP. V. ADMINISTRATION.

along which inspection tánahs under the management of the Forest department were placed to check the exports with the permits. These regulations still remain in force.

Minor forest produce for their own use may be collected by the Rampa people free of all charge; but on any which is exported, seigniorage is levied generally at the weekly markets outside Rampa where the produce is brought for sale, and from the traders and not from the hill men. The same procedure is adopted in the case of minor produce brought out of the Yellavaram division.

The Rampa people are also allowed to graze their own cattle in the forest free. But owners of foreign cattle driven to Rampa to graze have to take out permits and pay fees,[1] and the cattle have to be produced for check at the tánah specified in the permit. In 1900–01 the forest revenue from all these sources amounted to Rs. 5,500; in 1901–02 to Rs. 9,400; in 1902–03 to Rs. 10,800; and in 1903–04 to Rs. 6,700.

In the rest of the Agency.

In the Agency outside the Rampa country the forests are either wholly or partially reserved. In the latter, timber, as in Rampa, may be felled for agricultural and domestic purposes free, except that certain trees must not be touched. In Pólavaram nineteen species have been thus excepted, in Yellavaram fifteen, and in Bhadráchalam nine; while in this last taluk Kóyas and hill Reddis are allowed to fell any trees except teak and *Diospyros melanoxylon*. In unsurveyed villages any trees may be felled to prepare land for permanent cultivation and any except certain species (specified in each division) to clear it for *pódu*. In surveyed villages the rules usual elsewhere are in force.

Minor produce (except *rela* and *tangédu* bark, for which permits are required) may be gathered free for domestic use in this class of forests in Yellavaram, and in Bhadráchalam by Kóyas and hill Reddis. Seigniorage is collected, as in Rampa, at the weekly markets from the traders on any which is collected for export. In Pólavaram the revenue is collected on the permit system in both classes of forest.

The grazing rules differ in the different divisions of the Agency; but in all of them Kóyas and Reddis are allowed to graze their cattle free, and in all of them except Bhadráchalam (whither cattle are seldom driven on account of its remoteness

[1] This system was not instituted till 1899, when it was found that the hill muttadars were levying fees of this kind without authority. See the correspondence in B.Ps., Forest Nos. 318, dated 28th July 1897 and 264, dated 22nd June 1899. For the subsequent raising of the fees see B.Ps., Forest Nos. 89, dated 1st March 1901 and 19, dated 28th January 1904.

foreign cattle are charged full rates. People other than Kóyas and Reddis are charged one-quarter the full rates in Bhadráchalam, one-half in Pólavaram and one anna a head in Yellavaram.

The game rules are in force in the Pápikonda hill (Bison hill) reserve of the Pólavaram division, in order to protect the bison there, which are rapidly disappearing. It is in contemplation to extend the rules in course of time to the adjoining Kopalli and Kovvada blocks.

River transit rules.

The Gódávari (and, in a lesser degree, the Saveri) are important waterways for floating timber from forests belonging to other administrations, Native States, zamindars, and private individuals outside the district. But they also flow for many miles through the forests of this Collectorate, and this renders much care necessary to prevent them from being used for the illicit removal of timber from the forests of this district under the pretence that it comes from elsewhere. Inspection tánahs have accordingly been established at which all timber floated down these rivers is checked. Timber brought from forests other than those in this district belonging to Government has to be covered by vouchers signed by the owners of the forests or responsible authorities, and the wood is checked with these.

Fire protection.

Fire-protection, always a difficult problem, is rendered doubly troublesome in the Agency owing to the prevalence of the habit of smoking and the existence of *pódu* cultivation close alongside the reserves. Formerly patrols used to be employed during the fire-season, but during the past two years the money allotted for fire-protection has been spent in inducing the hill folk themselves to co-operate in checking fires, annual rewards being granted to the people of villages the reserves next which escaped damage from this cause. Villages are allotted certain limits within which they are expected to check fires by cutting lines, appointing patrols, and observing and enforcing prohibitions against burning *pódus* within 100 yards of any forest boundary line, burning the grass under *ippa* trees to facilitate the collection of the flowers when they fall, and throwing down live cheroot ends. If within the limits thus fixed a fire occurs, the villagers concerned lose their reward. The plan has met with a fair measure of success.

Artificial reproduction; casuarina.

The only artificial reproduction of forests which has been attempted is in the casuarina plantations near the coast. Two large blocks of this tree exist, in which over 85 acres are annually planted up. In the Kandikuppa block, in which the rotation has been fixed at fifteen years, the planting is at

CHAP. V. ADMINISTRATION.

intervals of six feet by six, the object being to produce long, straight poles for the river protection works of the Public Works department. In the Bendamúrlanka block, where the rotation is ten years, the seedlings are put out at an interval of nine feet by nine. In both areas thinnings are made after the fifth year to admit light to induce increase in girth ; and in both of them the method of reproduction employed is clear felling and replanting.

Mangrove.

The artificial regeneration of the mangrove has been undertaken during the past three years in the Coringa reserve, a valuable swamp forest about twelve miles from the important fire wood market at Cocanada. Natural reproduction is hindered by the unsuitability of the ground under the trees, which, being raised year after year by silt, becomes hard and dry during the season (the north-east monsoon) when the seed falls, and allows the seed to be carried away by the tide before it can take root. The higher and drier portions give very little hope of ever being restocked with anything except inferior species of *tilla (Excæcaria Agallocha)* which coppices freely. The mangrove itself gives poor result from coppicing, and consequently, in the lower and softer portions of the swamp, sowing and dibbling have been largely resorted to. The seed is sown broad cast wherever the sea recedes enough to leave the ground bare and the latter is soft enough for the seed to sink in; while where the surface is hard or permanently covered by water, the slower and more costly method of dibbling in the seed is followed. About 600 acres have been sown in three years at an average cost of twelve and a half annas per acre.

Introduction of exotics etc.

Experiments made with exotics and foreign varieties have not given satisfactory results. Log-wood plants raised from seed imported from Jamaica have been put down in the Coringa swamp forests in different localities, but without success. Attempts have also been made to re-stock elevated parts of the same marsh with dry-land species, but owing to want of rain the result was very disheartening. In the Pegha reserve in Bhadráchalam taluk some 25 acres were sown with teak seed from Coimbatore in August 1903, but a year later only 500 seedlings were to be found.

GENERAL CHARACTER OF THE FORESTS.

On the coast.

The character of the forests of the district naturally differs widely in different localities. Along the tidal creeks of the Gódávari river near the coast runs a mangrove jungle which extends southwards from Coringa for a distance of about 35 miles with an average width of five miles. About one-third of this area belongs to zamindars and the rest to Government. The zamindari portion is mere scrub jungle, having been

GENERAL CHARACTER OF THE FORESTS.

repeatedly cut over, and much of it is a waste plain containing no growth whatever. The Government portion is the main source of the fuel-supply of Cocanada. The species found in this forest consist chiefly of four varieties of *Avicennias*, and of *Rhizophoræ*, *Ægiceras*, *Lumnitzeras*, *Ceriops*, and other inferior trees. *Ceriops Candolleana* yields a bark ('*gedara* bark') which the villagers use for colouring fishing-nets. The barks of the other mangrove species, although said to be good tanning materials, are not used as such, probably because they contain a large percentage of colouring matter. The forest is useful only for the fuel it yields.

Mangrove wood is inferior as fuel to the ordinary upland jungle species, but *Lumnitzera racemosa* (though scarce) is extremely hard and burns excellently, and the *Ceriops* shrub burns even when green if the bark is removed. *Sonneratia apetala (kalingi)* is a soft wood which is useful in brick-kilns when newly cut, but rapidly rots. The worst fuel of all is the *tilla*, a pithy wood full of an acrid juice which smokes more than it burns.

Besides these natural jungles, the coast forests comprise the two large plantations of casuarina already mentioned, which yield firewood and poles or piles for the river-protection works of the Public Works department. The Kandikuppa plantation (532 acres in extent and only partially planted at present) lies on the coast about 30 miles from Cocanada and has direct water communication with that town. The Bendamúrlanka block (470 acres in extent) is 30 miles further down the coast, and is nearly planted up, but has only indirect and tortuous water communication with Cocanada.

In the uplands.

Proceeding northward from the coast, scattered blocks of forest are met with in the Rajahmundry and Peddápuram ranges. These chiefly contain wood fit only for fuel, though stunted specimens of timber-yielding trees are scattered here and there and provide small timber for building huts and so forth. Among these latter are *Terminalia tomentosa*, *Diospyros melanoxylon*, *Pterocarpus Marsupium*, *Anogeissus latifolia*, *Lagerstrœmia parviflora*, *Adina cordifolia*, *Chloroxylon Swietenia*, *Lebedieropsis orbicularis*, *Soymida febrifuga*, and a sprinkling of young *Xylia dolabriformis* and some patches of bamboo.

In Pólavaram and Yellavaram.

The forests of Pólavaram and Yellavaram are of a better character. In Yellavaram there are 47 square miles of good forest in which fairly large timber (three to five feet in girth) is found, and some 96 square miles containing trees (one and half to three feet in girth) providing timber of a smaller kind. The principal timber species are the *Xylia*, *Terminalia*,

CHAP. V. GENERAL CHARACTER OF THE FORESTS.

Pterocarpus, *Anogeissus*, *Chloroxylon*, *Lagerstrœmia* and *Adina* already mentioned as occurring further south. In the Pólavaram division, besides the above, teak (which never occurs in Yellavaram) is also met with. It may be said generally, however, that although these forests contain large timber trees, these are usually either unsound or situated in inaccessible places. The bulk of the crop consists of small growth which, owing to its distance from a market, is valueless either as fuel or timber.

The chief fruit-trees are the tamarind, gall-nut and *ippa*, and these forests also contain a quantity of the thin kind of bamboo (*Dendrocalamus strictus*) which is largely used for sugar-cane props.

In Rampa.

The Rampa forests, being unreserved, have been less studied than the others. They are in a worse condition than those of Yellavaram and Pólavaram, since unrestricted fellings are permitted for *pódu* cultivation, and their remoteness renders the extraction of any timber both difficult and costly. Small quantities are removed on permits by consumers on their borders, and the bamboos in them, which include quantities of both *Bambusa* and *Dendrocalamus*, are also utilized similarly.

In Bhadráchalam.

The forests in Bhadráchalam may be divided into (1) the Rékapalle or *Xylia* range, (2) the Marrigúdem or teak range, and (3) the Bhadráchalam range, of which three-quarters consists mainly of teak and one-quarter of *Hardwickia binata*. Besides these predominant and more valuable species, large quantities of other timber trees are found, among which are the *Terminaia*, *Pterocarpus*, *Adina*, *Anogeissus* and *Lagerstrœmia* already mentioned above, and likewise *Dalbergia latifolia* and *Terminallia Arjuna*. In the Bhadráchalam and Marrigúdem ranges, the teak, *Xylia* and *Hardwickia* are either comparatively young or unsound, the best trees having been felled in past years. The same is true of the less valuable species.

The best forest left is that in the inaccessible Rékapalle hills. For this a working plan[1] has been recently framed. The examination of the growth made in connection with this showed that over a fifth (sometimes nearly one-half) of the crop consisted of *Xylia*, that *Hardwickia* was very rare, that, among the inferior timber trees *Lebedieropsis orbicularis* was prominent, and that the rest of the forest was mainly made up of the trees already mentioned as prevalent in this part of the district, together with *Albizzia odoratissima* and *A. procera*.

[1] See B.P., Forest No. 222, dated 30th July 1902.

CHAP. V. GENERAL CHARACTER OF THE FORESTS.

The finest stock is found on the plateaus and in elevated situations generally, and the size of the trees increases as one goes northwards; but the growth along the western edge and near enclosures has greatly deteriorated from having been subjected to excessive *pódu* cultivation. Great difficulty is experienced in putting the working plan into practice, owing to the difficulty in extracting the produce from the more remote parts of these hills.

Timber and the market for it.

At present the Bhadráchalam forests give no large timber. Teak is rarely obtained in logs more than 30 inches in girth and 25 feet long, and even then is crooked, unsound, knotty and fibrous, and, except for boat-building, is unable to compete in the markets with Burma teak. That from Marrigúdem, however, is prettily grained and suitable for furniture. *Terminalia tomentosa (nalla maddi)* is procurable in about the same sizes and is useful for building; *Dalbergia latifolia (iruguduchaval)* is usually in shorter logs and is poor, unsound in the centre, and chiefly employed for furniture; and *Pterocarpus Marsupium (yégisi)* is procurable from 10 to 15 feet in length and from 4 to 5 feet in girth and is much used for planking, ceiling-boards and the like.

The chief markets for timber are Rajahmundry and Cocanada. Of these, the first is much the more important, and the timber is taken thence to Cocanada, Bezwada, Masulipatam and Ellore, as well as to smaller dépôts at Narasapur, Amalápuram and Rámachandrapuram.

Minor forest produce.

The bulk of the marketable minor forest produce comes from the Rampa and Yellavaram forests, Bhadráchalam and Pólavaram producing very little. Tamarind, gall-nuts, *nux vomica*, honey, wax, soap-nut, *síkáy*, platter leaves and skins and horns are the chief items, and the bulk of the revenue under this head is derived from tamarind and gall-nuts. The chief markets are again at Rajahmundry and Cocanada, whence the produce is distributed to many parts of India, Ceylon and Europe. Large quantities of *nux vomica* and gall-nuts are sent to London and Hamburg; wax goes to London, Colombo, Calcutta and Bombay; horns to London and France; skins to Madras; and *síkáy* to Madras, Cuddalore and Tuticorin. Most of the other produce is consumed locally.

Forest revenue.

The total revenue from the forests of the district amounted in 1904-05 to nearly two lakhs, of which Rs. 56,000 were derived from the sale of bamboos, Rs. 43,000 from minor forest produce, Rs. 35,000 from timber, Rs. 27,000 from firewood and charcoal, and Rs. 16,000 from grazing-fees and the sale of grass for fodder.

CHAPTER VI.

OCCUPATIONS AND TRADE.

ARTS AND INDUSTRIES—Silk-weavers—Cotton-weavers; their numbers—Their methods—Tape-weaving—Gunny-weaving—Cotton-dyeing—Chintz-stamping—Mats and tattis—Metal-work—Painting—Pith-work—Musical instruments—Wood and stone carving—Ropes—Oils—Tanning—Shoes—Baskets—Bangles—Pottery—Country sugar—Mercury—House-building—Printing-presses—Rice-mills—Indigo factories—Ship-building—Dowlaishweram workshops—District Board Workshops at Cocanada—Samalkot distillery and sugar-factory—Dummagúdem lace. TRADE—Markets—Grain-dealing—Exports—Imports—Trade of Cocanada—The harbour—Port conservancy—European business houses at Cocanada—European Chamber of Commerce—Steamers visiting the port—Amount of trade—Character of trade. WEIGHTS AND MEASURES—Goldsmiths' weights—Commercial weights—Measures of capacity—Miscellaneous commercial notations—Lineal measures—Land measures—Measures of time—Local monetary terms.

CHAP. VI. ARTS AND INDUSTRIES.

As in other districts, agriculture and the tending of flocks and herds employ the very large majority of the population. This is especially the case in the Agency. Precise statistics are not available for the district as it stands at present, as the census of 1901 was taken before its limits were altered. Agricultural methods have been referred to in Chapter IV above, and the breeds of cattle and sheep in Chapter I. Of the arts and industries, weaving employs a larger number of hands than any other.

Silk-weavers.

The weaving of silk is done on only the smallest scale. Silk borders are often given to cotton cloths, but the pure silk cloths worn in the district are imported. The best come from Benares and Calcutta, but commoner kinds are brought fróm Ganjám and elsewhere by local merchants and pedlars. Silk is rarely employed for ordinary wear, but is very commonly used by the higher castes for what are called *madi* cloths, that is, the ceremonially pure garments which are worn at home at meal times. The only silk fabrics made locally are the turbans and kerchiefs made by a few Dévángas and Karnabattus at Peddápuram. These seldom sell for more than Rs. 10. The silk is obtained from Calcutta and Bombay and is dyed locally with violet, red, green and yellow aniline dyes. These colours are popular; and, since the cloths are not often washed, the fugitive character of the aniline pigment does not matter. This industry is a small one, and does not appear to be increasing.

CHAP. VI. ARTS AND INDUSTRIES.

Cotton-weavers; their numbers.

Though silk-weaving is rare, the manufacture of cotton cloths is largely carried on. Almost every other village in the plains contains a few weavers, and a fair number of them possess a large contingent. In Rajahmundry some 400 households are so employed, in Jagannapéta (Nagaram taluk) 300, and in Tuni, Peddápuram, Bandárulanka (Amalápuram), Uppáda and Kottapalli (Pithápuram division) about 200 households. Four other villages each contain 100 weavers; and in about twenty other places the number of the craft is considerable. In the days of the East India Company, the exportation of cloth from the district was very large. Some seven lakhs of rupees were paid annually by the Company for local fabrics, and in some years the figure rose above ten lakhs, and in one year touched fourteen. The abolition of the Company's cloth trade had a most prejudicial effect on the weaving industry, and so on the prosperity of the district as a whole. The value of the piece-goods exported in 1825–26 was over fourteen lakhs; in 1842–43 it was less than two. In the import of cotton fabrics from Europe which followed, Gódávari shared to a much less extent than some other districts. English calicoes and longcloths are not now more popular there than the country fabrics, nor cheaper, and the use of them is very limited.

Their methods.

Most of the locally-woven cloths are white, and a visitor from the south cannot fail to be struck with the rarity of colour in the dress of the women. The men's cloths are often red, but the dye is applied after, and not before, the weaving. Of recent years the manufacture of coloured cotton tartans *(lungis)* for Muhammadans has been taken up by some of the weavers in a few centres. The white cloths worn by the women sometimes have coloured borders, but these are generally of the simplest kinds. They are very rarely of silk, but not uncommonly of 'lace,' that is, gold or silver thread; and the borders at the ends are sometimes embroidered with simple patterns in lace. This class of work is done at Uppáda, Kottapalli and Múlapéta in Pithápuram, at Totaramudi in Amalápuram and by a few weavers in Tuni and Rajahmundry.

The texture of the local work is often exceedingly fine. In Kottapalli and Múlapéta the weavers use counts as high as 200s, and 100s, 130s and 150s are employed in a good many places. The Kottapalli and Múlapéta fabrics are locally called Uppáda cloths, and under that name are well known as far south as Tanjore, and are said to be sent even to Calcutta and Bombay. Their prices run up to Rs. 10.

CHAP. VI. ARTS AND INDUSTRIES.

There is hardly anything worthy of mention in the methods of the local weavers. These are extraordinarily simple everywhere, and form a remarkable contrast to the complications entailed by the more elaborate work done in the great weaving centres of the south. Where special patterns are embroidered on the loom, the warp is given the necessary changes by the laborious method of picking out with the hand, at each passing of the shuttle, the threads which have to be lowered or raised. The great majority of the weavers are Dévángas by caste. In Kottapalli and Múlapétà Pattu Sáles monopolize the work; while there are a few Padma Sáles in Cocanada taluk, some Sáles in Samalkot and Peddápuram, and some Karnabattus in the last-named place.

Tape-weaving.

Tape for the cots so universally used in the district is largely manufactured, both in a number of scattered villages and in the Rajahmundry jail. It is woven from white cotton, and is of from half an inch to three inches in breadth. The work is usually done by Dévángas, but in the central delta Bógams (the dancing-girl caste), and elsewhere a few men of the Singam sub-caste of the Sáles are also engaged in it.

Gunny-weaving.

Gunny-bags are woven from hemp by a few Perikes in Vangalapúdi and Singavaram in the Rajahmundry taluk.

Cotton-dyeing.

The dyed cloths for men already mentioned are sold in quantities in the district and are also exported by the Cocanada merchants to Bombay, Calcutta and Rangoon. The places best known for this dyeing industry are Gollapálaiyam (in Cocanada taluk), where some 70 men are employed, and Cocanada and Samalkot, where the number of workers is about 30. Most of them are Kápus, and the next most largely represented caste are the Tsákalas, or washermen. A few Rangáris and Velamas also assist. None of them weave the cloths themselves.

The most popular colours are red, dark blue, and pink, or 'rose' as it is called. There are three shades of red, two of blue, and several of pink. Aniline and alizarine dyes, bought in packets or casks, are always used. In Cocanada chay-root *(sirivéru)* was employed until recently for red, but was abandoned because it involved more trouble and expense than the imported dyes. Black is still made sometimes with iron filings.

The methods of dyeing are much the same as elsewhere, the cloth being treated with oil emulsified with the ashes of certain pungent plants, soaked in a mordant (generally a solution of gall-nuts or alum) and then boiled in a pot of dye to which the dried leaves of sundry jungle shrubs, believed to brighten the colour, have been added.

Chintz-stamping.

The same castes which do this dyeing also engage in the stamping of chintzes. Only two colours, red and dark blue, are used. The former is made with imported dyes and the latter sometimes from iron or from copper sulphate. The processes are again the same as elsewhere. The pattern desired is stamped with a pattern-block which is pressed on a pad soaked in a mixture of alum and gum. The fabric is afterwards immersed in boiling dye and then washed in clean water. The dye only takes where the alum mordant has affected the cloth, and washes out of the other parts. Sometimes the whole cloth is soaked in the mordant and then stamped with the dye itself. White spots on a coloured ground are produced as follows: The spots are stamped on the cloth with a pattern-block dipped in hot wax, and the whole cloth is then dipped into the dye-tub. The dye does not act where the cloth is protected by the wax spots, and the parts under these latter come out white. The wax is then removed by boiling the cloth.

Mats and tattis.

Mats of grass are seldom made, the small demand being supplied from Madras and Bastar State. Plaited mats of palmyra, date and cocoanut leaves, and of split bamboo, are largely manufactured. Those of cocoanut leaves are chiefly made in the central delta, and the others everywhere in the plains. The date mats are generally used for packing, the cocoanut mats for tattis, and the palmyra mats for covering floors or, by the lower classes, for sleeping on. The first are made by Ídigas and Yerukalas; the second by Málas; and the last by Mádigas and (more rarely) by Ídigas; split bamboo work is done by Médaras.

Some 25 Málas weave kas-kas tattis at Samalkot. These are made of a scented grass called *vetti véru*, found in some of the tank beds, and supply the local demand at Rajahmundry and Cocanada.

Metal-work.

Metal vessels for household use are only manufactured on a very small scale. Kamsalas have a monopoly of the industry, which is stagnant, if not declining. Brass or bell-metal vessels are made by a few families in Cocanada, Gollamámidáda (in Cocanada taluk), Tuni, Rágampéta (in Peddápuram taluk), Pithápuram, Dowlaishweram, Rajahmundry and Peddápuram. At Marripúdi in the Peddápuram taluk ten or twelve men make bells of bell-metal. Copper is worked only by the Kamsalas of Cocanada. Vessels of lead and silver are made in that town and Amalápuram; and lead vessels by a few men in Rajahmundry and Peddápuram. Metal-work of

CHAP. VI. ARTS AND INDUSTRIES.

all sorts is imported in large quantities from the Vizagapatam district, especially from Anakápalle and Yellamanchili, and hawked for sale at all the important festivals.

Of the local manufactures, the brass-work of Peddápuram and the bell-metal work of Pithápuram and Rajahmundry are of good quality and well known. The bell-metal vessels are always cast, but the brass ones are made of three or more pieces soldered together. The lead-work is cast at Rajahmundry, but everywhere else both lead and silver vessels are hammered out of one piece.

Besides the manufacture of household vessels, a little ornamental metal-work is done at Rajahmundry, Cocanada, and Peddápuram. At the two former places brass and copper armour and canopies are made for idols, and at Peddápuram and Dowlaishweram idols of copper are made. In both cases the work is first cast, and then finished with the chisel.

Painting.

A little painting of a rude kind is done in the district. At Gollapálaiyam (eight miles south-south-west of Cocanada) a family of Kápus paint Hindu gods on curtains and punkah frills with a good deal of skill. Their only tool is a short sharp stick with a piece of cloth tied near the end; the point is used for drawing the outlines and the cloth for applying the colours, which are imported from Europe. Their work was considered worthy of being sent to the Delhi Durbar Exhibition, and they say that it is in demand in China, whither it is exported from Yanam. Two Múchis execute frescoes on walls at Rajahmundry, and one of them paints on cloth. A Múchi of Antarvédi in Nagaram taluk also paints figures on cloth gummed on to wood.

Pith-work.

A little inferior pith-work is done by a few Muhammadans at Nagaram and Jagannapéta. They make flowers and images out of *sóla* pith.

Musical instruments.

Tamburas and vinas are made (by one Kamsala at each place) at Pithápuram and Rajahmundry, and also at Rájavólu, Sivakódu and Tátipáka in Nagaram taluk. The sounding-boards are carved out of solid blocks of wood. Teak and jack are used, but preferably the latter. The work done at Sivakódu is good.

Wood and stone carving.

Wood-carving of excellent quality is done in a number of places. In almost all considerable villages there are a few Múchis or Kamsalas who can carve furniture and door-frames, and make the *váhanams*, or carved platforms on which gods are carried. The work at Cocanada, Drákshárámam, Rajahmundry, Dowlaishweram and Sivakódu is especially noteworthy.

A few stone-carvers are to be found at Rajahmundry, Jégurupádu in the same taluk, Venkatayyapálaiyam in Rámachandrapuram, and Vúbalanka in Amalápuram. They chiefly make images of the gods. The Jégurupádu work is well known in most parts of the district.

Ropes. Ropes are made from the fibre of the cocoanut and palmyra palms and the sunn hemp and 'jute' *(gógu)* plants. The coir ropes are mostly made in the central delta, especially at Bendamúrlanka, Ambájipéta and Pérúru. Large amounts of hemp, palmyra and date fibre are also sent to Europe from Cocanada.

Oils. Very large quantities of gingelly, castor and cocoanut oils are manufactured. The castor oil is generally made in iron mills in regular factories. There are twelve or thirteen of such factories at Cocanada, four or five at Rajahmundry and Peddápuram, and others at Pithápuram, Tuni and Dowlaishweram. Gingelly oil is made in a factory at Tuni; but everywhere else both it and cocoanut oil are made in the ordinary wooden mills. These are much smaller than those of the southern districts, are put up in the back-yards of houses, and are worked by a single bullock which is usually blindfolded to prevent its getting giddy from going round in such a small circle. Cocoanut oil is made in large quantities at Ambájipéta, Bódasakurru, Pérúru and Munjavarapukottu in the Amalápuram taluk. The oil-making castes are the Telukulas (who correspond to the Vániyans of the south), Kápus and Ídigas. Gingelly oil is commonly used for cooking and oil baths, cocoanut oil for the same purposes (especially in the central delta) and as a hair-oil, and castor oil for lighting. This last is being ousted by kerosine, and considerable quantities of it are exported. Castor and cocoanut cake are used as manures, especially for sugar-cane, and the former is exported to Cochin and Colombo for use on tea and coffee estates. Gingelly cake is given to cattle and is also used in curries. Curry made with it is a favourite dish with both rich and poor and is even offered to the village goddesses.

Tanning. Coarse leather for the manufacture of country shoes is made by the Mádigas all over the low country. Their method of tanning it is very elementary. The hides and skins are soaked in a solution of chunam to remove the hair, then in clean water for a day, next for ten days in a decoction of the bark of the babul *(Acacia arabica)* tree, and finally they are stitched into bags, which are filled with babul bark and soaked for a week in water.

In Rajahmundry three tanneries, owned by Labbais from the Tamil country, work in a less primitive fashion. The

CHAP. VI. ARTS AND INDUSTRIES.

hides and skins are first soaked in clean water for a night, then in chunam and water for twelve days so that the hair may be easily scraped off, next in clean water for two days, then for two more days in chunam and water, next in a decoction of *tangédu (Cassia auriculata)* bark for a fortnight, and finally in a solution of gall-nut for three days. They are then rubbed with gingelly oil and are smoothened by being scraped with a blunt copper tool. Most of the leather thus produced is exported to Madras.

Shoes.

Rough shoes of home-tanned leather are made by Mádigas in almost all the low-country villages. Those produced in Siripalli in the Amalápuram taluk are well known. Sanapalli-lanka in the same taluk had formerly a name for this industry. Good boots and slippers, excellent native shoes and Muhammadan slippers *(sadávu)* are manufactured in several centres. The common work is done by Mádigas, and the better class by Múchis, who ornament the Muhammadan slippers with elaborate designs in silk and bits of metal. The handiwork of the latter is exported to Hyderabad and Rangoon through the local Muhammadan merchants. Cocanada and Rajahmundry are the chief centres of the industry, but the work at Peddápuram is good, and some is done at Samalkot, Tuni, Pithápuram and Dowlaishweram. Good boots and slippers are also made at the Rajahmundry jail.

Baskets.

Baskets are made from date fibre, palmyra leaves and split bamboo by Yerukalas, Mádigas and Médaras respectively, and from rattan by Yerukalas in parts of Pithápuram taluk.

Bangles.

Black 'glass' bangles are made in several villages, notably by a few Linga Balijas in Sítarámpuram and Hamsavaram in the Tuni division and at Rágampéta in Peddápuram and by some Kápus in Duppalapúdi in Rajahmundry. At Rágampéta the Linga Balijas also blow simple flasks or retorts of this 'glass,' which are used in making sublimate of mercury (see below) in the neighbouring village of Jagammapéta. The 'glass' is imported from Nellore or Madras, and is manufactured by lixiviating alkaline earth, allowing the salts to crystallize out in the sun, and heating them in a crucible for some hours with flint and bits of broken bangles. The vitreous mass so produced is melted in this district in circular furnaces and the bangles are made by taking a small quantity of the molten 'glass' on the point of an iron rod, which is then twirled rapidly round until the glass assumes a roughly annular shape. This ring is transferred, while still glowing, to a heated conical clay mould, which the workman twists rapidly round with one hand while with the other he shapes the ring into a bangle with a tool resembling an ordinary awl. The finished article is often decorated with a coating of lac, and into this are sometimes stuck bits of tinsel or looking-glass. Better class bangles are all imported, many of them from Bombay.

Pottery.

Ordinary earthen pots are made everywhere, and a few potters at Rajahmundry make good water-bottles *(gújas)* out of a mixture of white alkaline earth *(suddamannu)* and ordinary potter's clay. The earth is said to be brought by Gollas from a village called Punyakshétram in the same taluk.

Country sugar.

At Rajahmundry a few families of Déwángas make sugar-candy and soft sugar. White crystallized sugar is made in the Deccan Sugar and Abkári Company's factory at Samalkot referred to below. Natives of the district are said to have some prejudice against this sugar because it is clarified with bone charcoal, but the prejudice disappears if it is converted into sugar-candy or soft sugar *(bura)*. The 'factory sugar' is therefore boiled in water, with the addition of a little milk, until it attains a treacly consistency, and is then poured into shallow plates, where it is left for ten days. It crystallizes in these into sugar-candy, and the liquid which remains among the crystals is again boiled with the addition of a little water, and is then well stirred with a wooden instrument until it turns into soft sugar. A precisely similar industry exists at Hindupur in Anantapur district, and no doubt elsewhere.

Mercury.

Some five or six persons, mostly Déwángas, make white sublimate of mercury at Jagammapéta in the Peddápuram taluk. Four varieties are made, namely *basmam* (a white crust), a white solid substance called *kárpuram*, and a red powder of two kinds, one called *sindúram* and the other *shadgunam*. The *basmam* is made by heating salt and quicksilver in the proportion of one to five for fifteen or sixteen hours, with a pot inverted over the mixture. The fumes form a crust on the inverted pot, which is the *basmam*. This is then put in retorts of bangle 'glass' which are coated with mud, and heated for the same period, when it turns into *kárpuram*. *Sindúram* is obtained by mixing quicksilver, sulphur, and *ardhalam* (mineral arsenic) in the proportion of one, one-half, and one thirty-second, and heating them for one and a half hours. The resultant matter is pounded in a mortar, and then heated in a retort like the *basmam*. For *shadgunam*, quicksilver and sulphur are taken in the proportion of two to one and are pounded in a mortar; the mixture is then heated in a retort like the *basmam*, only for a longer period. The quicksilver is got from Bombay and Calcutta. The existence of a large supply of cheap wood fuel in the neighbourhood is

CHAP. VI. ARTS AND INDUSTRIES.

a great advantage in this industry, and is not improbably the cause of its existence here.

House-building.

The art of house-building is much studied in the district. In every large town there are professional architects. Those of Rajahmundry and Dowlaishweram are well known and are employed in all the low-country taluks.

Printing-presses.

There are five printing-presses at Cocanada and the same number at Rajahmundry. Except two of those at Cocanada, namely the Sujana Ranjani press and Messrs. Hall, Wilson & Co.'s press, both of which employ about 25 men, these are very small affairs. In the former of the two, vernacular books and two Telugu periodicals, one weekly and one monthly, are printed; and the latter carries on a general business. Another monthly Telugu newspaper is printed at another press at Cocanada, and two more at Rajahmundry. At the latter town a weekly and a fortnightly paper are printed in English.

Rice-mills.

Several large rice-husking mills are at work in the district. The most important is that owned by the Coringa Rice Mills Company at Georgepet near Coringa, which employs a hundred men. There are also three more in Cocanada and four in Rajahmundry, two of which are not now working Another at Amalápuram has also stopped work for the present. The mills buy the paddy outright and export the husked rice, and do not husk paddy for payment, as is sometimes done.

Indigo factories.

There are several indigo factories in the Amalápuram taluk, of which seven employ 30 men or more in the season. Those at Vélanakapalli and Ayinavalli employ 75 and 150 hands respectively.

Ship-building.

At one time a large ship-building industry was carried on in Tállarévu on the Coringa river. Some two generations ago, it is said, about a hundred big ships used to be built, and four times that number repaired, every year; and boats came for repairs even from Negapatam and Chittagong. What with the increasing use of steam, and the silting up of the Coringa river, the industry is now almost dead. As recently as 25 years ago, it is said, ten or fifteen sea-going boats were built every year and some fifty repaired, but in 1903 only five were built, in 1904 only one, and in 1905 none at all, while only two ships were repaired in 1903 and in 1904. The boats built and repaired were native brigs of a hundred tons or so.

Dowlaishweram workshops.

Of the enterprises managed by European capital, the most important are the Public Works workshops at Dowlaishweram, which comprise a foundry, and carpenters', fitters' and smiths' shops. They employ a daily average of 145 men, and during the calendar year 1904 turned out work to the value of Rs. 1,63,600. The output consists chiefly of wood and iron-work and furniture for buildings constructed by the department; wooden and iron punts and staff boats for use on the canals; repairs to steamers and other floating plant; lock gates, sluice shutters and gearings; and repairs to engine boilers and machinery belonging to the department. The shops also undertake work for other departments, municipalities, and private persons. These are charged ten per cent. on the cost of the raw materials *plus* fifteen per cent. on the total cost of the work.

District Board workshops at Cocanada.

The District Board also has workshops of its own. These are at Cocanada, and the work done in them consists of such items as the construction of iron and wooden ferry boats and ballacuts, small iron bridges, doors and windows, office furniture and iron sheds for markets (of which latter a large number have been made), and of repairs to tools and plant, including the steam road-rollers and the two steam ferry-steamers owned by the District Board. The shops are in charge of an overseer, subject to the control of the District Board Engineer, and all the hands are temporary men on daily wages. The value of the work turned out in 1903-04 was approximately Rs. 30,000, inclusive of materials.

Samalkot distillery and sugar-factory.

An important industrial undertaking exists at Samalkot in the works of the Deccan Sugar and Abkári Company, Limited, established in 1897 and at present under the management of Messrs. Parry & Co., Madras. Excellent plant and buildings have been erected about half a mile south-west of the railway-station, and the capital of the company is ten lakhs. The manufacture of both refined sugar and spirit is carried on, and about 400 men are employed daily. Sugar is extracted from jaggery by the usual process, and the final residue molasses form the staple material of the distillery. Both palmyra and cane jaggery are used, the bulk of them being obtained in this and the surrounding districts. Three kinds of sugar are manufactured; namely, a white granulated, a soft, and a brown sugar, and the total output in 1903 was 8,600 tons. In the distillery two stills and a rectificator are in use, and the usual method of spirit manufacture is employed. During 1903, 198,000 gallons of proof spirit were manufactured. Arrack is supplied from the distillery to this district and Kistna, Nellore and Cuddapah, for the supply of which the company hold the contract. Two artesian wells have been recently sunk in the company's compound.[1]

1 See Chapter IV, p. 90.

CHAP. VI. ARTS AND INDUSTRIES.

Dummagúdem lace.

The wife of the Rev. J. Cain, the missionary at Dummagúdem, has started a lace-work industry at that station which is known even outside India. Lace-making was originally taught at the Church Missionary Society's boarding-school for girls; and during the famine of 1896-97 Mrs. Cain encouraged the young women who had learnt the art in the school to take it up as a means of livelihood. From that time forth, the industry spread among the wives of the natives round, and there are now 110 workers, most of whom are Christians. Mrs. Cain pays them for their work (Rs. 70 or Rs. 80 a week are expended in wages) and sells it in India, England and Australia. The lace is not the 'pillow lace' made elsewhere in South India, but what is called 'darned net work,' which somewhat resembles Limerick lace in appearance.

TRADE. Markets.

Fairs or markets are common in Gódávari. There are as many as 40 under the control of the taluk boards, and the right of collecting the usual fees at them sold in 1904-05 for over Rs. 21,600. Those which fetched the highest bids were the great cattle-markets at Drákshárámam and Pithápuram, which were leased for Rs. 3,165 and Rs. 2,500 respectively; the Tuni market, which fetched Rs. 2,010; and the Ambájipéta cattle-market, which sold for Rs. 1,625. The markets which chiefly serve the Agency are those of Yelésvaram in Peddápuram taluk and Gókavaram in Rajahmundry. To these resort the petty traders who have direct dealings with the hill men in the interior, and, to some extent, the hill men themselves.

Grain-dealing.

There are one or two centres in each taluk in which live the local merchants who collect grain from the ryots and either export it themselves or sell it to other and larger merchants. The money-lenders are generally also grain dealers, as their loans are often paid in kind. A common system, known as *jatti*, is that by which a ryot borrows money on the security of his crops and undertakes to sell these when harvested to the money-lender at less than the market price. Another usual arrangement, called the *várakam* or *pattubadi* system, is for a ryot to keep a sort of running account with the money-lender, getting small loans from time to time and clearing off the debt, principal and interest, at harvest. Here, again, the grain is sold at less than the market price, the difference being about ten rupees per garce. The ryot is also expected to graze his creditor's cattle and to supply him with vegetables when called upon.

Exports.

Almost the only noteworthy article of export from Gódávari is its surplus agricultural produce, but a fair quantity of the locally woven, dyed, or stamped cotton goods are sold outside the district, and so are the hides and skins from the tanneries of Rajahmundry. The distillery and sugar-factory at Samalkot also sends large quantities of its sugar and arrack to other parts of India. Of the agricultural products exported, rice is the largest item. Pulses, oils, fibres of various kinds and hemp are also shipped in great quantities.

Imports.

The chief imports into the district include metal vessels, kerosine oil, iron, European and other piece-goods, leather and cattle.

Trade of Cocanada.

The only considerable seaport in Gódávari is the flourishing town of Cocanada, which serves not only the district itself, but its neighbours to the north and south and an extensive hinterland which includes parts of the Nizam's Dominions.

The harbour.

The port of Cocanada is situated in the south-west corner of Coringa bay, a large but shallow sheet of water, five miles by five in extent, lying at the northernmost angle of the delta. The bay is something the shape of a horse-shoe and is only open from the north-east. The most northerly mouth of the Gódávari flows into it on the south, where it is gradually silting it up, and the everlengthening arm of Cape Gódávari, which is estimated to be advancing seawards at the rate of a mile in 20 years, encloses it on the east. The rapid shallowing of the bay has rendered it necessary for large ships to anchor five miles from the shore to the north-east of Cocanada town, but the anchorage is well-protected and exceptionally safe.

Goods have to be landed in cargo boats, but the channel leading from the anchorage to the harbour itself is deep enough to allow boats of 100 tons burden, and drawing as much as five feet of water, to reach Cocanada at certain states of the tide. The harbour consists of a tidal creek which receives the surplus of the Cocanada and Samalkot canals and the discharge of the Bikkavólu drain and the Yeléru river, which together enter the Samalkot branch of the creek just below the last lock of the Samalkot canal. The harbour shows a tendency to silt owing to deposits brought from above; and its mouth is also with difficulty kept clear of the sand and mud which is swept into the Coringa bay from the Gódávari on the south, from a drainage creek entering the bay just to the north of the harbour, and in stormy weather, from the open sea on the north-east. Two dredgers are therefore kept constantly at work, and it has also been found necessary to extend the mouth of the harbour by long groins. The harbour is revetted from the bridge leading to Jagannáthapuram, and the revetment is continued along the groins, its

CHAP. VI. TRADE.

total length being 3,680 yards on the north and 3,780 yards on the south side. Of this extent 2,700 yards of revetment and 87 yards of groin on the north and 2,500 and 260 yards of revetment and groin respectively on the south had been erected as early as 1855; and the groins were extended considerably in 1887 and very largely about 1893. The chief difficulty is experienced from the mud creek which, as just mentioned, flows into the bay just north of the harbour mouth. Its course and mouth have altered with the foreshore, going further and further towards the east. This is the result of its own action combined with the construction of the groins. The northern wall crosses its mouth, with the result that the silt it brings down has formed a solid sand bank along the groin. This bank has extended with each extension of the groin and now threatens to choke the harbour's mouth. The groins have been given a turn to the north to endeavour to counteract this tendency, but without success. Further means of dealing with the difficulty are now being considered.

The port had originally four light-houses and two port lights. The latter still stand on the ends of the two groins, but two of the former are no longer in use. The light-house at Cocanada itself has not been used since 1877 (though it has been left standing as a landmark) and the Hope Island light-house, on what was once the most north-easterly extremity of the delta, was abandoned in 1902. There are now revolving lights at Vakalapúdi, some five miles to the north of Cocanada, and on the Sacramento shoal, over twenty miles south of the present Point Gódávari, to warn vessels off the point and shoal.

Port conservancy.

Cocanada possesses a Port Officer, and he and his establishment are paid in the usual way from port funds chiefly derived from dues on vessels visiting the place. 'Landing and shipping dues' are also collected from the local merchants at certain fixed rates on all cargo landed and shipped; and this money, with the rent of certain ground within port limits, is devoted, as elsewhere, to meeting all expenditure involved in the improvement of the port, such as the maintenance of dredgers, groins and the foreshore. The fund so constituted is administered primarily by the Cocanada Port Conservancy Board, of which the chairman is the Collector and the vice-chairman one of the members of the European Chamber of Commerce. This body fixes the rates of dues to be paid, looks after the ordinary measures of port conservancy, and initiates measures for the improvement of the port. Its expenditure is, as usual, under the control of the Presidency Port Officer and ultimately of Government.

European business houses at Cocanada.

Several of the leading mercantile houses in the Presidency have agents in Cocanada (among them Messrs. Ralli Bros., Messrs. Gordon, Woodroffe & Co., Messrs. Volkart Bros., Messrs. Wilson & Co., Messrs. Ripley & Co. and Messrs. Best & Co.) and in addition the place is the head-quarters of several other substantial European firms, who are engaged in general trade and own local undertakings of various kinds. Messrs. Simson & Co. own a rice-mill and act as agents for the Asiatic Steam Navigation Company; Messrs. Hall, Wilson & Co. are agents for the British India line and were part-owners and local managers of the Oriental Salt Company, which until recently was working the salt-factory at Jagannáthapuram; Messrs. Innes & Co. are managers of the Coringa Rice Mills Company; and Messrs. Barry & Co. have a cheroot-factory where cheroots are made for export to Burma. There are also a great number of native merchants in the town. Indeed the mercantile importance of the place is so considerable that the Bank of Madras has a branch there under a European Agent, and both native and European Chambers of Commerce have been constituted.

European Chamber of Commerce.

The European chamber at Cocanada was established as long ago as 1868. Representatives of the leading European firms and the local Agent of the Bank of Madras are members. Its objects are 'to watch over and protect the interests of trade, to collect information on matters bearing thereon, to communicate with authorities and individuals upon the removal of grievances and abuses, to decide on matters of customs and usage . . . and to form a code of practice whereby the transaction of business may be facilitated,' and it has displayed much activity in all these directions. The practice of annually printing its chief proceedings, which was inaugurated in 1903, is to be continued. The native Chamber of Commerce is theoretically quite independent of the other; but generally the two bodies work hand in hand.

Steamers visiting the port.

The port is visited by the British India steamers, as many as six or seven of which often call in a week; by the Asiatic Steam Navigation Company's boats, two of which call every fortnight; and by the Clan Line steamers, three or four of which come every month. The Austrian Lloyd steamers and those of a Venetian company call occasionally.

Amount of trade.

In 1902–03 (see the figures in the separate Appendix to this volume) the total value of the export trade of Cocanada amounted, in round figures, to Rs. 1,22,80,000 and that of the imports to Rs. 25,10,000, making up a total trade of Rs. 1,47,90,000 or £986,000. In the statistics of that year the port takes the fifth place among those of this Presidency—

CHAP. VI. TRADE.

being passed only by Madras (total trade 1,406 lakhs), Tuticorin (388 lakhs), Cochin (320 lakhs) and Calicut (192 lakhs)—and the twelfth place among the ports of British India.[1] The trade has naturally varied considerably in different years; but in only three out of the 27 immediately preceding 1902-03 did it rise above 200 lakhs in total value. These were 1889-90 (201 lakhs), 1896-97 (216 lakhs) and 1892-93 (239 lakhs). In 1878-79 it fell below 75 lakhs, but in no other year was the figure less than 100 lakhs. In 1903-04 the imports were valued at Rs. 38,73,000 and the exports at Rs. 1,67,31,000, making a total of Rs. 2,06,04,000. The exports have always been largely in excess of the imports. The proportion in 1903-04 is fairly typical of other years.

In that year, out of a total export trade of 167 lakhs, goods to the value of 84 lakhs were sent to ports outside India (including Burma) and the rest to Indian ports; of the latter, 11 lakhs went to the ports of this Presidency. The foreign export trade has generally been equal to or larger than the Indian export trade, and often much larger. The trade with the rest of the Presidency has always been small, and it has very largely decreased in the last seven years, probably owing to the competition of the railway.

In 1903-04 the foreign imports made up rather more than half of the total import trade; but the figures of that year are rather exceptional, as the imports from abroad are usually nothing like so large as those from India and Burma. In former years the imports from other ports in this Presidency were considerable and averaged in value about one quarter of the total imports; but, like the exports to other places in the Presidency, they have much decreased in the last six years.

Character of trade.

Of a total foreign export trade in 1903-04 of Rs. 84,04,000, the exports of cotton were valued at Rs. 33,93,000; of rice and paddy (chiefly the latter) at Rs. 29,90,000; and of oil-seeds (castor and gingelly) at Rs. 9,25,000. Thus these commodities made up 73 out of the total of 84 lakhs. Food-grains accounted for Rs. 2,02,000, oil-cake for Rs. 1,69,000, fibre[2] for brushes for Rs. 1,56,000, and castor oil for Rs. 97,000. The cotton is chiefly sent to France (Rs. 9,06,000), Holland (Rs. 6,42,000) and Britain (Rs. 3,32,000) as well as to several other European countries and Japan. Rice and paddy is

[1] The larger ports outside this Presidency were Bombay (11,172 lakhs), Calcutta (10,381 lakhs), Rangoon (2,868 lakhs), Karáchi (1,929 lakhs), Moulmein (440 lakhs), Chittagong (283 lakhs) and Akyab (240 lakhs).

[2] Chiefly palmyra fibre extracted from the thick stem of the leaf. This item has much increased in the last year or two.

chiefly taken by Ceylon (Rs. 8,67,000), Réunion (Rs. 6,63,000) the Straits Settlements (Rs. 5,23,000), Mauritius (Rs. 4,88,000) and Japan (Rs, 2,76,000). Gingelly oil goes chiefly to Ceylon and France, and castor oil to Britain and Russia. The fibres and the oil-cake go almost entirely to Ceylon. An important item is tobacco, which is sent unmanufactured in large quantities to Burma to be made up into cheroots.

Nearly the whole of the foreign import trade of 1903–04 was made up of unrefined sugar (Rs. 9,69,000), kerosine oil (Rs. 7,47,000) and various kinds of metal and metalware (Rs. 1,40,000). The sugar all came from Java, and the kerosine oil from Russia (Rs. 3,32,000), the United States (Rs. 2,61,000) and Sumatra (Rs. 1,53,000). The metalware was chiefly from the United Kingdom.

The coastwise import trade is small. The largest items were gunny-bags from Calcutta (nearly five lakhs), cotton twist and yarn principally from Bombay (some three lakhs), kerosine oil chiefly from Rangoon (two and a half lakhs), ground-nut oil from Madras ports and cotton piece-goods from Bombay (each about a lakh), and cocoanut oil, also from Madras ports, Rs. 84,000.

The coastwise export trade included thirty-six lakhs' worth of grain and pulse of various sorts, of which five-sixths was rice and the greater part was sent to Bombay. Nearly sixteen lakhs' worth of tobacco leaf was sent to Burma, and gingelly worth nine lakhs (of which two-thirds went to Burma) and castor seeds worth two lakhs (nearly all of which went to Calcutta) were other considerable items.

WEIGHTS AND MEASURES. Goldsmiths' weights.

Outside the remoter parts of the Agency, where regular tables are little used, the following are the ordinary weights and measures in the district. The table employed by goldsmiths is generally :—

4 *visams* (grains of paddy) ...	=	1 *pátika*.
2 *pátikas*	=	1 *addiga*.
2 *addigas*	=	1 *chinnam*.
30 *chinnams*	=	1 tola (180 grains.)

Commercial weights.

The ordinary table of commercial weights is as follows :—

2 *pampus*	=	1 *yébulam*.
2 *yébulams*	=	1 *padalam*.
2 *padalams*	=	1 viss (=5 seers, or 120 tolas).
2 visses	=	1 *yettedu*.
4 *yettedus*	=	1 maund (of 25 lb.).
20 maunds	=	1 *putti* (or candy).

CHAP. VI. WEIGHTS AND MEASURES.

In Pólavaram, between the maund and the *putti*, come the *yédumu* of 5 maunds, and the *pandumu* of 10 maunds. These words are respectively corruptions of *aidu tumulu*, 'five tums' and *padi tumulu*, 'ten tums.' Wholesale merchants also buy and sell in terms of bags *(basthas)* supposed to weigh 166 lb.

Oil and ghee are sold retail by weight in the shops, and wholesale or retail by measure by the Telukulas and Gollas; milk and curds always by measure; long chillies by weight, and short ones by measure, though at Rajahmundry and Pólavaram both kinds are said to be sold by weight. Jaggery and tamarind are described in *kantlams* in addition to the above weights; one *kantlam* being equivalent to nine maunds everywhere in the district except at Peddápuram, where it is ten and a half maunds. Tape is sold by weight in terms of *yettus* and its submultiples (half, quarter, etc.). Fuel in large towns is sold by the following table:—

5 maunds	... ...	=	1 *kávadi*, *yédumu* or *pattu*.
4 *kávadis*	... ...	=	1 *putti*.

Weights below a *pattu* are described in submultiples of that weight.

The table used in Bhadráchalam is quite different. That taluk is situated above the Ghâts, and no doubt the influence of the Nizam's Dominions and the Central Provinces predominates. The weights are:—

2 *chatáks*	... ...	=	1 *pávu sir*.
2 *pávu sirs*	... ...	=	1 *ardha sir* (= ½ seer).
2 *ardha sirs*	... ...	=	1 seer (= 24 tolas).
5 seers	... ...	=	1 viss.
8 visses	... ...	=	1 maund.
20 maunds	... ...	=	1 *putti*.

Peculiar to this taluk is the selling of oil retail by weight. At Pólavaram a balance resembling the Danish steel-yard is used. One end of a longish stick is marked with notches denoting different weights. The article to be weighed is hung from this end of it, and the stick and article are lifted by a string loop which fits into the notches and is tried in one after the other of them until the stick hangs horizontally. The notch in which the loop then lies indicates the weight of the article.

Measures of capacity.

The following table of measures is recognized, with one or two exceptions, in all the taluks outside the Agency:—

5 tolas weight of rice	...	=	1 *gidda*.
4 *giddas*	... ...	=	1 *sóla*.
2 *sólas*	... ...	=	1 *tavva*.

CHAP. VI. WEIGHTS AND MEASURES.

2 *tavvas*	=	1 *mánika* or seer (holds 80 tolas weight of rice).
2 *mánikas*	=	1 *adda*.
2 *addas*	=	1 *kuncham* (320 tolas weight of rice).
20 *kunchams*	=	1 *yédumu* or *kávadi*.
2 *yédumus*	=	1 *pandumu*.
2 *pandumus*	=	1 *palle-putti* (= 80 *kunchams*).
7½ *palle-puttis*	=	1 garce (*garisa*) of 600 *kunchams* or 192,000 tolas weight of rice.

The *palle-putti* of 80 *kunchams* is only found in the north-east of the district, *i.e.*, in Cocanada, Peddápuram, Pithápuram and Tuni. In the other parts of the district the *malaka putti* of 200 *kunchams* (three of which go to the garce) is used, but not the *yédumu* or *pandumu*.

In Pólavaram the measures used are—

5 tolas weight of rice ...	=	1 *gidda*.
8 *giddas*	=	1 *tavva*.
8 *tavvas*	=	1 *kuncham* (of 320 tolas weight of rice).
10 *kunchams*	=	1 *túmu*.
4 *túmus*	=	1 *gonédu*.
5 *gonédus* or 20 *túmus* ...	=	1 *putti* of 200 *kunchams*.
3 *puttis*	=	1 garce of 600 *kunchams* or 192,000 tolas weight of rice.

In Bhadráchalam the scale recognized is—

10 tolas weight of rice ...	=	1 *gidda*.
4 *giddas*	=	1 *sóla*.
2 *sólas*	=	1 *tavva* or seer (holding 80 tolas weight of rice).
2 *tavvas*	=	1 *mánika* (of 160 tolas weight of rice).
10 *tavvas*	=	1 *kuncham* (of 800 tolas weight of rice).
2 *kunchams*	=	1 *irusa*.
2 *irusas*	=	1 *túmudu*.
5 *túmudus*	=	1 *yédumu*.
2 *yédumus*	=	1 *pandumu*.
2 *pandumus*	=	1 *putti* (of 80 *kunchams* or 640,000 tolas weight rice).

CHAP. VI. WEIGHTS AND MEASURES.

It will be noticed that the Bhadráchalam *gidda* and *tavva* are twice as large as those elsewhere, and the Bhadráchalam *kuncham* two and a half times as large.

Ghee and oil, as already stated, are sold wholesale by measure. The largest measure used for oil is the *kuncham*, and for ghee the seer. Butter-milk and curd are measured in small pots called *munthas*. It is the practice in this district to set milk for curd in a number of these small pots, instead of in one large pot as is done in some southern districts, and the pots are sold separately. There are four usual sizes of them; namely, the quarter anna, half anna, three-quarter anna and anna *munthas*, so called according to the price (and so the capacity) of each. An anna *muntha* holds about half a seer. Milk is sold by the seer and its submultiples. Large quantities of milk are sometimes spoken of in terms of the *kadava* or *kávadi*, which hold 20 and 40 seers respectively. Popular phrases to denote capacity are the closed handful, called *guppedu* or *pidikedu*, the open handful or *chárcdu*, and the double handful or *dósedu*.

Miscellaneous commercial notations.

Fruits (*e.g.*, mangoes, plantains, cocoanuts and guavas), palmyra leaves, and dung cakes are sold by 'hands,' one hand or *cheyyi* being equivalent to five. Twenty *cheyyis* make one *salaga*, and for every *salaga* one *cheyyi* extra is thrown in as *kosaru* or 'for luck.' *Kosaru* means 'bargaining.' Betel leaves are sold wholesale by the *móda*. This is a varying quantity equivalent generally to 200 or 300 leaves according to their thickness. It is supposed to be the quantity that can be held in the two hands, when the hands are pressed together at the wrist, as when catching a cricket ball. The leaves are sold retail by the *katta*, which contains 100 leaves.

Lineal measures

The old native scale of measures is in use alongside with the English inch, foot and yard. The native scale is:—

1 *angula*	... ...	=	the breadth of a man's thumb, or ¾ inch.
12 *angulas*	... ...	=	1 *jána* (span).
2 *jánas*	... ...	=	1 *mura* (cubit).
4 *muras*	... ...	=	1 *bára* (fathom).
2,000 *báras*	... ...	=	1 *kóss* (2¼ miles).
4 *kósses*	... ...	=	1 *ámada* (about nine miles).
6 *kósses*	... ...	=	1 *majili* (march, or halting place; about 13 miles).

Besides these, there are the *betta*, or the breadth of four fingers placed together, and the *loditha*, or half span, made by

CHAP. VI. WEIGHTS AND MEASURES.

extending the thumb and forefinger as far apart as possible. The *bára* is the distance between the tips of the fingers of the two hands when the arms are both stretched out horizontally to their greatest extent. In describing heights and depths above five feet or so, natives always use the terms *niluvu* and *ara* (half) *niluvu*. The *niluvu* is equivalent to the height of an average adult person. In the Agency *chalaka* and *mancha*, which (see below) are really square measures, are used to denote distances. They each represent about 70 yards.

Some of these measures of length are used much more frequently than the English standards. Thus the *jána* and the *mura* are very commonly used for measuring cloth, and the *mura* and *bára* for measuring ropes. Again the *kóss* and the *ámada* are in very common use for long distances, and the *majili* is not rare.

Land measures.

Acres and cents are only of recent introduction, and are less familiar to the natives than the English lineal feet and inches. The native table of land measures is the same throughout the district except in Tuni, Bhadráchalam, Yellavaram, Chódavaram and the wilder parts of Pólavaram, and is based on the quantity of seed required to cultivate a given area of land. Thus a *mánadu* is the quantity of land that can be sown with a *mánika* or seer of seed, and is equivalent to about two and half cents. An *addedu* is five cents, a *kunchedu* ten cents, an *iddumu neresa* is an acre, an *yédumu* two acres, a *pandumu* four acres, and a *putti* eight acres. A different and vaguer terminology is used in Tuni. There wet land is spoken of in terms of the out turn of paddy—or in 'garces'; and dry land in terms of the number of days it would take a pair of bullocks to plough it—namely in *yéllu* or ploughs. Thus one *yéru* or 'plough' of dry land is the quantity of land that a pair of bullocks can plough in one day, or about half an acre. A 'garce' of wet land is said to be about two acres.

There appears to be no precise table of land measure known in Bhadráchalam, perhaps because there is no need for one among the inhabitants of those uncivilized parts. The zamindars' accounts are said to be kept in acres and cents. In the wilder tracts of this taluk and of Pólavaram, and throughout the Agency, areas are described in terms of *chalakas*, *manchas* and *kattipódu*. *Mancha* is the raised bamboo platform put up in the middle of a field, on which the watcher sits to scare away birds and animals. The term is used to describe the amount of land which can be commanded by one watcher, or about two acres. The *chalaka* is the same as the *mancha* in extent. It literally means 'a piece.' *Kattipódu* has a reference to *pódu* cultivation, and denotes as much land as

CHAP. VI. WEIGHTS AND MEASURES.

can be cleared in one day by one *katti* or billhook. This extent is said to be about an acre.

English minutes and hours are well understood and are used equally with the native measures of time. The latter are :—

Measures of time.

60 *vigadiyas* ...	...	=	1 *gadiya* (or 24 minutes.)
$2\frac{1}{2}$ *gadiyas* ...	...	=	1 *ganta* (or English hour).
3 *gantas* ...	...	=	1 *jámu* (or watch).

Of these, the *vigadiya* is rarely, if ever, used, the term being only known to the educated. Periods shorter than twenty-four minutes are generally expressed in English minutes or in terms of fractions of the *gadiya.*

In telling the time of day or night a native calculates the number of *gadiyas* or *jámus* that have elapsed since 6 A.M., or 6 P.M., as the case may be. Thus 7–12 o'clock, whether A.M. or P.M., would be 'three *gadiyas*,' and 9 o'clock would be 'one *jámu*' or 'seven and a half *gadiyas*.'

There are also, however, in this as in every other district, a number of expressions in common use which denote various times of the day. Those which occur most frequently here are 'the rising of the star Venus' *(tsukka podichétappudu)*, which is of course variable; 'the time when the first cock crows' (3 A.M.); 'the time when the second cock crows' (4 A.M.); 'the time to begin ploughing' (6 A.M.); 'cock-crow time'; 'the time to sprinkle cow-dung-water' and 'the time to make butter-milk,' both of which indicate 6 A.M.; 'the time to milk the cows' (7 A.M.); 'the shepherds' breakfast time' (9 or 10 A.M.); 'the time to let the cattle out to graze,' which is very variable; 'the time when the feet burn' (midday); *muppoddu véla*, 'when three *jámus* have passed' (about 3 P.M.); 'time to begin cooking' (4 P.M.); '*sanda jámu*,' about three hours after nightfall, from *sanda*, evening; and 'the thief time' or midnight. A variation of the last, found in the Agency, is 'the time when the cock crows at the thief.' The Agency people also use the phrase *jáva vélu*, or '*kanji* time.' for 10 A.M. or breakfast time; and sometimes call it *muntha véla*, or 'porringer time,' from the vessel in which they eat it.

Local monetary terms.

Besides the ordinary currency, cowries *(gavvalu)* are very commonly used in making small purchases throughout the low country, except in Pithápuram and Tuni. They are imported from Bombay and sold by weight. Ninety-six cowries make one three-pie piece; but there are a number of terms denoting smaller numbers. Thus 4 cowries = 1 *punjam*; 3 *punjams* = 1 *toli*; 2 *tolis* = 1 *dammidi* (three-quarters of a pie); 2 *dammidis* = *égáni* (or 1½ pies); 2 *éganis* = 1 *dabbu*, *káni*, or *kotta dabbu*, which are the ordinary names for a three-pie piece. The value of a cowry, *punjam* and *toli* are not absolutely constant, but vary slightly with the market price of cowries. The *dabbu* is also a term of varying application. In Pithápuram, Tuni, and the Agency it means four pies, and is synonymous with a *páta dabbu* ('old *dabbu*'). In this case an *égáni* means two pies and a *dammidi* one pie ; but the *káni* and the *kotta dabbu* (' new *dabbu*') still denote three pies.

CHAP. VI. WEIGHTS AND MEASURES.

For sums above an anna a variety of curious terms are used. Thus,

4 *kotta dabbus*	=	1 anna.
2 annas	=	1 *béda.*
2 *bédas*	=	1 *pávula* or *dúlam* (=4 annas).
16 *páta dabbus*	=	1 *tankamu* (or 5 as. 4 ps.).
2 *pávulas*	=	1 half rupee or *chavulam.*
3 *pávulas*	=	1 *muppávula* (12 annas).
1 *pávu*	=	1 rupee.
1 *máda*	=	2 rupees.
1 *varáha* (pagoda) or *punji*	=	4 rupees.
1 *puli varáha*	=	$3\frac{1}{2}$ rupees.
1 *vanda*	=	100 rupees.

In Tuni, and perhaps elsewhere, the *dúlam* (4 annas), *chavulam* (8 annas), *pávu* (rupee), *máda* (2 rupees) and *punji*, or pagoda of 4 rupees, are used to denote percentages. Thus if a man wants to say he is giving 6¼, 12½, 25 or 50 per cent. he will say he is giving a *dúlam* (one-sixteenth of a pagoda), *chavulam* (one-eighth), a *pávu* (one-quarter) or a *máda* (one-half) respectively. No doubt the use of the pagoda as a unit of reference is the cause of the name *pávu* for a rupee, the word literally meaning 'a quarter.'

In Bhadráchalam, besides the usual British Indian coins, those of the Nizam's Dominions are also in common use.

CHAPTER VII.

MEANS OF COMMUNICATION

Roads—Their length and condition—Quarries—Maintenance, establishment and allotments—Bridges—Ferries. Water Carriage—The rivers—Upper Gódávari project—Navigable canals; their history—Expenditure and traffic—Nature of traffic--Conflicting interests of irrigation and navigation.' Madras Railway. Accommodation for travellers--Bungalows—Chattrams.

CHAP. VII. Roads.

Their length and condition.

THERE are just under 850 miles of road in the Gódávari district, most of which are shaded by fine avenues. Of these, 580 miles are metalled or gravelled, chiefly the former. The long lead from the quarries which has in most cases to be paid for, makes it the best economy to carry the best material available, and latterly gravel has for that reason been discarded. The rest of the roads are repaired with earth and sand. Nearly four-fifths of these earth roads are in the Agency divisions of Pólavaram and Bhadráchalam, the former of which possesses less than thirty, and the latter only six, miles of metalled road. On a good metalled road a cart will carry 1,500 lb. at about two miles an hour; on an earth road the load is about 1,000 lb. and the distance traversed in an hour about one and a half miles. The metalled roads in the uplands are generally good, and so are some of those in the delta; but the latter have great difficulties to contend with. They have usually to be made on a rich alluvial soil saturated by irrigation water for many months in the year, and the lead for metal is nearly always long, and in some cases amounts to as many as 40 miles. The numerous navigable canals enable this metal to be transported at less cost than usual, but it often has to be carted by road for four, five and even six miles from the canal-side dépôts to the places where it is required. Moreover, floods occasionally submerge the country and do a great deal of damage, and against these it is impossible to provide entirely except at enormous expense. Finally the material available is not of the best, being only laterite of fair quality.

Quarries.

The metal used in the delta is obtained from the laterite quarries of Kadayam and Samalkot. The uplands are as well supplied with quarries as most other districts, and some of those recently opened yield very good metal. Ordinarily the only material available is laterite and sandstone of poor quality.

CHAP. VII. ROADS.

Maintenance, establishment and allotments.

On the earth roads a hard surface crust is made by mixing sand and earth with water and then tamping the mixture with rammers. On the metalled roads the consolidation is done by the District Board's two six-ton steam rollers or by hand rollers of from two to three tons. Material is supplied, and generally spread, by contract, but the latter work is not popular and is only taken up as a necessary adjunct of a contract to supply. Petty repairs are done departmentally. Road maistries are posted to every sixteen miles of road and daily labour is obtained when necessary. Gang coolies are not employed. Avenue coolies are entertained to tend the nurseries and the young trees by the road-sides. The superior establishment consists of the District Board Engineer, two Assistant Engineers, five overseers and nine sub-overseers.

The usual grant for the maintenance of the roads is some Rs. 85,000. The minimum and maximum allotments per mile are Rs. 50 and Rs. 300 respectively; and the average for metalled roads is about Rs. 110. The above figures include Bhadráchalam; but that taluk has since been excluded from the operation of the Local Boards Act, and in future its roads will be managed by the Divisional Officer at Bhadráchalam.

Bridges.

In the delta there are few bridges. This fact, and the reason for it, are referred to as follows by Mr. Walch [1]:—

'There is probably no artificial irrigation and navigation system, except perhaps the neighbouring one of the Kistna, in which the provision of bridges per mile of canal and channel is so small as in the Gódávari delta.[2] This has arisen from the fact that when the works were commenced, and for long after, there was not a single made road in the delta, and the people were accustomed to wade through the streams and water-courses which crossed their path-ways, or when the water was too deep for wading to use dug-outs or rafts . . . . Bridges have however been provided over the tail-bays of almost all the locks, and of late years a few have been constructed at other places at the expense, or partly so, of local funds.'

Matters have been considerably improved recently. In the delta, on the main roads, bridges have now been built over all waterways except the actual branches of the Gódávari. The minor roads, however, have received much less attention.

Outside the delta, also, some fine bridges have been built in recent years. Of these, that at Yerravaram, which carries

[1] *The Engineering works of the Gódávari Delta* (Madras, 1896), p. 135.

[2] A very remarkable contrast is presented by the Tanjore delta, where fine bridges are very plentiful.

CHAP. VII. ROADS.

the great northern trunk-road over the Yeléru river, was constructed by the late Mr. P. H. Brown, M.I.C.E., District Board Engineer,[1] and was opened for traffic in 1887. It consists of sixteen spans of 32 feet with segmental brick arches on first-class coursed rubble piers and abutments. The bridge over the Tuni river at Tuni, on the same road and at the north-eastern extremity of the district, has ten spans of 30 feet. It was built over 30 years ago by the Public Works department. A fine bascule bridge crosses the Gódávari at Coringa. It is an iron construction 250 feet long with a 50-foot drawbridge in the middle, and is built on solid iron piles four to five inches in diameter and screwed down to from 30 to 45 feet below mean sea level. This also was designed and erected (in 1901) by Mr. Brown. The drawbridge consists of two bascules which when raised afford an opening of 50 feet for sailing ships. There has been no difficulty in passing through it the largest ships which can enter the river, which run up to 500 to 600 tons. As originally constructed, it took eight men to open and close the bascules, but recent improvements designed and carried out by the present District Board Engineer Mr. C. J. Lowry, enable each span to be easily opened and closed by one man. The flooring is of steel trough plates except over the drawbridge, which is floored with teak.

The only bridge across the Gódávari is that at Rajahmundry which carries the Madras Railway and is described below. Foot passengers are allowed to cross it. There is no separate footway, but it is floored and provided with a hand-rail, and there are refuges on every pier where people can wait for a train to pass.

Ferries.

The deficiency of bridges both over the Gódávari and over the many channels in the delta is supplied by ferries. The three steam ferry-boats which at present ply on the Gódávari are referred to below. Besides these there are 34 ferries under the control of the local boards, and eight more in the Bhadráchalam taluk. The local fund ferries are equipped with boats constructed by the local boards or by the Public Works department; the former contributing half the cost in the case of all natural waterways. Of these boats, fourteen are first-class, and the same number second-class, iron ballacuts.[2] A ballacut is a platform with hand-rails laid on

[1] To this officer, who was the first District Board Engineer and held that post from 1880 to 1901, the district owes the construction of most of its roads and of many minor bridges, as well as the planting of miles of fine avenues. He also erected the building now occupied by the branch of the Bank of Madras and St. Thomas' Church in Cocanada, as well as a number of other public buildings.

[2] Telugu *balla*, a plank and *kattu*, to tie; hence 'a platform.'

a broad-beamed punt, and is ordinarily of sufficient length and breadth to take a cart and its bullocks. The bigger river ferry-boats are large flats which will hold three or four carts with their bullocks. Long boats are used at some of the lesser ferries, and rafts laid on hollowed-out palmyra trunks (called *sangadis*) at a few insignificant ones. The round boats made of hides stretched over a bamboo framework which are used on some of the rivers of the Presidency (*e.g.*, the Tungabhadra, Cauvery and Bhaváni) are not employed in this district. Across narrow waterways the boats are propelled by poles, or, more rarely, are pulled across with the help of a rope tied from bank to bank. For crossing the wider and deeper channels, oars or (as sometimes on the Gódávari itself) sails are used.

CHAP. VII.
ROADS.

Thirty-four of the local fund ferries are leased out by auction by the taluk boards concerned to contractors, who are allowed to charge certain fixed fees. In 1904-05 the sums paid for the right to work these ferries amounted in round figures to Rs. 23,300. The eight ferries of Bhadráchalam fetched some Rs. 700 in the same year. The ferry across the Vasishta Gódávari at Kótipalli was leased for Rs. 4,020 and that across the Vainatéyam at Bódasakurru for Rs. 2,300. All the steam ferries were sold for large amounts.

All the other local fund ferries are allowed to be used by the public free of charge. They are managed by the villagers, who arrange for some one to work each of them and remunerate him themselves. For some of them the boat or ballacut is supplied by the District Board, and in that case the village headman is held responsible for its proper treatment.

WATER CARRIAGE.
The rivers.

The Gódávari river is largely used as a waterway. The three steam ferry-boats mentioned above do much passenger traffic. One of them, a stern-wheel boat with compound engines, plies between Rájavólu (Rázóle) and Narasapur; another, a large boat with an upper deck, of the usual river-steamer type, travels between Rajahmundry, Dowlaishweram, Bobbarlanka, Vijésvaram and Kovvúr; and the third, another stern-wheeler, touches at all the ferry stations on both sides of the Gódávari between Rajahmundry and Pólavaram and has recently been run experimentally as far up as Kunnavaram, to provide communication with Bhadráchalam. These boats are worked by crews paid by the District Board, but are generally managed by contractors who find the fuel, etc.,

[1] These are Kovvúr, Arikarevala, Kumáradévam, Tállapúdi, Sítánagaram and Gútála.

CHAP. VII. WATER CARRIAGE.

take the passengers' fees, and pay rent to the District Board. They are inspected by the District Board Engineer from time to time to ensure that they are maintained in a safe and proper condition. The Public Works department has one or two steamers at Dowlaishweram which are used by officials for inspections or journeys on the river.

A great deal of goods and passenger traffic is also carried on the river in native sailing-boats. These are generally 'dhónis,' which run up to 35 tons capacity. They go up by the Dummagúdem canal referred to below when there is enough water in the river and the canal is open (usually from June to January), and travel a long way above Dummagúdem. Going up stream they sail when the wind is favourable, and, when it is not, pole or, when possible, tow. Coming down stream they either sail or row, or drift with the current, rowing just enough to keep on steerage way. Rafts of timber (see below) come down the Upper Gódávari from December to May.

Upper Gódávari project.

The project of opening up the navigation of the Upper Gódávari was first urged on the attention of Government in 1851. A vast amount of money was expended on it; but it was eventually pronounced too expensive to be remunerative, and was abandoned.

Sir Arthur Cotton, a vigorous advocate and promoter of water carriage, was the first to broach the subject. He hoped that it might be possible to provide 'still-water steam navigation from the sea to Berar,' which would be, he said, 'the cheapest line of communication in the world.' It was decided in 1853 to investigate the project; and careful and repeated examinations of the river were carried out.[1] The great difficulty to be overcome was the existence of three remarkable barriers of rock, forming rapids which are only navigable during floods. The first of these, which is nine miles long, begins near Dummagúdem, at a distance of 143 miles from the sea; the second at Enchampalli, just below the junction with the Indrávati and 220 miles from the river's mouth; and the third, called the Dewalamurry barrier, at a point 310 miles from the sea. These barriers excepted, it was estimated that there was sufficient water in the river during nine months in the year for steamers drawing from two to four feet of water, according to the state of the river. The fall of the river is moderate; and during half the year the current was estimated to be only a mile and a half per hour, and rarely

[1] Among the fruits of these is Lieut. F. T. Haig's *Report on the Navigability of the River Godavery* (Madras, 1856), which contains elaborate plans and diagrams and a fund of information on the ways of the river.

CHAP. VII. WATER CARRIAGE.

to rise above three miles an hour. It was proposed to evade the obstruction caused by the barriers by cutting canals provided with locks along the side of the river past the impassable points.

The project was warmly accepted by Government, and, on their strong recommendation, was sanctioned by the Court of Directors. It was however never completed. The estimated cost of the whole scheme, which was designed to render the river navigable for 473 miles above the anicut for four or five months of the year, and to open out to traffic 300 miles of its tributaries, was £292,000. Up to 1861 £20,000 had been laid out in preliminary surveys, etc. In 1863, when Sir Richard Temple inspected the works, no less than £700,000 had been spent. He recommended that the works at the first and second barriers and up to the foot of the third barrier should be proceeded with at an estimated cost of £255,000, so that navigation might be opened so far; but in October 1871, at the request of the Government of India, the whole scheme was abandoned on the ground that it involved an expenditure which did not give promise of any adequate return.[1]

It has never been revived. There is a fine lock and anicut at Dummagúdem and a canal (two miles in length) which is still used. Cargo boats can as a rule pass through it between June and January, and small boats throughout the year, except when it is closed for repairs. At the second barrier at Enchampalli, are a partly-completed anicut and the remains of unfinished locks and excavations. The Dummagúdem works were damaged in the flood of 1900, and estimates, amounting to Rs. 1,26,800, for repairing them were sanctioned in 1905 and are now being carried out. It would be a great help to navigation if the canal there could be carried down to Bhadráchalam; but the work would be difficult and costly, as the excavation would be largely in solid rock.

Navigable canals; their history.

When the Gódávari anicut was being built, it was proposed that the canals taking off from it should be so constructed that they would serve for navigation as well as irrigation. Mr. Walch writes as follows on the subject[2]:—

"Even when sending in his first general estimate with his second report[3] Major Cotton had said that one of the results to be expected from the works which he contemplated would be that 'a complete

[1] Statement exhibiting the Material and Moral Progress of India during 1872-73, p. 79.

[2] Chapter XI of *The Engineering works of the Gódávari Delta* (Madras, 1896).

[3] Dated April 17th, 1845.

CHAP. VII. WATER CARRIAGE.

system of internal navigation intersecting the whole delta would be established throughout the year.' And besides the 'head-locks' the estimate included a provision of one lakh for 'sluices, locks, and other small masonry works.' The smallness of this provision, which could not have been intended for more than half-a-dozen[1] or so of even the small and inexpensive locks originally proposed, shows that there was but a very imperfect perception on the part of Major Cotton himself of what would be required to make the main irrigation arteries of the system into really efficient lines of communication. It is not therefore to be wondered at that when the detailed estimates for the various canals came in with large sums set down for locks and special arrangements for navigation, the Government should have regarded the provisions for that purpose as almost a new development of the original intentions to which sanction had been given. The Governor of the day, Sir Henry Pottinger, even went so far as to 'say I cannot shut my eyes to the fact that this is an entirely novel scheme which, so far as I recollect, had no existence in the original project for an anicut across the Gódávari.'

" But Colonel Cotton was determined that his chief canals should be made navigable . . . . . and so he went on with steady insistence, loyally backed up by the officers who followed him on the delta works, till at last opposition to his views on the subject was broken down, and there are now in the Gódávari system alone nearly 500 miles of canals which, besides carrying water for irrigation, are excellent lines of communication. Nor is this all; from the Gódávari system, navigation can at three places pass into the Kistna system with its 300 miles of navigable canals, and from it again into the Buckingham Canal, which runs along the coast for 196 miles from the end of the Kistna system to Madras, and for 65 miles further south. From Cocanada to the south end of the Buckingham Canal the length of canal navigation is 450 miles.

" There cannot be the slightest doubt that the provision for cheap carriage, not only in and about the district itself but also to the neighbouring districts and to an excellent sea-port, contributed largely to the rapidity with which the Gódávari irrigation developed and the district sprang into prosperity. In this way the cost of the works specially required for navigation has been repaid over and over again, quite irrespective of the direct returns from boat licenses, tolls and so on."

Expenditure and traffic.

The development of canal traffic has indeed been enormous. Sir Arthur Cotton wrote in 1852, 'I should not be surprised if, after a few years, the district be well managed and the canals kept in good order, the traffic were to average

[1] In his letter No. 184, dated 3rd August 1849, Captain Orr gives the number required as 10. There are *now* 54, exclusive of head-locks.

50 tons a day.' The traffic in 1893–94 amounted to 393,725 tons, or over 1,000 tons a day; and by 1902–03 it had risen to 576,643 tons, or nearly 1,680 tons a day, that is, more than 33 times as much as that anticipated by the founder of the canal system.

It was not till 1863 that tolls were levied for the use of the canals. Nowadays a considerable annual income is derived from them. The total receipts in 1902–03[1] were Rs. 85,600 and the total maintenance charges Rs. 63,900, leaving a net profit of Rs. 21,700. A navigation establishment (chiefly lock superintendents) costing Rs. 448 per mensem is kept up for the central and eastern deltas belonging to this district. In 1902–03 fees were paid on 458,000 tons of displacement; and cargoes worth 230 lakhs and over 345,000 passengers were transported on the canals. Timber rafts with a displacement of nearly 119,000 tons also used these waterways.

Nature of traffic.

The passenger traffic is carried in what are called *rádhári* boats, long covered craft holding from 40 to 70 passengers and entirely owned and directed by private enterprise. They are towed by regular staffs of coolies paid monthly wages and posted at stages of from ten to twelve miles in length. These boats also carry produce, and are patronized for this purpose when time is an object, as their pace averages three miles an hour. They all start from Rajahmundry or Dowlaishweram, and they constitute a regular boat service.

The cargo boats are numerous and range from 7 to 40 tons displacement. They all carry sails. Their charges for cargo are about four pies a ton a mile on the average. They are worked by crews of two or three men and one or two small boys, who tow, pole, or row the boats as convenient. On still water they can sail five miles an hour. Otherwise their pace is about three miles an hour down stream and one and a half up stream.

The timber rafts consist mostly of logs and bamboos from the forests of the Upper Gódávari, which are lashed together and floated down between December and May for export. Bamboos come down in December, but timber not until January. Of a total transported tonnage of 118,632 tons, only 418 tons were taken up stream.

The canals are used to a small extent by house-boats. These are nearly all Government boats employed by officials, but there are one or two private house-boats also. The only

[1] These, and except where otherwise stated the following, figures are for the whole delta system, including the part in Kistna district.

CHAP. VII. WATER CARRIAGE.

steamers on the canals at present are the inspection boats of the Public Works department. Mr. Walch[1] says that:—

'The introduction of steam power for the transportation of freight along the canals has often been considered, and it has to some extent been tried without success. It cannot compete with manual labour unless that becomes far less plentiful and cheap than it now is, and unless canals along the chief lines of communication be maintained *along their whole lengths and at all points* to a depth greater than is now the case. That steam or perhaps electricity will eventually supersede towing coolies on the Gódávari canals is most probable, but this will not be for many a long day.'

Conflicting interests of irrigation and navigation.

The combination of irrigation and navigation in these canals is not entirely without its drawbacks. Their requirements are necessarily to some extent conflicting.

'For irrigation, large quantities of water and consequently of silt have to be taken into a canal, and therefore the slope of the surface must be considerable; for navigation the less water taken into the canal the better, and its surface should have no slope. For irrigation, there are times when the canal should be kept low so that large quantities of water may not have to be passed into the drainages when they are already filled by rain-water; for navigation the canal should always be kept up to its full level. For irrigation, even when the river or other source of supply is low, it is often necessary to go on letting as much water as possible out of the canal to supply crops, thereby reducing the level and the depth in the canal, especially at its end; for navigation at such times the water should be kept in the canal so as to maintain as nearly as possible its full depth.'

These difficulties have been experienced in the Gódávari system. On the Ellore canal, which is the through line of communication to the Kistna river system, the silting was found to impede traffic, and the necessity of keeping enough water in the canal for navigation caused much tempting extension of irrigation to be abandoned. These facts were adduced in 1888 as arguments for the necessity of lightening that canal of some of its traffic and in support of a proposal for a railway between the Kistna and Gódávari rivers—a proposal which has since developed into the North-east line of the Madras Railway. As far as the present district is concerned, navigation is always subordinated to irrigation, and though every attempt is made to keep the canals full, navigation has to take its chance when water is scarce.

MADRAS RAILWAY.

The only railway which traverses the district is that which was originally called the East Coast Railway but is now

[1] *Op. cit.*, p. 152.

MADRAS RAILWAY.

known officially as the North-east line of the Madras Railway. It enters the district from the south at Rajahmundry over a fine bridge across the Gódávari, and, skirting the north-western edge of the delta, finally runs from Samalkot parallel with the coast till it passes out of the district at Tuni. From Samalkot a branch runs to Cocanada, the inhabitants of which have always protested vigorously against the chief commercial centre on the section being thus left off the main line. The bridge over the Gódávari at Rajahmundry is one of the finest in the Presidency. It is built of steel girders laid on masonry piers which are sunk from 48 to as much as 100 feet below low water level and stand over 44 feet above that level. It has a total length of no less than 9,000 feet, or over 1½ miles, between abutments, and consists of 56 spans of 150 feet each. It was opened to goods traffic in 1900. The railway was opened from Rajahmundry to Waltair (in the Vizagapatam district) in 1893 and the Cocanada branch in the same year.

ACCOMMODATION FOR TRAVELLERS.

Bungalows.

In 1904 there were altogether 110 travellers' bungalows in the district, of which 79 were maintained from local funds, 21 by the Forest department, and ten by the Public Works department. A detailed list is given in the separate Appendix. Of the local fund bungalows, nine were in Bhadráchalam taluk, and, since the Local Boards Act has been recently withdrawn from operation in that tract, are now managed by the Revenue department. Those maintained by the Forest department are designed primarily for the use of its own officers, but are also available for private individuals on payment of fees. Nineteen of them are in Bhadráchalam. That taluk contains 29 rest-houses in all, and Chódavaram eleven. These buildings are necessarily numerous in the Agency, where only short marches are possible and tents can only be carried with difficulty. Tuni and Pithápuram divisions only contain three and four bungalows respectively. The accommodation in the travellers' bungalows ranges from furnished and terraced buildings to empty thatched sheds, the latter predominating. With a few exceptions, the local fund bungalows are of an inferior type.

Chattrams.

There are eight endowed chattrams under the management of the local boards, six of which have considerable incomes. Their total annual revenues are some Rs. 18,000. They were all bequeathed by private individuals to the taluk boards. The largest is the Nallacheruvu choultry in Peddápuram taluk, the income of which is Rs. 5,500. There, and at two other large institutions at Peddápuram and Kottipudi, people of all

CHAP. VII. ACCOMMODATION FOR TRAVELLERS.

castes are fed. At two other considerable chattrams Bráhmans are fed. Three insignificant choultries are maintained by the municipality at Rájahmundry.

Private chattrams appear to exist in large numbers[1] in this district, and they are much less exclusively devoted to the needs of Bráhmans than is the case in some places. Indeed at several of them food (though not accommodation) is provided even for Málas. At many of them all Súdra castes are fed. Most of them, it seems, are supported by private liberality without regular endowments. Some are of a considerable size. Those at Cocanada (maintained by a Kómati), Samalkot (by a rich Reddi merchant), Pithápuram (by the zamindar) and Kótipalli (by the Pólavaram proprietor) are worthy of particular mention. The largest of all is supported by a Kómati at Rajahmundry. Another large one in that town, called the *chanda* ('subscription') choultry, is kept up by subscriptions from the local merchants, who set aside a percentage of their daily profits for the purpose.

[1] The Collector's office estimates the number of these institutions at 71.

CHAPTER VIII.

RAINFALL AND SEASONS.

RAINFALL. FAMINE—The conditions existing—Famine in 1791—The 'Guntúr famine' of 1833—Distress in 1835-38—Disasters of 1839-41—Improvement resulting from the anicut—Scarcity in the Agency, 1897. INUNDATIONS BY THE SEA—About 1706—In 1787—Its extent and effects—The accompanying hurricane—The landholders' losses—Inundation of 1839. CYCLONES. FLOODS—In 1614—In 1875, 1878, 1882, 1883 and 1884—Great flood of 1886—Floods of 1887 and 1892—Of 1895-96—Of 1900.

CHAP. VIII.
RAINFALL.

THE following table shows the average rainfall in certain seasons of the year in the various taluks and in the district as a whole. The seasons selected correspond roughly with what may be called the dry weather, the hot weather, the south-west monsoon and the north-east monsoon. The figures shown are the averages of a series of years. As will be seen, records have been kept at most of the stations for more than thirty years. Those where figures for only a few years are available have been entered separately and not included in the district average :—

Taluk.	Station.	Years recorded	January to March.	April and May.	June to September.	October to December.	Total.
Cocanada ...	Cocanada ...	1870-1903	0·93	2·36	21·98	15·60	40·87
	Còringa ...	1870-1903	0·58	1·95	21·09	18·67	42·29
Pithápuram ...	Pithápuram ...	1870-1903	0·50	2·19	20·41	11·36	34·46
Tuni	Tuni	1870-1903	0·96	2·74	21·39	10·70	35·79
Peddápuram.	Peddápuram.	1870-1903	0·65	2·41	23·22	10·52	36·80
	Prattipádu ...	1870-1903	0·97	2·90	23·96	9·79	37·62
Rámachandra-puram.	Álamúr ...	1886-1903	0·67	2·49	23·82	12·03	39·01
	Rámachandra-puram.	1870-1903	0·69	2·42	24·71	14·06	41·88
Amalápuram.	Amalápuram.	1870-1903	0·84	2·22	25·42	16·40	44·88
	Kottapéta ...	1886-1903	0·58	2·38	25·01	13·90	41·87
Nagaram Island.	Rájavólu (Sivakódu).	1870-1903	0·48	1·29	21·88	16·50	43·15
Rajahmundry.	Rajahmundry.	1870-1903	0·79	3·19	26·64	9·56	40·18
Bhadráchalam.	Bhadráchalam.	1875-1903	1·01	2·79	35·76	3·83	43·39
Chódavaram.	Chódavaram.	1870-1903	0·78	2·87	27·77	8·94	40·36
Pólavaram ...	Pólavaram ...	1870-1903	0·93	3·57	28·27	8·54	41·31
	Average for the district.		0·76	2·52	24·95	12·03	40·26
Amalápuram.	Mummidivaram.	1901-1903	2·03	1·25	27·73	20·89	51·90
Yellavaram ...	Addatígela ...	1895-1903	1·41	5·86	29·85	9·87	46·99

CHAP. VIII.

RAINFALL.

It will be noticed that the first three months of the year are practically rainless. April is almost as dry. In May, showers herald in the south-west monsoon, which begins in the middle of June and brings nearly two-thirds of the total yearly fall. It is naturally heavier in the Bhadráchalam taluk beyond the Gháts than in the rest of the district. Conversely, the north-east monsoon is hardly felt in that taluk. The latter current is much weaker in this district than in many other parts of the east coast. The rain it brings generally consists of a very heavy downpour on its first arrival, and after the 15th November rain worth mentioning rarely appears. The delta benefits more from this north-east monsoon than the uplands; whereas the latter get more rain in the hot weather than the former. The annual average fall for the whole district (40·26 inches) is moderately high for this Presidency. In only eight other districts is the amount greater. Vizagapatam on the north gets rather more rain, and Ganjám a good deal more; but Kistna on the south receives much less.

The highest fall on record is that at Chódavaram in 1893, which amounted to 86·02 inches. Twenty-two inches fell in September, over twelve in June, August and October, and over nine more in July and November. In the same year 85·85 inches of rain were registered at Amalápuram. The lowest fall recorded for any station is 13·40 inches at Tuni in 1876. No rain was received from January to April or from October to December, inclusive, in that year.

FAMINE.

The conditions existing.

The major part of the district is, humanly speaking, safe from anything in the nature of a famine. The Gódávari draws its water from vast and distant tracts and is not affected by any local failure of rain; and from the time that the anicut first made this river's supplies regularly available for cultivation, the delta has never felt the want of water. In the upland and hill tracts, however, the crops are precarious, and in the Agency the danger is aggravated by the improvidence of the inhabitants. The people there, on the other hand, are accustomed to eking out a livelihood in bad seasons on toddy, gruel made from the pulp of tamarind, jack and mango seeds, and jungle roots. The delta produces vast quantities more food than is required for the subsistence of its own inhabitants, and also provides a constant field for labour; so that no one in the uplands need ever starve for want of work if he will make up his mind to travel so far.

Before the construction of the anicut, however, the whole district suffered cruelly on several occasions from terrible famines due to drought. It was the recollection and the effects of these visitations which suggested the idea of constructing the anicut[1] and induced the Government to face the expense which that project involved. Inundations from the sea have also caused much loss of life and property in the past, and so have cyclones, though no serious damage caused by either has been experienced for many years; and a fourth variety of natural disaster to which the delta is particularly subject is floods in the Gódávari river, which have not only been common in past years, but even nowadays, in spite of the utmost efforts, frequently cause considerable loss and hardship. The various occasions on which serious disaster or suffering has been experienced from these four different causes will now be shortly referred to.

CHAP. VIII. FAMINE.

Famine in 1791.

Except for vague references by native historians, there is, as usual, no record of the famines which doubtless occurred before the days of British occupation. The first visitation of which particulars survive is that which desolated the Northern Circars in 1791-92. In January of the latter year the Board of Revenue said that the extreme drought had caused a large diminution of revenue and that 'though every alleviation in our power has been afforded by the suspension of duties on grain as well as on all necessaries of life, and every exertion is making by the Collectors to discover and distribute for the general consumption such grain as may be hoarded up by individuals for their private advantage, yet many of the poorer class of inhabitants are perishing from want.' Application was made to the Government to sanction the importation of rice from Bengal, and 'every effort seems to have been made by Government and individuals for affording temporary means of subsistence to the poorer class of people,' but in April 1792 the sufferings of the inhabitants still continued 'with little prospect of immediate relief.' Numbers had died and numbers more had emigrated; and the Board feared that the decrease of population and cultivation would long be felt.

At that time a large sum was due to pensioners in the zamindaris of Masulipatam; and Government ordered that any balance of this which remained unclaimed at the end of a month from the date of notice to that effect, should be devoted to relieving distress. Over 35,000 pagodas (Rs. 1,40,000)[2] were applied to this purpose, and the children of the poorer families were collected and fed at the public expense. Large remissions were also granted to the zamindars and extensions of their leases were sanctioned.

[1] See Chapter IV, p. 80.

[2] It is assumed that the pagoda was the local pagoda of four rupees.

CHAP. VIII. FAMINE.

The famine appears to have lasted from November 1790 to November 1792.[1] Its effect on the people was terrible. It was computed that one-fourth of them either emigrated or fell victims to starvation.[2]

The 'Guntúr famine' of 1833.

In 1833 a succession of unfavourable seasons culminated in the great 'Guntúr famine.' Though this did not affect Gódávari so severely as the neighbouring district of Guntúr after which it was named (where 'it covered the country with human bones from Ongole to Masulipatam'[3]) yet so deeply did the remembrance of it enter into the hearts of the people that it afterwards became an era from which they reckoned dates. The author of the original *Manual* of this district, who knew the country well, says[4] 'I have frequently asked a man his age, and he has been unable to state it; but he was quite ready to answer the question how old were you at the time of the Great Famine?'

The hardships appear to have begun with a hurricane in May 1832, which 'destroyed much produce stored, a large number of cattle, and many cocoa, palmyra and betel nut trees.'[5] This was followed by a failure of rain in western India and a consequent lack of freshes in the Gódávari, so that the paddy crop usually grown along the banks of that river was lost. A temporary rise of the river in the early part of the season had induced the ryots to commence this cultivation; and their disappointment was thus the more bitter. Gódávari, however, did not suffer either so soon or so severely as the districts to the south of the river. As late as April 1833 the Collector was able to report that though a great influx of distressed people had taken place from Masulipatam and Guntúr, and great distress prevailed on account of the high price of grain; yet 'the miserable creatures that everywhere meet the eye are principally other than the local inhabitants.'

But from that time forward matters gradually became worse. The contributions cheerfully given by the wealthier Europeans and natives were quite inadequate to the needs of the case. From March 1833 to the end of July private subscriptions enabled about 3,000 people to be fed every day, and it was hoped that a good monsoon might render Government relief unnecessary. But these hopes were disappointed, and assistance had at length to be demanded from the State.

[1] Mr. Benson's *Statistical Atlas* (Madras, 1895), p. 62.

[2] General reports of the Board of Revenue (Madras, 1871), ii, 130, 143, 145 iii, 2, 22, 31, 53, 73.

[3] *Statistical Atlas*, p. 84.

[4] P. 288.

[5] Sir Henry Montgomery's report, dated 18th March 1844, para. 30.

CHAP. VIII.
FAMINE.

Relief-works, chiefly the digging of tanks, were opened in August, but gratuitous relief was prohibited, and many of the higher castes preferred to starve rather than demean themselves by doing earth-work. The relief afforded seems in any case to have been quite inadequate to the distress. Thousands of persons emigrated to Madras and to other more fortunate districts. 'A stream of pilgrims flowed night and day towards the south . . . . The great northern road soon became one long graveyard. It was often most difficult to distinguish between the dying and the dead.'[1] Young girls were sold and sent away to Hyderabad; the scarcity of water added the torments of thirst to those of hunger; and grain could not be transported without armed escorts, since the villagers turned out *en masse* when they heard of the approach of grain merchants with a convoy of food, and tried to obtain possession of it by force. Happily the famine did not last more than a year, and seems to have come to an end before the beginning of 1834.

Distress in 1835-38.

The two following seasons were favourable, but there was a general failure of the monsoons between 1835 and 1838. In the first of these years the early rains were deficient and yet many of the crops were destroyed by inundations; in the next there was continued drought, and in 1837-38 the early showers again failed and the later rainfall was excessive.[2] The year 1838-39 is described in the report of Sir Henry Montgomery, who based his statements 'on his own observations, and enquiries from persons of all classes, confirmed by the periodical reports of the different Collectors,' as one of 'extreme distress little less than famine, equal if not exceeding in calamities that of 1832-33.' This however seems to have been an over-statement of the case. Want of sufficient rain ruined the 'white' paddy crop; and though in December a few showers saved the cholam harvest near Rajahmundry, in the north of the district that crop was lost too. Small relief-works (the deepening of tanks) were started by private philanthropy in Rajahmundry; and these were taken over by Government in February 1839, in which month 450 persons were daily employed upon them. Relief-works were also started at Samalkot in March. In June, good rain put a stop to the sufferings of the people. Altogether only Rs. 6,156 were spent on public relief, so the scarcity appears to have been far from severe. Two factors united to prevent more serious results: the area affected was not large, and the price of grain was kept down by liberal importations by sea.

[1] *District Manual*, p. 289.

[2] Sir Henry Montgomery's report already quoted, para. 30.

CHAP. VIII. FAMINE.

Disasters of 1839-41.

The season of 1839-40 began propitiously; but towards the middle of the year the district was visited by the disastrous cyclone and inundation referred to below. In 1840-41 'the early rains were again wanting, the north-east monsoon failed, and sickness was prevalent.'

Improvement resulting from the anicut.

This unfortunate cycle had thus lasted twelve years, and Sir Henry Montgomery summed up the case by saying that of these twelve 'five were marked by peculiar distress and three were bad.' The population, which in 1821 had amounted to 738,308, had decreased by 1839-40 to 533,836. Gódávari fell into a state even more miserable than that of the Northern Circars generally at that time, and at length Sir Henry Montgomery was deputed to take charge of the district as Special Commissioner[1] and to report what could be done to raise it from its lamentable state of depression. His report, as has already (p. 80) been seen, resulted in the construction of the anicut at Dowlaishweram, which changed the whole face of the delta and delivered it from any future fear of famine. No general distress has been experienced since it was built. Even the great famine of 1876-78 did not seriously affect this district, and men and cattle fled to it then in large numbers from the famine-stricken tracts in Kurnool, Bellary and Nellore.[2]

Scarcity in the Agency, 1897.

In 1896-98 failure of the monsoons caused a good deal of suffering throughout the Agency, especially in Bhadráchalam and Pólavaram. Indeed the jungle people were perhaps harder hit by this famine than by that of 1833. The Rev. J. Cain of Dummagúdem describes a conversation with an old man who remembered the latter, and who compared the two by saying, 'There were fewer of us then, and the forests had not been cut down, and there were plenty of roots.'

In 1896 Bhadráchalam and Yellavaram suffered from short rainfall, but a remission of 50 per cent. of the dry assessment was sufficient to enable the ryots to last out till the end of the year 1896-97, and no relief was necessary.

Things were much worse in the following year. The south-west monsoon stopped on the 18th June, and distress amounting to famine in Bhadráchalam, and verging upon famine in Pólavaram, was the result. Yellavaram and Chódavaram had rather more rain, and in these all that was needed was to assist for a short time a few aged or infirm people, who could not support themselves and had no one to maintain them. In Pólavaram and Bhadráchalam it was necessary to open

[1] See Chapter XI, p. 167.

[2] B.P. (Rev. Sett., L.R. and Agri.), No. 431, dated 12th March 1896, p. 12.

relief-works. Matters were made worse by the fact that, acting on a general belief (encouraged by the astrologers) that three whole years of famine were impending, the sowcars refused to give the hill people the usual advances on the security of their crops upon which they generally subsist in the interval between sowing and harvest.

Relief-works were opened, but, except in Bhadráchalam, the hill men absolutely refused to come to them. In Pólavaram they preferred to help themselves in their own lawless manner by plundering their richer neighbours. Collecting in gangs, they looted no less than 39 villages in seven days; and, as the local police were afraid to act, order was not restored till the District Superintendent of Police arrived with the Reserve, and marched a number of the rioters off to prison. The villagers had not resisted the robbers, so no blood had been spilt, but it was estimated that property worth Rs. 10,000 had been stolen during these riots. Meanwhile in Bhadráchalam works were opened in May 1897 and a fair number of Kóyas attended them.

Gratuitous relief was given on a large scale in this taluk, but to a less extent in the rest of the Agency where either the distress was not so acute, or the hill men had helped themselves by robbery. In Bhadráchalam nearly Rs. 12,000 were distributed in this way, and nearly Rs. 17,000 were spent from charitable funds when the distress was at an end in buying seed-grain, cattle, etc. and selling them at low rates to the impoverished people to enable them to start cultivating again.

It was not in the Agency alone that the pinch of these years was felt. Test works had to be opened in Rajahmundry and Cocanada taluks and in Ellore, then a part of this district; and nearly Rs. 7,000 were spent on works in these three areas. A little gratuitous relief was also given in Rajahmundry, and a poor-house was established at Cocanada.

INUNDATIONS BY THE SEA.

Inundations of the coast by the sea occurred fairly frequently in former times, and Mr. Topping, the astronomer, when making enquiries about them in 1789, found that they were so well known as to have a definite name, being called *uppena*.[1]

About 1706.

The earliest of which any record survives occurred in December about the year 1706, but all that is known of it is derived from the oral testimony of a very old man some eighty-three years later. The wind had been blowing very hard from the east for two days and the sea burst upon the

[1] *Selections from the Records of the Madras Government*, No. XIX (Madras, 1855), 23.

CHAP. VIII. INUNDATIONS BY THE SEA.

land during the night. A few lives were lost in the neighbourhood of Coringa, innumerable trees were blown down, the paddy was ruined, the springs of fresh-water were spoiled and quantities of salt were deposited upon the flooded ground.[1]

In 1787.

The next inundation which occurred was that of May 20, 1787. This was so extraordinary in its violence that it was commonly supposed to have been due to an earthquake, but Mr. Topping[2] ascribed it firstly to a 'violent and long-continued gale[3] from the North-East at a time when the South-West Monsoon should prevail, and had actually set in many weeks previous to it, checking the Northerly current and forcing the waters back upon the coast'; secondly to 'the configuration of the coast itself, peculiarly favourable to such an accident at such a crisis,' in particular 'the sudden projection of Point Gardewar (Gódâvari) and the situation of Coringa in the recess or *cul-de-sac* of a bay'; and finally to the fact that the inundation occurred at the spring tides of the new moon. 'In short there happened at that fatal juncture a union of almost every cause that could have a tendency to elevate the waters of the Sea.'

Its extent and effects.

Pitiable details of the havoc wrought by this hurricane and flood are to be found in the correspondence from the then Chief and Council of Masulipatam.[4] Coringa island and the country near Injaram were flooded, and so was Narasapur. The hurricane raged with increasing violence from the 16th of May onwards. On the 20th 'about ten in the morning,' writes the Resident of Injaram on the 22nd and 23rd May :—

'The sea rushed in upon us and inundated everything. On the morning of the 21st everything was desolation. The whole town of Coringa and all the little villages about, with the inhabitants, (were) carried away. Nellapillee is in not much better state. As yet I cannot ascertain what loss the Hon'ble Company may have sustained; but I suppose it is in proportion to the loss of individuals, which in fact amounts to everything we possessed. . . . . The poor black people are now running up and down crying and lamenting the loss of relations from the inundation The springs and wells all around are choked with salt water, and we have only to depend on the heavens for a supply of fresh water. Cattle, grain and everything carried away. . . I now request in the most earnest manner that you will with the utmost despatch send to this place by *dônis* or any other sea conveyance what quantity of grain you may be able to collect.

[1] *Selections from the Records of the Madras Government*, No. XIX (Madras, 1855), 23.

[2] *Ibid.*, p. 29.

[3] This blew for six days without intermission.

[4] See Extracts from the Public Consultations, pp. 1152-59 and 1202-10.

INUNDATIONS BY THE SEA.

The remaining part of the black inhabitants, who escaped from the inundation of the sea, are now dying by dozens for want of food; and, if we do not receive supplies very soon, very soon there will not be a native alive in the Nillapillee havelly.'

His letters also contain a distressing account of the sufferings of the European men and women in the place, all of whom, however, escaped with their lives. Five hundred bags of rice and other provisions were despatched to Injaram from Madras before the end of the month, and this terminated the immediate sufferings of the natives. Further down the coast, the inundation was much less felt; and the reports from Narasapur complain less of it than of the hurricane.

The accompanying hurricane.

This hurricane not only wrecked a great number of ships along the coast but was also felt far inland. As far north as Yernagúdem (now in the Kistna district) the camp of a detachment of sepoys was completely wrecked. 'The trees under which the tents were, fell upon them and tore them to pieces,' writes an officer on May 23rd. 'With the greatest exertion the ammunition was saved. The men were flying about like footballs endeavouring to find the village. Lieutenant Cuningham and I very nearly lost our lives in the same attempt. . . When we reached the village (we) found nothing but the walls of the houses and the greatest misery among the inhabitants.' A similar story is told of the effects of the storm at Samalkot. 'This dreadful hurricane has not left a roof standing even to the Commanding Officer's house. A range of barracks for two battalions, the guard-room and several other buildings are level with the ground.' So great was the force of the wind that near Yernagúdem scarcely a tree was left standing, and at Narasapur for some time no one could stand upright.

The landholders' losses.

The zamindars suffered very considerably from this visitation, but they seem all to have much overstated their losses in order to support extravagant demands for remissions of revenue, and the real amount of these seems never to have been even approximately ascertained. An officer who was directed to enquire into their extent in this district assessed them at over sixteen lakhs; but his data were of a very doubtful character, and both the Council of Masulipatam and the Board of Revenue considered his estimate 'entirely inadmissible.' In the end no remissions were given, but forbearance was shown in the collection of the kists.

Inundation of 1839.

In 1839 a cyclone raged all along the coast from Vizagapatam to Narasapur. It was accompanied by a tidal wave which burst upon the shore and inundated Cocanada and Coringa. Much of the shipping was driven on shore, some of

CHAP. VIII. INUNDATIONS BY THE SEA.

the wrecked vessels being carried, it was said, four miles inland. The loss of life and property was very great. The merchants' storehouses at Coringa and Injaram were ruined; cattle and crops were destroyed; large tracts of land were rendered unfit for cultivation by the salt water; and the tanks and wells were rendered brackish from the same cause. The force of the wind was also most destructive. Very many of the native houses in Samalkot were blown down, all the European houses except two were unroofed, and even in Rajahmundry some of the houses were nearly dismantled by the violence of the storm.

Since then no serious inundations from the sea have occurred in this district. The destructive tidal wave which desolated Masulipatam just a quarter of a century later did not affect Gódávari.

CYCLONES.

The inundations just described were usually accompanied (if not caused) by violent storms, and some of these were doubtless cyclonic in nature. In more recent times, four cyclones occurred in the ten years preceding 1878, all in the months between September and December. In November and December 1878, two others arrived which caused the sea to rise dangerously at Cocanada, destroyed a good deal of cultivation there, submerged some of the huts near the creek, blew down a number of mud houses and trees, and killed many cattle. In October 1904 a cyclone swept across the whole country levelling many trees in the Agency and thousands of cocoa and areca palms in the coast taluks. So universal was the damage to plantain gardens that plantains had actually to be imported from Tanjore. Since that year no violent cyclone has visited the district, but the barometer is always carefully watched in the months (September-December) when they are most to be expected.

FLOODS.

The fury of the Gódávari in full flood has always excited the wonder of those who have seen it. The irresistible torrent which pours through the deep gorges in the hills through which it forces its way has been referred to on p. 5. Sir Henry Montgomery, when pressing for the construction of an anicut across the river, could not deny that 'the Gódávari, when filled as it was in the early part of the present season (1843-44), is a fearful stream, overflowing the country through which it passes and carrying before it all impediments to its course.' Before the anicut was built and attempts to control the river were begun, destructive floods seem to have been constant, and even now, as has been more than once said, they occur every now and again.

In 1614.

The earliest of which any record is extant happened in and about Narasapur in 1614. The account of an English merchant, quoted in Sir H. Montgomery's report, says: 'In August there happened a greater overflow than had been seen in twenty-nine years. The whole Salt Hills, Towns, and Rice were drove away and many thousand men and cattle were drowned; the Water rising three Yards above the high way.'

In 1875, 1878, 1882, 1883 and 1884.

The damage done by floods in later years to various parts of the anicut system has already been briefly noticed in Chapter IV.

The flood of July 1875, 'the greatest fresh that has occurred in the Gódávery since the extraordinary floods of 1862 and 1863,' did no great damage to the crops, though there were three breaches in the embankment of the Vasishta Gódávari.

That of August 1878, however, breached the head-sluice of the Bobbarlanka canal and submerged a large extent of land in the Amalápuram taluk. That taluk was 'mostly flooded and was at one time in imminent danger, so much so that it was considered advisable to remove the people to the high lands. But the timely action taken by the Department of Public Works saved the people and their property.' The crops suffered much less than was expected, and only Rs. 8,000 had to be remitted.

In June 1882 a destructive flood in the river inundated a large tract of country in Amalápuram and Nagaram, and did much harm to villages and crops. In Nagaram six villages were entirely, and eight partly, submerged. On the Kistna side of the river the damage was even greater. The engineers again exerted themselves to the utmost to save life and property, and the loss of crop was not very large.

In August 1883 a breach in the Vasishta Gódávari caused considerable damage to the crops in Narasapur.

A dangerous flood occurred in the Gautami Gódávari in August 1884. Some 300 houses valued at Rs. 11,500 were washed away; other property worth Rs. 18,200 was destroyed in the villages of Pillanka and Mallavaram in the Rámachandrapuram taluk; and 23 villages were submerged between the river and the Injaram canal. The damage to crops was estimated at Rs. 30,000, and serious breaches were made in the Kótipalli road.

Great flood of 1886.

The highest flood on record occurred in August 1886. The river was 14·5 feet deep on the anicut on the night of the 19th. By noon of the 20th it had risen to 16·2, and by 5 A.M. on the 21st to 16·9 feet, above the anicut, or 1½ feet higher than any previously recorded flood. By 10 that night it had fallen to 16·5, by 6 A.M. on the 22nd to 16, and to 14·6 on the following

CHAP. VIII. FLOODS.

morning. The outer wall of the Dowlaishweram lock was carried away, and a breach 250 yards long was made in the bank of the main canal, which resulted in the whole of the south-eastern corner of the Rajahmundry taluk being submerged. Many breaches also occurred in the central delta, the worst being in the Gannavaram canal, and whole tracts of country were under water. Fortunately, the inhabitants, with very few exceptions, succeeded in making their escape to natural eminences and the river and canal banks. The river also breached its bank near Pólavaram, flooded Pólavaram, and did a great deal of damage there and in Tállapúdi and some other villages.

The loss of crop was again nothing like so great as at one time seemed likely. It was estimated that the damage in Amalápuram and Rámachandrapuram was Rs. 48,000, and that houses in those taluks and Rajahmundry had suffered to about the same extent. In the district as it was then constituted Rs. 16,500 of land revenue and Rs. 45,000 of water-tax were remitted, and damage estimated at Rs. 15,000 was done to the flood-banks, canals and channels.

Floods of 1887 and 1892.

In July of the next year a high flood lasted for about twelve days. The river was 15·8 feet above the anicut on the 19th. A number of breaches occurred in the left bank of the Vasishta and a large one in the Vainatéyam, and some 2,200 acres of wet crop were lost. This was mostly replanted again and the remission of revenue on account of the submersion of crops amounted to only Rs. 6,400.

On October 3rd, 1891, the river attained the unparalleled height of 16·9 feet above the anicut; but no breaches occurred. A flood of only 12·9 feet in September of the following year breached the Cocanada and Samalkot canals (the latter in thirteen places) as well as the river flood-banks above the anicut. Scarcely any harm was done to the crops; but the budget allotment for repairs to the delta works had to be increased by Rs. 30,000, chiefly on account of the repairs rendered necessary on the Samalkot canal.

Of 1895-96.

The crops in Amalápuram and Rámachandrapuram suffered from floods in 1895; but this was owing to excessive local rainfall, and not to the action of the river. Twenty inches of rain fell in 24 hours in Amalápuram on the 6th September. Remissions of revenue amounting to Rs. 10,000 were granted for submersion in these and the Rajahmundry taluks, and roads and trees suffered much more than the crops.

More serious damage was done by the river next year. Rising to 13·8 feet above the anicut on the 2nd August, the water made a large number of breaches in the canal and river banks, and rising again to 13·7 on the 16th much increased the harm already done.

Of 1900.

The last of this long list of calamities occurred in 1900. Before daylight on the 14th August the river overtopped the lock and canal banks at Dummagúdem and completely flooded out that village, driving the inhabitants to the higher ground and drowning a few women and children. It breached its bank near the Vijésvaram anicut and did great damage to the works of the western delta in the present Kistna district; and the central delta was inundated through numerous breaches in the Gautami, Vasishta and Vainatéyam. Little harm was done to the eastern delta, though parts of Rajahmundry taluk were inundated by a breach in the flood-bank. The repairs to the breaches had not been finished before a slightly higher flood on the 22nd September (15·8 feet over the anicut) opened many of them again. The damage done to the delta and Dummagúdem works was estimated at Rs. 10 lakhs. Only about Rs. 40,000 had to be remitted for submerged crop in the present district. The taluk worst affected was Amalápuram, where 4,000 houses were destroyed and some 70,000 acres of land were more or less damaged.

CHAPTER IX.

PUBLIC HEALTH.

CHAP. IX. PREVALENT DISEASES.

Malaria; in the Agency.

THE most noticeable of the diseases which afflict the district is malaria. This is worst in the Agency. The Gháts there are densely wooded and the valleys are filled with a tangle of damp jungle, so that during the rains the country is eminently suited to the propagation of the malaria-bearing mosquito. Beyond the Gháts, the lower parts of Bhadráchalam appear to be equally malarious, the villages along the valley of the Saveri river and those lying between it and the Rékapalle hills being the worst parts of the taluk.

Even the Kóyas, who have resided for untold generations in the Agency, are not immune to malaria. The disease is said to be chronic among them, and its effects are particularly noticeable in the case of the children. People from the plains suffer far more severely, however; and from the earliest times up to the present day the country has retained a most unenviable reputation for its unhealthiness. The Board of Revenue referred to its 'putrid fever' as far back as 1794; and of the party of 25 men who were recently engaged in inspecting the forests of Rékapalle preparatory to the preparation of the working-plan for their exploitation, almost all subsequently suffered from low fever of a malignant and lingering type, several were dangerously ill, and as many as one-fourth died. It is characteristic of this malaria that it does not as a rule show itself when the victim is in the hill country, but appears in all its virulence as soon as he descends to the plains. One explanation of this fact avers that the system is braced to resist the disease by the cooler air of the hills, but as soon as the patient reaches the hotter plains becomes relaxed, and allows the latent malaria to obtain the upper hand. The agency malaria is generally said to be more prevalent in the cold than in the hot weather, but no season of the year is free from it.

CHAP. IX. PREVALENT DISEASES.

In the uplands.

The upland taluks adjoining the Agency also suffer, though to a much less extent, from malarial fever. In 1869–70, before the advent of the theory that all malaria is conveyed by the anopheles mosquito, elaborate enquiries were made as to the prevalence and causes of the disease in these parts of the district, and the Sanitary Commissioner arrived at the conclusion that the fever in the plains was due to the northerly winds which sweep over the malarious forests of the hill tracts. He pointed out that the taluks which were most open to breezes from the sea had the least fever, while those which were most exposed to wind blowing across unhealthy jungles had the highest ratios of sickness and death from malaria.

In the delta.

The question had also been raised at that time whether the great increase of irrigation under the recently-constructed anicut was in any way responsible for the insalubrity of the district. It was known that in some places (the Punjab, for example) irrigation was invariably accompanied by malaria. Enquiries were therefore directed at the same time to the elucidation of this point. The conclusion arrived at was that the irrigation had had no effect upon the prevalence of malaria. The result of five years' registration of vital statistics 'demonstrates in a very clear manner that the intensity of fever in any taluk has no relation to the extent of irrigation of the land, but is solely due to its geographical position and its exposure to malarious winds during the north-east monsoon.' The irrigated taluks were in fact found to suffer in very varying degrees. For five years the death-rate in Rámachandrapuram taluk had been 11·9 per thousand, while in Amalápuram and Narasapur it was 6·5 and 4·6 per thousand respectively. The difference was attributed entirely to the position of the taluks, the former being exposed to winds from the north, while the latter are swept by sea-breezes.[1] Theories regarding the dissemination of malaria have doubtless changed since those days, and vital statistics in rural areas are seldom sufficiently accurate to afford a firm foundation for debatable propositions ; but the fact remains that the delta taluks (unlike irrigated areas in some places in this Presidency—the valley of the Tungabhadra, for example) are not greatly subject to malaria and are, in fact, the part of the district in which it is least prevalent.

Cholera.

Cholera, however, is endemic throughout the delta. It is chiefly conveyed from place to place along the lines of communication, that is, by the movement of persons affected with

[1] Proceedings of the Madras Government, Public Department, June 14, 1871 nd G.O. No. 143, dated 30th December 1872.

CHAP. IX. PREVALENT DISEASES.

it, and by the irrigation channels, which are used for drinking purposes. At times the disease has broken out in a very serious manner. In 1892 as many as 13,600 persons died of it in the Gódávari district as then constituted, and in 1878, 1879 and 1889 its victims numbered between nine and ten thousand. But such visitations have been rare; and, though in nearly every one of the last 35 years cholera has claimed some victims, the number of these has, as a rule, been less than that even in less populous districts. It exceeded one thousand in 17 of the 32 years between 1871 and 1902 inclusive, but on only four occasions was it higher than in any other district.

Small-pox.

The ravages of small-pox have on the whole been less serious than those of cholera, but on more than one occasion they have been very grave. In 1878 over 18,000 persons died of the disease in the district as then constituted, and in 1884 over 11,300. In six of the 32 years between 1871 and 1902 more deaths occurred from small-pox in this district than in any other; in fifteen of these years the mortality exceeded one thousand; and in only one year did it fall below one hundred.

A serious epidemic of the disease broke out in the delta taluks and the Tuni division in 1900, and after that compulsory vaccination was extended to a number of the unions. It is now in force in the municipalities of Rajahmundry and Cocanada and the unions of Dowlaishweram, Amalápuram, Kottapéta, Peddápuram, Rámáchandrapuram, Pithápuram and Tuni.

Other diseases.

Certain other less virulent diseases are common in Gódávari. Dysentery and diarrhœa are frequent, but perhaps not more so than elsewhere. Elephantiasis and hydrocele are also prevalent, and the town of Peddápuram has a bad name for the former. Guinea-worm is rare. A few cases of black-water fever have occurred in the Bhadráchalam taluk. A peculiarity of the district is the prevalence of beri-beri, the Telugu name for which is *ubbu vayuvu*. Though endemic in many localities, it is frequently epidemic, and it is commonest along the coast. It is said to confine its attacks to males and to be most frequent among the middle-aged.

Sanitation.

A good deal has been done in the municipalities to improve sanitation, and with satisfactory results. In rural villages, as in other districts, matters are still backward and even the state of the unions leaves much to be desired. The difficulties are greatest in the delta, where the pressure of cultivation leaves little waste land round the village sites and the population is thickest. Drinking-water is also usually

PREVALENT. DISEASES.

obtained there from the irrigation canals, which are liable to pollution. The water-works recently constructed in Cocanada municipality are referred to in Chapter XIV.

MEDICAL INSTITUTIONS.

Public hospitals and dispensaries.

The public medical institutions in the district comprise seven hospitals and seventeen dispensaries. Of these, two hospitals and a dispensary are maintained by the municipalities, and the rest by the local boards. Statistics regarding all of them will be found in the separate Appendix to this volume.

Mission institutions.

Besides the above, the missions maintain several medical institutions. The American Lutheran Mission at Rajahmundry keeps up a dispensary for women and children in which some 3,000 cases are treated annually. Connected with the dispensary is a small hospital, and the erection of a larger one has been resolved upon. The Canadian Baptist Mission manages, and in part maintains, the Kellock Home for lepers at Rámachandrapuram, which was founded in 1899 by the liberality of Mrs. Kellock, the widow of Dr. Kellock, a Canadian Baptist. At the end of 1904 the patients attending it numbered 94. It contains three large wards for men and a smaller one for women, and is owned, and largely supported, by the Mission to Lepers in the East. At a distance of a mile from it, is the Phillips Memorial Home for the untainted children of the lepers, which was erected from the subscriptions of the children attending Sunday schools in Great Britain in memory of the first Secretary of the Indian Sunday School Union. The Canadian Baptist Mission also has a dispensary at Rámachandrapuram, and is erecting at Pithápuram a hospital to contain 21 beds.

Institutions in Cocanada.

The medical institutions in Cocanada town comprise a hospital, a branch dispensary and a dispensary for women and children.

The first of these is situated in the suburb of Jagannáthapuram. It was founded in 1856 and has 32 beds for male, and 14 for female, patients; in the out-patient department is a room with six beds set apart for Europeans. The main block is well ventilated and lighted; but there are no caste, or special contagious, wards. The hospital is jointly maintained from Provincial, local, and municipal funds. It is in charge of a Commissioned Medical Officer aided by an Assistant Surgeon and two hospital assistants, and is under the general control of the municipal council.

The branch dispensary in the same town was founded in 1888 and is maintained by the municipality. It treats over 20,000 patients annually. The building was erected in memory of M.R.Ry. Kommireddi Narasinga Rao by his son.

CHAP. IX. MEDICAL INSTITUTIONS.

The dispensary for women and children at Cocanada was established in 1895 and the attendance is over 11,000 annually. Its expenditure is nearly all met from local funds and it is under the control of the District Board.

Rajahmundry hospital.

The Rajahmundry hospital has been in existence since 1854. It contains twenty beds for men and twelve for women. The attendance is larger than that at any other medical institution in the district, and compares favourably with the figures for most of the mufassal institutions in the Presidency. Its expenditure is met from municipal and local funds; it possesses an invested capital of Rs. 5,560; is under the general control of the municipality; and is managed by a Civil Surgeon and two hospital assistants.

CHAPTER X.

EDUCATION.

CENSUS STATISTICS—By taluks—By religions. EDUCATIONAL INSTITUTIONS—Early beginnings—Schools now existing—The Government college, Rajahmundry—The Government training college, Rajahmundry—The Pithápuram Rája's college.

CHAP. X. CENSUS STATISTICS. By taluks.

SEVENTY-SEVEN in every thousand of the male, and 7 per mille of the female, population of the district can read and write. The figures are greatly reduced by the inclusion of the Agency, where education is at a discount and only 30 per mille of the males and three per mille of the other sex are literate. Excluding this tract, they come to 83 and 8 per mille of the two sexes respectively, or about equal to the average in the plains of the east coast districts taken as a whole. Taking the statistics for the taluks separately, it is found that the highest figures in the lowlands are those of Rajahmundry (105 and 15) and Cocanada (103 and 12), while the lowest are those of Peddápuram, namely 51 and 3. In the Agency all the figures are very low, but Bhadráchalam and Pólavaram take a far higher position than Chódavaram and Yellavaram. In this last only 11 per mille of the males and 1 per mille of the females can read and write.

By religinos.

If the statistics of literacy among the adherents of the chief religions are examined, it will be found that both the Muhammadans and Christians are far better educated than the Hindus. Among the Hindus, the literate persons per mille of the male and female population, respectively, number 74 and 6; among the Musalmans, 180 and 20; and among the Christians, 400 and 317. It will be noticed that these last are the only people whose girls have received an education in any way equal to that given to the boys.

EDUCATIONAL INSTITUTIONS. Early beginnings.

Gódávari was the pioneer among the Madras districts in educational matters. As far back as 1826 the Collector, Mr. Bayard, under instructions from Government, established schools at both Rajahmundry and Cocanada; but these were both abolished after a short life of ten years. In 1854, the year when the Court of Directors issued its memorable despatch about education, Mr. George Noble Taylor, who was the Sub-Collector of the district as it then existed, and

CHAP. X. EDUCATIONAL INSTITUTIONS.

resided at Narasapur, formed a society at that town for the purpose of advancing education, and established schools in Narasapur (the nucleus of the existing Noble high school) and three others of the chief towns of his charge, all of which were supported by local subscriptions. His system spread throughout his subdivision, largely owing to the interest taken in the matter by the ryots themselves. Attracted by the novelty of the institutions already established, they applied to Mr. Taylor to open primary vernacular schools in a number of villages, and proposed to defray the cost by a fixed annual addition to the revenue demand of each village at the time of the annual settlement, which should form a permanent fund to be applied solely to educational purposes. The movement was brought to the notice of Sir Walter Elliott, then Commissioner[1] of the Northern Circars, who recommended it warmly to the attention of Government; and a scheme was ultimately sanctioned by which this addition to the revenue demand was levied in the three taluks of Mogalturru, Tanuku and Undi (all now in the Kistna district) and schools were maintained from the proceeds.[2]

Schools now existing.

The higher educational institutions now in existence in the district comprise three colleges (namely the Government arts and training colleges at Rajahmundry and the Pithápuram Rája's college at Cocanada); seven upper secondary schools for boys; and 53 lower secondary schools, of which eighteen provide ordinary instruction for boys, fifteen similar instruction for girls, and twenty are Sanskrit schools for boys. There is only one district in the Presidency (Tanjore) in which there are more colleges, and only four where there are more lower secondary schools. The number of pupils under instruction in these two grades, and also in the upper secondary schools, is also very much above the average. Primary education, on the other hand, both in the number of institutions and of pupils, is considerably below the average of other districts. Detailed statistics regarding the subject will be found in the separate Appendix to this volume.

The Government college, Rajahmundry.

The most important educational institution in the district is the Government college at Rajahmundry. This was originally established by Government in 1853 as a Zilla school for imparting instruction to the children of the four districts of the Northern Circars up to the present secondary standard. In 1868 it was raised to the rank of a Provincial school, but owing

[1] See Chapter XI, p. 169.

[2] The correspondence will be found in *Selections from the Records of the Madras Government No. XXVI.*

to various unfortunate circumstances it remained in effect a Zilla school till 1873, when an F.A. class was started. A B.A. class was formed in 1877 and the Provincial school became a first-grade college. It is now one of the three first-grade colleges in the Presidency which are Government institutions, the other two being the Presidency college and the college at Kumbakónam. The high-school classes were discontinued in 1885. The college was affiliated to the University in 1891 in mathematics, physical science and mental and moral philosophy.

The institution is entirely supported from fees and Provincial funds. It is managed by a European Principal (an officer of the Indian Educational Service), who is under the control of the Director of Public Instruction, and its assistant staff consists of three lecturers, all officers of the Provincial Educational Service, six assistant lecturers, three munshis for Telugu, Sanskrit and Hindustáni, and a gymnastic instructor. A carpentry class is also attached to it, where the students work out of college hours under the guidance of a qualified mechanic. Its total strength is about 230, of whom some 160 are reading in the F.A., and 70 in the B.A., classes. The fees are Rs. 40 each term for the B.A. course, and Rs. 32 for the F.A. Over 200 of the boys are Bráhmans.

A hostel, rented from private persons, is attached to the college, and in this Bráhman students are boarded and lodged. It is under the direct control of the Principal, assisted by a Superintendent and two members of the college committee, and has a manager who attends to the details of its working. The boarding fees vary from Rs. 7 to Rs. 9 a month, according to the market price of rations, and the building accommodates fifty boys. Arrangements are being made for the construction in the college compound of a hostel for all classes. The students in the college come from the four districts of the Northern Circars, but the majority belong to Gódávari.

The college is endowed with three annual prizes founded in honour of, and called after, respectively, the late Mr. B. H. Young, formerly Executive Engineer of the district, and two former head-lecturers of the college, the late M.R.Rys. Sundara Rao and Subrahmanya Aiyar. Two scholarships are given by M.R.Ry. G. V. Subbaráyadu Sástri, at present Assistant Inspector of Schools, Guntúr Division, in memory of the late M.R.Ry. B. Gavara Rázu, B.A., of this college, after whom they are named. Their value is respectively Rs. 60 and Rs. 30 per annum, and they are given, on the result of

CHAP. X. EDUCATIONAL INSTITUTIONS.

a competitive examination held every alternate year, to necessitous students of the Junior B.A. and Junior F.A. classes respectively.

The Government training college, Rajahmundry.

The training college at Rajahmundry was originally established as an elementary normal school by the Gódávari District Board in 1883. Its status was raised in 1890 to that of a second-grade normal school. In 1892 it was taken over by Government and in February 1894 it was raised to collegiate rank with the Union high school, transferred to Government by the managing committee, as its practising school. In May 1904 it was affiliated to the University of Madras for the degree of Licentiate in Teaching. Its aim is twofold: to supply the educational institutions of the Northern Circars and Ceded Districts (Cuddapah excepted) with trained Telugu teachers, the want of whom has long been a bar to education in those districts; and to work (as a practising school) a large and efficient high school at Rajahmundry with classes as large as the needs of the town and the neighbourhood require.

The college is maintained from Provincial funds and the general management is in the hands of the Principal of the Rajahmundry college. The teaching staff consists of a Vice-Principal—a member of the Provincial Educational Service—eleven Licentiates in Teaching, two matriculates, a drawing-master, an agricultural instructor (who holds a diploma in agriculture), two pandits and a gymnastic instructor.

When transferring the Union high school to Government with all its properties, the managing committee also handed over a site, measuring two and a third acres, purchased by them in the heart of the town. On this, the Government began in 1897 to construct a building at a cost of about Rs. 65,000; and, on its completion in 1899, it was occupied by the training college classes, which had been before located partly in the arts college and partly in a rented building. With a view to providing a recreation ground for the boys of the practising school and the students of the training college, and to secure healthy surroundings for the latter, the authorities negotiated with the Rajahmundry municipality for the acquisition of the whole of the Potter's tank, situated in front of the college, and in 1895 submitted proposals for its acquisition. The scheme however fell through then owing to its prohibitive cost. In 1901 the subject was re-opened; and in the following year a portion of the Potter's tank and the house-sites in front of the college were acquired, and this area was reclaimed and enclosed within a compound wall at a cost of about Rs. 18,500. In 1902 proposals estimated to cost Rs. 12,000 were submitted for the extension of the building at its northern end and the carrying out of certain alterations in the existing structure. These were sanctioned, and the work is now proceeding. No hostel is attached to this college. The fees in the practising section range from Rs. 19-6 to Rs. 7-6 a term, and the rates of stipends to students under training from Rs. 5 to Rs. 15.

The arts college possesses certain endowments for the benefit of Muhammadan students; and when it contains no boys of that faith who are eligible for these, they are given to Muhammadan pupils in the practising section. They consist of two 'Yeomiah scholarships,' each of the annual value of Rs. 46, constituted from the funds of an ancient yeomiah which lapsed to Government. The interest on Rs. 7,200, being the amount of a boarding-house fund collected by the late Saiyid Ali Sáhib Bahádur, a retired Deputy Collector, supplemented by a grant from Government, is also devoted to forming Muhammadan scholarships open to poor Muhammadan pupils, and ranging in value from Rs. 3 to Rs. 7 per mensem according to the class in which the pupil is reading.

The Pithápuram Rája's college.

The Pithápuram Rája's college at Cocanada was founded in 1852, as a general English and vernacular school, through the exertions of the then Collector, Mr. Prendergast, and his sheristadar, M.R.Ry. Tulasinga Chettiyár. It depended entirely on private subscriptions, gradually declined, and ultimately collapsed for a time in 1862. In the following year, however, through the efforts of the Collector, Mr. Purvis, whose bust is now placed in a prominent position in the northern block of buildings in memory of his interest in the institution, the school was resuscitated and was formally re-opened on the 28th October 1863. Government made a monthly contribution of Rs. 70 towards its expenses, and the late Rája of Pithápuram, who had been one of its earliest pupils, added a further sum of Rs. 100 a month.

It was located in a rented building till 1865, when the increasing attendance rendered it necessary to provide better quarters for it. The late Rája of Pithápuram again showed his interest in the promotion of education by presenting the institution with a munificent endowment of Rs. 28,000, the extensive and valuable site which it now owns, and a sum of Rs. 3,700 for the building and its furniture. Further contributions were collected and a building grant of Rs. 5,000 was obtained from Government, and with these and the Rája's donation the northern block of buildings was constructed.

CHAP. X. EDUCATIONAL INSTITUTIONS.

This was soon found insufficient, and shortly afterwards the western block was erected and was called the 'Linton Memorial School' in memory of the late Mr. Linton, an Assistant Collector who had evinced great interest in the welfare of the institution. This block cost Rs. 7,000, of which one half was contributed by Government and the other by the public.

The necessity of additional buildings was felt again in 1882, and a two-storied house was erected at a cost of Rs. 12,000, of which a moiety was contributed by the late M.R.Ry. Pydah Rámakrishnayya, another of the earliest students of the school, and a moiety by Government. The building was opened by the then Governor, Sir Mountstuart Grant Duff, on March 3rd, 1883.

In 1897 a hall was constructed from college funds, at a cost of Rs. 6,000, and in 1902 a hostel was completed at a cost of Rs. 7,550, of which Rs. 2,500 was given by Government. The latter is divided into two blocks (containing six rooms each) which are called respectively the Brodie and Sweet Homes, after Messrs. V. A. Brodie and H. Sweet, a Collector and a Superintendent of Police of the district who took much interest in the improvement of the college.

The school taught up to the 'middle school standard' (corresponding to the present lower secondary course) till 1866, when it was raised to the matriculation standard. In January 1884 the school committee opened an F.A. class, and the institution was duly affiliated to the Madras University and styled the 'Pithápur Rája's College' in honour of its liberal patron. In order to place the institution on a satisfactory financial basis, the committee registered itself on the 29th August 1892 under the Indian Companies Act under the name of 'The Pithápur Rája's College, Limited.'

The institution is managed by a council of which the Collector of the district, the Chairman of the municipal council, a representative of the Rája of Pithápuram, the Inspector of Schools and the Principal of the college are *ex-officio* members. A separate committee of seven disposes of all matters not expressly reserved for the decision of the council.

The college is supported mainly by school fees, which in 1903-04 amounted to nearly Rs. 15,000. Other important items of income are the interest (Rs. 1,400) on certain Government pro-notes and a mortgage loan of Rs. 400; and a monthly grant from Government of Rs. 90. The college is generally self-supporting, but is sometimes worked at a small loss. The deficit in 1903-04, for example, was Rs. 370.

The establishment consists of a Principal and sixteen assistant masters.; two Sanskrit, and two Telugu, pandits; two gymnastic instructors; and copy, drawing and music masters. The attendance, according to recent figures, amounts to 487, of whom 39 are reading in the senior, and twelve in the junior, F.A. class. The fees paid vary, according to the class in which the boy is reading, from Rs. 60 per annum for the F.A. classes to Rs. 14 for the first class. The boys come mostly from the adjacent taluks of Cocanada, Rámachandrapuram, Peddápuram and Pithápuram. The hostel buildings completed in 1902 will accommodate 24 boys, who pay twelve annas each per mensem for the use of them. They have not yet boarded there, but a kitchen has recently been built at a cost of Rs. 1,000 to enable them to do so.

Liberal scholarships are given in the college. They amount in all to Rs. 492 a year and vary from Rs. 40 to Rs. 5 per annum according to the class to which they are open. They are tenable for terms varying from two to four years, and are awarded by competitive examinations. They are only open to boys who are too poor to prosecute their studies without pecuniary help; and entrance to the examinations is also subject to certain age limits.

CHAPTER XI.

LAND REVENUE ADMINISTRATION.

EARLY HISTORY—The zamindars—Their administration—The *havili* land—Committee of Circuit, 1785-87—Settlement with the zamindars in 1789—Abolition of the Chiefs and Councils, 1794—Collectors of the *havili* land. THE PERMANENT SETTLEMENT, 1802-03—Its failure—Its effect on the ryots—Special Commissioner appointed, 1843. RYOTWARI SETTLEMENTS—Before 1865—Settlement of 1865-66—Its scope—Grouping of villages—Classification of soils—Standard crops, grain outturns, commutation prices—Cultivation expenses and money rates—Financial results—Water-rate in the delta—The existing settlement; its scope—Reclassification of delta soils—Water-rate problems—Settlement of wild tracts—Financial results—Bhadráchalam taluk—Proprietary rights—Fixing of the peshkash—Settlement of 1890 in Bhadráchalam—Agency tracts and rented villages. DISTRICT AND DIVISIONAL LIMITS. VILLAGE ESTABLISHMENTS—Re-organized in 1866—Revised in 1885. INAMS.

CHAP. XI. EARLY HISTORY.

AS has already been mentioned on p. 34 above, the district, when it was at length definitely acquired in 1768, was not at once administered directly by the Company but was leased out to native renters called zamindars, over whom was a head renter named Hussain Ali Khán. The latter's lease expired in 1769 and the newly-acquired territory was then placed under the direct administration of the servants of the Company. The agents of the old factories and their subordinates were converted into Provincial Chiefs and Councils, and the Rajahmundry and Ellore Circars were put under the Chief and Council of Masulipatam, who for the next 25 years controlled the entire political, civil and revenue administration. They found that the land of the district was of two classes; namely, the *havíli* ('havelly') land, which consisted of household estates, situated round the chief towns, which had been appropriated by the Musalmans to the upkeep of their numerous garrisons and establishments and administered directly by them; and the zamindari land, the collection of the revenue in which was leased out on a commission to zamindars.

The zamindars.

These zamindars, in theory, were merely agents of the Musalmans,[1] created for the sole purpose of collecting the

[1] See Higginbotham's reprint (Madras, 1883) of the *Fifth Report on the affairs of the East India Company* (1812) and Mr. Grant's *Political Survey of the Northern Circars* appended thereto, both of which have been freely utilized in the following pages.

CHAP. XI. EARLY HISTORY.

revenue. Theoretically, they were removable at pleasure; but they were generally permitted to remain for generation after generation in possession of their estates. They were often charged with the raising of local troops, who were consequently devoted to them, and during the lax administration of the later years of Musalman rule they had become so powerful that they had usurped hereditary rights and come to regard themselves as the legal owners of the soil. They maintained the semblance of state, residing in mud forts in which their palaces were situated, moving abroad only on elephants or in gorgeous palanquins, and being accompanied on their excursions by a rabble of armed peons and a posse of relatives and followers mounted on horses or borne in palanquins. Their practice was to exact by force or fraud all the revenue they could, to pay a certain fixed sum to the Government, and to appropriate the balance themselves. The Chief and Council of Masulipatam treated these zamindars as the owners of their estates, subject to the payment of a money peshkash to Government which was settled from time to time on what was called the *mámúl* jamabandi, *i.e.*, a customary sum assessed on no scientific basis. The *havíli* land was kept under direct management as in the time of the Musalmans.

Their administration.

The zamindars undoubtedly oppressed their ryots. The 'ancient established custom' of collecting the revenue in the zamindari land was by a division of the crop *(ásará)*, but in practice several different modes were adopted by the zamindars.[1] In some cases the crop was shared; in others, particularly on the more fertile soils producing paddy, there was a fixed rent; and garden land, or land producing tobacco, cotton, betel, sugar-cane, oilseeds, palmyra or fruit trees, was assessed on special principles. Where the paddy crop was divided between the zamindar and the ryot, the division was theoretically supposed to leave the cultivator 40, 50 or 60 per cent. of the crop, the higher rates being allowed to Bráhmans and other favoured classes. But as a matter of fact the cultivator's share rarely exceeded 20 or 25 per cent. The fixed rents were also maintained at an oppressively high level.

The *havíli* land.

The *havíli* land appears to have been managed on a somewhat similar system, a renter being substituted for a zamindar. Division of the crop was more common, but arbitrary assessments called *sist* and *malavati* were in some places substituted in its stead. Here again however it was the

[1] See the reports of 1786 and 1787 of the Committee of Circuit referred to below.

CHAP. XI. EARLY HISTORY.

practice rather than the theory which was of essential importance to the ryot. In the division of crops the proportions theoretically allowed to the cultivator were the same as in the case of paddy in zamindari land; but 'many after collections were made, and the renter usually exacted a higher price for his proportion than that of the market, which reduces the ryot's share to a fourth or even a fifth part of the produce.' The cultivators, in fact, were as much under the thumb of the renters as of the zamindars. They had no right in the soil, and the renter let the land to the highest bidder. Bad as was the condition of the zamindari ryots, their fields were better cultivated than the *havíli* farms immediately dependent on the Company.[1]

Committee of Circuit, 1785-87.

The Chief and Council at Masulipatam did little or nothing to check this maladministration and oppression, and in 1775 the Court of Directors, aware of the evils of the existing system, and anxious both to protect the ryots and to secure a more adequate revenue from the zamindars, ordered that a Committee of Circuit, to be composed of five Members of the Council of Fort St. George, should be appointed 'to inquire into the state of the Northern Circars by ascertaining with all possible exactness the produce of the country, the number of inhabitants, . . . the gross amount of the revenues, the articles from which they arose, the mode by which they were collected and the charges of collection.' The Directors further ordered that enquiries should be made into the military strength and financial position of the zamindars; and intimated that, while not desirous of depriving these latter of their revenue, they were determined to protect the ryots from violence and oppression.

Hardly, however, had this Committee begun its labours than its work was interrupted by the intervention of the new Governor of Madras, Sir Thomas Rumbold, who in 1778 decided to summon the zamindars to Madras and himself make a settlement with them there. The arrangement made accordingly was for five years at a rate 12½ per cent. above the '*mámúl* jamabandi,' *i.e.*, the amounts the zamindars had hitherto been paying.

Sir Thomas Rumbold ceased to be Governor in 1780 and in 1783 the Committee of Circuit was reappointed. It conducted a lengthy enquiry into the resources of the district and the other points referred to in its instructions, and its reports on the *havíli* and zamindari lands dated respectively December 18, 1786 and February 15, 1787 contain a full and valuable

[1] Circuit Committee's Report, dated February 15, 1787, para. 43.

description of the country. The immediate effect of its enquiry was that the increment of 12½ per cent. imposed by Sir Thomas Rumbold on the zamindars was confirmed, and in 1786 his settlement was extended for a period of three years till 1789; so that it was actually in force for eleven years.

Settlement with the zamindars in 1789.

In 1789 the Chief and Council reported that a just assessment on the zamindaris would be two-thirds of their gross revenue. The Board of Revenue (which had been established in 1786) and the Government agreed, and a settlement was made on these terms except in the case of the zamindari of Pithápuram, the lease of which had not expired and which was then being administered by renters.

In 1791, however, famine devastated the country,[1] the zamindars fell into arrears, large remissions were granted them, and their settlements were extended from three to five years wherever the shorter of these terms had been fixed.

Abolition of the Chiefs and Councils, 1794.

The Chief and Council at Masulipatam had distinguished themselves during this trying time neither by their knowledge of the conditions of their charge, nor by their loyalty to superior authority; the reports of the Committee of Circuit had also proved the inefficiency of their administration; and in 1794 they and the other Chiefs and Councils in the Northern Circars were abolished, and the country was divided into Collectorates. At first, three Collectorates were formed with head-quarters at Cocanada, Rajahmundry and Mogalturru, now in Kistna; but shortly afterwards the greater part of the present district was placed under one Collector at Rajahmundry and was named the Rajahmundry district.

Collectors of the *havili* land.

Collectors had already been appointed in 1787 for the management of the *havili* land. Till 1792 they were independent of the Chiefs in Council, but from that year till 1794 were subordinated to them. They introduced much-needed improvements, reducing the size of the areas leased to renters, and in some cases dealing directly with the ryots by sharing the actual crop with them in fixed proportions without the intervention of middlemen. The latter practice, though a great improvement on the system it succeeded, had many drawbacks, as it involved, among other things, the maintenance of a large establishment of native officers who generally combined with the inhabitants to defraud the State.

From 1794, land which fell under the immediate management of Government was leased out in appropriate farms on joint rents to the leading ryots, the rents being fixed

[1] See Chapter VIII, p. 137.

CHAP. XI. EARLY HISTORY.

in grain and commuted into money at the market price or the average price for a number of years. This plan, however, still left much to be desired, since no precautions were taken to prevent the head ryots from oppressing their poorer neighbours—the besetting evil of all joint rent systems. Moreover the famine of 1791 had denuded the country of cultivators, and though much land had thus gone out of cultivation the ryots had to pay for it just as if it had yielded a crop.

THE PERMANENT SETTLEMENT, 1802-03.

Meanwhile the Court of Directors and the Government of India had been pressing the Madras Government to introduce permanent settlement which had been adopted in Bengal in 1793 and which was supposed to provide a solution of the vexed questions of the amounts which the zamindars should receive from their ryots and should pay to Government. The system was introduced in the Rajahmundry district in 1802–03. The estates of the existing zamindars were confirmed to them in perpetuity on a peshkash which was generally fixed at two-thirds of the average gross collections of land revenue in preceding years, the period of calculation varying from eight to thirteen years according as accounts were available. The *havíli* land was divided into proprietary estates (or 'muttas') of convenient size yielding from Rs. 3,500 to Rs. 17,500, and these were sold in public auction to the highest bidders on permanent tenure subject to the payment of a peshkash calculated on the best available data. In both cases the rights of the under-tenants were protected by a legislative enactment (Regulation XXX of 1802) which enforced the grant of pattas and the observance of customary rights. The land-customs, salt, abkári and other miscellaneous sources of revenue, which had been included in former assessments, were resumed by Government and excluded from the assets of the new estates.

Twenty-seven muttas and thirteen ancient zamindaris were thus formed. Two other small zamindaris[1] were subsequently added to this number. The hilly and thinly populated estates of Rampa, Tótapalli, and Jaddangi, whose owners were called mansabdars and whose revenues were trifling, were not brought under the permanent settlement like the other parts of the district, and their existence was in fact almost ignored.

The greater part of the district was included in the Peddápuram estate, which was assessed with a peshkash of nearly seven lakhs. Large areas were also included in the

[1] Vilasa, and Jampalli and Bantumilli.

CHAP. XI. THE PERMANENT SETTLEMENT.

Pithápuram, Pólavaram and Kóta Rámachandrapuram zamindaris, which were assessed respectively at two and a half lakhs, one lakh, and one and a quarter lakhs. The other properties were inconsiderable in extent. There were in all fourteen ancient zamindaris and twelve muttas in those parts of the present Gódávari district which were then included in the district of Rajahmundry.[1]

The Pithápuram zamindari is the only large property which retains anything like its old proportions. Much of the Peddápuram estate has been bought in by Government for arrears, and what remains of it has been divided into nine small zamindaris which altogether pay a peshkash of less than one and a half lakhs. The whole of the Kóta Rámachandrapuram estate was bought in by Government in 1846, and Pólavaram has been reduced by sales for arrears to a petty estate paying a peshkash of less than Rs. 7,000. The other properties have suffered similarly from sales and subdivisions. Excluding the agency hill muttas and Bhadráchalam, eighteen zamindaris and eleven muttas are still in existence.

Its failure.

This permanent settlement was a dismal failure. Both the ancient zamindaris and the newly-created proprietary estates were speedily involved in financial difficulties. In the case of the former this appears to have been less the effect of over-assessment than of extravagance and mismanagement. Indeed the most lightly-assessed of them all was the first to collapse. The newly-created proprietors not only imitated the extravagance of the ancient zamindars, but had also to struggle against over-assessment. Their estates quickly began to be put up to sale in satisfaction of arrears of peshkash, and usually passed at first into the hands of speculators who eventually came to the same end. In 1813–14 the first of them was purchased on behalf of Government at auction by the Collector, and thenceforward, as the figures in the margin show,* an ever-increasing area came, by the same process, under the direct administration of Government. Though the proprietary estates were the first to fall, several of the ancient zamindaris eventually shared their fate.

* *Year.*	*No. of Government villages.*
1813	10
1817	59
1820	133
1832	150
1840	361
1844	580
1851	876

[1] These figures exclude Bhadráchalam and parts of Yellavaram, which were not added to the district till later. The figures of peshkash include areas which have since been handed over to Kistna, and are only roughly correct.

CHAP. XI. THE PERMANENT SETTLEMENT.

The political results of the permanent settlement were equally disastrous. In 1822, Sir Thomas Munro, then Governor of Madras, examined in a characteristic minute the causes of the frequent disturbances of the peace which occurred, and attributed much of the disorder to the attempts of Government to enforce the rights of traders and other speculators who had lent money to the zamindars and proprietors on the security of their estates. He wrote:—

'They are not dishonoured, they think, by their possessions falling into the hands of Government, but they consider themselves disgraced by seeing the abodes of their ancestors become the property of a low trader. As the Regulations now stand, we must, whenever a sowcar obtains a decree against a zamindar for a part or the whole of the zamindari, support him by force both in getting and maintaining possession of it; and hence we are every day liable to be dragged into a petty warfare among unhealthy hills, where an enemy is hardly ever seen, where numbers of valuable lives are lost from the climate, and where we often lose but never gain reputation.'[1]

He was emphatically of opinion, none the less, that the great hope for the future lay in the gradual extension of the area of the Government land. 'No zamindari once forfeited for rebellion should ever be restored. All estates falling in should invariably be kept and annexed to the Circar lands.'

Its effect on the ryots.

Nor did the permanent settlement bring peace and plenty to the cultivators. Few of the zamindars interested themselves personally in the management of their estates; they entrusted everything to the care of managers, whose policy it was to render their masters entirely dependent on them and to prevent their interfering in the administration. There was no system of management; the only object was to extort from the ryots the utmost possible amount of revenue. A second middleman was often introduced by renting villages annually or for a term of years, preference being given to such proposals as ensured the highest amount of rent and afforded security for its punctual payment, and little regard being had to the class of persons tendering or the influence rack-rents must have on the resources of the villages. In adverse seasons all that could be taken of the ryots' produce was claimed on the part of the zamindar, and in ordinary years the demand purposely exceeded their means. The deficiencies of bad years were made up in good ones, and in both the ryot was left only a bare subsistence.

The inherent evils of this system were soon exaggerated by a succession of natural calamities which is described in more

[1] Arbuthnot's *Munro* (London, 1881), i, 213.

detail in Chapter VIII. An unfavourable season in 1831–32, culminating in a destructive hurricane in May of the latter year, was followed by the disastrous famine of 1833; the three years 1835–38 were far from prosperous, the scarcity in the last of them almost amounting to famine; in 1839 a cyclone did great damage all along the coast and far inland; while the season of 1840–41 was almost equally calamitous. Moreover a great decline in the weaving trade had taken place owing to the abolition of the Government factories. The value of piece-goods exported decreased from 14 lakhs in 1825 to less than 2 lakhs in 1842. Numbers of people were thus thrown out of work.

Special Commissioner appointed, 1843.

The impoverishment of the district and the decline in its revenue at length, in 1843, led Government to send Sir Henry Montgomery, Bart., an able member of the Civil Service, to make enquiries. His report, dated March 18, 1844, dealt fully with the evils of the existing system. He attributed them chiefly to the inefficient management of the zamindars and proprietors, and the consequent rack-renting and impoverishment of the villages. He also lamented the want of adequate means of irrigation—especially the neglect of the Gódávari water—and the disrepair of the existing works; and his report led to the enquiries which ultimately resulted in the construction of the great anicut at Dowlaishweram and the transformation of the delta of the Gódávari consequent thereon.

RYOTWARI SETTLEMENT. Before 1865.

The most important part of his report, however, was that devoted to a consideration of the revenue policy which should be adopted in the constantly increasing area which, as has been seen, was coming under the direct administration of Government.

The first villages which came (in 1813–14) into Government hands were rented out to the principal inhabitants jointly, on the system approved by the Board of Revenue in 1794. In 1817 that plan was relinquished, and for a number of years the Government land was administered under the *ásará* system of sharing the crops or the *vísabadi* system of annual or periodical rents. In both cases the settlement was made with the ryots directly and without the intervention of a middleman; and the Collector was only authorized to rent the villages in the event of the inhabitants refusing to come to reasonable terms.

The *ásará* or sharing system was simply the conversion into money of the Government share, ascertained by estimate or by actual measurement of the grain, of the actual crop

CHAP. XI.
RYOTWARI SETTLEMENTS.

harvested each year. It was apparently almost universal on wet land. Its drawbacks, as already mentioned, were that it involved the entertainment of a large native staff who cheated the Government and bullied the ryots.

Under the *vísabadi* system, which was generally applied to dry land, the assessment on the village as a whole was fixed annually by the Collector with reference to the probable prospects of the harvest, but was frequently revised at the jamabandi in accordance with the actual state of the season. This lump assessment was distributed among the different fields by the ryots themselves, individual agreements being taken by the Collector from each ryot for the rent apportioned to his holding.

The fairness of this distribution was in theory maintained by the introduction of the peculiar system of 'challenging,' under which any ryot who considered that his own holding was over-assessed and that of his neighbour too leniently rated could demand that the latter should be made over to him at an increased rate which he named. If the ryot in possession consented to pay the enhanced demand he could retain the land, and in that case a proportionate reduction was made in the assessment of the fields held by the ryot who challenged. If, however, the ryot in possession refused to agree to the increased rate, he was compelled to give up the land to the challenger, who took it on the higher terms he had himself named.

This challenging necessarily rendered occupation insecure, and it moreover failed to meet every case of unfairness, since the unit of challenging was the entire holding and not a particular field; and a small ryot whose one or two fields were over-assessed could not afford to challenge a wealthy cultivator with a large holding, however sure he might be that the latter was too leniently rated. 'Accordingly,' wrote the Collector in 1825, 'the substantial ryots invariably contrived that their own lands should be lightly assessed and the burden thrown on those of the poorer ryots.'

This apportionment of the lump village assessment among the different holdings was made either annually or periodically. If the latter, it was generally accompanied by a redistribution of the fields among the various villagers every three, four or five years (according to the custom of each village), somewhat in the same way as under the *karaiyídu* form of the mirási tenure in Tanjore, of which relics even now survive. This was done chiefly to prevent the land held by the smaller ryots from being exhausted by continual poor farming, but also to counteract the frequent changes of possession rendered possible by the challenging system.

The *vísabadi* leases did not work satisfactorily. Arrears usually accumulated owing to the inability of the poorer classes to pay their rents, and then alterations were made in the total amount of the lump assessment; but apparently nothing was done to render its incidence more fair.

Both the *ásará* and the *vísabadi* systems therefore had their drawbacks, and more than one Collector proposed a return to the renting methods. This was indeed authorized in 1839, though it was not actually carried out.

Sir Henry Montgomery's report of 1844 already referred to recorded the opinion that the only satisfactory way of dealing with the Government land was by a survey and scientific settlement. Meanwhile, as a temporary measure, he advocated a system of joint village rents, and this was introduced a year or two later and remained in force for some 20 years. The challenging system, curiously enough, was retained, and the main modifications introduced were the abolition of the *ásará* system and the insistence of the joint responsibility of the village community as a whole for the default of any of its members. Sir Henry Montgomery's view was that these joint village rents would afford protection to the poorer ryots in so far as their interests were mixed up with those of the richer, and he was also anxious to remove the obnoxious interference of Government servants which was an essential part of the *ásará* system, and had also grown up round the *vísabadi* system owing to the ryots being unable themselves to arrange the apportionment of the lump assessments among the different holdings.

Meanwhile notable changes had been effected in the administration of the district. In 1849 a Special Commissioner with the powers of a Board of Revenue was appointed to the charge of it, and the post was continued until 1855. In 1859 the Rajahmundry, Masulipatam and Guntúr Collectorates were formed into the two districts of Gódávari (with Cocanada as head-quarters) and Kistna, the boundary between which followed the course of the Upputéru and Tamaléru rivers. The anicut across the Gódávari had also been completed in 1853.

Settlement of 1865–66.

Proposals for the first scientific settlement of the taluks comprising the new Gódávari district were submitted by Mr. R. E. Master, Deputy Director of Revenue Settlement, in two schemes, one in 1860 dealing with the western delta, and the other in 1861 relating to the rest of the district.[1] The two

[1] Printed in No. XXII of the *Selections from the Madras Records.*

CHAP. XI. RYOTWARI SETTLEMENTS.

schemes, with certain modifications, were introduced in 1862-63 and 1866-67 respectively.

Its scope.

It was not considered desirable to survey or settle the whole of the villages belonging to Government. The scheme did not deal with 148 Government villages in the Agency and elsewhere in which patches of land were only cleared for temporary cultivation and abandoned after a year or two for fresh ones. These were left to be settled from year to year. Waste land, even in surveyed villages, was often left unclassified on the ground that it was not likely to be soon occupied; and many of the *lankas* in the Gódávari were omitted from the scheme, because their limits were continually fluctuating, and were ordered to be leased out annually by auction—a system which still obtains.

Grouping of villages.

The remaining area was divided into the 'upland' and the 'delta,' according as it lay outside or within the influence of the Gódávari irrigation. In each of these tracts the villages were grouped into classes with reference to their general fertility and the quality of their irrigation sources. All the delta land was classed as dry, a uniform water-rate of Rs. 3 per acre being imposed on irrigated fields in addition to the dry assessment.

Classification of soils.

The soils were grouped into fourteen classes,[1] the arenaceous series amounting to four per cent. of the whole, the alluvial to six, the red ferruginous varieties to 29 and the regar to 59 per cent. There was also an exceptional class, making up two per cent. of the whole, in which were placed the lankas in the Gódávari and the land irrigated by the Yeléru river in Peddápuram taluk.

Standard crops, grain outturns, commutation prices.

The grain values of each of the 'sorts' into which these classes were subdivided were ascertained by experiment. The crops taken as the standard for each class were as under:—

Lankas.	Upland wet.	Delta land and upland dry.			Exceptional land under the Yeléru.
		Red.	Black.	Sandy.	
Tobacco.	White paddy.	Cholam. Cambu. Horse-gram.	Cholam. Cambu. Ragi. Black paddy.	Cambu. Ragi. Black paddy.	White paddy. Sugar-cane.

From the grain values, a deduction was made of one-sixth in the delta and one-fourth in the uplands to allow for vicissitudes

[1] B.P. (Rev. Sett.), No. 43, dated 12th May 1896, p. 6.

CHAP. XI. RYOTWARI SETTLEMENTS.

of season and unprofitable areas. Commutation prices were calculated from the prices of past years and independent enquiries, and worked out as shown in the margin.* The ultimate grain values were reduced to money in accordance with the commutation prices, and the gross annual money value per acre of each soil was fixed by taking the average of the money equivalents of the grain values of each kind of standard crop. For the special class of land under the Yeléru river the calculations were made on the assumption that sugar-cane would be cultivated once in four years and paddy in the others, the aggregate outturn being estimated for four years and the average for one year taken from this.

* *Grain.*	*Rs. per garce.*
White paddy ...	72
Black paddy ...	60
Cambu	60
Ragi	66
Horse-gram ...	96
Cholam	84
	Rs. 20 per maund.
Tobacco ...	40
Sugar-cane ...	15

Cultivation expenses and money rates.

Deductions were next made for cultivation expenses, the expenses per acre on each class of soil being taken as the average cost of cultivating an acre with each of the standard crops. The result worked out in ordinary cases to between Rs. 5-8-0 and Rs. 2 per acre, but in the case of tobacco it came to Rs. 35, and in that of sugar-cane to Rs. 95, per acre. Both the gross and the net value of each 'sort' of soil having thus been ascertained, rates of assessment per acre were framed. The share of Government generally approximated to half the net produce. The rates arrived at were modified in their application to actual fields according to the classification of the villages already referred to, the same soils paying less in villages which were classed low in the scale of fertility. In the end, the eighteen rates for dry land and fourteen for wet shown in the margin * were arrived at. The first three of the former applied only to the exceptional soils in the lankas, etc.

* *Dry.*		*Wet.*	
RS.	A.	RS.	A.
20	0	10	0
12	0	8	0
5	0	7	0
4	8	6	8
4	0	6	0
3	8	5	8
3	0	5	0
2	8	4	8
2	4	4	0
2	0	3	8
1	12	3	0
1	8	2	8
1	4	2	4
1	0	2	0
0	12		
0	8		
0	6		
0	4		

Financial results.

The result of the settlement was an increase in the revenue demand amounting, on the whole, to four lakhs, or 23 per cent., over the figures of 1859-60, though there was a decrease in the dry upland villages. In the area which at present makes up the district, the approximate increase in the delta land amounted to Rs. 99,000, or 12 per cent., and in the upland

CHAP. XI. RYOTWARI SETTLEMENTS.

wet land to Rs. 41,000, while in the upland dry land the decrease was Rs. 14,000. The net increase in this tract was thus some Rs. 1,26,000. The water-rate in the delta was raised almost immediately (1865) from Rs. 3 to Rs. 4 per acre, and eventually in 1894 to Rs. 5; and this resulted in a further increase.

Water-rate in the delta.

This separate water-rate on regularly irrigated wet land was quite exceptional, the method usual in other districts being to charge such land a consolidated wet assessment. It was introduced under the orders of the then Secretary of State, Sir Charles Wood. His idea appears to have been that, though Government was selling the water, it had no concern with the use made of it, and was only required to fix a 'fair commercial value' for it. But to some land the water was worth much more than to others (since fields which grew excellent dry crops did not always do well when irrigated), and in effect the greatest inequalities of assessment grew up among the delta fields.[1] These considerations led the Government to reclassify the delta land when the present settlement was introduced.

The existing settlement; its scope.

The settlement continued in force for 30 years and in 1896 proposals for its revision were made. The chief factors calling for consideration[2] were the enormous increase in prices (they had more than doubled in most cases), and the great improvement in means of communication, which had occurred since the last settlement. The anomalies caused by the water-rate system in the delta also called loudly for removal. In the uplands no reclassification of soils was considered necessary, and the chief change was an all round enhancement of the existing rates by one-third, so that Government might share in the profits resulting from the great increase in prices.

In the delta, however, both wet and dry land soils were reclassified and a consolidated wet assessment was substituted for the existing dry assessment plus water-rate.

Reclassification of delta soils.

In reclassifying these soils three series (alluvial, regar and arenaceous) were adopted, the first containing two classes and each of the two latter three. Each class was subdivided into 'sorts.' The standard crops taken for wet and dry land were white and black paddy respectively. For the former the grain outturns which had been arrived at for the same classes of soils in Tanjore were adopted; they were rather

[1] See G.O. No. 623, Rev., dated 27th August 1894 and B.P. (Rev. Sett.), No. 16, dated 29th January 1895, p. 1.

[2] See the exhaustive report in B.P. (Rev. Sett.), No. 43, dated 12th March 1896.

CHAP. XI. RYOTWARI SETTLEMENTS.

less than those worked out at the first settlement. For black paddy the outturns adopted were also rather below those calculated at the earlier settlement. For vicissitudes of season and unprofitable areas allowances of 10 per cent. were made in wet, and 20 per cent. in dry, land. The delta crops never fail and the ryots there obtain very high prices for their crops in famine years; but their assessment was not enhanced on that account. The estimated cost of cultivation was raised, the maxima for wet and dry crops being Rs. 14 and Rs. 8 against Rs. 5-8-0 and Rs. 4 respectively under the old settlement. The commutation prices were taken at Rs. 118 and Rs. 96 per garce for black and white paddy respectively. The average prices of the last twenty non-famine years were actually much higher than these figures, but fifteen per cent. was deducted from the averages to allow for merchants' profits. Half the net annual money value of the outturn of each field as thus ascertained was taken as the Government share and rounded off to the nearest standard rate of assessment. The result was the marginally-noted * fourteen rates for dry, and twelve rates for wet, lands. The two highest dry rates were only applied to lanka or *padugai* (river bank) lands, which are of exceptional fertility. For purposes of dry assessment, the villages were divided into two groups with reference to their means of communication and their proximity to markets; while wet land was grouped in blocks (irrespective of village boundaries) into four 'classes' with reference to the quality of the irrigation and drainage. When the rates of assessment were applied to particular fields, they were modified according to the groups and classes in which the fields were included.

* *Wet.*		*Dry.*	
RS.	A.	RS.	A.
12	0	11	0
10	0	9	0
9	0	7	0
8	0	5	0
7	0	4	0
6	0	3	0
5	0	2	8
4	8	2	0
4	0	1	8
3	8	1	4
3	0	1	0
2	8	0	12
		0	8
		0	4

The general result of the settlement was that in the whole of the Gódávari delta—including those portions since transferred to Kistna district—there was a gross increase in the assessment of Rs. 2,35,000, or eight per cent.

Water-rate problems.

The change from the system of water-rate to a consolidated wet assessment caused some difficulties. The first doubt which arose was as to what land should be assessed as wet and what as dry, since under the former system the ryot had been able to please himself as to whether he would grow dry crops or wet. It was eventually decided that all land which had been continuously under wet cultivation for the five years

CHAP. XI. RYOTWARI SETTLEMENTS.

1893–99 (but excepting 1895–96), or from which Government water could not be excluded, should be classed as wet. The next question was what water-rate should be imposed on the remaining delta fields when they were irrigated. In the case of this land the option of using or refusing the water was continued, and; in consideration of this concession, the water-rate was fixed at one rupee per acre more than the difference between the wet and dry assessment. No land was classed as permanent double-crop land. The charge for a second crop on wet land was fixed at half the wet assessment, and specific rules were made for the charges for irrigated dry crops and second wet crops on dry land.

The levy of water-rate in zamindari and inam land occasioned some discussion. A ruling of the High Court had raised a doubt as to the right of Government to levy the rate on land of these two classes from which water could not be excluded, and this had to be removed by legislation (Act V of 1900); and the rate was eventually fixed at the old uniform figure of Rs. 5 per acre.

Settlement of wild tracts.

Besides reassessing the areas dealt with at the former settlement, the existing settlement assessed to revenue many villages which either did not then belong to Government or had been left out of account owing to their jungly nature. Some 41 proprietary villages had been resumed by Government[1] since the original settlement, and many jungle villages had so far advanced in civilization as to justify their assessment. The large areas of waste land in the surveyed villages of the upland taluks, which at the original settlement had been left unassessed on the ground that they were not likely to be brought under cultivation within a reasonable period, were now brought into line with the fields adjoining them.

Financial results.

On the whole, then, 320,000 acres which had been settled in 1866 and assessed at Rs. 11,38,000 were charged Rs. 18,36,000 in the new settlement of 1900; 19,000 acres which had come newly under cultivation between the two settlements, and had been provisionally assessed at Rs. 16,000, were now charged Rs. 23,000; and some 42,000 acres were assessed for the first time in 1900 at Rs, 34,000.

Bhadráchalam taluk.

The existing taluk of Bhadráchalam beyond the Gháts became British territory in 1860, and till 1874 was administered as part of the Upper Gódávari district of the Central Provinces. It is made up of the old Bhadráchalam and Rékapalle taluks. In 1874 it was decided, in view of its racial and geographical affinities to the Gódávari district of

[1] Thirty-seven villages of the Tótapalli estate in 1881 and four of the Rampa estate in 1882.

this Presidency, to transfer the taluk to this latter. Its revenue history is therefore distinct from that of the rest of the district.

Proprietary rights.

Bhadráchalam is a portion of a large zamindari estate which is said to have been in the possession of the present family since 1324, and the rest of which remained, at the time of the cession in 1860, a part of the Nizam's Dominions. The possession of the property by the present owners has on several occasions been seriously, though not permanently, interrupted by feuds with a rival family. Rékapalle, which was formerly a separate taluk but is now embodied in Bhadráchalam, was leased out in 1815 by the proprietors of the latter estate to renters who subsequently set at nought their authority and even rose in arms against them. These people were accordingly registered as inferior proprietors at the settlement which followed the cession in 1860. Another class of inferior proprietors were the 'Doras,' to whom the owners of the estate had been wont to rent out certain areas on short leases on a commission of from 20 to 40 per cent. of the gross produce. Their position was also defined at the settlement.

Besides fixing the position of the superior and inferior proprietors, this settlement also determined the status of the ryots. Some of these possessed varying degrees of occupancy right in the soil,[1] but the rest were tenants-at-will. The occupancy rights conferred ranged from a conditional right (in the case of those who had held their land for twelve years) to an absolute right, and in all cases the proprietors were prohibited from raising the ryots' rents during the currency of the settlement.

Fixing of the peshkash.

The assessment of the peshkash to be paid by the proprietors was calculated by regular settlement operations. The villages were grouped for purposes of assessment into *chuks* (subdivisions) with reference to their fertility and locality, and the land was surveyed and the soils classified field by field. The rental which each class of soil in each *chuk* might be assumed to be able to pay was then calculated with reference to the money rents actually paid during the last five years, and to the value of rents paid in kind. Of the assumed rental thus arrived at, one half was taken as the peshkash.

The Doras above referred to had to pay the superior proprietors the whole of the peshkash so fixed on each village, together with road and school cesses each amounting to two per cent. on the peshkash, a dák cess of a half per cent., and

[1] These are clearly set out in the papers printed with G.O. No. 122, Revenue, dated 29th January 1885, pp. 4 and 5.

CHAP. XI. RYOTWARI SETTLEMENTS.

a tribute of from 10 to 40 per cent. called *malikhána*. The amount and description of rent due from the cultivators to the proprietors was also prescribed, even in the case of the tenants-at-will upon whom no permanent arrangement was binding. Waste lands and forests were declared to belong to Government; after a liberal deduction of waste (from 100 to 200 per cent. of the cultivated area and called the *dupati* land) had been set apart round each village for the extension of cultivation, firewood and grazing purposes. The abkári revenue was also resumed, and the ráni of Bhadráchalam was granted a deduction of Rs. 4,428 from her peshkash as compensation for the loss she suffered through the resumption of this and the forests. This settlement was thus altogether different in principle from those carried out in zamindaris in this Presidency.

Besides the occupied proprietary tracts, the country contained a vast extent of waste land and small area of occupied land the proprietary right in which was vested in Government. The latter consisted of a number of small and neglected villages in the heart of the forest, in which only shifting cultivation *(pódu)* was practised. The ryots in these were given occupancy rights over all fields which they could prove to have been continuously held by them, and a small assessment —apparently four annas on the extent culturable with one axe, about three acres—was levied.

Settlement of 1890 in Bhadráchalam.

After Bhadráchalam became part of the Gódávari district, the question of its re-settlement arose. The original settlement had been far less favourable to the proprietor than those carried out in this Presidency, and the proprietor pressed for a reduction of his peshkash and the restoration of his former rights to the revenue from abkári and the forests. The general lines upon which the re-settlement should proceed were ultimately laid down in 1885; but it was not carried out till 1888-89 nor introduced till 1890. The inferior tenures were not interfered with—indeed ryots with provisional occupancy tenures were granted absolute occupancy rights. The average rates on Government wet and dry land were put at 8 annas and 4 annas respectively, and cultivation is now measured up annually. The peshkash was fixed at two-thirds of the various superior and inferior proprietors' assets, ascertained by a scrutiny of their accounts, subject to the proviso that no curtailment exceeding 15 per cent. should be effected in any proprietor's income. The abkári and forest revenue were again retained in the hands of Government, but as an act of grace an allowance of Rs. 4,000 a year was made to the zamindar of Bhadráchalam as compensation therefor, the deduction from the ráni's peshkash above referred to having lapsed at her death. The cost of the village establishment was deducted from the assets on which the peshkash was calculated. The *malikhánas* were fixed at a uniform rate of 10 per cent. on the peshkash. The road and other cesses were continued and formed into a fund called the Bhadráchalam Road Fund, which was to be administered by the Collector.

The net result of this settlement was a loss to Government of just over Rs. 1,000 annually.

Agency tracts and rented villages.

The present Agency tracts of Gódávari consist of the whole of the old mansabs (estates) of Rampa and Jaddangi, the more hilly parts of the old Peddápuram and Pólavaram zamindaris, the Dutcharti and Guditeru muttas of the Golgonda Agency transferred from Vizagapatam in 1881 and the Bhadráchalam taluk transferred from the Central Provinces. As has already been seen, the mansabs were disregarded, as being unimportant, both at the permanent settlement in 1802-03, and at the settlement of 1861-66, and since that time they have all been resumed in circumstances described in the account of each in Chapter XV; the land which formerly belonged to the two zamindaris of Peddápuram and Pólavaram is held either by muttadars or direct from Government; and the revenue system in Bhadráchalam has just been described.

The Government villages, generally speaking, have not been surveyed or settled, but are rented out from year to year to the highest suitable bidder, who is debarred by the terms of his annual patta from raising the rents of the ryots. The auction is merely a form, as there is seldom any competition. Some of these villages are being surveyed and it is proposed to introduce an experimental settlement direct with the ryots on the basis of existing rents. The muttadars pay a small quit-rent. They hold their land[1] on a service tenure of the same nature as that of the former mansabdar (*i.e.*, *kávalgári* or watch and ward) for any breach of which they are answerable to the Government. The holders of the muttas transferred from Vizagapatam are on somewhat similar ground, their tenure being conditioned for service and defeasible at the will of Government. Government can remove them and can appoint whom they choose as their successors. The Agency also includes a few mokhása villages granted by Government on favourable terms for services performed—generally during the Rampa rebellion.

[1] G.O. No. 103, Revenue, dated 3rd February 1890

CHAP. XI.
DISTRICT AND DIVISIONAL LIMITS.

It has already been mentioned that the area which now makes up the Gódávari district was originally placed under the Chief and Council at Masulipatam; was divided in 1794 into the Collectorates of Cocanada and Rajahmundry; was included in 1802 in the new Rajahmundry district; formed part of the Gódávari district first formed in 1859; and was increased by the addition of Bhadráchalam taluk in 1874 and two muttas of Golgonda Agency in 1881.

The district thus constituted increased enormously in wealth, population and importance when the irrigation from the Gódávari anicut took full effect, and became a heavier charge than one Collector could efficiently administer. Accordingly in 1904 the portion of it which lay south and west of the Gódávari river (with the single exception of the Pólavaram division) was transferred to the Kistna district, which latter in its turn was lightened by the formation of the new district of Guntúr. The existing divisional charges are as under:—

Division.	Taluks.	Area in square miles.	Population in thousands.
Rajahmundry (Sub-Collector) ...	Rajahmundry, Amalápuram, Nagaram.	993	542
Bhadráchalam Agency (Head Assistant Collector).	Bhadráchalam ...	911	49
Pólavaram Agency (European Deputy Collector).	Pólavaram, Yellavaram, Chódavaram.	2,229	111
Peddápuram (Deputy Collector).	Peddápuram, Rámachandrapuram.	800	387
Head-quarter (Cocanada) Deputy Collector.	Cocanada, Pithapuram, Tuni.	701	357
	Total ...	5,634	1,446

VILLAGE ESTABLISHMENTS.
Re-organized in 1866.

It was not till 1866 that the village establishments of the district were thoroughly re-organized on modern lines. At that time the village servants were paid partly by certain customary fees and partly by the profits of the cultivation of inam lands granted them free of assessment. The customary fees had been collected with, and included in, the old joint-rent settlements; and then deducted under the head of ordinary remissions and disbursed to the village servants entitled to them. At the settlement of 1862-67 these fees were not included in the assessments fixed upon the land, and the Government expressly reserved the power to levy a regular cess for the proper remuneration of the village officers. It

VILLAGE ESTABLISHMENTS.

was decided in 1866[1] that this cess should be levied under the recent Village Service Cess Act of 1864 at the rate of 8 pies in every rupee of the land revenue on Government lands and of water-rate on inams. It was ordered that the inam lands which had up to then formed part of the remuneration of the village servants should be enfranchised (*i.e.*, surrendered to the then holders) at a quit-rent of five-eighths of the land revenue assessment which would have been charged upon them had they not been inams. The proceeds of the cess and the quit-rents on the inams were set aside to constitute a fund (since abolished) for the future payment of the village establishments.

Before these changes were introduced, the existing establishments were revised. The number of villages was greatly reduced by clubbing small ones with larger ones adjoining, and the establishments were greatly modified, being in every case much reduced. A munsif, a karnam, a talaiyári (called in this district a náyak) and one or more vettis (according to the amount of the revenue demand) were allowed to each village; an additional talaiyári was sanctioned for 29 large villages; and nírgantis (distributors of irrigation water) were largely increased in number, but were only employed for tanks in upland villages in which the ryots applied for them, and were not allowed in delta villages. The payment of munsifs and karnams varied, with the revenue demand of the village, from Rs. 1½ to Rs. 12, and from Rs. 5 to Rs. 20 a month, respectively. The lower rates for munsifs (Rs. 1½, Rs. 2, Rs. 3 and Rs. 4) were confined to villages where the revenue demand was small and the work of the headman consequently light. The pay of the talaiyáris, nírgantis and vettis was fixed at a uniform rate of Rs. 4 a month. The old village shroffs were abolished.

Village barbers and Chamars (leather-workers) had also been formerly remunerated with land inams. These were not enfranchised, but were left to their holders to be enjoyed as service inams on condition that the holders rendered to the villagers the services, as barbers and leather-workers, which had been customarily required of them. Specific services were usually specially paid for in grain by the villagers, and these payments formed an addition to the income obtained from the inams.

Revised in 1885.

In 1885 a new scheme of village establishments was sanctioned. The essential alterations effected by this were the increase of the munsifs' pay and the appointment of monigars to help them; the appointment of assistant

[1] See G.O. No. 1237, Revenue, dated 23rd May 1866, and also Nos. 963, dated 29th June 1870, and 1097, dated 26th July 1885.

CHAP. XI. VILLAGE ESTABLISHMENTS.

karnams; a moderate increase in the number of the talaiyáris and nírgantis and a decrease in that of the vettis; and the payment of those village officers in whole inam villages and zamindaris who did work for Government. Villages were graded into six classes, and the pay of munsifs and karnams varied between Rs. 5 and Rs. 12 and Rs. 8 and Rs. 20 respectively. In some cases the munsifs were paid as much as Rs. 15. The number of villages was altered by regrouping and by making provision for some resumed villages in the Rampa and Tótapalli mansabs, and the net result was that the total was reduced by ten. Subsequent to the reforms of 1885 the number of monigars was slightly reduced by regrouping;[1] and finally in 1898[2] the minimum pay of karnams was raised to Rs. 8.

In Government villages in Bhadráchalam an establishment of headmen (patéls), karnams (patwáris) and talaiyáris is paid from a fund constituted from a deduction of one anna in the rupee on the land revenue collections in those villages.

INAMS.

The inams of the district were settled by the Inam Commissioner between 1860 and 1870. One peculiar class of inam then dealt with was the ferry inams, which had been granted to remunerate the boatmen who worked ferries on the Gódávari. The enfranchisement at a quit-rent of two-thirds of the assessment, of such of these as had been rendered unnecessary by other ferrying agency was ordered in 1865.[3] Ferry inams still exist, notably in zamindari villages. As has been said, the village service inams in Government villages were enfranchised at a quit-rent of five-eighths of the assessment, and the inams of the quasi-private servants of the villagers in such villages—the barbers and the chucklers—were not interfered with.[4]

Since 1902 a special officer has been engaged upon the enfranchisement of the village service inams proper in the proprietary estates. The principles followed differ in two important particulars from those adopted in the case of village service inams in ryotwari villages. The enfranchisement is at a quit-rent equal to the full assessment leviable on such lands, instead of at five-eighths of this amount; and the enfranchised lands are liable to re-assessment at the resettlement of the district. The work is practically completed and the revised village establishments nearly all introduced.

[1] G.O. No. 691, Revenue, dated 25th August 1890.

[2] G.O. No. 207, Revenue, dated 15th April 1898.

[3] Proceedings of Government, dated 21st February 1865, para. 21.

[4] See the correspondence ending with G.O. No. 541, Revenue, dated 3rd April 1872.

CHAPTER XII.

SALT, ABKARI AND MISCELLANEOUS REVENUE.

SALT—The systems of administration—Methods of manufacture—Markets—Salt for Yanam—Fish-curing yards—Contraband salt-earth. ABKÁRI AND OPIUM—Arrack—Arrack in the Agency—Toddy—Toddy in the Agency—Foreign liquor—Opium and hemp-drugs—In the Agency. CUSTOMS—Land-customs—Sea-customs. INCOME-TAX. STAMPS.

CHAP. XI. SALT. The systems of administration.

THREE systems of administering the Government salt monopoly are in force in the Gódávari district; namely, the excise system, the monopoly system and the modified excise system.

Under the first of these, which is in force in the factory at Jagannáthapuram (Jagannàikpur) and the major part of that at Penugudúru (these are the only two factories in the district), the salt is manufactured by licensees who are allowed, subject to certain restrictions, to make any quantity they choose, and dispose of it how and when they like, after they have paid to Government the excise duty on it, plus a small cess per maund to cover interest on the capital cost of permanent works connected with storage and manufacture which have been carried out by Government. This system was introduced into the district in 1885-86. It has two drawbacks; namely, that the quantity manufactured by the licensees may be inadequate to the demand, and that by manipulating the market the licensees (or outside capitalists) may unduly raise the price of salt. The former of these disadvantages is met by the provision of penalties for neglect to manufacture, and the latter by the retention of a part of the Penugudúru factory under the old monopoly system, the second of the two systems above referred to.

Under this, the pans are worked by license-holders who are required to hand over all the salt they make to Government, and are paid for it a stated rate per garce called the *kudivâram* ('cultivator's share') which is calculated to cover all expenses of manufacture and leave the license-holder a reasonable profit.

Of late years the third of the above systems, the modified excise system, has been introduced in an extension of the Penugudúru factory. Under this, the Board of Revenue announce, before the manufacturing season begins, what quantity (if any) Government is prepared to buy, and the licensees are bound to make and deliver this quantity.

CHAP. XII. SALT.

Having done so, they are allowed to manufacture on their own account in the same manner as under the excise system.

Methods of manufacture.

The figures in the margin show the extent in the two factories which is worked under each of these three systems. The Jagannáthapuram factory is within Cocanada municipality and that at Penugudúru is near that town. In both of them, the salt is made by the ordinary methods. The pans are supplied with brine from channels connecting with the sea or tidal creeks; and not from brinepits. At Jagannáthapuram a steam pump is used for lifting the brine, and, at Penugudúru, picottahs. The soil at Penugudúru is nearly all of a clayey description, and is sandy in only a very few parts. The result is that the salt made there is dark in colour and rather dirty. That made at Jagannáthapuram is also darker than usual. In both places, however, the quality is good and the salt has the commercial advantage of being rather light, which, since salt is bought wholesale at the factories by weight and retailed in the bazaars by measure, renders it popular with the dealers. The Jagannáthapuram factory used to be worked entirely by the Oriental Salt Company, Limited, which endeavoured, by the use of certain patent processes, to purify the local product so as to enable it to compete in the Calcutta market with 'Liverpool' salt. The attempt failed and the company was voluntarily wound up at the end of 1904. The factory is now worked, under a lease running for 20 years from January 1889, by Messrs. Hall, Wilson & Co., who have been recognized as receivers on behalf of the debenture-holders in the company.

	Acres	Cents.
Jagannáthapuram, excise ...	127	8
Penugudúru, excise	669	87
Do. , monopoly ...	77	8
Do. , modified excise.	88	18

Markets.

The salt made in the two factories is largely consumed within the district itself. Out of 780,000 maunds of salt manufactured there in 1905-06, nearly half was consumed within it. The balance was sent to Vizagapatam, Kistna, the Central Provinces and Orissa. The exports by sea used formerly to include large quantities sent to Rangoon; but in recent years cheap salt, mostly from Germany, has reached that town and reduced prices to a stage which leaves no profit on this trade. When the stock of Bombay salt is short, salt is sometimes exported from Cocanada to Calcutta. In 1903-04 about 126,000 maunds were sent there; but this figure is quite exceptional, and the exports by sea rarely exceed 50,000 maunds in all.

Salt for Yanam.

The supply of salt to the French Settlement of Yanam is governed by the rules which apply to the other French

CHAP. XII. SALT.

Settlements in this Presidency. Under a treaty of 1815 between France and England, modified by two subsequent conventions entered into in 1818 and 1837 between the Governments of Madras and the French Possessions,[1] it was agreed that the French, in consideration of an annual payment, should undertake to manufacture no salt in their territories, that the Madras Government should supply them with such salt as they required 'for domestic use and consumption' at cost price, and that they should retail this 'at nearly the same price' as it fetches in adjoining British territory.

Fish-curing yards.

In Gódávari, as elsewhere, fish-curing yards have been established in which salt is sold at a little over cost price for use in the curing of fish caught in the sea. There are four of these; namely, at Coringa, Gudarugunta (near Cocanada), Uppáda (near Pithápuram) and Konappapéta, further north up the coast. At least three-quarters of the fish cured are small. The larger kinds chiefly include mango fish, sharks and skates. The demand for salted fish is great and exceeds the supply, though the method of curing is primitive if not inadequate. Prices, however, are kept down by the merchants, who make the fishermen advances and so have them in their power.

Contraband salt-earth.

Salt-earth is at present declared to be contraband only in the Pithápuram and Tuni divisions, certain villages in the Tótapalli zamindari in Peddápuram taluk, the Cocanada and Nagaram taluks, and the Amalápuram taluk less the division under the deputy tahsildar of Kottapéta. Elsewhere the saline soils are neither plentiful enough nor rich enough in salt to constitute a danger to the revenue. The Salt Act is not in force in the Agency, but no saline earths exist there and the supply of salt is all obtained from the low country.

No saltpetre is made in the district, either crude or refined.

ABKÁRI AND OPIUM.

The abkári revenue consists of that derived from arrack, toddy, foreign liquor and hemp-drugs. Statistics regarding each of these items, and also concerning opium, will be found in the separate Appendix.

Arrack.

The arrack revenue is managed on what is known as the contract distillery supply system, under which the contract for the exclusive privilege of the manufacture and supply of country spirit in the district is disposed of by tender, an excise duty is levied on the spirit issued from the contractor's distillery or warehouse, and the right of retail sale in licensed shops is sold separately by auction every year. Wholesale vend dépôts are opened by the contractor at places fixed by the Collector, and the number of retail shops is definitely limited. The rates at which the spirit should be sold to the

[1] The first two of these papers are printed *in extenso* in Aitchison's *Treaties, etc.* (1892), viii, 214-22.

CHAP. XII. ABKÁRI AND OPIUM.

retail vendors are fixed by Government and embodied in the terms of the contract. The contract is held at present by Messrs. Parry & Co., Managers of the Deccan Sugar and Abkári Co.'s distillery at Samalkot,[1] who make the spirit at that distillery from molasses.

The consumption of arrack in Gódávari, when compared with that in other districts in which the still-head duty is the same (Rs. 4-6 per gallon of proof spirit), is moderate. In 1903-04 the average incidence of the arrack revenue per head of population in the district as formerly constituted was as. 2-7 against as. 3-11 in the then Kistna district, as. 2-1 in Nellore, and 3 annas in the Presidency as a whole.

Up to 1900 the arrack consumed in the district was made from toddy and on the out-still system. The change to the spirit made from molasses in the distillery, which was dearer than the other and had a less popular flavour, caused a fall in the consumption and revenue (which however was more than counterbalanced by a rise in the revenue from toddy) and also offered a strong temptation to illicit distillation. The consumption of the molasses arrack, however, is now steadily increasing, and it would seem that the vigilance of the protective staff of the Salt and Abkári department has resulted in the transition from the one system to the other being safely tided over.

Arrack in the Agency.

In the Agency, the arrack revenue is differently administered. Three systems are in force; namely, the ordinary excise system, the nominal fee system, and the out-still and shop system.

The Abkári Act I of 1886 has been extended to 47 villages in Yellavaram, Chódavaram and Pólavaram—chiefly the more civilized villages near the plains—and the excise system has been introduced into 30 of these—two in Yellavaram, four in Chódavaram and 24 in Pólavaram.

In the rest of the Agency only the old Abkári Act (III of 1864) is in operation, and the abkári administration is in the hands of the Revenue officials. Outside Chódavaram, the second of the two systems above mentioned is in force in the Kóya and Reddi villages, the inhabitants of which are allowed to make arrack for their own consumption on payment of a nominal fee of two annas a head per annum for every male over fourteen years of age. The rules require that the village headman should take out the license and make and supply arrack to the Kóya and Reddi residents, but in practice no actual license is granted. In Chódavaram little abkári revenue is derived from the muttas, since a toddy tax *(chigurupannu)* is supposed to be included in the quit-rent levied from

[1] See Chapter VI, p. 111.

the muttadars; but the out-still system is in force in some of the muttas.

In all parts of the Agency in which neither of the aforementioned systems is in force, the arrack revenue is managed on the out-still system, whereby the right both to make and to sell arrack in licensed premises is sold annually by auction.

In Bhadráchalam the arrack is distilled from the flowers of the *ippa (Bassia latifolia)* tree, but elsewhere in the Agency from toddy.

Toddy. In the plains, the toddy revenue is now managed on the usual tree-tax system, under which a tax is levied on every tree tapped and the right to open retail shops is sold every year to the highest bidder. The toddy is nearly all drawn from date and palmyra palms, the number of each of these which is tapped being about equal. Date toddy is used from October to the end of January and from July to September, when palmyra toddy is scarce. The toddy-drawers are generally of the Idiga and Gamalla castes.

A fair number of trees are tapped for sweet juice in the delta taluks, since the demand for jaggery at the Samalkot distillery and sugar factory is very large. Many more are tapped in the western delta lately transferred to the Kistna district. Licenses have to be taken out for tapping for sweet juice. The low price of jaggery formerly retarded the industry; but recently (probably owing to the effect of the countervailing duties on sugar) the price has risen from Rs. 14 per candy of 500 lb. to Rs. 21 or Rs. 22, and this may result in an extension of sweet-juice tapping. The tappers, however, are very usually in debt to capitalists from whom they have received advances, and are perhaps not likely to benefit much themselves.

Toddy in the Agency. In the Agency, the tree-tax system is in force in the 30 villages already mentioned where the excise system of arrack administration has been introduced, but elsewhere no separate revenue is derived from toddy. Toddy is drawn by the hill people from date, palmyra and sago *(Caryota urens)* palm trees.

Foreign liquor. Six taverns have been opened in Rajahmundry and Cocanada for the sale of foreign liquor to be consumed on the premises. The right to sell in them is disposed of annually by auction. In the Agency, a few shops have been opened on payment of fixed fees.

Opium and hemp-drugs. The sale of opium, preparations of the hemp plant and poppy-heads is controlled under the system usual elsewhere. Supplies are obtained from the Government storehouses. There is an opium storehouse at Rajahmundry, the only one in the Presidency outside Madras. Licenses for wholesale

CHAP. XII. ABKÁRI AND OPIUM.

vend dépôts are issued by the Collector on payment of a fee of Rs. 15 per annum, and retail shops are sold annually by auction. The retail price of opium is fixed by Government at 2¼ tolas for a rupee.

The amount of opium consumed is very large. In the old Gódávari district the average consumption per head of the population in 1903-04 was ·619 tola against ·082 tola in the Presidency as a whole, and the incidence of the revenue was 2 as. 2 ps. per head against 4 ps. for the whole Presidency. It has been suggested that smuggling to Burma (most difficult to prevent) is responsible for much of this abnormal consumption. Parcels of opium sent by post from this district were seized in Rangoon in 1902-03 and previous years, and the many emigrants who go to Rangoon from Cocanada are believed to smuggle the drug with them. The Rangoon authorities have been particularly on the alert recently. Another explanation is that opium is used in the district as a prophylactic against malaria; but against this is the fact that the drug is not consumed more largely in the malarious than in the healthy taluks.

The consumption of hemp-drugs per head of the population is smaller in Gódávari than usual. In 1903-04 the incidence of revenue in the old Gódávari district per head per annum was one pie against two pies in the Presidency as a whole.

In the Agency.

In the Agency, the villages to which Act I of 1886 has been applied are supplied with ganja from two shops in Pólavaram which get their stock from the plains. Elsewhere there are no restrictions on the cultivation of ganja; but as a fact it is little grown or consumed. There are a few opium shops. They are supplied from Rajahmundry and are managed in the ordinary manner, but by the Revenue department instead of by the abkári authorities.

CUSTOMS. Land-customs.

Under native rule, and even in the early years of British administration, land-customs were levied at frequent stations along the main lines of communication, and had the most baneful effects upon trade. In their report of 1787, the Circuit Committee[1] wrote:—

'Numerous chowkis are placed on all the roads, where, besides the zamindars' dues, many russooms are exacted, which is the cause of much vexation and inconvenience to the trader. The enormous duties exacted on teak deserve particular notice. From Pólavaram to Yanam they amount to 200 per cent. That carried by the Narasapur branch pays 250 per cent. at nine places. Hence teak timber is frequently brought from Pegu at a cheaper rate than can be afforded by the merchants who trade in this article to Rékapalle.'

[1] See Chapter XI, p. 162.

CUSTOMS.

The only land-customs now collected are those on goods passing into the district from the French Settlement of Yanam. These are levied at two stations (chowkis) established at Nílapalli and Injaram, on the east and west frontiers of the Yanam Settlement. The tariff of rates in force is the same as that for sea-borne imports from foreign countries. The only articles which are ever charged an export duty in this Presidency are paddy and rice; and by an arrangement entered into many years ago the export of these to Yanam, in quantities sufficient for the consumption of its inhabitants, is permitted free of duty.

Sea-customs.

There is only one considerable port in the district, that of Cocanada, and there a regular sea-customs etablishment is maintained. Coringa is also open to foreign trade, but the business done is very small. The sea-customs work is supervised by the ordinary establishment of the Salt, Abkári and Customs department. The small sub-ports of Uppáda and Bendamúrlanka are open only to coasting trade.

INCOME-TAX.

The Income-tax Act does not apply to the Agency tracts. Figures for the rest of the district will be found in the separate Appendix to this volume. The incidence of the tax per head of the population in the present district in the triennium ending 1904–05 was as high as one anna six pies, against 10½ pies in the mufassal districts as a whole. Madura and the exceptional case of the Nilgiris were the only areas in which the figure was higher. Of the various taluks, the incidence was highest in Tuni, Cocanada and Rajahmundry, and lowest in Pithápuram and Rámachandrapuram. The great wealth of the delta taluks comes from agricultural pursuits, the income from which is not liable to tax, and the incidence in several of these is low.

STAMPS.

The revenue from stamps is very large in proportion to the population, the receipts per mille of the inhabitants from judicial stamps being higher in only two other districts and those from non-judicial stamps in only four others. Of the total stamp revenue, by far the largest amount is paid by the Cocanada and Rajahmundry taluks, owing no doubt to the existence of the Judge's and Sub-Judge's courts at their head-quarters. Considerable contributions are also made by Amalápuram and Peddápuram, and, to a less extent, by Rámachandrapuram. In the Agency, the revenue from stamps is exceedingly small, especially in Yellavaram and Chódavaram. The Collector (and, during his absence from head-quarters, the Treasury Deputy Collector) have been empowered to affix impressed labels to documents presented by the public.

CHAPTER XIII.

ADMINISTRATION OF JUSTICE.

EARLY METHODS—Under native rule—Under the Chiefs and Councils. THE PRESENT SYSTEM—In the plains—In the Agency. CIVIL JUSTICE—Existing Courts—Amount of litigation—Registration. CRIMINAL JUSTICE—The various Courts—Crime—The Yánádis or Nakkalas—Other criminal classes. POLICE—Former systems—The existing force. JAILS.

CHAP. XIII. EARLY METHODS.

UNDER native rule, and also in the early days of British administration, the regular courts of justice were few. The Committee of Circuits,[1] in its report of December 1786, describes as follows the system which was in force:—

Under native rule.

'During the Mogul Government there were courts of justice established at Rajahmundry and Ellore, where Kazis administered justice according to Muhammadan law. The Foujidars[2] reserved to themselves the infliction of capital punishments and the determination on causes of considerable property. There was also at each place a Cutval (kotwál) with an establishment of peons to superintend the police, and a Nurkee whose duty it was to regulate the price of provisions.

'Of these nothing but the names remain, and the inhabitants are without any Courts of Justice. Trifling disputes are settled by the Karnams and head inhabitants. Matters of greater consequence are referred to the Renter or the Chief and Council; but the distance at which some of the farms are from the seat of Government renders an appeal to the latter troublesome and expensive. For heinous crimes (which are seldom perpetrated) the only imprisonment at present inflicted by cur Government is confinement of the culprit's person.'

Under the Chiefs and Councils.

In the early days of British rule the only civil court having any jurisdiction within the district was that of the Chief and Council at Masulipatam, and the activities of this were confined almost exclusively to the limits of Masulipatam town and factory. 'Of criminal jurisdiction there was none. There was no law providing for the infliction of death or any other penalty. . . . The Chiefs in Council had very little authority in their districts; and of course every zamindar could interfere in the direct administration of justice.' A brief but vivid picture of the lawlessness which naturally

[1] See Chapter XI, p. 162.

[2] *I.e.*, The Faujdārs, sometimes called also Nawábs, who were in charge of each of the five Northern Circars.

CHAP. XIII. EARLY METHODS.

resulted from this state of things is afforded by a contemporary account of the condition in 1789 of the port of Coringa, then a busy place. There, owing to the number of ships and sailors that visited the port and the 'general want of police,' fighting, thefts and murder were common. 'When any wrong is done the injured party has no one of sufficient authority to apply to for redress. Every one here is judge of his own cause. The Honorable Company's Resident lives at Comprapollam (Sunkarpálaiyam near Injaram), eight miles off; and when applied to on such occasions urges want of due authority to remedy abuses and to take cognizance of offences.' [1]

THE PRESENT SYSTEM. In the plains.

The beginning of the last century withessed a salutary change in the state of things. The supine Chiefs and Councils had been replaced in 1794 by Collectors; and in 1802 Lord Cornwallis' system of judicial administration was introduced into this Presidency and a Zilla Court was established at Rajahmundry. It was subordinate to a peripatetic Provincial Court at Masulipatam, the judges of which used to come on circuit from time to time and hold criminal sessions. In the same year (1802) native commissioners were appointed to hear petty civil suits. A few years later they received the designation of district munsifs, which, though their powers have been much increased, they still bear. In 1827 Auxiliary Courts were established and native judges (later called Principal Sudder Amins) were appointed with extensive authority. In 1843 the Zilla and Provincial Courts were abolished and a Civil and a Subordinate Court were created in their stead at Rajahmundry. The latter was abolished in 1859; but in 1873, when the existing District Courts Act became law, the name of Subordinate Courts was given, as elsewhere, to the courts of the Principal Sudder Amins, and the chief court in the district was designated the District and Sessions Court. The Sub-Court at Rajahmundry was temporarily abolished in 1877.

In the Agency.

In the Agency, both civil and criminal justice are differently administered. This tract consists of the deputy tahsildars' divisions of Pólavaram, Yellavaram and Chódavaram and the taluk of Bhadráchalam, all of which are remote tracts covered with hill and jungle, sparsely provided with communications, shunned by the dwellers in the plains, and inhabited by backward tribes who are most illiterate and ignorant of the ways of the world, and yet ready to go out on the warpath if once any of their many peculiar

[1] *Selections from the Records of the Madras Government* (Madras, 1855), xix, 24.

CHAP. XIII. THE PRESENT SYSTEM.

susceptibilities are wounded. In country, and to people, such as these, much of the ordinary law of the land is unsuited, and a special system has consequently been introduced.

A precedent existed in the case of the Agencies of Vizagapatam and Ganjám. In consequence of the unceasing turbulence in them which led at length to the appointment, in 1832, of a Special Commissioner, with special powers, to restore order, these two tracts were excluded, by Act XXIV of 1839, from the operation of much of the ordinary law and were placed under the direct administration of the Collectors of those districts, who were endowed with special and extraordinary powers within them in their capacity as 'Agents to the Governor.'

A similar method of administration was extended to the greater part of the present Gódávari Agency in 1879, advantage being taken of the Scheduled Districts Act (India Act XIV of 1874) to constitute an Agency in the then Bhadráchalam and Rékapalle taluks, which make up the present Bhadráchalam taluk, and 'the Rampa country,' which is practically the present Chódavaram division.

The Agency thus formed has been three times extended; namely, in 1881, when the muttas of Dutcharti and Guditéru (now in Yellavaram division) were transferred to it from the Vizagapatam Agency; in 1883,[1] when the villages of the resumed mansab of Jaddangi and large portions of the Pólavaram division were added; and in 1891,[2] when the Pólavaram and Yellavaram divisions attained substantially their present shape.

In the Agency thus constituted the Collector of the district, in his capacity as Government Agent, is both District Magistrate and District and Sessions Judge; the tahsildar and deputy tahsildars have minor civil jurisdiction within their respective charges, corresponding (with certain modifications) to that of district munsifs; and the Agency Deputy Collector of Pólavaram and the Divisional Officer at Bhadráchalam, in their capacity as Assistant Agents, hear appeals from them and have powers similar to those of Subordinate Judges. The tahsildars and deputy tahsildars (and the taluk sarishtadar at Bhadráchalam) are second-class magistrates, and the Divisional Officers, as elsewhere, are first-class magistrates; but appeals from the decisions of the latter lie to the Collector as Agency Sessions Judge. The village munsifs have the ordinary criminal, but no civil, powers. The

[1] See notification in the *Gazette of India* for 1883, i, 265.
[2] See notification in the *Gazette of India* for 1891, i, 248.

CHAP. XIII. THE PRESENT SYSTEM.

procedure in civil suits is not governed by the usual Civil Procedure Code, but by a simpler set of rules framed under section 6 of the Scheduled Districts Act. Rules under this same enactment have also been drawn up for the guidance of the Agent in other branches of the administration.

CIVIL JUSTICE. Existing Courts.

Outside the Agency, the civil tribunals of the district are of the usual four grades; namely, the courts of village and district munsifs, the Sub-Court and the District Court.

District munsifs' courts have been established at Rajahmundry, Cocanada, Peddápuram and Amalápuram. That at Amalápuram has a heavier file than any of the others.

The Sub-Court is stationed at Cocanada. It was established in 1874. Another Sub-Court was in existence at Rajahmundry for a few months in 1895; began regularly working there in 1903; but was abolished in 1905.

The District Court is held at Rajahmundry. Before the district was reduced in size by the transfer to Kistna of the taluks south of the Gódávari, the file of this court was very heavy. In 1902 the number of suits instituted in, and of appeals disposed of by, it was greater than in any other District Court in the Presidency.

Amount of litigation.

As in other wealthy districts, the amount of litigation in Gódávari is great. In 1902, in the district as then constituted but excluding the Agency, more suits were instituted per unit of the population than in any other in the Presidency excepting Tanjore, North Malabar and Tinnevelly. In the Agency, on the other hand, litigation is rarer than in any other tract in Madras except the Agencies of Vizagapatam and Ganjám.

Registration.

The registration of assurances is effected in the usual manner. A District Registrar is stationed at Cocanada and sixteen sub-registrars are located at Rajahmundry; at Amalápuram, Kottapéta and Mummidivaram in Amalápuram taluk; at Rázóle in Nagaram; at Peddápuram and Prattipádu in Peddápuram; at Rámachandrapuram, Drákshárámam, Álamúr and Bikkavólu in Rámachandrapuram; at Cocanada and Coringa in Cocanada taluk; and at Pólavaram, Pithápuram and Tuni. There are no sub-registrars in the Chódavaram or Yellavaram Agency tracts but in Bhadráchalam the Registration Act was extended to certain villages in 1906 and the taluk sheristadar acts as sub-registrar.

CRIMINAL JUSTICE. The various Courts.

The criminal tribunals are of the same classes as elsewhere. The village magistrates have the usual powers, both within and outside the Agency. Bench Courts, invested with third-class powers to try offences under the Towns Nuisances Act, the Municipalities Act and the conservancy clauses of the

CHAP. XIII. CRIMINAL JUSTICE.

Police Act, have been established at Rajahmundry and Cocanada. The latter also tries cases of assault and voluntarily causing hurt under the Penal Code.

All the tahsildars and deputy tahsildars in the district have second-class magisterial powers, but in Amalápuram, Cocanada, Peddápuram, Rajahmundry and Rámachandrapuram there are stationary sub-magistrates, and the tahsildars of these taluks hear few cases. At Bhadráchalam, also, there is a second-class magistrate in addition to the tahsildar. Deputy tahsildars with second-class magisterial powers are stationed at Kottapéta in Amalápuram taluk, Coringa in Cocanada taluk, Prattipádu in Peddápuram taluk and Álamúr in Rámachandrapuram and independent deputy tahsildars with similar authority at Pithápuram and Tuni. As elsewhere, appeals from the second-class magistrates, and practically the whole of the first-class cases arising in the district, are decided by the Divisional Officers, who are severally stationed at Cocanada, Peddápuram, Rajahmundry, Pólavaram, and Bhadráchalam. The District Magistrate and the Sessions Judge have the usual jurisdiction, except that, as already mentioned, the latter has no powers in the Agency, his place in that area being taken by the District Magistrate.

Crime.

Gódávari occupies a rather unenviable position among the Madras districts in respect of the total amount of registered crime which occurs within it, but a very large proportion of the offences committed are common thefts, and another considerable percentage are simple house-breakings. In crime of the graver kinds—robberies, dacoities and murders—its position is not exceptional, and indeed dacoities are rare outside Pólavaram.

The Yánádis or Nakkalas.

The nearest approach to a criminal tribe is afforded by the Yánádis or Nakkalas. These people are called indifferently by either of these two names, though they themselves resent the appellation Nakkala. This word seems to be derived from *nakka*, a jackal, since the tribe is expert in catching these animals and eats them. The Nakkalas are generally of slight physique, dark of complexion and very dirty in their habits. At Pithápuram there are some of them who are more strongly built and perhaps spring from a different strain. On the register of criminal gangs kept by the police there are at the present time 114 men, 121 women and 236 children belonging to this caste. The most troublesome sections of them are those in the Rámachandrapuram and Peddápuram taluks.

The Nakkalas are by nature wanderers and dwellers in fields and scrub jungle, who make a scanty living by catching jackals, hares, rats and tortoises, by gathering honey, and by

CHAP. XIII. CRIMINAL JUSTICE.

finding the caches of grain stored up by field-mice. To people with such slender means of subsistence the gains of petty pilfering offer a strong temptation; but the Nakkalas seldom commit any of the bolder kinds of crime, though now and again they have been known to rise to burglary, more rarely to robbery, and sometimes even to dacoity. Of late years most of them have settled down permanently in villages. They live in very small huts made of palmyra-leaves. They add to their earnings from their hereditary occupations the wages to be earned by light cooly work in the villages, and are consequently looked upon by the rest of the community as rather an acquisition when cheap labour is in demand. They are sometimes employed as horse-keepers by subordinate officials; and their women are very useful as sweepers, since, though they are exceedingly dirty in their persons, they are not considered to carry ceremonial pollution. If treated well, they live in this hand-to-mouth fashion and give no trouble to the authorities, and their present unfortunate notoriety as a criminal tribe is largely due to the performances of one notorious gang of them in Rámachandrapuram taluk. This gang, led first by one well-known criminal and later by another, consisted of about fifteen men and lived an entirely nomadic life, subsisting on the proceeds of its thefts and burglaries. It has now been broken up, ten of its members being in jail (most of them on long sentences) and the others, with one exception, being in hiding; and probably the criminal propensities of the Nakkalas will henceforth be less in evidence.

Other criminal classes.

Three other classes of people, namely, some of the Málas, the 'Pachayappas,' and the 'Peddinti Gollas,' have pronounced criminal tendencies. Two small sets of Málas in the central delta (one in the limits of Kottapéta station, and the other in those of Nagaram station) have a decided turn for burglary. A number of convictions are on record against them. The Pachayappas consist of six wandering gangs, containing 68 registered male members, who are constantly on the move and are under police supervision. They originally came from the direction of Guntúr. They ostensibly live by begging, but there is little doubt that the proceeds of crime contribute to maintain the men in the robust condition they exhibit and to support the crowd of children who belong to them. Cases are from time to time established against them, and some of them have been convicted of burglary and theft. The Peddinti Gollas comprise four gangs who appeared in the district in 1902. They are said to have come from Kurnool, and to

CHAP. XIII. CRIMINAL JUSTICE.

have committed a large dacoity in Kistna. Only thirteen male members of these now remain.

POLICE. Former systems.

Up to the time of the permanent settlement in 1802, such police as existed were under the orders of the renters and zamindars, and were in some cases remunerated by grants of land on favourable tenure. In the larger towns kotwáls with separate establishments were maintained. At the permanent settlement, the zamindars' control over the police was withdrawn, and Government assumed the responsibility of enforcing law and order. In the hill country, which was excluded from the permanent settlement, the muttadars were, however, still expected to keep order within their muttas, and this responsibility is even now insisted upon. The muttadars of Chódavaram and Yellavaram are bound by their sanads to 'afford every assistance to the Sircar in maintaining quiet and order, by giving timely information of any disturbance or offence against the laws, and apprehending and delivering up to the authorities robbers, rebels and other bad characters.'[1] As a matter of fact they perform this service indifferently, and are of little use in suppressing or detecting crime.

The existing force.

The existing police force, which like that in other districts was constituted by Act XXIV of 1859, is in charge of a District Superintendent stationed at Rajahmundry, aided by an Assistant Superintendent at Bhadráchalam who has immediate control over the police in the Agency.

Statistics of the force, and of its distribution among the various taluks, will be found in the separate Appendix. A reserve about one hundred strong under an inspector and two sergeants is maintained at Rajahmundry, and consists of picked men, better armed and drilled than the others, who are qualified to deal with disturbances. As a rule the inspectors' divisions are included within the limits of only one taluk or revenue division, but a few unimportant exceptions occur. Dowlaishweram in Rajahmundry taluk, for example, is included in the limits of the Álamúr station, and Pithápuram lies entirely in the Súriyaraopéta (Cocanada) police division.

Besides the regular police, there are 477 talaiyáris or rural constables, who, as in other districts, are required to afford help to the police, especially by reporting the presence of suspects within their villages and the occurrence of crime, and by aiding in the detection of offences committed within their limits. They are reported to be of little real assistance.

[1] See Chapter XI, p. 177.

POLICE.

At Chódavaram is located the Special Hill Reserve, who are armed with Martini-Henry rifles and are kept up primarily to cope with any overt disturbances which may occur in the wild Agency country. They number about 40 men, are in charge of the divisional inspector, and perform the ordinary duties of the station.

JAILS

At Rajahmundry is one of the eight Central Jails of the Presidency. It was established in 1864, is constructed on the radiating principle, and will hold 1,089 criminal, and 20 civil, prisoners. Cellular accommodation has been provided for 400 convicts, and the rest are kept in wards. The convicts are employed in a variety of industries, manufacturing, among other articles, carpets, coarse woollen blankets, sandals, tin and brass work, furniture of various kinds, and fabrics woven from cotton, such as sheeting, rugs, table-cloths, napkins, etc. Fly shuttles are used in some of the looms. They enable double the ordinary quantity of work to be accomplished, but have not yet been rendered suitable for the finer fabrics.

Thirteen sub-jails exist in the district; namely, one at each of the taluk head-quarters and at the deputy tahsildars' stations of Álamúr (Rámachandrapuram taluk), Kottapéta (Amalápuram), Prattipádu (Peddápuram), Pithápuram, Tuni and Pólavaram. These have accommodation for 186 prisoners in all.

CHAPTER XIV.

LOCAL SELF-GOVERNMENT.

THE LOCAL BOARDS—The Unions—Finances of the Boards. THE TWO MUNICIPALITIES—Cocanada municipality—Rajahmundry municipality.

CHAP. XIV
THE LOCAL BOARDS.

OUTSIDE the two municipalities of Cocanada and Rajahmundry referred to below, and excluding Bhadráchalam taluk in the Agency, local affairs (roads, hospitals, schools and sanitation) are in the hands of the District Board and four taluk boards subordinate to it. The areas in charge of these latter have been changed from time to time, and the most recent alteration was effected in April 1905. The four boards are now those of Cocanada, in charge of the Cocanada taluk and the Pithápuram and Tuni divisions; Peddápuram, with jurisdiction over the taluks of Peddápuram and Rámachandrapuram; Rajahmundry, comprising the Rajahmundry, Amalápuram and Nagaram taluks; and Pólavaram, which administers matters in the Agency divisions of Pólavaram, Chódavaram and Yellavaram.

Prior to 1902 none of the Agency tracts were included within the operation of the Local Boards Act, and the roads, educational and medical institutions, and sanitation within them were in charge of the Revenue authorities, aided by advice from the Public Works and other expert departments. In 1902 the whole of the Agency as it then existed was brought under the Act; but in 1905 [1] Bhadráchalam was withdrawn again from its operation and is to be managed henceforth on the same system as was in force before 1902. The taluk is remote, thinly-populated and covered with jungle; and the income derivable within it from the ordinary sources of taxation provided for by the Local Boards Act is quite insufficient to meet the expenditure which is necessary. Heavy contributions towards its local needs have consequently always been made from Provincial funds. The same state of things exists in the three Agency divisions which make up the charge of the present Pólavaram taluk board, and a similar contribution to its exchequer has been necessary to save it from insolvency.

[1] See G.O. No. 227 L., dated 27th February 1905.

The Unions.

Fifteen of the larger towns in the district have been constituted unions with the usual powers and functions. These are Dowlaishweram, Amalápuram and Kottapéta under the Rajahmundry taluk board; Peddápuram, Jagapatinagaram, Yelésvaram, Jaggampéta, Rámachandrapuram, Drákshárámam, Mandapéta and Bikkavólu under the Peddápuram board; and Gollamámidáda, Samalkot, Pithápuram and Tuni under the taluk board of Cocanada. The chief item in their receipts is (as elsewhere) the house-tax, which is everywhere levied at the maximum rates. The average tax per house for 1905-06 is estimated to work out to As. 12-1.

Finances of the Boards.

The separate Appendix to this volume contains statistics of the receipts and expenditure of the various local boards. The chief source of income is, as usual, the land cess, which is levied at the ordinary rate of one anna in every rupee of the land assessment. The chief item of expenditure is the upkeep of the roads and the medical and educational institutions. These have already been referred to in Chapters VII, IX, and X respectively.

THE TWO MUNICIPALITIES.

The only two municipal towns are Cocanada and Rajahmundry. In the separate Appendix appear particulars of the receipts and expenditure of their councils.

Cocanada municipality.

Cocanada was one of the municipalities established under the first regular municipal act (Madras Act X of 1865) and the council was constituted in 1866. It now consists of twenty members of whom eight are nominated and twelve elected. The privilege of electing its own chairman was conferred upon the council in 1886, was withdrawn in 1893, but was restored again in 1897. The appointment of a paid secretary was sanctioned in 1899. He is selected by the municipal council subject to the approval of Government.

Several considerable permanent improvements have been effected in the town by the municipality. First in importance come the Victoria water-works, which were completed in June 1903. The water is obtained from the Samalkot canal, and a large reservoir to contain two months' supply has been excavated in the water-works premises. The scheme was designed to supply 400,000 gallons of water per diem (at the rate of 10 gallons per head of the population of the town) and the supply is expected to be perennial. The water is drawn from the reservoir just mentioned through filter beds into a second reservoir, and is thence distributed throughout the town by cast-iron pipes and fountains. Three Worthington engines of 10 horse power each are employed in the works. The cost of the scheme was estimated at Rs. 4,66,200, but actually

CHAP. XIV. THE TWO MUNICIPALITIES.

amounted to only Rs. 4,44,800. Of this sum Rs. 1,44,500 were lent by Government. The scheme was carried out by the Public Works department.

Other permanent improvements effected by the council are the construction, at an outlay of Rs. 18,137, of the bridge across the Yeléru; the revetting of the harbour creek for a length of some 270 yards at a cost of Rs. 8,000 in 1902-03 and the reclamation and laying out of a considerable strip of ground formerly covered by the creek; the building of three public markets, the two larger of which cost Rs. 15,000; and the erection of two slaughter-houses costing Rs. 4,000 and of three municipal school-houses at an average cost of some Rs. 1,500 apiece. The clock tower near the bridge was constructed by a private gentleman some 20 years ago, but the municipality contributed Rs. 1,000 to its erection and it now has charge of the building.

No drainage scheme has yet been prepared for Cocanada, but a portion of the town is served by the main sewer leading into the harbour creek which was constructed by the Public Works department at a cost of Rs. 10,000 out of Provincial funds some years ago. Some smaller branch drains lead into this, and the municipality has kept both these and the main sewer in repair at considerable cost.

The council's chief contributions to the medical and educational institutions within the town include the aiding of ten primary schools, the management of a lower secondary and twelve more primary schools, and the upkeep of a hospital and dispensary.

Rajahmundry municipality.

The municipality at Rajahmundry was also founded in 1866. The council originally consisted of ten members, but since 1895 the number has been eighteen. The right of electing some of the members was granted in 1884, and twelve councillors and the chairman are now appointed by election. A paid secretary was first entertained in 1897-98. He is selected by the council, subject to the approval of Government.

Very few permanent improvements of any magnitude have been executed by the municipality. Drinking-water is obtained from the Gódávari river and the Kambala tank, and nothing of note has been done from municipal funds to improve the supply. Similarly no considerable improvement in the drainage has been effected or worked out. Three markets have been constructed and two slaughter-houses. A choultry founded in 1873 by Mr. H. Morris, a former Judge, and called by his name was completed by the municipality in 1874 at a cost of Rs. 1,500. A rest-house for homeless poor has been constructed at an outlay of Rs. 500, and additions are being made to it in order to accommodate lepers and persons suffering from other incurable diseases.

The council has partly supported the hospital in the town since 1871, and keeps up four upper primary, four lower primary, and one lower secondary school. It also maintains the Morris choultry, two other small institutions called the Kambham and Durbha choultries, and a travellers' bungalow.

Government have sanctioned Rs. 16,000 for revetting the river bank to prevent further erosion, which was becoming alarming, and a bund to protect the town from inundation during heavy floods is in contemplation.

CHAPTER XV.

GAZETTEER.

AMALÁPURAM TALUK—Amalápuram—Ambájipéta—Ayinavalli—Bandárulanka—Bendamúrlanka—Gannavaram—Késanakurru—Mandapalli—Muramalla—Palivela—Pérúru—Ráli—Vádapalli—Vánapalli—Vyágrésvarapuram. COCANADA TALUK—Bhímavaram—Chollangi—Cocanada—Coringa—Gollapálaiyam—Injaram—Nílapalli—Samalkot—Sarpavaram—Tállarévu—Yanam. NAGARAM TALUK—Antarvédi—Jagannapéta—Kadali—Nagaram—Rájavólu—Sivakódu—Tátipáka. PEDDAPURAM TALUK—Annavaram—Dháramallápuram—Jagammapéta—Kándrakóta—Kattipúdi—Kirlampúdi—Peddápuram—Prattipádu—Rágampéta—Rangampéta—Tallúru—Tótapalli—Víravaram—Yelésvaram. PITHÁPURAM DIVISION—Chandurti—Kóttapalli—Múlapéta—Pithápuram—Ponnáda—Uppáda. RAJAHMUNDRY TALUK—Dowlaishweram—Gókavaram—Kórukonda—Kottapalli—Rajahmundry. RÁMACHANDRAPURAM TALUK—Bikkavólu—Drákshárámam—Gangavaram—Kótipalli—Márédípáka—Rámachandrapuram—Rámaghattálu—Végayammapéta. TUNI DIVISION—Bendapúdi—Hamsavaram—Kottapalli—Tallúru—Tátipáka—Tétagunta—Tuni. BHADRACHALAM TALUK—Bhadráchalam—Dummagúdem—Gundála—Kumárasvámigúdem—Kunnavaram—Parnasála—Rékapalle—Srí Rámagiri. CHODAVARAM DIVISION—Bandapalli—Birampalli—Bodulúru—Bolagonda—Chavala—Chidugúru—Chódavaram—Chopakonda—Dandangi—Dorachintalapálem—Geddáda—Kákúru—Kondamodalu—Kundáda—Marriváda—Musurumilli—Nádunúru—Nimmalapálem—Pálem—Pámuléru—Péta—Rampa—Sirigindalapádu—Tádapélli—Tunnúru—Vádapalli—Velagapalli—Válamúru—Vémulakonda. POLAVARAM DIVISION—Gangólu—Gútála—Jangareddigúdem—Páta Pattisam—Pólavaram—Táduváyi. YELLAVARAM DIVISION—Addatígela—Anigéru—Dutcharti—Gurtédu—Jaddangi—Kóta—Móhanapuram—Nelipúdi—Pandrapóle—Rámavaram—Vírabhadrapuram.

AMALÁPURAM TALUK.

CHAP. XV. AMALÁPURAM.

AMALÁPURAM taluk is a triangular island enclosed between the Vasishta, Vainatéyam and Gautami branches of the Gódávari and the sea. With the smaller Nagaram island, which is similarly bounded, it comprises the whole of the central delta of the Gódávari river. Statistics regarding it will be found in the separate Appendix to this volume. It is the most populous taluk in the district and the density of its inhabitants to the square mile (548) is well above the average of the plain taluks. Most of the wet land is irrigated by the central delta canal, but the area under wells, hough not considerable, is far greater than in any other taluk in the district.[1] Of the classified area, 87 per cent. is made up of

[1] See Chapter IV, p. 89.

alluv.al earth and the rest of arenaceous soils. The average rainfall is the highest in the district, namely 44·88 inches in the year.

The taluk is an agricultural area, and boasts few other industries. Dévángas weave white cloths in fair quantities in several villages, but the industry has greatly declined since the days when Bendamúrlanka was a busy port and one of the outlets for the great trade of the East India Company in cotton piece-goods. A large cattle-fair, known beyond the district, takes place at Ambájipéta. A number of places of local religious interest exist; but only two of these, namely Vánapalli and Vádapalli, are known much beyond the limits of the taluk. Pérúru is the home of a class of Bráhmans who have immigrated from the Tamil country and are called Kóna Síma Drávidas. Relics of the Jains are found at Nédunúru and Átréyapuram; and the large wells so common in the taluk are popularly ascribed to the followers of that creed.

Amalápuram.

Amalápuram, the head-quarters of the taluk and a union, is situated on the main canal of the central delta 38 miles south-east of Rajahmundry. Population 9,510. It contains the offices of a tahsildar, sub-registrar, stationary sub-magistrate and district munsif, a travellers' bungalow, a coronation rest-house for natives, a local fund hospital (founded 1880) and high school, and a police-station.

Popular legends say that Amalápuram was the capital of the king of Pánchála, the father-in-law of the Pándava brothers; and the taluk is known throughout the district as the 'Pánchála country.' Another name for it is the *Kóna Síma*, or the 'end country.' The town contains two temples of local repute. One was built for an idol of Venkatasvámi which was found there some years ago by a man of the place, who, as usual, stated that he was told of its existence in a dream; the other is a shrine to the serpent god, Subbaráyudu, the festival at which, held in Márgasiram (December-January) is fairly attended. A little weaving of white cloths goes on, counts as fine as 150s being used for the best work, and a little wood-carving of a good class.

Ambájipéta.

Ambájipéta: A hamlet of Máchavaram (population 5,661) which lies five miles west by north of Amalápuram. Contains a police-station and is famous for its large cattle-fair, which is held every Wednesday and is visited even by buyers from other districts. The place is a centre for the manufacture of cocoanut ropes and oil, and a large number of general traders live there.

CHAP. XV. AMALÁPURAM.

Ayinavalli.

Ayinavalli: Eight miles north of Amalápuram, population 3,363. Its temple to the belly-god Siddhi Vináyaka is well known to the people of this and adjoining districts, and vows are frequently made therein, scarcely a day passing when pilgrims do not visit it to discharge their obligations by breaking cocoanuts before the god. The temple is supposed to have been built to propitiate the belly-god by Daksha, the father-in-law of Siva, before he performed the famous *yágam* at Drákshárámam referred to in the account of that place on p. 250 below. Ayinavalli is also well known to natives as the birth-place of two famous Sanskrit pandits, Bulusu Achayya and his son Pápayya Sástri, who died not long ago.

It has a hamlet called Muktésvaram ('the place of beatitude') or Kshana Muktésvaram ('the place of instantaneous beatitude') and the names are accounted for by a local legend. The wife of a sage, says this story, was seduced by some celestial being and cursed in consequence by her husband. She purified herself by a bath in the Gódávari and took to a life of contemplation. Ráma, when returning from Lanka, took compassion on her forlorn state and persuaded Siva to give her *mukti* or beatitude.

Bandárulanka.

Bandárulanka : Four miles west by north of Amalápuram. Population 2,796. The village is known for the manufacture of excellent white cloths. Some 200 Déványa houses are engaged in the industry, and use thread of the finer counts, up to 130s.

Bendamúrlanka.

Bendamúrlanka: Twelve miles by road south-south-west of Amalápuram. It is a hamlet of Komaragiripatnam (population 5,757) and contains a police-station, a travellers' bungalow and a vernacular lower secondary school for girls. It is situated at the mouth of the Vainatéyam branch of the Gódávari, and was selected as the site of an English factory in 1751. This was seized without resistance by Bussy in 1757, but was recovered after the battle of Condore. It was once an important centre for the trade with Europe in cotton piece-goods. Bendamúrlanka is still technically a port; but has no harbour and has not been visited by any ships for a long time.

Gannavaram.

Gannavaram: Nine miles west by north of Amalápuram. Population 2,101. Contains a small market and a travellers' bungalow. It gives its name to the fine aqueduct which crosses the Vainatéyam Gódávari there and is described in Chapter IV. According to the local legend, it was at Gannavaram that the sage Vainatéya stole some of the water of the Vasishta Gódávari to make the river of his own which goes by his name. The sage Vasishta cursed the Vainatéyam, and a bath in it is only sanctifying if taken on a Sunday. The lingam in the Siva temple is said to have been brought from the Nerbudda river by the kite Garuda, and the supposed marks of the bird's claws are pointed out on it.

Késanakurru.

Késanakurru: Eleven miles north-east of Amalápuram in a straight line. Population 3,556. A bath in its tank is supposed to confer religious merit. The sage Vyása, who (see p. 250) is said to have founded Drákshárámam, once, say the local legends, intended to establish a second Benares at Késanakurru; but heard a voice saying 'Kási nakuru,' 'do not make a Benares.' He accordingly founded Drákshárámam instead; but Késanakurru was named after the words of the divine warning, which have since become corrupted to their present form.

Mandapalli.

Mandapalli: Fourteen miles north-west of Amalápuram. Population 542. The god at the Siva temple here, Mandésvara, is bathed in oil every Saturday; and a common form of vow consists in a promise to provide the oil for this bath. Saturdays coinciding with the second day before full-moon day are particularly propitious for the fulfilment of this vow.

Muramalla.

Muramalla: Thirteen miles north-east of Amalápuram. Population 1,448. The Siva temple here is visited by numerous pilgrims, and the usual vow taken by the devout is a promise to celebrate the marriage of the god. Hardly a day, it is said, passes without this ceremony being performed; and there is a proverb to the effect that at Muramalla there is a marriage every day and the garlands are always green. The temple is rich, and is said to have been founded and endowed 'about 500 years ago' by the widow of a Kóna Síma Drávida Bráhman.

Palivela.

Palivela: Twelve miles north-west of Amalápuram. Population 7,509. The Koppésvara temple here contains a number of inscriptions, some of which have been copied by the Government Epigraphist (Nos. 498 to 505 of 1893). The oldest records a gift by a minister of one of the Vélanándu family and is dated 1172 A.D. None of the others are earlier than the fourteenth century. One on the east wall of the shrine belongs to the time of the great Kákatíya king Pratápa Rudra, and is dated in 1317, or not long before his fall.[1] The *nandi* in front of the temple is popularly declared to have been mutilated by order of Aurangzeb.

In former times dancing-girls used to sleep three nights at the commencement of their career in the inner shrine, so as to

[1] See Government Epigraphist's Annual Report for 1894, pp. 22 and 23.

CHAP. XV. AMALÁPURAM.

be embraced by the god. But one of them, it is said, disappeared one night, and the practice has ceased. The funeral pyre of every girl of the dancing-girl (Sání) caste dying in the village should be lit with fire brought from the temple. The same practice is found in the Srírangam temple near Trichinopoly.

Palivela forms part of the union of Kottapéta (population 10,369), in which Vádapálaiyam and Kammareddipálaiyam are also included. Kottapéta contains the offices of a sub-registrar, a deputy-tahsildar and sub-magistrate, a local fund dispensary (founded 1892), a police-station, a small market, and an English lower secondary school for boys The travellers' bungalow is in Palivela itself.

Pérúru.

Pérúru: Five miles south-west of Amalápuram. Population 5,864. Contains a Sanskrit school. The place is noteworthy as being the home of a colony of Tamil Bráhmans, called Kóna Síma Drávidas, who came, at some date unknown, from Valangimán near Kumbakónam in Tanjore district. The story of their emigration is recounted (with impossible details) in the village itself and is also known in Madras. They no longer speak Tamil, but their village, both in appearance and in general arrangement, is so like a village of the south that it is popularly declared that if a Tanjore man could be suddenly transported thither and set down in the middle of it, he would think he was in his native country.

The original emigrants are said to have been fifteen families of twelve *gôtras*, seven of which belonged to the Vadama, and five to the Brahacharnam, subdivision of the Tamil Bráhmans.

They first settled at Ráli, but difficulties arising, they eventually obtained from a rája a grant of as much land as an elephant could traverse in a given space of time. Thus they secured possession of the village of Pérúru. They increased and multiplied, and many of them emigrated to Ganjám and Vizagapatam, where they call themselves 'Pérúru Drávidas.' They are not popular in the district, and stories in disparagement of them are common. The part they play in the festival at Antarvédi in Nagaram taluk is referred to in the account of that place below.

Pérúru, like Amalápuram, is connected by legend with the Mahábhárata, for it is believed that the tank in the hamlet of Chindádu Garuvu is the identical sheet of water in which Arjuna saw the reflection of the flying fish which he shot in order to win the hand of Draupadi. A bath in this tank on the four Sundays succeeding the New Year's day is considered to have a sanctifying effect.

Numbers of large and ancient revetted wells exist in the village, and are known as the Reddis' wells. The story goes that a Bráhman who had the philosopher's stone was murdered by a Reddi, and that his ghost haunted the murderer and gave him no peace until he built a number of large wells at which it might quench its thirst.

The village is a centre of the export of cocoanuts and cocoaunt oil. One family of. Múchis does some good wood-carving.

Ráli.

Ráli: Twenty miles north-west of Amalápuram, population 4,045. Contains a travellers' bungalow. A section of the Dowlaishweram anicut was originally called the Ráli anicut, and the name occurs frequently in the early accounts of the work. The village was once the head-quarters of a taluk. It is also said to have been one of the first halting-places of the Kóna Síma Drávida Bráhmans just referred to. There is a 'Tamil street' *(Arava vídi)* in it even now. The image of Vishnu in the local temple is represented as half male and half female, and the legend connects this fact with the well-known story of how the *asuras* and *dévatas* churned the sea to obtain the nectar of immortality. When the nectar rose to the top, Vishnu appeared in the form of a beautiful woman, so as to divert the attention of the *asuras*, was seen by Siva and was pursued by him as far as Ráli.

Vádapalli.

Vádapalli: Three miles north by east of Ráli. Population 915. It is well known for its temple to Venkata or Venkanna, which is considered by the people of this neighbourhood to be almost as sacred as the famous shrine of the same god at Tirupati in North Arcot. The festival to commemorate the marriage of the deity lasts for five days in Chaitra (April-May), is very largely attended, and is a great occasion for the performance of vows.

Vánapalli.

Vánapalli: Eight miles north-north-west of Amalápuram. Population 4,686. A large festival in honour of the village goddess Pallálamma takes place there every year. Marvellous stories are told about this deity: the size and age of her image alter according to the size and age of the worshipper; it sweats profusely and its clothes have to be wrung out every morning; 'an engineer officer' (name unknown) was turned blind some 40 years ago for entertaining the idea of demolishing the temple to make room for a canal; and the stone jackal in the shrine is one which used to defile the holy precincts every night, and was petrified in consequence.

CHAP. XV. AMALÁPURAM.

At the great festival, which lasts for a week in the month of Chaitra (April-May), a hook-swinging takes place, but nowadays the man is swung in a basket, or by a hook run through his belt. The festival is a great occasion with the jungle 'Chentzus,' who go there to celebrate their marriages and settle their caste disputes.

Vyágrésvarapuram.

Vyágrésvarapuram: Ten miles north-north-west of Amalápuram. A hamlet of Pullétikurru, the population of which is 3,516. The name means 'the place of the tiger god.' It is explained by a legend to the effect that a Bráhman, being pursued by a tiger, climbed a sacred *bilva* tree; and thence addressed the animal with mantrams and prayers, which so affected its feelings that it turned into the stone lingam which is still worshipped under the name of Vyágrésvara.

A fairly large festival takes place in the village on the Sankránti (*i.e.* Pongal) day, when some fifteen of the neighbouring gods come to visit this deity.

COCANADA TALUK.

CHAP. XV. COCANADA.

COCANADA lies on the coast north of the Gódávari, and all but the northern portion of it is included within the delta of that river. Over 86 per cent. of the soil is consequently alluvial, and most of it is irrigated. Statistics regarding these and other points will be found in the separate Appendix. The taluk is one of the most densely populated in the district and the average revenue payable on each holding is over Rs. 40, or higher than in any other.

Most of the taluk belongs to Pithápuram zamindari. It is well supplied with means of communication. The Madras Railway crosses the north of it, and a branch runs through the heart of it to its head-quarters, the busy sea-port of Cocanada. This town and the old port of Coringa are connected with the interior by good waterways. Roads are plentiful and, on the whole, good. Trade is consequently large, and many important firms are located at Cocanada, but industries are few. Rice-milling at Cocanada and sugar-refining at Samalkot are the only considerable undertakings, and the indigenous industries are of an elementary kind. Coarse weaving goes on at several places; chintzes are largely stamped at Gollapálaiyam, Cocanada and Samalkot; and metal vessels are made at Cocanada, Gollamámidáda and Peddáda. The taluk contains several temples of no small local reputation. These are referred to below.

Bhímavaram.

Bhímavaram is now a portion of Samalkot, but it has a character of its own. The full name of the place as given in inscriptions is Chálukya Bhímavaram. Under the Mughals it appears to have been called Mrúthyujánagar.[1] The Bhímésvara temple is locally famous both for its architectural beauty and for its sanctity. It possesses a huge lingam which is said to be similar to those in Drákshárámam (in the Rámachandrapuram taluk), Amarávati (or Amará-ráma) in the Guntúr district, Pálakollu (also called Kshíra-ráma) in the Kistna district and 'Kumará-ráma,' a place not identified. The story goes that the god Subrahmanya killed a demon named Tárakásura who was wearing a huge lingam round his neck, and that this was broken into five pieces, one of which fell at each of these villages. The place is sacred on this account, and a bath in the Bhímagundum tank in front of the temple is believed to confer holiness.

[1] Mackenzie MSS., Local Records, i, pp. 496–98.

CHAP. XV. COCANADA.

There are a number of ancient inscriptions in both the Bhímésvara and Náráyanasvámi temples in the village. Thirty of these have been copied by the Government Epigraphist (Nos. 460 to 489 of 1893). Some others, mostly of a private nature, are given in one of the Mackenzie MSS.[1] The most ancient is one among the former dated 1087 A.D. A few of them mention members of the Reddi dynasty. The Mackenzie MS. gives what purports to be a copy of a copper-plate grant of Kátama Véma Reddi to the Náráyanasvámi temple dated 1393 A.D.

Chollangi.

Chollangi: Lies six miles south of Cocanada, near the coast, and on one of the traditional seven holy mouths of the Gódávari. It is the first place visited by those who are making the 'pilgrimage of the seven mouths.'[2] The branch of the river which has its mouth here is said to have been brought down by the sage Tulya, and is accordingly called the Tulya-ságara-sangam. It is really nothing but the Tulya Bhága drain. The village is otherwise quite insignificant, and its population is only 577.

Cocanada.

Cocanada, the head-quarters of the taluk and district, is a municipality of 48,096 inhabitants and one of the busiest sea-ports in the Presidency. It is situated on the western side of the Coringa bay, and is connected by a branch with the North-east line of the Madras Railway. Its trade has been referred to in some detail on pp. 113-7. It is the head-quarters of the Collector (the Judge resides at Rajahmundry), the District Forest Officer, Local Fund Engineer, Assistant Commissioner of Salt, Abkári and Customs, District Medical and Sanitary Officer, District Registrar, head-quarters Divisional Officer (either a Deputy Collector or an Assistant Collector) and Government Chaplain, and of the Port Officer in charge of the harbour and port. The minor officials stationed there are the tahsildar, district munsif and stationary sub-magistrate. The place is also the head-quarters of a company of the East Coast Rifle Volunteers, and contains a municipal hospital (founded 1856), a dispensary (founded 1888), a women and children's dispensary (founded 1895), two police-stations, a travellers' bungalow, a large private choultry, a private native rest-house, the Pithápuram Rája's college, an English lower secondary school for boys, and two English, and four vernacular, lower secondary schools for girls. Its medical and educational institutions have been referred to in Chapters IX and X respectively, and the doings of its

[1] Local Records, ii, 213-30.
[2] See Chapter I, p. 6.

municipal council in Chapter XIV. The salt factories in the suburb of Jagannáthapuram and Penugudúru are mentioned in Chapter XII. The town is situated in the Pithápuram zamindari.

Jagannáthapuram, which lies south of the harbour, is the only part of the place which possesses any historical interest. It was the site of a Dutch Factory which, with Bimlipatam in Vizagapatam and Pálakollu in Kistna, were 'represented to be held under Fermans granted by the Nizam and confirmed by the Mogul or Emperor of Delhi, bearing various dates from A.D. 1628 to A.D. 1713 and by a Cowle granted by Hajee Houssun in A.D. 1734 and A.D. 1752 by Jaffur Ally Khan. The two last mentioned persons were Naibs or deputies of the Nizam in the Circars. The Dutch are stated to have first occupied these factories about the year A.D. 1628.'[1] Their factory included the dependent villages of Gollapálem and Gundavaram and they had a mint, at which were made the coins issued from Bimlipatam.[2]

In 1781 war broke out between the English and the Dutch, and the settlements of the latter on the Coromandel coast were seized. Jagannáthapuram was in that year 'a place of some consequence. The factory house, fortified I believe,[3] and all the public buildings were demolished in that year.'[4]

In 1784 peace was declared, and their factories were handed back to the Dutch in the following year. During the wars of the French Revolution (1789-95) the settlements were again captured by the English, but were once more handed back in 1818 by a convention of 1814. They were finally made over to the English Company in 1825, with the other Dutch possessions in India, under the operation of a treaty of 1824 between Holland and England.

The Dutch factory played a small part in the campaign of 1758-59 by which the Northern Circars were taken by the English from the French. French officers wounded at the battle of Condore were permitted to go to Jagannáthapuram on parole. In 1759 a small force of Frenchmen landed at Cocanada to intrigue with Jagapati Rázu at Samalkot; but, as has been mentioned in Chapter II, they were driven by the English to take refuge in the Dutch fort, and their surrender was enforced under protest from the Dutch.

[1] Hodgson's report on the Dutch Settlements, quoted in Mr. Rea's '*Monumental remains of the Dutch East India Co.* (Madras, 1897), 52.

[2] Mr. Rea's book, 65, 66.

[3] Apparently by rude ramparts of earth, Pinkerton's *Collection of Travels*, xi, 303.

[4] Hodgson's report.

CHAP. XV. COCANADA.

The first impetus to the town of Cocanada was given by the silting up of Coringa bay and the consequent decline of Coringa as a port and dockyard. Cocanada gradually took its place. A second impulse was given during the American Civil War (1861), when the town suddenly rose into great importance as a place of shipment for the cotton pressed at Guntúr.

Cocanada is the head-quarters of the Canadian Baptist Mission and contains a Roman Catholic church and convent. In the Protestant church is perhaps the finest organ in the Presidency outside Madras City. It was built from private subscriptions, of which a large portion was given by Messrs. Simson Bros., about twenty years ago. A cemetery near the Collector's house contains some old European tombs, the earliest of which is dated 1825 and a list of which is in the Collector's office. In the Jagannáthapuram cemetery are many more graves, the oldest of which is a monument to a Dutch family the members of which were buried between 1775 and 1778. From the latter of these years up to 1859 the churchyard does not seem to have been used, but from that year onwards the burials have been numerous.

Of the industrial concerns in the town, the Local Fund workshops (near the Collector's office) have been referred to in Chapter VI. The town also contains three rice mills and five printing presses. Of the latter, only two (one called the Sujana Ranjani press and one managed by Messrs. Hall, Wilson & Co.) are of any importance. The latter prints general matter and the former Telugu books, and a weekly newspaper and a monthly magazine called respectively the Ravi and Sávitri. In another press a monthly magazine called Sarasvati is printed. There are also about a dozen native factories which each employ several handpresses for making castor oil.

The vernacular name of the town, Kákináda, is supposed to have some connection with the phenomenal number of crows which live in it. A merchant recently opened his rice godowns to trap these marauding birds, and then, closing the doors, had the intruders killed. No fewer than 978 were accounted for in one morning in this way, but without sensible diminution of the nuisance.

Coringa.

Coringa (vernacular *Kórangi*): Nearly ten miles south of Cocanada. Population 4,258. It contains a travellers' bungalow, a native rest-house, a police-station and the offices of a deputy tahsildar who is also a sub-registrar. It was once one of the greatest ports and ship-building centres on this coast; but, owing to the silting up of the channel which leads to it, it is now of no commercial importance. Coringa appears in Pliny's pages as the name of a cape, but the village is now several miles from the sea. It was for long the residence of British merchants, but little now remains to call them to mind. There are a few old tombs in the graveyard—some dating back to 1816[1]—and portions of a few bungalows survive. One forms the present deputy tahsildar's office. Two others, one of which must have been a fine building, belonged to a certain Mr. Graham, whose name is still well known. The latest date in the churchyard is 1857, and apparently English merchants did not live in the place long after that.

An interesting account of the town as it was in its busiest days was given by Mr. Topping, an astronomer in the service of the Madras Government, who visited it in 1789. He deplored in particular the want of police, which he said were badly needed owing to the number of ships—English, French, Dutch and Portuguese—that anchored in the road and the many disorderly people that landed from them. 'Nothing is more common,' he said, 'than night broils and frays among people under the influence of intoxication. Frequent thefts and even attempts to assassinate happened during my short stay, which induced me to apply for a guard of sepoys, to protect myself and the Company's property from violence and rapine.' A curious contrast, this, to the quiet country village of to-day!

It appears that the present town of Coringa, which is on the east of the river, was 'built' about 1759 by Mr. Westcot, a resident of Injaram; while what is known as 'old Coringa,' on the western bank, is older than this.[2] The bulk of the inhabitants and the deputy tahsildar live in the former, but there are a few good houses in the latter. The village suffered severely from the hurricane of 1839, and has twice (in 1787 and 1832) been nearly swept away by tidal waves. The old village was also damaged by the tidal wave of 1706.

The place is indeed a shadow of its former self. Its sea-borne trade was valued in 1877–78 at Rs. 8,22,000, and in 1880–81 at Rs. 3,20,000; but by 1884–85 it had fallen to Rs. 33,000; and since 1898–99 it has ceased altogether.

Moreover the neighbouring village of Tállarévu has now monopolised the ship-building that was formerly the pride of Coringa. In 1802 Mr. Ebenezer Roebuck, a private gentleman residing at Coringa, constructed at a great cost a dock near

[1] See the list in the Collector's office.

[2] *Selections from the Records of the Madras Government* (Madras, 1855), xix, p. 24.

CHAP. XV. COCANADA.

the old town capacious enough to receive any ship of the Royal Navy not drawing more than fourteen feet. H.M.S. *Albatross* and other ships were repaired in this. It was 155 feet long, and its breadth was 51 feet at the bottom, and 76 feet at the top. The masonry at the bottom was five feet thick. It used to be pumped dry, after a ship had been admitted, by two steam engines in a few hours. Now it is choked to the level of the ground with earth, and nothing is to be seen of it but the tops of the brick walls surrounding it. No one seems to remember its being used. Till quite recently, however, ships were repaired in mud docks at old Coringa.

The silting up of the port has progressed very rapidly in recent years. Between 1806 and 1861 the anchorage for big ships had to be moved five or six miles to the north. At the beginning of the last century a frigate drawing thirteen and a half feet was got over the bar; and a report to Government written in 1805 records the opinion that 'any ship not drawing more than twelve and a half feet of water may easily enter the mouth of the river in two springs at any time of the year.' Nowadays, however, it is only with great difficulty that a ship drawing six feet can be got over the bar, and it takes a month to warp a vessel of that size up the river.

Coringa is of some religious importance, since the neighbouring village of Masakapalli is one of the places at which pilgrims bathe when performing the *sapta-ságara-yátrá* or 'pilgrimage of the seven mouths,' already referred to. The river Coringa is said to have been brought to the sea by the sage Atri, and the bathing place is called the Átréya-ságara-sangam. It is also believed that the demon Márícha, who was sent by Rávana in the form of a golden deer to Ráma, when he and Síta were at Parnasála, was killed by Ráma at this place. Ráma is supposed to have founded the Siva temple of Korangésvarasvámi.

Gollapálaiyam.

Gollapálaiyam (eight miles south-south-west of Cocanada, population 1,817) is of interest as the home of the cloth-painting described in Chapter VI. Some seventy households are also engaged in the stamping and dyeing of chintzes, and a little weaving of fair quality is carried on. There are some Jain remains in the neighbouring village of Áriyavattam.[1]

Injaram.

Injaram: A zamindari village near Yanam, fifteen miles south by west of Cocanada. Population 2,042. A factory, an offshoot of the settlement at Vizagapatam, was founded

[1] For others, see Chapter III, p. 39.

there by the East India Company in 1708, was soon afterwards abandoned, but was re-established in 1722. It was captured by the French under Bussy in 1757—the garrison numbered only twenty men and no resistance was offered—but it was ceded by the Nizam to the English in 1759 after the battle of Condore. It continued as a mercantile establishment of the East India Company till 1829. Its two great qualifications as a factory were that it was situated near one of the principal mouths of the Gódávari and that very good cloth was made there. Indeed Captain Hamilton, who visited India at the beginning of the eighteenth century, stated that it produced the best and finest longcloth in all India. With the abolition of the Company's factory the prosperity of Injaram declined. It has now no sea-borne trade whatever. No traces, it is said, exist of the European settlement.

Injaram is the head-quarters of a small zamindari estate containing three villages and paying a peshkash of Rs. 2,832. It was part of the old Peddápuram zamindari and was acquired by sale by the present holders' family in 1845.

Nílapalli.

Nílapalli: An old sea-port near Yanam, on the eastern bank of the Coringa river where it joins the Gautami Gódávari. Its population is 3,936 and it contains a vernacular lower secondary school for girls. The Company established a factory here in 1751, but it was captured by Bussy in 1757. A quantity of good cloth was formerly manufactured in the neighbourhood, and a considerable sea-borne trade existed; but now the place is of little importance commercially and has no sea-borne trade at all. In it are the remains of several old bungalows once occupied by English merchants, and four English tombs ranging in date from 1807 to 1865.

Its hamlet of Georgepet, which was clearly so named by Englishmen, contains a large mill belonging to the Coringa Rice Mills Company, where about one hundred men are employed and which is in charge of two European superintendents. The rice is sent in boats to be shipped from Cocanada. The mill is said to have been started by a French engineer from Káraikkál in 1854. Before that time the buildings are said to have been used as an indigo factory.

Nílapalli is the only remaining village of the old Nílapalli proprietary mutta (created in 1802-03) which formerly contained nine other villages and paid a peshkash of Rs. 6,300. The peshkash is now only Rs. 480.

Samalkot.

Samalkot (vernacular *Chámárlakóta*): Seven miles north of Cocanada, and the junction between the branch line from

CHAP. XV. COCANADA.

that place and the North-east line of the Madras Railway. It is connected by canal with both Rajahmundry and Cocanada. Its population was 16,015 in 1901. It contains a police-station, a small market, a travellers' bungalow and a fine private choultry near the railway-station. Its educational institutions comprise the Canadian Baptist Mission seminary,[1] a vernacular lower secondary school for girls and a Sanskrit school. The town is a union, and comprises the villages of Bhímavaram and Jaggammagáripéta.

Samalkot is included in the Pithápuram estate, was the original residence of the family of sirdars who founded that property, was apparently the first capital of the zamindari, was deserted in favour of Pithápuram for a time, but became the capital once more in the eighteenth century. Its fort was the scene of some exciting by-play in the great drama enacted by the English, French and Muhammadans in 1759, and seems to have more than once changed hands. Further particulars will be found in the account of Pithápuram below. In the latter half of the eighteenth century the place was made a sanitarium for the British troops in the district. Barracks were built in 1786, and it was at that time 'the principal garrison of the English in the Circar of Rajahmundry.'[2] The fort was demolished in 1838 and the place was abandoned as a military station in 1868. Owing however to the Rampa disturbances of 1879, two companies under a British officer were afterwards stationed there, and they were only withdrawn in 1893. Samalkot is now of some commercial importance owing to the establishment within it, in 1899, of the large sugar-refinery and distillery which is described in Chapter VI. A large number of Dévángas in the town weave plain cotton cloths, and a few make cotton cloths with lace borders. A little chintz-stamping and dyeing, and manufacture of kas-kas tattis also goes on. A Government experimental agricultural farm[3] was started in the place in 1902 and has recently been made into a permanent institution.

Sarpavaram.

Sarpavaram (snake town) lies 4¼ miles north of Cocanada and contains 1,681 inhabitants. It is locally famous for its sanctity. The temple is known by the name of Nárada Kshétram after the rishi Nárada, who is supposed to have

[1] See Chapter III, p. 41.

[2] Grant's *Political Survey of the Northern Circars* appended to the *Fifth Report of the Select Committee on the affairs of the East India Co.*, 1812 (Madras reprint, 1883), p. 215.

[3] See Chapter IV, p. 75.

founded it. This sage was turned into a woman by Vishnu and married a Pithápuram Rája who was killed in battle with all his children. Thereupon Vishnu pitied him and turned him back into a man. Both transformations were effected by bathing in tanks at Sarpavaram, the former in the Nárada Gundam, the latter in the Muktika Sarasu tank. To bathe in the Nárada Gundam is considered a holy act. The name of the town is locally said to be derived from the fact that it was in this place that, as the Mahábhárata relates, Paríkshit the son of Arjuna was bitten by a snake and died. His son performed the *sarpa yágam* (serpent sacrifice) to effect the destruction of all those reptiles, but one snake was spared by Indra's mercy.

The temple is a plain building of no beauty. A late Rája of Pithápuram built its gópuram at a great cost. Eight inscriptions in it (Nos. 452–59 of 1893) have been copied by the Government Epigraphist. The oldest of these, on a pillar in the mantapam in front of it, is in Tamil and is dated in the 46th year of Kulóttunga Chóla Déva—apparently Kulóttunga I (A.D. 1070–1118)—or 1116 A.D. One, dated A.D. 1414, is a record of Véma Reddi, and several others of the early part of the thirteenth century are grants of a Vishnuvardhana Mahárája, who is probably the same person as the local chieftain Mallapa III.

Tállarévu.

Tállarévu: Two miles south of Coringa, on the east bank of the river of that name. This village, like so many on this river, appears to have once been an important trading centre. It is now only interesting as the scene of a small indigenous ship-building industry.

Yanam.

Yanam (French, Yanaon) is a small French Settlement which is entirely surrounded by British territory. It is situated about twelve miles from the mouth of the Gautami Gódávari, at the point where the Coringa river branches off from the main stream. The Settlement extends along the banks of these rivers for seven or eight miles, and its area is returned at 2,258 acres. Besides Yanam, it includes the four hamlets of Adivipálem, Kánakalapéta, Mettakúru, and Kursammapéta. Its population in 1901 was 5,005 against 5,327 in 1891. The town contains a few handsome European buildings, including a fine church: and there is a spacious walled parade on the south side facing the Gódávari.

Yanam is a comparatively modern town, and was not in existence in 1706. The French established a factory there about 1750, and the place was formally ceded to them in 1752. It shared the vicissitudes of their other possessions on this coast; and from 1793 onwards, save for a short period in 1802-03, was in the occupation of the English till the treaties of 1815 restored it to its former owners. It was then finally handed back in 1817. In 1839 the town was laid waste by a hurricane which was accompanied by an inundation of the sea.

Subject to the control of the Governor of the French Possessions at Pondicherry, Yanam is administered by an official called the *Administrateur* who is assisted by a local elective Council of six members. The *Administrateur* is the head of the magistracy and police and president of the criminal court. Local affairs are managed by a communal council, also elective, of twelve members. Two free schools, one for boys and the other for girls, having an attendance of 202 and 248 respectively, are maintained in the town. The area of cultivated land in the Settlement in 1903 was 664 *hectares* or about 1,000 acres. Land is held in absolute ownership subject to the payment of an assessment of Rs. 37-8 per candy (about 4½ acres) for cultivated land, and Rs. 5 for pasture land. Water is supplied free of cost from the British canal which passes through Yanam. Little trade is now carried on at the place, and in 1903 the exports were valued at only Rs. 22,300 and the imports at Rs. 53,625. The seaborne trade is carried northwards down the Coringa river into the Cocanada bay, as the mouth of the Gautami Gódávari is much silted up.

The special arrangements connected with customs and salt which are necessitated by the existence of the Settlement are referred to in Chapter XII above.

NAGARAM TALUK.

CHAP. XV. NAGARAM.

NAGARAM taluk consists of the small island of that name which lies in the south-west corner of the delta and is surrounded by the Vainatéyam and Vasishta branches of the Gódávari and by the sea on the east. It is sometimes known as the Tátipáka Síma (' country '), after the village of that name within it. It is called after the unimportant village of Nagaram, but its head-quarters is Rájavólu. Till October 1st 1904 it was part of the Narasapur taluk, and the usual statistics are not always available for it. Certain figures appear in the separate Appendix, however. It is now the charge of a temporary tahsildar. It is the smallest and the most densely peopled taluk in the district. It is particularly fertile and is irrigated entirely by means of the great Gannavaram aqueduct referred to on p. 86.

Nagaram contains an important centre of pilgrimage in the Vaishnavite temple at Antarvédi, and several other places of religious interest. A fair amount of weaving is done in Jagannapéta, Mori, Sivakódu and Tátipáka ; and the work of the first of these is well known. Tátipáka has a certain historical interest.

The whole of the taluk belongs to Government with the exception of Lankala Gannavaram village, which forms a part of the Palivela *thána* of the Pithápuram estate, and the whole inam village of Gudumulakhandrika. This originally belonged to the old Peddápuram zamindari, was purchased at a sale for arrears, and, after one more sale, was left by will to the late zamindar of Pithápuram.

Antarvédi : Lies in the south-west corner of the taluk at the mouth of the Vasishta Gódávari. Population 6,583. It is the last and the most important of the sacred bathing-places comprised in the *sapta-ságara-yátrá* already referred to, and has other distinct claims to sanctity which are widely recognized. The god of the place is Lakshminarasimha-svámi, an incarnation of Vishnu, who at the prayer of the sage Vasishta and with the help of a local goddess killed another giant called Rakta Vilóchana. The local goddess' name was Asvarúdámba or Gurrálakka ; a small stone image of her, mounted on a horse, is to be seen in the village. Lakshminarasimha-svámi was entreated by Vasishta to remain in the locality, and he accordingly concealed himself in an ant-hill, where the existing image of him was found. This was originally enshrined

Antarvédi.

CHAP. XV. NAGARAM — in a shed by a shepherd, who had miraculously discovered it by the extraordinary insight of one of his cows; and one of its earliest devotees was a Srí Vaishnavite pilgrim who spent his life worshipping it, and from whom the Srí Vaishnavites of Antarvédi claim to be descended. The present temple, as is mentioned in an inscription within it, was built in 1823 by a pious Palli of Bendamúrlanka.

A well-known festival occurs in the village in Mákha (February-March), and at this the marriage of the god is celebrated. It lasts about a week, and is the largest in the district, as many as 80,000 people sometimes attending it. The car is dragged round on the second day; and on the last the god is taken down to the sea-shore, where his bronze quoit *(chakram)* is laid on the head of each of the pilgrims, who afterwards bathe in the sea.

A curious feature of this festival is the importance accorded thereat to the Kóna Síma Drávidas of Pérúru mentioned in the account of that place above. When the marriage of the god is performed they represent his bride's relations, and they are also allowed to go to considerable lengths in making fun of the Srí Vaishnavite Bráhmans of Antarvédi, who are the leading religious party in the place and represent the god himself at the marriage. On the last day but one of the festival they put on Vaishnavite sect-marks and sing abusive songs about the Vaishnavites, who show no resentment. The reason for all this is said to be the fact that long ago the *chakram* of the god was lost in the sea, and that one of the Tamil Bráhmans of Pérúru earned the everlasting gratitude of the people of Antarvédi by getting it back by the use of powerful charms *(mantrams)*. It is even believed that the car cannot be drawn without the help of one of these privileged persons. It is solemnly asserted that 'in the year Vijaya' (1893-94) the villagers could not move the car in spite of all their efforts, because no one from Pérúru was pulling. Some men from there were sought out and prevailed upon to touch the ropes, and the car at once started; and nowadays they take care to have some one from Pérúru to help pull. The temple is a handsome building with a number of gópurams, but it is not of any great size. It is endowed with some 800 acres of land and receives an annual tasdik allowance of about Rs. 3,000.

Antarvédi is of no industrial importance. The painting done there is referred to in Chapter VI.

Jagannapéta. **Jagannapéta**: Four miles north-north-east of Rájavólu. Hamlet of Mogalikudúru, the population of which is 2,524. The place is noted for its weaving, which, though now said to be declining, still employs some 300 families of Dévángas. They weave white cotton turbans and cloths, ornamented with cotton or lace borders and sometimes with simple embroidery. They work with counts as fine as 150s, and their fabrics are noted for the closeness of the weaving.

Kadali.

Kadali: Three and a half miles east-south-east of Rájavolu. Population 3,687. Contains a small local fund market. The god of the place is named Kapótísvaradu and is said to have been first recognized by a certain hermit, who, with his wife, used to worship him in the form of a *kapóta* bird. One day the hermit was mistaken by a shikári for a real bird and shot while at his prayers. He fell into the pool called the *Kapóta gundam* at this place, and his wife flung herself in after him. It is considered a holy act to bathe in this pool on Sundays.

The village is known as 'the place of the five K's' *(Kakára panchakam)*, from five names of local importance which begin with that letter; namely, those of the god, of the village itself and of three families (the Kádambri family of Niyógi Bráhmans, the Kásibhatlu family of Vaidíki Bráhmans, and the Katika-reddi family of Kápus) which are largely represented in the village.

Nagaram.

Nagaram: Five miles north-east of Rájavólu. Population 2,241, of whom about a quarter are Muhammadans. Contains a police-station and a small local fund market. It was presumably once of importance, as for at least the last 120 years it has given its name to the Nagaram island, but now, except that it does a certain amount of local trade, it possesses hardly any features of interest. It contains the remains of an old fort which is said to have been built by the Muhammadans.[1]

Rájavólu.

Rájavólu (commonly called Rázóle by Europeans) has been the head-quarters of the Nagaram taluk since it was split off from Narasapur in 1904. It contains 2,553 inhabitants, a police-station, a sub-registrar's office, a local fund dispensary (opened in 1881) and a local fund choultry.

Sivakódu.

Sivakódu: Two miles south-east of Rájavólu. Population 3,541. Contains a travellers' bungalow and an English lower secondary school for boys. The Siva temple, like that at Rámésvaram still further south-east, is supposed to have been built by Ráma on his return from Ceylon in expiation of his sin of killing king Rávana, who was a Bráhman. It is supposed to be the very last one he made for this purpose, and to have completed the crore *(kóti)* of temples the construction of which was needed to cleanse him thoroughly of his

[1] Sewell's *Lists of Antiquities*, i, 41.

CHAP. XV. NAGARAM. sin. The name Sivakódu is supposed to mean 'the crore of Siva' and to be derived from this fact.

There are about 50 Dévángas in the village who weave plain cloths, using thread of counts as fine as 150s. A local carpenter carves wooden figures, bed-steads and door-frames well, and also makes musical instruments of fair quality.

Tátipáka. **Tátipáka**: Three miles north-north-east of Rájavólu. Population 2,838. A small local fund market is held there. In one of the streets is a Jain image, buried up to its neck, the head of which is more than life size. Several large wells in the neighbourhood are called 'Jain wells.' The place is a centre of trade and of the jaggery industry. Some 50 Dévánga families weave plain cloths.

Tátipáka seems at one time to have been a place of some importance, since the local name for the Nagaram island (Tátipáka Síma) is derived from it. It is referred to in the accounts of the Muhammadan invasion of 1562-64. It was then held by a powerful zamindar, Narasinga Rao, and was strongly fortified and protected by a deep moat. The Muhammadans were detained a month in front of the walls and were finally driven to raise the siege. The place was attacked next year when the rains were over, and was then captured.

PEDDÁPURAM TALUK.

PEDDÁPURAM taluk lies in the north-east of the district, south of the Yellavaram Agency and west of Pithápuram and Tuni. The northern part of it is very like the Agency in character, and is, in particular, exceedingly malarious. The greater part of the taluk, as well as the Pithápuram country, is known to the natives as the Porlunádu. Very little of Peddápuram is irrigated. More than half the wet area is under the Yeléru river, and over 4,600 acres under the large Lingamparti tank. Eighty per cent. of the soil is red ferruginous, eleven per cent. black regar, and only six per cent. alluvial. The average rainfall is 36·80 inches a year. The comparative barrenness of the taluk results in many contrasts to the delta tracts: the incidence of the land revenue, for example, is only Rs. 1-13-7 per head; the density of the population (331 per square mile) is unusually low for this district; education is more backward than in any other taluk on the plains; and only 5 per cent. of the male population can read and write. CHAP. XV. PEDDÁPURAM.

Of the few industries in the taluk, the most important is the manufacture of jaggery, which is exported in large quantites to the refinery at Samalkot.

The taluk was originally a part of the large zamindari of Peddápuram, the history of which is sketched below. It is now nearly all Government land. The small estates of Kirlampúdi, Víravaram, Dontamúru and Ráyavaram, one village of the Pithápuram zamindari and the Jagammapéta estate are the only areas that are still zamindari land.

Annavaram: Twenty-five miles north-east of Peddápuram. Population 605. Possesses a small choultry and a temple of some local fame. The latter contains an image of Satya Náráyanasvámi which was discovered on a hill near by as the result of a vision seen in a dream by a local Bráhman, and many people, especially those desirous of children, go on pilgrimages to it. Annavaram.

Dhárамallápuram: Forty miles north by east of Peddápuram among the hills. Population 86. Contains the ruins of an old mud fort, oval in shape and half a mile in diameter, which is declared by local tradition to have been built by Bussy after his expedition against Bobbili. Dháramallápuram.

CHAP. XV. PEDDÁPURAM.

Jagammapéta.

Jagammapéta: Eight miles north-west of Peddápuram; population 4,638. Chief village of a union which also comprises Kóttúru, Rágampéta and Rámavaram. Contains a police-station, two travellers' bungalows (one for natives and the other for Europeans), a small choultry, a small local fund market, and a lower secondary school for boys. The sublimate of mercury made in it is referred to in Chapter VI. One or two Kamsalas make brass vessels.

Jagammapéta is the chief village of the zamindari of the same name, which consists of 28 villages and pays a peshkash of Rs. 33,062. Along with the Dontamúru estate (one village, peshkash Rs. 3,267) and the Ráyavaram estate (two villages, peshkash Rs. 1,998) this zamindari was purchased from the Peddápuram estate by the Rája of Pithápuram. He gave them to a certain Rao Venkata Rao, and the present holder is the widow of the latter's grandson.

Kándrakóta.

Kándrakóta, six miles north of Peddápuram, population 2,664, is celebrated for its festival to the village goddess Núkálamma, which lasts for a month and end with the last new-moon day before the Telugu New Year's Day in March or April. Many pilgrims visit the place on this occasion and vows of many kinds are made to the goddess, generally, it is said, to secure alleviation from disease. A buffalo is sacrificed, a wound being first made in its throat and the blood caught in a pot, and its head being then cut off.

Kattipúdi.

Kattipúdi: Seventeen and a half miles north-east of Peddápuram. Population 1,470. Contains a police-station, a travellers' bungalow and a large choultry with an income of Rs. 3,000 from land bequeathed to the taluk board, which is devoted to feeding travellers of all classes.

Kirlampúdi.

Kirlampúdi: Nine miles north-north-east of Peddápuram. Population 4,316. Has a small market. Is included in the Jagapatinagaram union. Chief village of a small estate, consisting of ten villages paying a peshkash of Rs. 23,186, which was purchased from the old Peddápuram zamindari at a sale for arrears. It has changed hands since then and is now held in shares by two brothers. One share has been sold to the Mahárája of Bobbili.

Peddápuram.

Peddápuram, the head-quarters of the taluk, lies three miles from Samalkot railway-station and contains a population of 12,609. In it are the offices of a Deputy Collector, a tahsildar, a district munsif, a sub-registrar, and a stationary sub-magistrate, and also a local fund dispensary (established 1881), a fair-sized market, a police-station and a fine taluk board choultry where Bráhmans and Súdras are fed. This last is endowed with an income of Rs. 3,400 from land, and was bequeathed to the taluk board. The town also contains a high school belonging to the American mission and a vernacular lower secondary school for girls.

It was for nearly three centuries the capital of a great zamindari estate which seems at one time to have extended from north of Tótapalli to Nagaram island. About 1785 it 'comprised nearly one-half of the whole Circar of Rajahmundry, both in extent and value, and contained 585 villages.'[1]

The old zamindars of Peddápuram are said to be descended from Vachchavaya Musali, the perfidious minister of Vidiádri, the last Gajapati ruler of Rajahmundry, whose treachery is said to have been one of the factors which facilitated the Muhammadan conquest in 1571. The line of descent was unbroken till 1734, when the estate was apparently in the hands of a woman, the zamindarni Vachchavaya Rágamma who was defeated near Peddápuram by the Muhammadans for joining in the rebellion of the chiefs of Ellore, Mogalturru and Pithápuram.[2] The Muhammadan general then enticed the sons of Rágamma into his camp and tortured them to death 'by drizzling on them hot-boiled oil with brushes.'[3] Rágamma burnt herself alive when she heard the news. 'Challa Peddy, a faithful servant, made haste to the palace and took permission from the Ranee to set the palace on fire to prevent the ladies being maltreated by the barbarous soldiers of the Sirlushkar.'[4] Her grandson was sent for safety to Vizianagram. In 1749 the family was re-established by the amildar, Nimat Ali, who for a bribe of Rs. 90,000 appointed one Ráyappa Rázu, a grandson of Rágamma, as zamindar. Ráyappa Rázu, like most of the other zamindars, hated the Vizianagram Rája and so opposed the English in their advance in 1758. He was either killed at Condore,[5] or was deposed by Ananda Rázu of Vizianagram in the following year, and his son Timma Rázu, then a boy only seven years old, succeeded to the estate. Timma Rázu ruled till 1797 and was followed by Ráya Jagapati Rázu, with whom the permanent settlement was made. He died in 1804 without issue, and left the estate to a minor child adopted by him.[6]

[1] Grant's *Political Survey of the Northern Circars* already several times cited.

[2] See p. 235.

[3] MS. history of Pithápuram (Cocanada, 1881), p. 30.

[4] *Ibid.*

[5] Grant's *Political Survey*.

[6] Selections from the Records of the Gódávari district (Cocanada, 1891); Mr. Hodgson's report, dated 23rd November 1805, para. 3.

The estate was eventually sold for arrears of revenue in 1847. Much of it is now Government property, but parts of it went to make up nine small estates which are still in existence. These are : Kottam, Víravaram, Kirlampúdi, Dontamúru, Jagammapéta, Ráyavaram, Gollaprólu, Palivela and Injaram. The ancient line of zamindars still maintain something of their former position in the Kottam zamindari, which was split off from that of Peddápuram in 1810.

Peddápuram town is an important centre of the jaggery trade and sends large quantities of that commodity to the factory at Samalkot. A little silk-weaving is also carried on there; some 200 households are employed in weaving cotton cloths with lace borders; a few families stamp and dye cotton cloths; a fair amount of metal-work is done; and a little good shoe-making. The town has a bad name for elephantiasis.

The ditch and parts of the walls of the old fort are still to be seen. It was built of stone, was oval in shape and about three-quarters of a mile across. The land inside the walls is now under cultivation.

A hill in the neighbourhood, called the *Pándavulametta* ('the Pándavas' hill'), contains a cave which is supposed to be the mouth of an underground passage leading to Rajahmundry. It is popularly supposed that the Pándavas used to haunt this hillock and go to Rajahmundry through this passage.

Prattipádu.

Prattipádu : Eleven miles north-north-east of Peddápuram. Population 2,100. Contains the offices of a sub-registrar and a deputy tahsildar, a police-station and a native travellers' bungalow. It is the chief village of the Jagapatinagaram union which comprises also Kirlampúdi, Simhádripuram, Jagapatinagaram, Chillangi, Rámakrishnápuram and Vélanka, and the total population of which amounts to 11,329. It enjoys considerable local celebrity owing to its possession of an idol of Rámalingasvámi, which was recently found on a neighbouring hill by a Kamsala who had been told in a dream that it was there. A cobra is said to have been shading the idol with its hood. About two miles from Prattipádu on the road to Jagammapéta are two idols under a cluster of trees which are known in the neighbourhood as Páthalamma (the foot goddess). These are visited by large numbers of pilgrims who in satisfaction of vows sacrifice fowls and animals to the goddess and hang up the victims' heads in front of her. A number of stories are told about the malignant powers of this goddess: a Local Fund Engineer (name not specified) who ventured to cut down one of the trees near by some twenty years ago was thrown from his horse in consequence; another man who committed the same offence was at once seized with fever and died within the week; and some ryots of Yerravaram who removed one of the idols to their village were struck with blindness.

Rágampéta.

Rágampéta : Eight miles north-west of Peddápuram; population 865. Is included in the Jagammapéta union. Some ten Linga Balijas make bangles and 'glass' bottles here, an industry not common in this district. Brass vessels are made by a few Kamsalas.

Rangampéta.

Rangampéta : Ten miles west of Peddápuram, population 2,017. Contains a large choultry called the Nallacheruvu choultry (from the tank on the bank of which it is situated) which has an income of Rs. 5,500 from land, and in which travellers of all classes are fed. There is a travellers' bungalow close to it.

Tallúru.

Tallúru : Eleven miles north-west of Peddápuram; population 1,768. Is called Taidoor in old maps. The present Vaishṇavite temple in the village is said to have been originally built above a rock-cut cave, by a saint called Bhárgava, as a shrine to Siva. The local chief, a Dúdéku named Sitab Khán, who was a Saivite, was afterwards converted to the Vaishnavite faith by the famous Rámánujáchári, and in consequence overthrew the Saivite lingams (which now lie buried in a mound known as the *lingala dibba*) and turned the temple into a Vaishnava place of worship.

Tótapalli.

Tótapalli, eighteen miles north-east of Peddápuram, population 94, was the former capital of one of the three ancient mansabdaris of the Gódávari district. The original holder of this was a mokhásadar under the zamindar of Peddápuram, who was bound to pay his suzerain a quit-rent of 1,000 pagodas a year and attend on him when required with a body of 700 peons. It was this military service which caused him to be denominated a mansabdar.[1]

His estate comprised 100 villages, of which 37 were held by inferior mokhásadars.[2] Mr. Grant (writing about 1785) speaks of the property as a 'region of tigers,' and mentions that in 1771, at the instigation of the Peddápuram zamindar, 'this little territory, with the sacrifice of almost the whole detachment to the unhealthiness of the climate, was reduced by the English to pay a future tribute to the zamindar.'[3] As this quit-rent was not punctually paid, the Peddápuram zamindar in later times resumed certain of the Tótapalli villages. The

[1] G.O. No. 559, Judicial, dated 19th March 1881.

[2] G.O. No. 2425, Judicial, dated 23rd November 1881.

[3] *Political Survey of the Northern Circars*, 214.

CHAP. XV. PEDDAPURAM.

quit-rent of 1,000 pagodas on the property was one of the assets of the Peddápuram zamindari on which the peshkash payable to the Company was assessed at the permanent settlement. That settlement did not recognize the mansabdar save as a subordinate of the Peddápuram zamindar, nor deal with him direct. In 1847 the Peddápuram zamindari was sold for arrears of peshkash and bought in on behalf of Government, and from that date the feudal service of the mansabdar was due to Government and was occasionally demanded. In 1859 a money payment of Rs. 6,500 per annum, being one-fourth of the assumed rental of the villages, was substituted for this service. The estate thus became an unenfranchised inam from which no service was required. Subsequently the mansabdar ran into debt and alienated a number of his villages. Government accordingly decided in 1881 [1] to assess the whole estate fully and take it under their own management, and, while remitting the demand fixed in substitution of the former military service, to pay the mansabdar annually the difference between the estimated cost of that service and the estimated value of the estate, or Rs. 19,500. The ruins of the mansabdar's fort still exist in Tótapalli. It was built of mud and stone, was oval in shape, and covered some 200 acres. The land inside it is now under cultivation.

Víravaram.

Víravaram : Eight miles north of Peddápuram. The chief village of a small estate which previously formed part of the Peddápuram zamindari and was purchased at a sale for arrears by a certain Rao Bhanayyamma, from whom the present holder has inherited it. It contains eleven villages and pays a peshkash of Rs. 26,759.

Yelésvaram.

Yelésvaram : Fifteen miles north of Peddápuram on the border of the Yellavaram division. Population 5,180. It is the chief village of a union which also includes Appanapálaiyam, Ráyavaram, Lingamparti and Náráyanapatnam, and the population of which is 8,531. The village contains a local fund dispensary (established 1882), a travellers' bungalow and a local fund market. This last is much used by the hill tribes, and the village has been appropriately called 'the gate of the Agency.' It is the scene of a large festival in honour of the village goddess Núkálamma in Vaisáka (May-June), which is also largely attended by the agency people.

[1] G.O. No. 559, Judicial, dated 19th March 1881.

PITHÁPURAM DIVISION.

CHAP. XV. PITHÁPURAM.

THE Pithápuram division lies along the coast, north of the Gódávari delta, and, except Nagaram, is the smallest in the district. Most of it is included in the Pithápuram zamindari. Though it adjoins the delta, where the rainfall is heavy, it receives only 34·46 inches annually on an average, the lowest figure in the district. Part of it, however, benefits from the excellent irrigation provided by the Yeléru river. The head-quarter town is of much historical and archæological interest. Good weaving is done at Múlapéta, Uppáda and Kottapalli, and excellent bronze-work at Pithápuram. Chandurti was the scene of the great battle of 'Condore.'

Chandurti.

Chandurti: Seven miles north by east of Pithápuram. Population 1,087. It is called Condore by Orme, and has given this name to the decisive battle which took place near it on the ninth of December 1758, which resulted in the wresting of the sovereignty of the Northern Circars from the French by the English. The battle is described in detail by Orme,[1] and in somewhat different terms by Cambridge[2] and Malleson.[3] A very precise local tradition survives in the village to this day as to the locality in which it was fought, and old swords, bullets, cannon-balls, remains of pewter vessels, and elephants' bones have been found in quantities in the neighbourhood by the villagers while cultivating their fields. The account given by Orme is more detailed than the others and agrees more closely with the local tradition.

When the English under Colonel Forde entered the Pithápuram division they found the French under M. Conflans encamped at Gollaprólu,[4] some four miles north-east of Pithápuram on the main road. This was on December 3rd. The French force consisted of 500 Europeans, 500 native cavalry, 6,000 sepoys and a great number of local levies.[5]

[1] Orme (Madras, 1861), ii, 378 ff.

[2] *The War in India* (London, 1761), 204 ff.

[3] *Decisive battles of India*, 80–87.

[4] Cambridge says 'near Tallapool' (*i.e.*, Tatiparti); and local tradition places the French camp at the now deserted village of Vodulapenta. The latter may refer to the temporary occupation of that village by the French on the morning of the battle.

[5] Orme says 'a great number of the troops of the country, of which 500 were horse and 6,000 sepoys;' Cambridge says '8,000 sepoys and a great many of the country powers.'

CHAP. XV. PITHÁPURAM.

They had had 36 pieces of cannon and some mortars, in fact, 'many more pieces of cannon than they could use at once.' The English force consisted of 470 Europeans and 1,900 sepoys; while their ally, the Rája of Vizianagram, had with him '500 paltry horse and 5,000 foot, some with awkward firearms, the rest with pikes and bows,' as well as a small force of 40 Europeans in charge of four guns, who, in the event, proved of more assistance than all the rest put together.

The French did not move from Gollaprólu, and on the sixth the English occupied Chebrólu, which was also on the main road and lay about three miles north of Gollaprólu. For the next three days the two armies remained in their respective camps; but on the early morning of the tenth they both made a movement. Forde desiring to draw the enemy from their camp to a general action, and to lead them to ground where their cavalry would not be of much assistance to them, marched off at 4 A.M., followed at some distance by the Vizianagram forces, who were not ready to start at the proper time, and at about eight in the morning took possession of Chandurti, which lay some two miles north-west of Chebrólu and well off the road. Meanwhile Conflans had been induced by an intelligent deserter, who had told him that the English force was raw and undisciplined and who had noticed a spot from which their camp could be commanded, to send off six guns the same night to cannonade Chebrólu; and he followed with the rest of his army and artillery to support them. The advance detachment of the French army came across the Vizianagram troops as they were leaving Chebrólu about daybreak, and fired upon them for some little time, but apparently without doing much harm. When Conflans came up he imagined that the English intended to take possession of the now deserted village of Vodulapenta, which lay midway between Gollaprólu and Chandurti and some two miles nearly due west of Chebrólu, and would have afforded them a strong advanced post in any attack upon Gollaprólu. He at once marched across the plain to prevent this, and had no difficulty in doing it, as Forde remained at Chandurti, two miles north of Vodulapenta, resolved 'to regulate his future movements by the enemy's.' Conflans imputed this inactivity to fear, and supposing that, with the advanced post in the enemy's hands, the English would now return to their camp at Chebrólu, he hurried forward to cut them off. Forde, nothing loth, advanced to meet him about nine o'clock, and the two armies came face to face about a mile south-south-west of Chandurti.

The spot which tradition identifies as the scene of the battle which followed is locally known as Angleyulapádu, 'the place of the English,' and is at present covered by a small tope of babul trees. It is a little to the east and north of a small pool which lies about equidistant from Chandurti and Vannipúdi, is due east of the latter, and about one and a half miles north-north-east of Tátiparti.[1]

Orme gives the following account of the battle which ensued :—

'The French Battalion of Europeans was in the centre of the line, with 13 field-pieces, divided on their flanks, the horse, 500, were on the left of the battalion ; 3,000 sepoys formed the right wing, and the same number the left, and with each wing were five or six pieces of cumbrous cannon. The English army drew up with their Europeans in the centre, the six field-pieces divided on their flanks ; the 1,800 sepoys were likewise equally divided on the wings. Colonel Forde placed no reliance on the Rajah's infantry or horse, and ordered them to form aloof, and extend on each flank of the sepoys : all this rabble kept behind, but the renegade Europeans under Bristol, who managed the four field-pieces belonging to the Rajah, advanced, and formed with the division of artillery on the left of the English battalion. The line having had time, were in exact order, and had advanced a mile in front of the village of Condore [Chandurti], during which, the enemy cannonaded hotly from all their guns. At length the impetuosity of the enemy's approach, who came on, outmarching their cannon, obliged the English line to halt for action ; and it chanced that the whole of their battalion stopped near and opposite to a field of Indian corn, which was grown so tall that it entirely intercepted them from the enemy ; but the sepoys on the wings were free in the plain on each hand. For what reason is not known, Colonel Forde had ordered his sepoys to furl their colours, which, besides the principal flag, are several small banners to a company, and to let them lay on the ground during the action.

The sepoys and horse of the enemy's wings greatly outstretched the wings of the English line, and came on each in a curve to gain their flanks ; the French battalion in the centre, instead of advancing parallel to where by the wings they might judge the centre of the English line would be, inclined obliquely to the right, which brought them beyond the field of Indian corn, opposite to the English sepoys on the left wing ; whom from their red jackets,[2] and the want of their usual banners, they from the first approach mistook for the English battalion ; respecting them as such, they halted to dress their ranks

[1] Mr. B. McCormack, Engineer of the Pithápuram estate, has kindly given much assistance in locating the site.

[2] They were from Bengal and wore red ; the Madras sepoys' tunics were usually white.

before they engaged, and then began to fire in platoons advancing, but at the distance of 200 yards. Nevertheless, this was sufficient; for the sepoys, seeing themselves attacked without cover by Europeans in front, and the horse and multitude of the enemy's sepoys gaining their rear, or coming down on their flank, scarcely preserved courage to give their fire, hurried, scattered, and without command; and then immediately broke and ran away to shelter themselves in the village of Chambole (Cnebrólu), and were followed by the nearest of the enemy's horse. This success was greater than even the confidence of the enemy expected; and several platoons of the French battalion were setting off to pursue them likewise, when they saw a line of men with shouldered arms marching fast and firm from behind the field of Indian corn across their way, to occupy the ground which the sepoys had abandoned.

Colonel Forde had been with the sepoys before their flight, encouraging them to resolution; but saw, by the usual symptoms of trepidation, that they would not stand the shock, which prepared him to order the judicious movement which the officers were now performing with so much steadiness and spirit. Captain Adnet, commanding on the left, led the line, and as soon as the last files were got clear of the corn the word was given, when the whole halted, and faced at once in full front of the enemy. This motion was quickly executed; for the foremost man had not more than 300 yards to march, and the field-pieces were left behind. During this short interval, the French battalion were endeavouring with much bustle to get into order again; for some of their platoons had advanced a considerable distance before others; and thus the fire of the English line commenced before the enemy's was ready; it was given in divisions, that is, the whole battalion divided into five, and began from Captain Adnet's on the left, which was within pistol shot, and brought down half the enemy's grenadiers; the fire ran on, and before the time came for Adnet's division to repeat theirs, the whole of the enemy's line were in confusion, and went about running fast to regain their guns, which they had left half a mile behind them on the plain.

The ardour of the English battalion to pursue was so great, that Colonel Forde judged it best to indulge it in the instant, although not certain of the success of the sepoys on the right, but concluding that the enemy's sepoys who were to attack them, would not continue long, if they saw their Europeans completely routed. The order was given for the battalion to march on in following divisions, the left leading. Nothing could repress their eagerness. All marched too fast to keep their rank, excepting the fourth division commanded by Captain Yorke, who to have a reserve for the whole battalion, if broken, as the enemy had been, by their own impetuosity, obliged his men to advance in strict order. The French battalion rallied at their guns, which were 13 in number, spread in different brigades, or sets, as they chanced to stand when left by the troops advancing to the action. This artillery began to fire as soon as the ground was clear of their own troops, and killed some men, which only quickened the approach of the divisions to close in with the guns, of whieh several fired when the first division was within pistol shot, and Adnet fell mortally wounded; but his men rushing on drove the enemy from the guns they attacked, and the other divisions following with the same spirit, obliged them to abandon all the others.

The day, if not completely victorious, was at least secured from reverse by the possession of all the enemy's field artillery fit for quick firing; but their camp [at Gollaprôlu], to which they were retiring, still remained to be attacked; and Colonel Forde halted until joined by his sepoys, and, if they would come, by the Rajah's troops.

The sepoys and horse of the enemy's right wing were in their turn panick-struck by the fire of the English battalion routing their own, and all turned to gain the rear of the guns, keeping aloof to the left of the English divisions; and then went off again with the French battalion to the camp. Their left wing of sepoys behaved better, advancing to the use of musketry against the English sepoys of the left, with whom the battalion, when filing off to oppose the French, left the three field-pieces of their right; and the sepoys, encouraged by this assistance, the ardour of the Europeons marching off, and the spirit of their own commander Captain Knox, maintained their ground, facing and firing in various directions behind the banks of the rice fields in which they had drawn up. The enemy's wing nevertheless continued the distant fire, until they saw their battalion of Europeans quitting their guns, and the sepoys and horse of the right retreating with them to the camp; when they went off likewise; stretching round to the left of the English battalion halting at the guns, and keeping out of their reach. Captain Knox then advanced to join the battalion with his own sepoys, and the six field-pieces, and had collected most of the fugitives of the other wing. Messages had been continually sent to the Raja's horse to advance, but they could not be prevailed upon to quit the shelter of a large tank,[1] at this time dry, in which they, his foot, and himself in the midst of them, had remained cowering from the beginning of the action.

As soon as the sepoys joined, and all the necessary dispositions were made, which took an hour, Colonel Forde advanced to attack the enemy's camp; but, not to retard the march, left the field-pieces to follow. A deep hollow way passed along the skirt of the camp, behind which appeared a considerable number of Europeans regularly drawn up, as if to defend the passage of the hollow way, and several shot were fired from heavy cannon planted to defend the approach. Just as the English troops came near, and the first division of the Europeans stept out to give their fire, the field-pieces were arrived

[1] The Chandurti tank.

CHAP. XV. PITHÁPURAM.

within shot; on which all the enemy went to the right-about, abandoned their camp, and retreated, seemingly every man as he listed, in the utmost confusion; but the English battalion crossing after them, many threw down their arms, and surrendered themselves prisoners. Mr. Conflans had previously sent away four of the smallest field-pieces; and the money of the military chest, laden for expedition on two camels. The spoil of the field and camp was 30 pieces of cannon, most of which were brass; 50 tumbrels, and other carriages laden with ammunition; seven mortars from thirteen to eight inches, with a large provision of shells; 1,000 draught bullocks and all the tents of the French battalion. Three of their officers were killed in the field, and three died of their wounds the same evening; 70 of their rank and file were likewise killed, or mortally wounded: six officers and 50 rank and file were taken prisoners, and the same number of wounded were supposed to have escaped. Of the English battalion, Captain Adnet and 15 rank and file were killed; Mr. Macguire, the paymaster, and Mr. Johnstone, the commissary, who joined the grenadiers, two officers, and 20 of the rank and file were wounded; the sepoys had 100 killed and more wounded. No victory could be more complete; Mr. Conflans, the commander of the French army, changing horses, arrived on the full gallop at Rajahmundrum before midnight, although the distance is 40 miles from the field on which the battle was lost; the troops took various routes, but most of them towards Rajahmundrum.'

Kottapalli.

Kottapalli: Five miles east-south-east of Pithápuram. Population 1,203. Good muslins are woven here by 200 households of Pattu Sáles. The work is referred to in Chapter VI.

Múlapéta.

Múlapéta: Seven miles east of Pithápuram. Population 2,002. About 100 households of Pattu Sáles weave good cotton cloths in the village. The Mondi Jaganna temple there is widely known. There are two gods and a goddess in the temple, namely Bála Ráma, Jagannátha, and his sister Subadra. All the images are of wood and are without hands or feet and are therefore called *mondi*, or 'crippled'. Whence the name of the temple. Popular tradition says the images were washed ashore in the village. It is said that the idols in the great Jagannátha temple at Púri in Orissa are changed once a year, the old ones being thrown into the sea, and that these are a set of the old ones from that place. In Phálguna (March-April) a five-days' festival takes place at the temple and the pilgrims bathe in the sea on the newmoon day. It is declared that married women of the lower classes who are desirous of children are permitted, without discredit attaching to them, to indulge in promiscuous intercourse at this feast, and respectable people consequently resent being asked whether they attended it. A curious feature of the worship is that suppliants do not clasp their hands before the deities in the conventional Hindu form of reverence, but salaam to them as in the Muhammadan fashion of greeting. Nor do they address the usual praises to them, but actually insult them with the most vulgar abuse. No reasons are forthcoming for these customs.

Pithápuram.

Pithápuram: A union of 13,220 inhabitants. The head-quarters of the great Pithápuram zamindari, of a deputy tahsildar and of a sub-registrar. It contains a police-station, a large choultry maintained by the Rája, another kept up from local funds, a local fund hospital (founded 1879), an upper secondary school for boys, an English lower secondary school for boys, a Government lower secondary school for girls and a large cattle market. The Rája owns a bungalow near the station which is generally placed at the disposal of travellers. Close by are his experimental farm and veterinary dispensary.

Its antiquity.

Pithápuram is mentioned as a sovereign city in very early times. In the Allahabad pillar inscription of the Gupta king Samudragupta, which belongs to the middle of the fourth century A.D., the chieftain Mahéndra of Pistápuram is mentioned along with the kings of Conjeeveram and Vengi. He was almost undoubtedly a Pallava chief and a semi-independent feudatory of the Pallava king Vishnugópa of Conjeeveram. Again 'the strong fortress of Pishtápura' is one of the places mentioned in the Aihole inscription of the Eastern Chálukya emperor Pulakésin II as having been subdued by him when he conquered the Vengi country. But from this period onwards a wide gap occurs in the history of the place. Inscriptions ranging from 1186 to 1391 A.D. and belonging to the Vélanándu chiefs, the Kónas, Mallapa's Eastern Chálukya line, and Reddi kings are found in it; but they throw no light on its history.

In comparatively modern times Pithápuram reappears as the head-quarters of an important zamindari. Mr. Grant, in his *Political Survey of the Northern Circars* already quoted, states that the ancestors of the Rája of this estate were established as renters of part of it as early as 1571, but that the family was involved in the general proscription of Indian landholders under the rule of Rustum Khán until in 1749 one of its members obtained a sanad for the zamindari from the amildar Nimat Ali.

History of the Pithápuram

A detailed history of the estate has recently been published at Cocanada by order of the Rája. Up to the end of the eighteenth century, this consists entirely of a translation of one of the Mackenzie MSS. The dates and names (especially the former) in this are evidently confused, but it may be relied on

CHAP. XV. PITHÁPURAM.

where it refers to events in the latter half of the eighteenth century. Further materials for a historical sketch of the estate are provided by the appointments and title-deeds given to the family by successive Muhammadan rulers which are still preserved in its archives, and by an old genealogical tree kept there.

Origin of the Pithápuram family.

The family is of the Velama stock and its ordinary titles (like those of the Kálahasti zamindars) are Rao or Ráya-Nimgár. It claims descent from one Anupótama Náyudu, about whom some remarkable stories are told. His existence is proved by orders of the Báhmani kings—one of Ala-ud-dín (1435-58) dated 1454, 'pardoning him for his misbehaviour' and granting him and his brother Mádhava certain lands, and the other by the son of Muhammad Shah II (1463-82) dated 1464-65 and confirming or modifying the former grant—but these do not connect him with Pithápuram. The grants confer villages in the Nizam's Dominions, and the former directs him to come to the court of the Sultan. The 'misbehaviour' perhaps consisted of the exploits (mentioned in the MS. history) of his son, who collected a large army and conquered forts in the west, which were afterwards held by the family as a jaghir. The names of two of these forts are given in the MS. as Kailása and Metukúr, and a Metukúr is mentioned in the grant. Anupótama's brother, Mádhava Nayudu, is said in the MS. to have founded the family of Venkatagiri in Nellore. The family were afterwards ousted from their jaghir by 'some Delhi sirdars', but one of them, Ranga Rao (of the third generation after Anupótama Náyudu), won back Metukúr and Kailása by force of arms and his son and grandson ruled them more or less independently. The sons of the latter were ousted again and served the king of Golconda as sirdars. This must have been about the end of the sixteenth century.

Grant of the zamindari, *circa* 1684.

It is from Mádhava Rao, one of these sirdars, that the Pithápuram family is descended. His sons 'lived for a long time at Samalkot,' and one of them, Tenugu Rao, was appointed Sirdar of the Rajahmundry Circar at the head of 4,000 troops with Anaparti (in Rámachandrapuram taluk) as a jaghir.[1] He is said to have been appointed by king Abu Hassan of Golconda (1672-88), who was undoubtedly well disposed to his family. He had seven sons. One of them, Jaga Rao, was made a sirdar over 350 men and the letter of

[1] The Pithápuram MS. professes to quote an inscription from Anaparti confirming this appointment, and dated 1598. But this date must be too early, and the list of Muhammadan rulers in the Rajahmundry MS. referred to below does not support the appointment.

appointment, dated 1676–77, is still kept at Pithápuram. Both the MS. history and the genealogical tree agree in saying that the nucleus of the present zamindari of Pithápuram was given to another son named Rámachandra Rao; the former ascribes the gift to king Abu Hassan, but the latter gives the date as 1647. The sanad then granted is not forthcoming, but the MS. gives what purports to be a copy of it. According to this, the grant included the 'pergunnas' of Cocanada, Selapáka (7 miles south of Cocanada) and Porlunádu (*i.e.*, apparently, Pithápuram).[1] Samalkot and two other villages were also given as mokhása.

The MS. goes on to describe the fortunes of Tenugu Rao's children in some detail. Two more of his sons, Krishna Rao and Rangasáyi Rao, were intimates of king Abu Hassan, being particularly good chess-players. The latter killed himself in the presence of the king rather than survive the insults which that ruler, being out of humour, one day heaped upon him.

Rebellion of the zamindar about 1733.

Various descendants of the seven sons of Tenugu Rao held the estate for some years. One of them, Venkata Krishna Ráya-Nimgár, at length obtained an exemption from the payment of peshkash and 'ruled over the estate as if it were independent.' Certain zamindars of the country having failed to pay their revenues, an expedition was sent by the Muhammadans under Rustum Khán,[2] the subordinate of Anwar-ud-dín, about 1733 to suppress them. The zamindars of Mogalturru and Ellore were defeated at Ellore and called in the help of Venkata Krishna Ráya-Nimgár and the zamindarni of Peddápuram. The united forces of the zamindars fought the Muhammadans twice near Peddápuram, but were defeated and driven into exile. The Rája of Pithápuram 'lived for some time among the hills of Tótapalli on predatory excursions.' His cousin Bachchanna was captured with the remnants of the army by Rustum Khán and he and his followers were beheaded at Pithápuram.

His restoration about 1750.

Venkata Krishna Ráya himself is said in the MS. to have died of jungle fever in Tótapalli. But this is apparently wrong. The genealogical tree makes him rule till 1759, and his existence in 1754–55 is proved by nine Muhammadan

[1] Pórlunádu is nowadays used to designate those parts of the Cocanada, Peddápuram and Pithápuram country which are watered by the Yeléru. The word is locally explained to mean 'the land of floods,' from *porlu*, 'to overflow.'

[2] Called in the MS. 'Haji Hussain,' but evidently identical with Rustum Khán. The Rajahmundry MS. represents him as Nawáb of Rajahmundry from 1730 to 1737, and Mr. Grant (p. 208) gives the date of the defeat of the Mogalturru zamindar as 1733.

CHAP. XV. PITHÁPURAM.

grants to him, ranging from 1749–50 to 1754–55, which are still kept at Pithápuram.[1] His estates and jaghirs were apparently regranted to him in the first of these years by Nimat Ali, who was Nawab of Rajahmundry from 1749–50 to 1751–52. The gap between 1734, when he was defeated by the Musalmans, and 1749, when he was restored, is hard to fill. Anwar-ud-dín had quieted the country, and the people were 'in enjoyment of peace of mind and freedom from predatory incursions.' Rustum Khán had been killed by his own son, Núr-ud-dín, and the latter was beheaded by Anwar-ud-dín. But whether Venkata Krishna Ráya was allowed to return to his estate before 1749 and, if not, who ruled the property in the interim, is not clear.

The estate during the Anglo-French war.

The authorities do not say what happened to the estate while the French held the Northern Circars, but when the Vizianagram Rája induced the English to invade the country in 1758–59, the Pithápuram zamindar, like the other chiefs of this district, suspected that he wished to extend his dominions at their expense, and accordingly opposed the invasion. He apparently took no part in the battle of Condore; but hearing that the English were advancing against Samalkot with the Vizianagram Rája he obtained the help of the Dutch of Cocanada to resist them. The MS. says that the Samalkot fort held out for three months, but then submitted. Very shortly afterwards, however, the French landed some troops at Cocanada and these were received into the fort at Samalkot, and were joined there by Jagapati Rázu, a relative and enemy of the Vizianagram Rája. This coalition fought an action at Undúr with the Vizianagram forces, but was defeated. Samalkot was re-taken by the English and the French were driven to Cocanada. All this must have taken place in 1759. The Rája of Pithápuram took refuge in Rághavapuram, but, on the death of the Vizianagram Rája soon afterwards of small-pox, he returned to Pithápuram.

Meanwhile the Nizam had again become possessed of the district, and about 1761 the zamindar was re-established in his property.

Subsequent history.

Who held the property during the next few years is not clear, and there seems to have been some fighting over the successions. In 1765 the then Rája, Kumára Mahípati, died, and his uncle Níládri succeeded. He seems to have been a man of character and to have taken a strong line in the disturbances of the preceding years.

[1] Four of these bear the seal of the Mughal emperor Ahmad Sháh (1748–54) and one of Alamgir II (1754–59).

The next zamindar of any interest is Kumára Venkata Mahípati Rao[1] (1786–93), of whom we are told that he 'did away with the peshkash and ruled over the estate as if he were an independent ruler without any disturbance and in the enjoyment of the greatest delights.' This was too much for the 'Nawáb of Masulipatam' (the Chief of the English Council there) who summoned the zamindar to appear before him. The zamindar started for Masulipatam; but on his way he halted at Nallacheruvu and uttered the following native soliloquy: 'It is not proper to proceed any further; for if the Nawáb were to question me why I did not remit the peshkash and I could not give him satisfactory answer; then it would be very difficult to say what steps the Nawáb might take.' So he retired to the hills by way of Rampa where, 'the climate of the place being unsuited' to him, he was attacked by jungle fever and 'died prematurely there.'

The story is confirmed by the general report of the Board of Revenue of that day. The Board recommended that the late zamindar's young cousin, Venkata Níládri, should succeed him, and it was with this man that the permanent settlement was made in 1803. From his death, which occurred in 1828, till 1841 the estate was under the Court of Wards; and it was again under management from 1850 till 1861, when it was handed over to the then owner Venkata Mahípati Gangádhara Ráma Rao with a balance of four lakhs. This zamindar died in 1890, and, with a brief interval, the estate continued under the Court of Wards until October 1906, when it was handed over to its present proprietor.

The estate at present.

The estate is a remarkably fine one. In the early years of British administration it was no doubt overshadowed by the more important zamindari of Peddápuram; but while the latter has ceased to exist Pithápuram has greatly extended. Not only does it now comprise nearly the whole of the Pithápuram division and the Cocanada taluk, but it also owns fourteen villages in Amalápuram, twelve in Tuni, nine in Rajahmundry, eight in Rámachandrapuram and four in Chódavaram, as well as others in North Arcot and other districts. Its total area is 383 square miles and its income in 1903–04 was Rs. 9,14,000, and the peshkash Rs. 2,44,000.

For purposes of administration the estate is divided into six *thánas*, each under a *thánadár*. The cultivators have no admitted occupancy right in their holdings, though they have shown a tendency to claim this, and until recently what

[1] This is the Mahípati mentioned by the Committee of Circuit, 1787.

CHAP. XV. PITHÁPURAM.

is known as the *vantavâradi* system of land tenure has been enforced by the estate. This is, in effect, the joint-rent system in vogue in ryotwari lands prior to 1866 and described in Chapter XI. It included the 'challenging' there referred to. This undesirable method was practically abandoned under the Court of Wards. Rentals were fixed, whenever complaints were made about them, by holding a kind of public auction and giving the land to the man who offered the highest figure. When once thus settled, they were not altered until the holding changed hands by succession or otherwise, and the successful bidder was not interfered with in his possession. The estate has now been surveyed; and it may be hoped that the Rája will introduce a regular settlement on the basis of the survey.

The town.

The town of Pithápuram is one of the least attractive places imaginable. The streets are narrow, winding, uneven and dusty, and the houses are poor in appearance. The Rája's residence is in striking contrast, being an imposing building of great size.

The town possesses some religious and archæological interest. It is known throughout the Northern Circars as a place of pilgrimage. The particular point of sanctity is the *páda gaya* pool in front of the Kukkutésvara-svámi temple. According to the legend, a giant named Gayásura, who was so big that when he lay down his body stretched from Gaya to Pithápuram, once ruled southern India. He was killed by Siva while his feet were resting in Pithápuram near this pool. The pool is accordingly called the *páda* ('foot') *gaya*. The local Hindus speak of three gayas, where different parts of the dead giant were found. One of these is the place of that name in Bengal, and it is held throughout this district that any one who bathes there ought also to bathe in the *páda gaya* pool at Pithápuram. Three large images of Buddhist or Jain origin, sitting cross-legged in the usual contemplative attitude, stand at the side of one of the main streets of the town. They are known as *sanyási dévulu* ('ascetic gods') and a festival is held in honour of them in times of drought; by which means, it is supposed, they are induced to send rain. Four interesting inscriptions have been found in the Kunti-mádhava temple. These give some historical information and the genealogies of three lines of chieftains who ruled in the twelfth and thirteenth centuries.[1] A small mosque in the bazaar street has evidently been built with the materials of

[1] See Government Epigraphist's annual report for 1894, pp. 2 ff., and inscriptions Nos. 490 to 493 of 1893.

an old Hindu shrine. It is locally supposed that the pillars came from the Kuntimádhava temple. There are some inscriptions on the pillars.

One of the largest cattle markets in the district takes place in the town every Saturday. The sale of the right to collect the fees at this fetches over Rs. 3,000 annually. The excellent bell-metal work done in the place is referred to in Chapter VI. About fifty households of Dévángas weave plain but fine cloths and about the same number of Sénápatis make coarser stuffs.

Ponnáda.

Ponnáda: Lies near the sea coast eight miles east by north of Pithápuram. Population 2,927. Its ancient importance is attested by the fact that three spots in Pithápuram town, namely, one of the fort gates, a well, and a cattle-stand, bear its name. A building erected round a banyan tree in the village is held sacred both by the Muhammadans and the Hindus of the locality. The legend says that long ago a Muhammadan widow wished to be buried with her husband, was prevented, but was permitted to live in this building, which was erected over his tomb. After her death the entrances to the building were closed.

Uppáda.

Uppáda: Seven miles east-south-east of Pithápuram; population 3,912. Contains a police-station. The travellers' bungalow recently collapsed owing to the encroachments of the sea. It is noted for its muslins, which are known throughout a large part of the Presidency. They are referred to in Chapter VI. About 200 Dévángas are engaged in this industry.

The village gives its name to a small zamindari estate with an income of Rs. 2,700 and a peshkash of Rs. 660. This was given by the late Rája of Pithápuram to his sister.

The erosion of the coast and the existence of a submerged town here have been referred to in Chapter I.

RAJAHMUNDRY TALUK.

CHAP. XV. RAJAH-MUNDRY.

RAJAHMUNDRY taluk lies along the left bank of the Gódávari just above the head of the delta. Most of it is not a particularly fertile upland, and as much as 71 per cent. of the soil is ferruginous. Nearly all the rest is regar. The taluk is irrigated chiefly by tanks, of which 28 of fair size are in charge of the Public Works department. The largest are those at Kottapalli (ayacut 970 acres) and Kápavaram (823 acres). Rice is the most widely grown crop, but the areas under tobacco and castor are considerable. Nine per cent. of the cultivable land is unoccupied, and the incidence of the land revenue per head is only Rs. 1-10-11. The number of educational institutions in Rajahmundry town results in the people being more literate than in any other taluk, and over ten per cent. of the male population can read and write. The industries of Rajahmundry town and Dowlaishweram are referred to below. At Rájánagaram and Káteru a fair amount of weaving is done, at Duppalapúdi black bangles are made by twenty Kápus, and the stone-carving of Jégurupádu is well known. Large taluk board chattrams have been established at Rájánagaram and Dowlaishweram.

Nearly the whole of the taluk is Government land. It includes nine villages of the Pithápuram zamindari and also nine other small proprietary estates, but of these latter all but one consist of only one village. The exception is Vangalapúdi, which comprises three villages.

Dowlaish-weram.

Dowlaishweram: Four and a half miles south of Rajahmundry. Population 10,304. It appears to have been a place of importance during the early struggles between the Hindus and Muhammadans and is now widely known as the site of Sir Arthur Cotton's great anicut across the Gódávari, referred to in Chapter IV, is the head-quarters of two Executive Engineers, and contains the Public Works department's workshops mentioned in Chapter VI. The town is a union and contains a local fund dispensary (established 1892), a large local fund choultry, a fair-sized market, an English lower secondary school for boys, and a Sanskrit school. The choultry (called, after the house-name of the donor, the Kruttivantivári choultry) is endowed with land bringing in an income of Rs. 2,100 annually, and was bequeathed to the taluk board. The income is devoted to feeding Bráhmans. There are a small European church and cemetery in the village. What looks like a town wall and is pierced by the road entering the place is really only the bank of the old railway constructed to bring materials from the quarry to the river for the building of the anicut.

Dowlaishweram possesses considerable religious interest for Hindus. The name Dowlaishweram is derived from that of the neighbouring hill Daulagiri. There, it is said, a saint named Nárada used to live; and he is credited with the foundation of the Vaishnavite temple of Janárdhanasvámi on the hill, as well as of many other shrines to the same god in the villages on the river bank in this and the Rámachandrapuram taluk. That in Dowlaishweram has an annual festival lasting six days in February or March. A cave on the side of the hill is supposed to be the mouth of a subterranean passage leading to Benares. In it is a stone image called *Konda Nivásudu* or *Santána Gópálasvámi*, which is visited by women who desire to have children. The temple of Anjanéya contains two *rávi* trees said to have been planted by Ráma and Síta respectively; and there are two footsteps in the rock there which are supposed to be those of these two deities. Dowlaishweram is in consequence sometimes called *Ráma páda kshétram*, 'the holy place of Ráma's feet.' The sanctity of the village is also enhanced by the fact that it is the last place at which the waters of the Gódávari flow down united and undiminished, and by a fanciful legend that 108 Siva temples lie buried somewhere or other in the neighbourhood. The result is that Dowlaishweram is one of the holiest of the bathing-places along this holy river, and is thronged by pilgrims during the *pushkaram* festival.[1]

A feast to the village goddess Mutyálamma is held in the village once every three years. A buffalo is sacrificed and afterwards votive offerings of pots of buttermilk are presented to the goddess, she is taken outside the village, and the pots are emptied there. The head of the buffalo and a pot of its blood are also carried round the village by a Mála, and a pig is sacrificed in an unusual and cruel manner. It is buried up to its neck and cattle are driven over it until it is trampled to death. This is supposed to ensure the health of men and cattle in the ensuing year.

A few industries flourish in the place. Two Kamsalas make brass and bronze vessels, and about 25 persons of various castes do really good wood-carving. The place is also known for its architects, who are said to be employed

[1] See Chapter I, p. 6.

CHAP. XV. RAJAHMUNDRY.

throughout the plain taluks of the district when houses are built.

Gókavaram.

Gókavaram: Nineteen miles north-north-east of Rajahmundry. Population 2,425. Contains a local fund rest-house and a large weekly market to which the hill people bring the produce of the Rampa country for sale.

Kórukonda.

Kórukonda: Eleven miles north-north-east of Rajahmundry. Population 3,952. Contains a police-station. A travellers' bungalow is kept up in the neighbouring village of Gónagúdem. A pilgrimage to the temple of Narasimhasvámi at Kórukonda is supposed to be of unrivalled efficacy in granting offspring to childless women, and the place is often thronged with suppliants of this class. Rumour avers that the Bráhmans of the place take a personal and direct share in ensuring that their prayers shall not be fruitless, and the belief has passed into a proverb. A festival which lasts for fifteen days takes place at the temple in the months of January and February.

Kórukonda and its neighbour Kóti[1] appear once to have been of some political importance. One of the Mackenzie MSS. which deals with the ancient history of the district[2] gives some account of their early fortunes. It says that Kóti and 101 Siva temples were founded by king Rájarája of the Eastern Chálukya line, who reigned from 1022 to 1063 and is prominent in the traditional history of Rajahmundry, and that about two hundred years later a fort was built in Kóti by an early Reddi chief named Annala Déva. The MS. goes on to quote a local inscription of 1322–23, apparently still in existence at the end of the eighteenth century, which recorded the revenue arrangements made in the village by the Kákatíya king, Pratápa Rudra, who reigned till 1324. The Kórukonda fort was built some time afterwards by Kúna Reddi, 'a good Súdra who became ruler of the adjoining country,' and who governed wisely and well. He was succeeded by his son Mummidi Reddi, one of whose servants erected the Lakshminarasimha temple. The date of this event is given both in the MS. and in an inscription quoted by Mr. Sewell as 1353.[3] Mummidi Reddi's three immediate successors ruled for the next 40 years. One of them rebuilt the Ranganáthasvámi temple in 1394-95 A.D.

[1] Said to be short for Kótilingam ('a crore of lingams') and to be derived from the number of Saivite emblems about the place.

[2] Local Records, vol. ii, p. 231 and vol. xix, p. 75. See also Chapter II, p. 25.

[3] *Lists of Antiquities*, i, 21. The MS. only gives the cycle year.

From this point until Muhammadan times are reached, the MS. is silent, but it gives details of the lessees of the place under the Musalmans. The fort was apparently destroyed by the vigorous and cruel Rustum Khán (1730-37) referred to on pp. 29-30. Its ruins are still to be seen, and there is another ruined fortress at Kóti. On the Pándava hill west of Kórukonda are two rock-cut caves. The MS. says that the Pándavas lived in them during their exile.

Kottapalli.

Kottapalli: Twenty-two miles north-north-east of Rajahmundry. Population 3,900. Contains a travellers' bungalow and a large tank which irrigates some 970 acres. The village gave its name to one of the 'pergunnas' of the old Pólavaram zamindari. For many years this was divided from the rest of that estate and managed by a díwán; but in 1781 it was reannexed to it and shortly afterwards was placed under Narasimha, a brother of the Pólavaram zamindar. During the fighting in 1785 at Gútála, described in the account of Pólavaram, two usurpers wrested Kottapalli from Narasimha and the Government troops had to interfere. They captured the place and put Narasimha over it once more. He stood aloof from the disturbance of 1790 referred to in the account of Pólavaram, but joined in the more considerable rebellion of Mangapati at the close of the century. Kottapalli was then occupied by a company of sepoys to keep the hill people of Rampa in check, and the young zamindar was ultimately captured and deposed. His estate was then again united with Pólavaram. It was however once more separated from it afterwards, and its 36 villages were sold in 1808 for arrears of revenue. The purchaser himself fell into arrears in 1829, and the estate was attached and remained under management till 1841, in which year it was put up to auction and purchased by Government. The village now belongs to Government. It was formerly the head-quarters of a deputy tahsildar.

Rajahmundry.

Rajahmundry, the head-quarters of the taluk, stands on the left bank of the Gódávari at the head of the great railway bridge (see p. 133) which carries the Madras Railway across that river. It is a municipality of 36,408 inhabitants, and the second most important town in the district.

The earliest mention of Rajahmundry in any extant literature is in the introduction to the Telugu translation of the Mahábhárata, which was composed by Nannayabhatta in the reign of the Eastern Chálukya king Rájarája (1022-62) who is known to popular tradition as Rájarája Naréndra. In this the town is called Rájamahéndrapattanam ('the city of Rájamahéndra') and is referred to as the capital of the Eastern

CHAP. XV. RAJAHMUNDRY.

Chálukya kingdom and 'the central gem of the Vengi country.' Rájamahéndra was a title borne by two of Rájarája's predecessors, namely, Amma I (918–25) and Amma II (945–70), and the town was perhaps founded by and called after one or other of these kings. But one of the Mackenzie MSS. attributes its foundation to an earlier king named Vijayáditya Mahéndra.

The extension of the Eastern Chálukya dominions into the kingdom of Kalinga on the north must have rendered Rajahmundry an important strategical point. It is described in comparatively recent times as 'the barrier and key to the Vizagapatam country'.[1] On the downfall of the Kákatíya dynasty of Warangal before the armies of the Muhammadans in 1323, the conquerors made their way as far as Rajahmundry, and the 'Royal masjid' there contains an inscription dated 1323–24 which mentions Muhammad Tughlak of Delhi. Local tradition says that this building was formerly a Hindu temple and was converted to its present use by these Musalmans.

Rajahmundry next comes into prominence as the capital of one of the lines of Reddi kings.[2] Its first independent sovereign of that line has left inscriptions in it the dates of which range from 1385 to 1422. By 1458–59 a minister of the Gajapati king Kapilésvara was ruling at Rajahmundry; and in 1470–71 the town was captured by the armies of the Muhammadan Sultan of Kulbarga. About 1478 the Hindus revolted and the Muhammadan garrison was besieged and perhaps reduced. The Vijayanagar chieftain Narasimha seems to have occupied the town at this time and to have been driven thence by a relieving force from Kulbarga. In any case the Muhammadans soon recaptured Rajahmundry and king Muhammad of Kulbarga made the town his head-quarters for some three years (1478–80).

Soon after, during the dissensions among the Musalman powers in the Deccan, Rajahmundry was taken by the king of Orissa. About 1515, however, the town was captured by Krishna Déva, the king of Vijayanagar, in the course of his campaign against the Orissa dynasty.

By 1543 Rajahmundry was the frontier town of the Orissa country and lay on the borders of the new Muhammadan conquests south and west of the Gódávari river. It was ruled by a prince of the Gajapati house, one Vidiádri, who seems to have affected independence. He was ill-advised enough to join in an attack upon his Muhammadan neighbours some time between 1550 and 1564, and paid a heavy penalty. Defeated in

[1] Cambridge's *War in India* (London, 1761), 207.
[2] *Ep. Ind.*, iv, 319.

the field, he was shut up in Rajahmundry. The Muhammadan powers of the Deccan then combined to deal a death-blow to the Vijayanagar kingdom, and he obtained a short respite. But on the return of the Musalman invaders he was again defeated outside the walls of Rajahmundry. At their first onset in this battle his troops broke the right wing of the enemy, but, on their reserve coming up, the fugitives rallied and drove their assailants inside the fort. Vidiádri was besieged there for four months, and at last (1571-72) was compelled to surrender. The fire of the heavy artillery of the Musalmans had made a breach nearly fifty paces in length in the curtain of the fort, and further resistance seemed useless. Vidiádri was permitted to go unharmed and Rajahmundry was never again a Hindu possession.

The neighbourhood was the scene of a stubborn battle a few years later, when the Muhammadan governor defeated the insurgent rája of Kasimkota. The fate of the day hung long in the balance and victory was only secured by a charge of Muhammadan cavalry which had turned the flank of the Hindu army.

On the disruption of Aurangzeb's empire, Rajahmundry became the head-quarters of a Nawábship of the province of Golconda. The names of the Nawábs, and indeed of all the Musalman governors of the town from 1572 to 1769, are given in the Mackenzie MS. referred to above.

After the cession of the Northern Circars to the French in 1753, Rajahmundry, on account of its central position, was chosen by Bussy as his head-quarters in preference to Masulipatam. It remained the French capital till the English invasion of 1758. On the evening after the battle of Condore, a force of 1,500 sepoys was sent on by Colonel Forde to occupy the town. They arrived on the following evening (December 10th 1758) and found the French, who imagined the whole English force to be upon them, in the act of evacuating the fort. One boat laden with several Europeans was in the middle of the Gódávari river, and some others with a few small field-pieces had just reached the opposite bank, when the English arrived. The English sepoys opened fire on them from the walls of the fort, and this deterred them from carrying off their guns, or remaining in the vicinity. Fifteen Frenchmen were taken prisoners in the fort, and also a quantity of ammunition and stores. The town was shortly afterwards, however, retaken by the French. When Colonel Forde advanced southwards against Masulipatam in February 1759, only a small garrison, some sick and wounded, and some

CHAP. XV. RAJAHMUNDRY.

treasure had been left there; and a detached French force made a dash for the place and easily captured it. The Commandant had only just time to send his treasure to Cocanada and his able-bodied men in retreat towards Vizagapatam before the French arrived. The latter, however, did not attempt to hold the place.

During the few years thereafter in which the district was again in the hands of the Nizam, Rajahmundry was the head-quarters of his local representative, Hussain Ali Khán. The latter's position was precarious, and an English force of 200 sepoys and twelve artillery men under Lieutenant (afterwards Sir Henry) Cosby was sent to Rajahmundry to support him. Two rival claimants were at that time competing for the position of Nawáb. A near relative of one of them was commandant of the fort at Rajahmundry, and had 500 Arabs, ready for any mischief, under him. He had entered into a conspiracy to take the town and hold it for his relative, but his design was defeated by the vigour and promptitude of Cosby, who, despite the insignificance of his force, took him prisoner. Reinforcements were soon received from Masulipatam, and Cosby maintained his position at Rajahmundry till the country was ceded to the English.

Though Masulipatam then became the centre of the administration, troops appear to have been stationed at Rajahmundry for many years. When, in 1794, the Chief and Council at Masulipatam were replaced by Collectors, one of the latter was stationed at Rajahmundry. When the 'Rajahmundry district' was constituted, the Collector did not live in the town which gave his charge its name, though from the very first this had contained the court of the Zilla Judge appointed in 1802,[1] and it was not until 1867 that even the Sub-Collector was stationed there. The Sub-Collector, the District and Sessions Judge and the District Superintendent of Police are stationed there now. The place moreover contains the usual taluk offices, a sub-registrar and a district munsif. It is the head-quarters of the American Evangelical Lutheran Mission, which keeps up a high school there, a station of the Roman Catholic Mission, and contains several Christian churches and two European cemeteries. The older of the latter is near the old Civil Court, and the tombs in it go back to 1771. The other contains a large number of graves dating from 1862 down to the present day.

The town also contains two travellers' bungalows, one belonging to the municipal council and the other to the taluk

[1] Chapter XIII, p. 189.

board; several private chattrams, two of which are important institutions; two police-stations, a police school and a large Special Police Reserve; a municipal hospital and a mission dispensary; a first-grade college, a training college, two high schools, three English lower secondary schools for boys, one English and three vernacular lower secondary schools for girls, and a Sanskrit school. The choultries are referred to in Chapter VII, the chief medical and educational institutions in Chapters IX and X respectively and the municipal council and its doings in Chapter XIV.

Rajahmundry is not only of interest historically and as an administrative centre, but is also of importance to Hindus from a religious point of view. It is held that all pilgrims going from this district to Benares should also visit Rajahmundry, and most of these people bathe in the river there on their way back from the holy city. They also observe the curious custom of emptying half the contents of the pots of Ganges water they bring back with them into the Gódávari, and fill them up again from the latter river. It is believed that if this is not done, the Ganges water will quickly dry up in the pot. The sanctifying effect of a bath in the Gódávari at Rajahmundry is placed so high that people come by train all the way from Madras for the purpose, often going back the next day. The bathing place is called the Kótilingam ('crore of lingams') ghat. The name is explained by a story that the Bráhman sages at one time wanted to make the place as sacred as Benares, where there are supposed to be a crore of lingams, and therefore set themselves to found the same number here in a single night. Unfortunately the day dawned before the last one was made. The lingams are supposed to lie buried in the bed of the Gódávari opposite the ghat. The river is held to be particularly sacred at Rajahmundry (and Dowlaishweram) because, like the Cauvery above the delta, it is still undiminished by division into many branches. It is called the Aganda ('entire') Gódávari, just as the other is called the Aganda Cauvery. The Rajahmundry ghat is one of the centres of the great *pushkaram* festival, which takes place once in thirteen years.[1]

The place is also noted for the worship of a very widely known village goddess called Chamalamma, whose image reposes under a tree about a mile away. A fortnight's festival in her honour is celebrated in the last month of the Telugu year (March-April), and at this a mud pot which her spirit is supposed to enter is taken round the town every day

[1] See Chapter I, p. 6.

CHAP. XV. RAJAHMUNDRY.

and worshipped. Various peculiar rites are performed at the festival. The buffalo which is sacrificed is not killed outright; but a wound is first made in its neck and a potful of its blood is collected. A hook-swinging is conducted, but a sheep is the victim, and not a man, and it is swung by a rope tied round its body. The ordinary offerings of sheep, fowls, buffaloes, etc., are also made in fulfilment of vows. Another local deity is called Kannamma Pérantálu ('housewife Kannamma'). She was a Reddi woman. She, her husband, and her six sons all died on one day of cholera about 40 years ago, and her soul appeared to one of her relatives and said she had been deified. Ever since then she has been worshipped by all the non-Bráhman Hindus of the place, who offer her sheep, fowls, cloths, etc. Her shrine is an unpretentious tiled house.

The industries of the place are of some note. Some 400 households of Dévángas weave coloured cloths for men and women, and some of them can do simple embroidery. A few Rangáris stamp chintzes, and some thirty Kamsalas make vessels of brass, bell-metal and lead. One or two Múchis are said to paint with skill, and thirty Kamsala and Odde carpenters do excellent wood-carving. Three fair-sized tanneries, managed by Labbais, are at work, and good shoes are made by Mádigas and Gódáras. A few potters make good gújás.

RÁMACHANDRAPURAM TALUK.

RÁMACHANDRAPURAM taluk lies along the left bank of the Gautami Gódávari just below the head of the delta.

Almost all its soil (91 per cent.) is alluvial, it is irrigated by the Gódávari water, nearly the whole of it is cultivated, and the density of its population is second only to that of Nagaram island. Paddy is naturally the chief crop, but tobacco is grown in fair quantities, and the area under sugar-cane is greater than in any other taluk in the district. Detailed statistics regarding the crops and other matters will be found in the separate Appendix.

Local industries are few. Kótipalli and Drákshárámam are sacred places, and tne temple in the latter contains many ancient inscriptions.

Nearly the whole of the taluk is now Government land. Eight villages belong to the Pithápuram zamindari, eight others to the Végayammapéta estate, and five more each make up a small estate.

Bikkavólu.

Bikkavólu: Nine miles north of Rámachandrapuram. Population 7,994. It is a union, and containts a sub-registrar's office and a small local fund market. Two Múchi wood-carvers do good work. The village is said in one of the Mackenzie MSS.[1] to have been the capital of the earlier Eastern Chálukya kings before they moved to Rajahmundry. It is said to contain extensive ruins and some deserted temples.[2]

The place is now famous as a centre of snake-worship. The snake-god Subbaráyadu has a three days' festival there in the *sashti* (sixth day) following the new moon in Margasira (December-January), which goes by the name of the *Subbaráyadi sashti*. People attend this in the hope of obtaining relief from small bodily ailments (such as boils and pains in the ears, eyes, etc.) and in order to get children. Childless women spend a night fasting in the temple clothed in a particular kind of cloth (called *nágula kókalu)* in which the colours are mixed in a peculiar way. All castes appear to resort tó the temple for the purpose. In former times a cobra was supposed to come out and show itself on one of the days of the festival.

[1] Wilson's, *Catalogue*, p. 397. No. 12, 4,
[2] Sewell's *Lists*, i, 25.

CHAP. XV. RAMACHANDRAPURAM. — Drákshárámam.

Drákshárámam: Four miles south by east of Rámachandrapuram; population 11,213. Contains a private chattram for feeding Bráhmans, a police-station, a sub-registrar's office and a large cattle-market. The union of which it is the chief village also includes Vélamapálaiyam, Tótapéta, Jagannáyakulapálaiyam and Végayammapéta. Two Múchi wood-carvers do particularly good work, and a little weaving of tape and cloths is carried on.

The village is noted for its fine temple and for its sanctity. Its name is said to be more correctly 'Daksharáma' and to mean 'the Garden of Daksha.' According to the well-known story in the *Sivapuránam*, this Daksha was a Bráhman, the father-in-law of Siva. Thinking that he had not been properly treated by that god, he performed a *yágam* (sacrifice) without inviting him to be present. His daughter attended uninvited, he treated her discourteously, and she accordingly plunged into the fire of the sacrifice. Siva burst into a sweat on hearing the news, and from this perspiration was born Vírabhadra, who went and killed Daksha. Orthodox Bráhmans will not perform a *yágam* inside the village, as it is held to be an ill-omened place.

The real centre of the religious interest of Drákshárámam is the temple of Bhímésvara-svámi. It contains a particularly big lingam, some fourteen or fifteen feet high. This is supposed to be part of a lingam which broke into five pieces and fell at five holy places, namely at Bhímavaram or Bhíma-ráma in Cocanada, Pálakollu or Kshíra-ráma in Kistna, Amarávati or Amara-ráma in the Guntúr district, and Kumára-ráma, which is not identified. It is supposed to have been erected by the sun and worshipped by the seven sages who made the seven mouths of the Gódávari.[1] So it is sufficiently holy. The seven sages are supposed to have each brought water from their respective rivers underground to the tank at Drákshárámam, which is called the *sapta Gódávari*, 'seven Gódávaris.' There is a sacred bathing ghat in this tank which confers in a condensed form all the sanctity which is to be obtained by separate baths in each of the seven rivers.

Like many other holy places in this and other districts, the town is called the southern Benares. It is supposed to have been founded by the sage Vyása, and a *rávi* tree and a lingam planted by him are still shown. So great is its sanctity that a night's halt in it is believed by some to render

[1] Chapter I, p. 6.

future births unnecessary. A festival is held in honour of the god every Mákha (February-March), and lasts for five days beginning on the eleventh day after the new moon day.

The temple is a rather handsome two-storeyed building. Its erection is ascribed by popular tradition to an unknown Chóla king. In the porch round the shrine in the upper storey are black granite Chálukyan pillars, a great rarity in this district. The lower porch is also of black granite. On the northern side of the temple a figure of a Jain tirthankara, sitting cross-legged, is carved on a stone slab. The stone *Nandi* (bull) and Hanumán in the temple have had their heads knocked off, and it is said that this was done by the Marátha marauders[1] when hunting for treasure. In the temple is a curious well, the mouth of which is the shape of a strung bow. It is called the *rudra tírtam*, and a bath in it is holy. The lingam at the side of the western gate is supposed to go to Benares every night.

The temple has an annual allowance of Rs. 1,000 from Government, and some of the servants in it have inam lands. But it is a large building and is not in particularly good repair. It contains a great number of ancient inscriptions. No less than 271 of these have been transcribed by the Government Epigraphist (Nos. 181 to 451 of 1893). The earliest appears to be No. 185, which is dated in A.D. 1055, or during the reign of the Rájarája whose capital was at Rajahmundry. The latest appears to be No. 426, which belongs to the Reddis' times, and is dated in the year corresponding to 1447 A.D.

Drákshárámam is sacred to Muhammadans also. The mosque and tomb of a saint called Saiyid Sháh Bhaji Aulia are much revered by the Muhammadans of the neighbourhood, who are often buried within their precincts. This saint is said to have been a contemporary of the famous Míra Sáhib of Nagore near Negapatam, and, like that rather shadowy personality, to have lived some five hundred years ago. He was born, it is said, at 'Gardez,' near Medina, and visited Drákshárámam with four disciples. Being hungry, the visitors slaughtered the bull belonging to a *math* of the local Saivite priests. In the disputes which ensued the comparative holiness of the Muhammadan saint and the Saivite head-priest was called in question; and to test the matter a lingam was thrown into a pond (the *Lingála cheruvu*) and each was told to charm it back again. The saint succeeded, was given the *math* to live in, and turned it into a mosque. A very similar tale is related

[1] See Chapter II, p. 30.

CHAP. XV. RÁMACHANDRAPURAM.

of the Bábayya darga at Penukonda.[1] The saint had a daughter, and her descendants are still living. They are said to receive an endowment from the Nizam of Hyderabad. In former times a festival of some importance used to be held at the mosque, but of recent years it has ceased to be observed.

Two Dutch tombs stand in the village on what is called the *Ollandu dibba* ('the Holland mound'). They are dated 1675 and 1728 respectively and are covered with the sculptured slabs which are characteristic of Dutch tombs in this Presidency.

Gangavaram.

Gangavaram: Seven miles south of Rámachandrapuram. Population 1,532. The name is supposed to mean 'Ganges blessing;' and to explain it a legend has been invented to the effect that the Gautami Gódávari blessed the Ganges at this place. Defiled by the sins of the many wicked people who bathed in her, the latter river used to come every day in the form of a crow to be purified by the Gautami, and used to return in the form of a *hamsa* bird. At last the Gautami took pity on her and blessed her, and now she can purify herself.

Kótipalli.

Kótipalli: Nine and three-quarter miles south of Rámachandrapuram. Population 2,476. It contains a travellers' bungalow and a large private choultry maintained by the proprietor of Pólavaram, at which travellers are fed. Tape and *kusa* mats are manufactured on a small scale in the village. Its correct name seems to be Kódipaili, which Dr. Macleane translates 'border village,' apparently from the Tamil *kódi*. It is also sometimes called Kótipali, which means 'a crore of benefits' and is explained by the assertion that the value of a good deed done there is increased one crore-fold by the sanctity of the place. The place is in fact held very sacred by Hindus. A bath in the Gódávari here has virtue to expiate the most terrible of sins, even incest with a mother, and the bathing-ghat is called *mátrigamanághahári* for this reason. A story is told of a Bráhman who inadvertently committed this sin, and was in consequence turned into a leper until he bathed here.

The temple is dedicated to Sómésvara, 'the moon god,' and is supposed to have been built by him to expiate his sin of having seduced the wife of his teacher Brahaspati. The injured husband cursed the moon and caused it to loose its brightness. In the same precincts is a shrine to Kótísvaradu, 'the god of crores.' This was built, it is declared, by Indra

[1] *Anantapur District Gazetteer*, 193.

to atone for his seduction of the wife of Gautama. The erring god brought 'crores of waters' underground to the Gódávari at this place; andt he deity of the temple took his name from this act. There is a local festival there every year on the Sivarátri day. The great *pushkaram* festival held once in every thirteen years is celebrated here with great éclat.

Kótipalli forms a proprietary estate which pays a peshkash of Rs. 5,831. It belongs to the Rája of Vizianagram.

Márédipáka.

Márédipáka: Seven miles west by north of Rámachandrapuram. Population 1,005. Some Singams do a little tape-weaving there. After Kándrakóta in Peddápuram taluk, this is the greatest centre for the worship of the village deities in the district. The goddess of this village is called Mávullamma. She was originally a mortal maiden who was persecuted by her mother. Unable to bear the latter's cruelty, she hid in a cave by a mango tree, and disappeared for ever. Some days later she was seen in a dream by her parents, and informed them that she had become one with the divine, and must henceforth be worshipped as a goddess. This has been done, and the priests at her temple are supposed to belong to her family. The annual festival in her honour, which lasts for a fortnight, attracts many pilgrims. One peculiar feature of the ceremonies is that the blood of the sacrificed buffalo is left in the temple all night, with various kinds of grain scattered around it, and the door secured and sealed. In the morning, it is said, a foot-step is seen in the temple, and some of the grain is found thrown into the pot. This is considered to afford a forecast of the coming season; those grains being expected to do well which are found in the pot.

Rámachandrapuram.

Rámachandrapuram: Head-quarters of the taluk, and once the chief village of a large ancient zamindari which was eventually bought in by Government. The place is a union of 10,692 inhabitants, the other component villages being Pasalapúdi and Mutsumilli, and contains a travellers' bungalow, a local fund rest-house for natives, a police-station, an English lower secondary school for boys and a local fund hospital founded in 1876. A tahsildar, stationary sub-magistrate and sub-registrar are stationed there. Some 25 Dévánga households weave cloths of a fair quality. The village is a centre of trade in local produce.

Rámaghattálu.

Rámaghattálu: Four miles east of Kótipalli. It is a hamlet of the village of Masakapalli, the population of which is 2,244. It contains one of the many temples supposed to have been founded by Ráma to expiate the sin of having killed the Bráhman king Rávana. Ráma's foot-steps are said

CHAP. XV. RÁMACHANDRAPURAM.

to be visible on a rock there. A bath at this place on the Sundays in the month of Mákham (February-March) is considered holy.

Végayammapéta.

Végayammapéta: Five miles south-south-east of Rámachandrapuram and part of Drákshárámam union. Population 2,004. Contains a lower secondary school for boys. It is the chief village of an ancient zamindari, which comprises ten villages and pays a peshkash of Rs. 8,055. The present holder says that the estate was originally given by 'Haidar Bádsháh'—apparently the Nizam of Hyderabad—to one of his ancestors for his literary ability. It was permanently settled in 1802 on a peshkash of Rs. 8,750. The estate was diminished by a partition in 1809, and in 1879 a suit about it went up as far as the Privy Council. The present zamindarni says that she is the eleventh in descent from the original founder.

TUNI DIVISION.

CHAP. XV. TUNI.

TUNI division lies in the north-east corner of the district. It is the most sparsely populated tract in the district outside the Agency, and education is very backward in it.

It is a hilly tract and contains little irrigated land. One large tank waters nearly 2,000 acres near Hamsavaram, and a few channels take off from the Tandananadi river. The local rainfall averages only 35·79 inches, which is low for this district. The incidence of land revenue per head of the population is only seven and a half annas. The weaving at Tuni is as good as is to be found anywhere in the district, and a considerable manufacture of oil is carried on at the same place. Bangles are made at Hamsavaram and Kottapalli.

The division contains the whole of the Kottam or Tuni estate and twelve villages belonging to the Pithápuram estate.

Bendapúdi: Twelve and a half miles south-west of Tuni. Population 1,477. It contains the ruins of what must at one time have been a very large fort. Old copper coins (and, more rarely, gold ones) are found there after rain. People believe that the philosopher's stone *(parsavédi)* is also to be found there. The ruins include many dilapidated temples. Popular legend ascribes the building of the fort to the Kákatíya king Pratápa Rudra, and the same account of it is given in one of the Mackenzie MSS.[1] called the 'Kórukonda *kyfeat*,' which gives a description of that place. The fort at Bendapúdi is said in this to have been founded by two brothers, Pedda Malla Rázu and Chinna Malla Rázu, who ruled the country under Pratápa Rudra. They were an effeminate and tyrannical couple, if the account is to be credited. They drew upon themselves the vengeance of the king of Cuttack by abducting the bride of one of his relatives, who was passing through the district. An army came from Cuttack to exact vengeance, and the fort was besieged. It fell after a siege of six years, the water-supplies being cut off. The affair is described in some detail in the manuscript. Bendapúdi.

In the hamlet of Tirupati Agraháram is a temple to Venkatésvarasvámi, in honour of which a five days' festival is held every year in Chaitra (April-May). This is largely attended and is well known to people living north of Cocanada.

[1] Wilson's *Catalogue*, 396, 8 (3).

CHAP. XV. TUNI.

Hamsavaram.

Hamsavaram: Six miles south-south-west of Tuni. Population 1,909. Lime is collected there in large quantities and taken to Tuni to be burnt, and glass bangles are made there.

Kottapalli

Kottapalli: Nine miles south-west of Tuni. Also called Ayyapparázu Kottapalli. Population 2,449. There is a mound by the roadside near the village, which is known as the tomb of one Mála Bucchamma, a Mála woman who is said to have burnt herself to death many years ago, no one knows why. People of all castes make prayers and vows at this tomb. In the hamlet of Sítarámpuram glass bangles are made.

Tallúru.

Tallúru: Two miles west-north-west of Tuni. Population 248. A cave in a hill there contains the image of Talupulamma ('door mother'), a goddess very much revered in this division. The adjoining valley is called Talupulamma lóva. From the hill a perennial spring flows down into the jungle. This is a very favourite bathing-place, and the local people pretend that they do not know where the stream goes to. They declare that the torrent shrinks or widens in proportion to the number of people bathing in it! The goddess is especially appealed to in time of drought, her favourite days being Tuesdays, Thursdays and Sundays. She is worshipped with the usual animal sacrifices.

Tátipáka.

Tátipáka: Six miles north-north-west of Tuni. Also called Tátipáka-Jagannáthanagaram. Population, 346. A tomb there is called the *gundam* (pit) of Lakshmamma, a woman who is supposed to have committed *sati* at this spot. It is reverenced by the people of the locality, and a small festival is held there in February or March.

Tétagunta.

Tétagunta: Seven and a half miles south-west of Tuni. Population 2,600. A hill there called the *Parnasála konda* is supposed to have been inhabited by the Pándava brothers. It contains a large cave about a hundred yards in length and consisting of two compartments.

Tuni.

Tuni: Head-quarters of the division, and the chief town of the Tuni or Kottam estate. Besides the offices of the deputy tahsildar and a sub-registrar, the town contains a police-station, a travellers' bungalow, a private choultry for feeding Bráhmans and Súdras, a large local fund market, a local fund dispensary (established 1879), and the zamindar's high school for boys. It has been constituted a union and has a population of 8,842. Good weaving of the same kind and quality as in Uppáda is done there by about 200 Dévángas; a few Kápus do simple dyeing and chintz-stamping; five or six blacksmiths make ordinary household vessels of brass; a large manufacture of castor and gingelly oil is carried on, and there are two factories for the purpose; and the place is a considerable trading centre.

The Kottam estate is interesting as being the only remnant of the old Peddápuram zamindari which remains in the hands of the original family. It was created in 1810. A claim was advanced in that year to the zamindari of Peddápuram by a relation of the then zamindar; and, in settlement of that claim, the Kottam estate, till then a portion of the Peddápuram zamindari, was severed from the rest of the property and made over to the claimant's father, Vatsavaya Súrappa Rázu. The two estates were once again for a short time under the same proprietor. In 1838 one Súrya Náráyana, grandson of Vatsavaya Súrappa Rázu, was recognized as proprietor of the Kottam mitta and soon afterwards succeeded also to the Peddápuram zamindari; but the latter estate had been held for but a short time by him when it was sold for arrears of revenue. The present zamindar, Rája Vatsavaya Venkata Simhadri Jagapati Rázu, is the second son of Súrya Náráyana, and succeeded to the estate after the death of his elder brother in 1879. He is now (1906) fifty-two years old. The property consists of 38 villages situated within a radius of twelve miles of Tuni. It pays a peshkash of Rs. 26,219.

BHADRÁCHALAM TALUK.

CHAP. XV. Bhadrá chalam.

BHADRÁCHALAM taluk runs along the left bank of the Gódávari above the Gháts, by which it is cut off from the rest of the district. It is intersected by the Saveri, an important tributary joining the Gódávari at Kunnavaram. Owing to its position beyond the Gháts its climatic conditions are rather different from those of most of the district. The variations in temperature are greater, and the rainfall, which is almost all brought by the south-west monsoon, is 43·39 inches at Bhadráchalam, a high record for this district, and probably much greater in other parts of the taluk. The officer who drew up the working-plans for the Rékapalle forests inferred 'from an examination of the undergrowth and the general factors of that locality that 70 inches would be a closer estimate' of the annual rainfall among them. The taluk is for the most part covered with low hills and forest. Some high hills rise to the west of the Saveri river adjoining the Gháts, and a smaller cluster stands some way from the Gódávari and to the east of the Saveri near Bódugúdem in the centre of the taluk. The whole of the taluk is malarious, especially the villages along and to the east of the Saveri river, but the scope for irrigation is considerable, and with more energetic ryots and a better land system cultivation might be largely extended.

Cholam is the staple crop of the country, though paddy and a little tobacco are grown along the river banks. The taluk appears to contain no indigenous industries whatever. The lace-work of the Dummagúdem mission is referred to in Chapter VI.

The taluk is of interest in several unusual directions. The curious Kóya people (see p. 60) make up a large proportion of its inhabitants; its revenue system, inherited from the Central Provinces administration, is in most respects (p. 174) unusual in this Presidency; coal has been mined for at Gaurìdévipéta (sixteen miles east of Bhadráchalam), albeit (p. 10) without much success, and plumbago has been worked at Pedakonda; garnets, rock-crystal, sapphires and gold are found; the country possesses many legendary associations with the story told in the Rámáyana of Rávana's stealing Síta, the wife of Ráma; and in it, from fifteen miles below Bhadráchalam to four miles north of Dummagúdem, are a number of rude stone monuments. No weapons have yet been found in these, but they contain half-burnt pottery, charred bones, and beads of ivory and glass. From the position of skeletons around them it would appear that human sacrifices accompanied the funeral ceremonies.[1] Forts ascribed to the Reddi dynasty are found at Nallapalli, four miles north-east of Dummagúdem, and at Vaddigúdem near Rékapalle. There are also the remains of a fine stone fort at Dévarapalli, nine miles east of Bhadráchalam; but it was largely demolished by the engineers engaged in the Upper Gódávari navigation works.

As is mentioned in Chapter XI, the zamindar of Bhadráchalam has a semi-proprietary right over the whole of the taluk. Beneath him, but still recognized by Government, are a number of other proprietors of larger or smaller estates. The only one of these which is of any size is Rékapalle, which was for some time independent of its suzerain, and the history of which is sketched below. The others only contain a village or two apiece. The largest are those of Nandigáma, which contains ten villages and pays a peshkash of Rs. 1,308, and Tripurapantavídu, with seven villages and a peshkash of Rs. 1,195. No other inferior proprietor pays as much as Rs. 400 peshkash.

Bhadráchalam.

Bhadráchalam: Head-quarters of the taluk and of the Head Assistant Collector. Population 1,783. It is the chief town of the zamindari of the same name. The original holder of this is said to have been one Anapa Ashwa Rao, who received it in free jaghir from the Emperor of Delhi in A.D. 1324 on condition of keeping up a body of 500 foot for service, and it is stated that the property has remained almost ever since in the families of the founder or his kinsmen. The taluk formed part of a large estate which is called by Captain Glasfurd[2] the Hussanabad Sankaragiri zamindari, and is also spoken of as the Palavancha estate, from the town of that name in the Nizam's Dominions in which a large portion of it lay. The zamindar of Bhadráchalam is zamindar of Palavancha also.

In 1769 one of the Nizam's officers put the then zamindar to death and took the estate under management till his own death in 1778, when it reverted to the founder's family. In 1809 an adoption, said to have been the first in the family, was made. This was the cause of a great deal of disturbance

[1] Sewell's *Lists*, i, 20.

[2] See his settlement report on this taluk (Nagpur, 1869), para. 41.

CHAP. XV. BHADRÁCHALAM.

and even bloodshed. The adopting zamindar belonged to the Damara Ashwa Rao family, and selected as his heir a boy of the Kundemulla family. This choice was resented and resisted by another family, called by Captain Glasfurd the Setpilly Ashwa Raos, who thought one of their members ought to have been selected. The struggle between the members of these families went on for more than forty years. The Setpillys were at first victorious; but their representative made a raid into British territory and was taken prisoner and carried off to Hyderabad in 1811. The Damara adoptee was now appointed zamindar by the Nizam; but he was so harassed by the Setpillys that in 1819 a European officer (Mr. Ralph) was sent with a body of local troops to Palavancha, where he remained to keep order for three years. The Nizam soon intervened again, this time granting a small portion of the estate to the Setpillys and one village to the Damaras, and taking the rest under his own management. The Setpillys defied the local authorities in 1844 and seized the greater part of the estate; but their representative died in 1851; and, after a little disturbance and some negotiation the property was handed over finally to the Damaras on a decision being passed in their favour (in 1852) by an influential pancháyat of zamindars. The Damara appointed in 1852 was succeeded by his mother in 1859, who was followed before her death in 1874 by her daughter's son, Parthasarathi Appa Rao, who is the present zamindar. The estate at one time (see p. 175) also included the present Rékapalle zamindari.

Until the taluk was handed over to the British Government by the Nizam in 1860 the Bhadráchalam zamindar always kept up a troop of Rohillas, who received very little pay for their services and lived chiefly by looting the country round. The taluk was divided into ten *samutús*, each of which theoretically contained twenty-five Kóya villages and each of which had to supply for a month, without pay or batta, a hundred Kóyas to carry burdens, fetch supplies, etc., for the Rohillas, and a hundred Mádigas to act as horse-keepers. The whole country appears to have been at the mercy of these undisciplined Rohillas. 'All was grist,' writes Mr. Cain,[1] 'that came to their mill, even the clothes of the poor Koi women, who were frequently stripped and then regarded as objects of ridicule. The Kois have frequently told me that they never could lie down to rest at night without feeling that before morning their slumbers might be rudely disturbed, their houses burnt and their property carried off. As a rule they hid their grain

[1] *Ind. Ant.*, v, 303.

in caves and holes of large trees . . . . The last great plundering took place in 1859 not far from Parnasála.'

The present position of the Bhadráchalam zamindar is in many respects unlike that of most other zamindars in this Presidency owing to his estate having been first settled by the Central Provinces Government. The point is referred to in Chapter XI.

Bhadráchalam is considered a holy spot, since Ráma is supposed to have lived there for some time after the abduction of Síta. The name means 'the hill of Bhadra,' and is said to be derived from the fact that a saint of that name was living there at the time of Ráma's sojourn. Ráma promised to return when he had found Síta, and did so after many years, and gave the saint salvation. The temple in the village, which is built on the top of a small hillock and is not remarkable architecturally, is supported by an endowment from the treasury of the Nizam of Hyderabad, which amounts to Rs. 19,000 a year but small sums from which are diverted to the upkeep of the temple at Parnasála and those in Hyderabad territory at Mótigadda and Viruvandi opposite Chintalagúdem and Turubáka in this taluk. Legend says that the first beginnings of the Bhadráchalam shrine were made by a *bairági* who took up his abode there, built a small temple and carved a rude image of Ráma. More authenticated history commences about 1725, when Ráma Dás, an official of the Nizam's government, was sent to collect the revenues of this taluk. Instead of transmitting the money, he spent it in enlarging the shrine and building the *gópuram*. His superiors at last objected to this, and sent a number of Rohillas who carried him to Hyderabad, where he died after an imprisonment of twelve years. Tradition, however, declares that he was miraculously ransomed by Ráma and Lakshmana (who appeared before the then Nizam in person) and returned to Bhadráchalam, where he disappeared and became one with the god. His adventures are the subject of a book of Telugu poems, called the Ráma Dás *kírtana*, which is widely known throughout the country. The poems in this are often sung by the Telugu bards (*bhágavatas*) who are in such favour at social gatherings throughout south India.

Ráma Dás was succeeded in his office by a certain Túmu Lakshminarasimha Rao who, wiser than his predecessor, annually despatched part of the tribute and devoted the rest to finishing the work the latter had begun. He also commenced another temple. While he was thus engaged a wealthy man from Madras, named Varadaráma Dás, brought two lakhs of rupees to Bhadráchalam and agreed to help him to complete the work. Before this could be done, however, the Nizam's government, dissatisfied with the small amount of revenue received, sent a number of sowars to take Lakshminarasimha Rao to Hyderabad. He bribed the sowars to give him a little grace, promising to follow them shortly to Hyderabad. The rich man from Madras died soon after their departure; and Lakshminarasimha Rao embarked on rafts to cross the river, taking with him the dead man, his widow and mother, his own mother and a number of servants. Half way across he threw the corpse into the river and plunged in himself, followed by the widow, her mother-in-law and most of their followers.

The Nizam originally endowed the temple with a lakh of rupees, but the endowment was gradually reduced till in 1840-41 it was fixed at Rs. 19,125, for which a sanad was given. An important festival takes place at the temple in the month of Chaitra (March-April) and is said to be attended by as many as 20,000 people from all parts of India, in spite of the difficulties of the journey thither. A common object of the pilgrimage is to obtain children; the childless women sleep behind the temple and draw an augury of the future from their dreams.

Dummagúdem.

Dummagúdem: Thirteen miles north of Bhadráchalam. Population 2,556. It was the head-quarters of the old Upper Gódávari Navigation project referred to in Chapter VII. Operations on this were discontinued in 1871, but while they were in progress Dummagúdem was a busy town. It is now an insignificant village. The anicut is in good condition and a large lock stands close to the village and a canal runs parallel with the river there for two miles. The lock is in fair condition, but was much damaged by the floods of 1900. The village is also the head-quarters of the Church Missionary Society in the district (see p. 41) and the centre (p. 112) of a lace-making industry fostered by this. A number of roughly carved idols have been dug up near the place.

Gundála.

Gundála: Four and a half miles east of Bhadráchalam. Population 359. This (like Sarpavaram in the Cocanada taluk) is said to be the place where king Janaméjaya, the son of Paríkshit, performed the sacrifice described in the Mahábhárata because his father had been bitten by a snake. A hot spring in the bed of the Gódávari near by is pointed out as the pit (*gundam*) where the sacrifice was performed. Pilgrims to Bhadráchalam bathe in this, and the name Gundála is supposed to be derived from it.

Kumárasvámigúdem: Twenty-six miles south-east of Bhadráchalam. Population 110. Contains a very old and sacred temple to Kumárasvámi, son of Siva. He was devoted to the fair sex more than was seemly, and his father cured him by contriving that any woman he looked upon should at once assume the shape of his mother, Párvati. The first occasion on which this happened was at Kumárasvámigúdem, and Kumárasvámi induced Siva to direct that a bath in the Gódávari at that spot should have great sanctifying virtue. The temple has no income and is very much out of repair.

Kumárasvámigúdem.

Kunnavaram: Stands at the junction of the Saveri and Gódávari rivers; population 1,107. Formerly the station of the Special Assistant Agent and now the head-quarters of the District Forest Officer, Upper Gódávari. It is an important point for the river-borne trade, as it is beyond the Gháts and the unbridged Saveri and carts can travel from it to Bhadráchalam.

Kunnavaram.

Parnasála: Twenty-two miles by road north of Bhadráchalam. Population 276. It is widely believed in the district that this is the spot on the banks of the Gódávari described in the Rámáyana where Rávana carried off Síta.

Parnasála.

In a stream bed near the village the people show the stone on which Síta is supposed to have sat while bathing. Certain marks on a rock resemble foot-prints, and these are therefore called Síta's foot-prints, and are revered accordingly. On another rock are yellow stains which are attributed to the yellow dye from Síta's clothes when they were laid out to dry, or, according to another account, to the saffron she used to adorn herself withal. The black stain left by Ráma's sash when put out to dry is also shown on another rock. The Nalugu gutta hill on the opposite side of the river is supposed to have been formed by an accumulation of *nalugu* (a kind of soap) left by Síta after her daily bath. Behind the Vishnu temple is a hollow which is pointed out as the exact place where Síta was seized; some of the earth is said to have been carried off with her. There is also a Siva temple in the neighbourhood where, it is said, Rávana used to pretend to worship, disguised as a mendicant.

A small festival is held at Parnasála in Chaitra (March-April) at the same time as the Bhadráchalam festival, and those who visit the latter place go on to Parnasála.

Rékapalle: Twenty-eight miles east-south-east of Bhadráchalam, and below the junction of the Gódávari and Saveri rivers. Population 617. The name means 'wing village' and is explained as referring to the abduction of Síta which

Rékapalle.

CHAP. XV. BHADRACHALAM.

tradition locates in this taluk. It is supposed that the wings of the bird Jatáyu, who tried to oppose Rávana's flight but was killed by him, fell here.

Rékapalle is still important as the chief village of the most considerable of the inferior proprietors of this part of the country. The Rékapalle estate formed only a part of the large possessions of the Ashwa Raos of Palavancha and Bhadráchalam referred to in the account of the latter place above, and it was leased in 1574 to a family of Kórukonda (in Rajahmundry taluk) who enjoyed it for nearly two and a half centuries. In 1814 the then holder was murdered by his four díwáns, who seem to have enjoyed the estate thereafter either jointly or successively. Three of the four having died, the survivor, Venkayya, became for a time the sole proprietor; but in 1857 he was compelled to hand over a portion of the estate, then known as the Marrigúdem taluk, to one Rájaji, the son of one of his deceased accomplices. Rájaji misconducted himself, and his share was given over to the Bhadráchalam zamindar's direct control by the Central Provinces Government in 1862. The present proprietor of Rékapalle is the son of Venkayya. The relations of the inferior to the superior proprietors in this taluk are referred to in Chapter XI. Rékapalle was formerly the head-quarters of a taluk which comprised that part of the Bhadráchalam taluk which lies to the east of a line running due north from a point a little to the east of Gauridévipéta.

This country joined in the Rampa rebellion of 1879, and at one time gave a great deal of trouble to the authorities. The causes of the rising were quite different from those which operated in Rampa. Under the Central Provinces administration, *pódu* cultivation had been almost unrestricted, and the assessment on it had been only four annas an axe. The Madras Government almost trebled the assessment, excluded the cultivators from certain tracts, and levied a tax on the felling of certain species of reserved trees. These new taxes and restrictions were considered a grievance, and it was for this reason that the Rampa leaders found adherents in the Rékapalle country. On the tenth of July some Rampa insurgents under Ambul Reddi, aided by a number of Rékapalle people, attacked the Vaddigúdem police-station. They were driven back, and a party of armed police was directed to proceed up to the river from Rajahmundry in a steamer and launch. The steamer which was without a guard or arms, incautiously went on ahead, was attacked a little above the gorge, and was taken by the insurgents. A

CHAP. XV. BHADRÁCHALAM.

force of 125 sepoys was then sent up the river, the Gódávari and Saveri were patrolled by steamers, and posts were established along their banks. By September the people had resumed their ordinary occupations and quiet was restored. The Rékapalle country was again disturbed by an incursion of Tamman Dora in October 1880. He looted a few defenceless villages, but his stay in this quarter did not last long.

Srí Rámagiri.

Srí Rámagiri ('holy Ráma's hill') lies .orty-four miles south by east of Bhadráchalam. It is supposed to have been here that the bird Jatáyu, who had tried to hinder Rávana's abduction of Síta but been mortally wounded in the attempt, told the news of the abduction with his dying breath to Ráma as he passed that way. The grateful Ráma performed the funeral rites of the faithful bird at Srí Rámagiri. The god is known as Kulása ('the joyful') Ráma, because he here had news of his lost wife; while the Ráma at Parnasála is Sóka ('the sorrowful'), because his bereavement occurred there. The temple is supported by the zamindar of Rékapalle, who devotes to its maintenance the net income derived from the village of Kúnnavaram, which ordinarily amounts to about Rs. 800 a year.

The neighbouring hill called Váli Sugríva is so named from the legend that it was there that Ráma obtained further news of Síta from Sugríva, the brother of Váli and king of the monkeys.

CHÓDAVARAM DIVISION.

CHAP. XV. CHÓDAVARAM.

THE Chódavaram division comprises most of what was in former times known as 'the Rampa country,' from the village of that name which stands just north of Chódavaram village. Its history is sketched in the account of Rampa below. Almost all the division is occupied by the Eastern Gháts, and four-fifths of it consists of forest. The density of the population is as low as 32 persons to the square mile. There is only one metalled road in the division, namely that from the headquarters to Rajahmundry, but the road from the former to Dévipatam is partially maintained.

Only one village in the division is on ryotwari tenure, four are held as mokhásas direct from Government, 50 belong to zamindaris, and the rest, some 300 in number, consists of hill muttas held on the *kával* tenure referred to in Chapter XI. The zamindari villages are said to have belonged long ago to some Reddi chiefs called the Reddi Rázus, and to have been sold by them, apparently before the permanent settlement of 1802–03, to various lowland zamindars. At present 20 villages belong to the Pólavaram estate, four to Pithápuram, and two to Gútála ; while the independent estates of Dandangi and Toyyéru and the disputed mokhása estate of Kondamodalu contain respectively twelve, eight and four villages. The hill muttas are 24 in number and often have a separate history of their own. A brief description of them will be found below.

As there is only one Government village in the division, the ordinary statistics of soils and cultivation are not available. The chief crops are said to be paddy, pulses, ragi, cambu and maize. In the hills, *pódu* cultivation is the rule.

Bandapalli.

Bandapalli: Four miles east-north-east of Chódavaram. Population 223. It is the head village of a hill mutta comprising thirteen villages. In the *fitúri* of 1840 the then muttadar and his eldest son took a prominent part among the insurgents. A reward was offered for their capture, but they disappeared and were never seen again. The mansabdar of Rampa, on coming into power in 1848, annexed the mutta on the plea that there were no heirs to it, though the vanished muttadar had left an infant son. In the settlement of 1879, made by Mr. Sullivan at the end of the Rampa rebellion, this son was given a sanad and his quit-rent was fixed at Rs. 42.

Birampalli.

Birampalli: Head village of a hill mutta of eleven villages. Lies seven miles south-east of Chódavaram, and contains 166 inhabitants. The people of this mutta joined the rebellion of 1879; but they seem to have been driven to this act by the rapacity of a renter to whom the muttadar had sub-let the property. This renter admitted having made Rs. 300 a year out of it, though the quit-rent was only Rs. 40. At the settlement of 1879 no punishment was imposed upon the people for having joined the late rebellion, as it was conceded that they had some excuse for their action, but the muttadar was deposed for maladministration and the property was given to his brother on a quit-rent of Rs. 42.

Bodulúru.

Bodulúru: Head village of a hill mutta of the Rampa country, containing 36 villages and paying a quit-rent of Rs. 60. It lies 25 miles north by west of Chódavaram, and contains 90 inhabitants. The muttadar joined in the Rampa rebellion, and had not 'come in' at the time of Mr. Sullivan's settlement. His quit-rent was accordingly raised from Rs. 40 to Rs. 60.

Bolagonda.

Bolagonda: Head village of a hill mutta; lies eight miles north-east of Chódavaram; population 218. The mansabdar of Rampa obtained possession of this estate in 1867 by means of a forged document purporting to be a deed of resignation by the muttadar. He obtained an income of Rs. 306 out of the property, though the quit-rent was only Rs. 40. The mutta was restored in 1879 to its former owner, but as he had joined in the *fitúri* of 1858, and in the 1879 rebellion had been constantly seen with the notorious Tamman Dora and only escaped arrest owing to the absence of direct evidence to connect him with the atrocities committed, his quit-rent was raised to Rs. 60, and the mutta was reduced by granting the village of Vádapalli as a reward to a loyal munsif.

Chavala.

Chavala: An uninhabited village forty-two miles north by west of Chódavaram. Gives its name to a hill mutta, though the chief village of this is now Jájilanka, population 23. The mutta contains 13 villages and pays a quit-rent of Rs. 50. The muttadar joined in the Rampa rebellion and had not 'come in' at the time of Mr. Sullivan's settlement.

Chidugúru.

Chidugúru: Uninhabited village ten miles north-west of Chódavaram, which gives its name to a hill mutta containing 36 villages and paying a quit-rent of Rs. 40, the chief village of which is Badagunta. For participation in the rising of 1838-40, the then muttadar was hanged and was succeeded by his brother. In 1872, the Rampa mansabdar took possession of the property on the plea that it had been relinquished

CHAP. XV. CHODAVARAM. by the owner, but in 1879 a descendant of the man who had been hanged was appointed muttadar.

Chódavaram. **Chódavaram**: Head-quarters of the division. Population 377. It contains a local fund dispensary (established in 1902), and a police-station garrisoned by a Special Hill Reserve 40 strong, The siege it underwent at the beginning of the 1879 rebellion is briefly described in the account of Rampa below. Chódavaram was strongly held by troops throughout the greater part of the rebellion. It is situated on one side of an extensive plateau.

Chopakonda. **Chopakonda**: Eight miles south-west of Chódavaram. Population 67. Chief place in a hill mutta paying a quit-rent of Rs. 21 and containing six villages. In 1849 the mansabdar of Rampa obtained possession of this on the ground that the muttadar has disappeared, and by a village settlement obtained an income of Rs. 116 per annum from it. In 1879 the real muttadar, who had been alive all the time and was well known to the hill people, was restored.

Dandangi. **Dandangi**: Twelve miles south-south-west of Chódavaram. Population 161. Is the head-quarter village of a zamindari estate consisting of ten villages and paying a peshkash of Rs. 565. The estate forms part of a property of 26 villages which was sold by the Reddi Rázus, apparently before the permanent settlement, to the then zamindar of Nuzvíd. This passed by sale in later years to the ancestors of the present owners of the Gútála zamindari, and from them (some time before 1855) to the ancestors of the present zamindars of Dandangi.

Dorachintalapálem. **Dorachintalapálem**: Fourteen miles north-east of Chódavaram. Population 27. Gives its name to a hill mutta of fourteen villages the chief place in which is Narasápuram. In 1871 the then muttadar died without legitimate issue and the mansabdar of Rampa at once annexed the property. An illegitimate son of the late owner accordingly took a prominent part in the rebellion of 1879; and would not come in at the time of the settlement. The villagers were allowed to elect one of their own number as muttadar, and the quit-rent was raised from Rs. 50 to Rs. 70.

Geddáda. **Geddáda**: Four miles north-west of Chódavaram. Population 275. Chief village of a hill mutta of the old Rampa estate, containing nine villages and paying a rent of Rs. 21.

Kákúru. **Kákúru**: Twenty-eight miles north of Chódavaram. Population 78. Chief village of a hill mutta of the Rampa country, which pays a quit-rent of Rs. 40 and contains eight villages. The muttadar joined in the Rampa rebellion and had not come in at the time of Mr. Sullivan's settlement. His mutta was settled by Mr. Carmichael in 1881.

Kondamodalu.

Kondamodalu: Twenty-seven miles west of Chódavaram. Population 332. The head-quarters of a mokhása estate at the entrance to the gorge on the Gódávari. The present owner is the grandson of the Linga Reddi who assisted Government in the Rampa rebellion.

'The Government are aware,' wrote Mr. Sullivan in 1879, 'that Linga Reddi has from the very commencement of the rising shown himself a most loyal adherent of the Government. Not only has he supplied information and messengers, but he has brought into the field 50 or 60 well-trained matchlockmen who have been of great use as scouts and envoys. With his following he himself on more than one occasion accompanied parties of troops and police . . . and has done everything he could to render assistance. It was he who at the commencement of the outbreak surprised and brought in Jangam Pulicanta Sambiah.'

His services were rewarded by the grant, as a mokhása, of the village of Rávilanka, which is held on the condition that the grantee attends the Collector with peons when required to do so,[1] and pays a quit-rent of Rs. 300. Linga Reddi had previously, in 1858, been granted an allowance of Rs. 50 a month to compensate him for the withdrawal of his right of collecting fees on goods passing up and down the Gódávari. This grant is conditional on good behaviour. Linga Reddi had just then earned the gratitude of Government by holding aloof from the *fitúri* of his partner Subba Reddi.[2]

Kondamodalu comprises four villages and pays Rs. 110 annually to the zamindar of Pólavaram. Its precise relations with the latter are at present the subject of a law suit.

Kundáda.

Kundáda: Eighteen miles north-west by north of Chódavaram. Population 129. Chief village of a hill mutta belonging to the old Rampa estate, containing eight villages and paying a quit-rent of Rs. 21. The muttadar was loyal during the 1879 rebellion, and his village was plundered and burnt by the insurgents.

Marriváda.

Marriváda: Three miles east of Chódavaram, which gives its name to a hill mutta containing three villages of the old Rampa mutta. This was granted to the family of one Karam Dhulu Dora, who during the first few months of the Rampa rebellion was of the greatest service to the authorities. 'He

[1] G.O. No. 2297, Judicial, dated 11th November 1881.

[2] G.O. No. 1240, Revenue, dated 11th September 1858.

CHAP. XV. CHODAVARAM.

was always with me,' wrote the Sub-Collector, 'giving such assistance as guide, etc., as was in his power.' The grant imposed a quit-rent of Rs. 15, but not the service conditions attached to most of the other hill muttas. This same family were also given, free of rent, the mokhása village of Darimadugula in the Bandapalli mutta, which had formerly been their property but had been taken from them by the mansabdar of Rampa.

Musurumilli.

Musurumilli. Five miles south of Chódavaram. Population 188. Is the chief place in a hill mutta of 18 villages. The people of this behaved well during the 1879 rebellion, and it was settled on the old quit-rent of Rs. 42.

Nédunúru.

Nédunúru : An uninhabited village nine miles north-west of Chódavaram which gives its name to a hill mutta of the Rampa country, the chief place in which is Dévarapalli and which pays a quit-rent of Rs. 42 and contains eleven villages. The muttadar joined in the Rampa rebellion and had not come in at the time of Mr. Sullivan's settlement. The mutta was settled in 1886.

Nimmalapálem.

Nimmalapálem : Twelve miles north-east of Chódavaram. Population 170. A mokhása village which the present holder says was given to his ancestor about 1858 by the muttadar of Geddáda, to whom he was related. It was confirmed free of quit-rent in the possession of the holder at the settlement of 1879.

Pálem.

Pálem : Six miles south-west of Chódavaram. Population 319. Gives its name to a hill mutta containing nine villages and paying a quit-rent of Rs. 21. See also Velagapalli.

Pámuléru.

Pámuléru : Twenty-four miles north by west of Chódavaram. Population 15. Gives its name to a hill mutta of the old Rampa country, containing eleven villages and paying a quit-rent of Rs. 40, the chief place in which is Kutruváda. This surrendered to the Rampa mansabdar about 1874, and was sub-let by him to an outsider who was arrested as a ringleader in the rebellion of 1879. In the settlement of that year, however, no one else was willing to take the property and it was given to his son on a quit-rent of Rs. 50. The quit-rent was reduced to Rs. 40 again about ten years ago.

Péta.

Péta : Twenty miles south of Chódavaram. Population 728. Chief place in a small zamindari estate containing two villages and paying a peshkash of Rs. 546. Its history, *mutato nomine*, is precisely the same as that of the Dandangi estate.

Rampa.

Rampa : A little hill village just north of Chódavaram. Population 177. Near it, beside a waterfall about 25 feet high, is a shrine formed of three huge boulders, two of which make a kind of roof, and fitted with a doorway and one side-wall of cut stone. The water of the fall pours continually between the boulders. A rough lingam and other holy emblems have been carved out of the rock.

Rampa was once the chief place in the small mutta of the same name and the residence of its muttadar. This man was chieftain over the whole of the old Rampa country and controlled the other muttadars there, and the rebellion in this which occurred in 1879 and is referred to below was in consequence called 'the Rampa rebellion.'[1]

In the earliest records which mention him, the zamindar, mansabdar, or rája of Rampa is described as an independent ruler. Mr. Grant, in his *Political Survey of the Northern Circars* already several times referred to, calls him as independent as the rája of Bastar; and the Committee of Circuit, writing in 1787, said that, though the zamindari of Rampa belonged to the Circar of Rajahmundry, yet neither the Company nor the Nizam's government received any tribute from it. 'The country,' said this body, 'is represented to be extremely mountainous and full of jungle, the natives rude and uncultivated, frequently making incursions on the adjacent countries, plundering the villages during the harvest, and driving off the cattle.'

At the time of the permanent settlement of 1802-03 the Rampa country was as entirely disregarded as if it had not existed, and no settlement of any part of it was made. During the disorders which arose in this district early in the nineteenth century, the mansabdar, Rámbhúpati Dévu, descended with an armed force from the hills and took forcible possession of some villages in the plains. He was driven out of these and submitted, offering to acknowledge 'for ever the sovereignty of the Company.'

Then (1813) for the first time a settlement was made with him. The villages he had taken were restored to him as mokhásas and, along with his ancestral possessions in the hills, were confirmed to him free of peshkash on condition that he maintained order in them and prevented incursions into the low country.[2] He appears to have leased his villages to certain subordinate hill chiefs or muttadars, whom he

[1] The following give accounts of the early history of Rampa, the causes of the rebellion and its course: G.Os., Judl., Nos. 1036, dated 5th May 1879; 755, dated 3rd April 1879; and 109, dated 16th January 1880. Also the report of Mr. D.F. Carmichael, when Special Commissioner, dated November 1st, 1881; and the Presidency Administration Reports for 1879-80 and 1880-81.

[2] G.O. No. 1036, Judicial, dated 5th May 1879, appendix, p. 11.

CHAP. XV. CHODAVARAM.

required to keep order in their own charges and from whom he received an income of Rs. 8,750 per annum.[1] These were the ancestors of the present muttadars.

He died in 1835 leaving a daughter and an illegitimate son named Srí Madhuvati Rámbhúpati Dévu, and the former was recognized by the muttadars as heiress to the zamindari. She declined to marry, declaring her intention of following the example of a former zamindarni of the country who had remained unwedded all her life.[2] Some time afterwards, however, her chastity was suspected, and she and her brother, both of whom were apparently detested, were driven out of the country.

They were maintained by the Government, and in 1840 the estate was placed under the Court of Wards. Grave disturbances followed (a police force was cut up in 1840)[3] but by 1845 the more turbulent of the muttadars had been apprehended or driven to flight. The zamindarni surrendered the estate in favour of her illegitimate brother[4]; and in 1848, after protracted negotiations, the muttadars agreed to accept this man as mansabdar and to perform their old police duties, on condition that their united quit-rents should not exceed Rs. 1,000 and that the mansabdar should never attempt to exact more from them.

The mansabdar agreed to this, but quickly broke his promise. His confiscations of muttas and oppressions of the people resulted in risings against his authority in 1858 and 1861; and such was the hatred he inspired that when, in 1862, he attempted to go and reside in his property an insurrection arose which had to be put down by a strong force of police. He continued his depredations, however, and by 1879 had succeeded in getting eight muttas into his own enjoyment, had doubled the quit-rent in several others, and was deriving a considerable revenue from taxes on fuel and grazing and other unauthorized cesses.

He succeeded in doing this largely by making it appear, sometimes by disgraceful devices, that all his actions had the sanction of Government; and unfortunately the officers of Government neither adequately realized what was going on in his country nor made sufficient endeavours to protect the muttadars.[5] They forgot that the agreement of 1848 was made under the authority of Government; and some of the

[1] G.O. No. 109, Judicial, dated 16th January 1880, p. 75.

[2] G O. No. 1036, Judicial, dated 5th May 1879, appendix, p. 3.

[3] *Ibid.*, appendix, p. 5.

[4] *Ibid.*, p. 11.

[5] G.O. No. 109, Judicial, dated 16th January 1880, p. 8.

muttadars who complained of the mansabdar's exactions were referred to the Civil Courts, though the hill men are notorious for their dread of the plains. The growing discontent among the people was increased by new abkári regulations preventing the drawing of toddy for domestic purposes and leasing the toddy revenue to renters. These renters demanded that the muttadars should pay fees (called *chigurupannu*) for the right to tap toddy, and the mansabdar threatened to levy an additional tax, called *modalupannu*, at the rate of one-half or two-thirds of the *chigurupannu*.

This was the last straw, and was the immediate cause of the 'Rampa rebellion' of 1879. The unpopularity of the police, who had assisted in introducing the new toddy rules and also oppressed the people on their own account, was a contributory cause. The people said that 'they could not stand all the taxes that were being imposed; that three years ago came the *chigurupannu;* that this year the mansabdar was demanding *modalupannu;* that the constables were extorting fowls; and that, as they could not live, they might as well kill the constables and die.'[1] The operation of the civil law of the country was an additional grievance. Traders from the low country had taken advantage of the simplicity of the hill men, 'who would much sooner walk into a tiger's den than put in an appearance in the Rajahmundry court,' to make unfair contracts with them, and then, if these were not fulfilled according to the traders' own interpretation, to file suits against them, obtain *ex parte* decrees, and distrain as much of their property as they could lay hands on. In satisfaction of a debt of Rs. 5, cattle and produce worth Rs. 100 had been sometimes carried off in this manner, and sometimes, it was said, the formality of a suit was dispensed with, and the trader, accompanied by a friend personating an officer of the court, made the distraint without any authority whatever. The hill people laid the blame for all this injustice on Government and Government rules and regulations, and thought that their only remedy lay in rising against the authorities.

On the 9th March 1879 the police inspector of Rampa reported that there was reason to apprehend a disturbance. The Collector had gone to Bhadráchalam, so the Sub-Collector and Superintendent of Police set out for the hills with a small body of police. At Gókavaram they met one of the muttadars who was suspected of disaffection, but he tried to allay their suspicions and accompanied them to Chódavaram. The next day, however, two policemen were stopped near that place by

[1] G.O. No. 109, Judicial, dated 16th January 1880, p. 19.

CHAP. XV. CHÓDAVARAM.

a body of armed men, and news was received of the capture by some insurgents of a body of police near Bodulúru. Early on the 13th March a large party of hill men came close to Chódavaram and stated their grievances to the Sub-Collector, who went out unarmed to meet them. He attempted to reassure them and they expressed themselves satisfied; but a few minutes later they called out that they could not trust the Sircar's promises, and began firing on the camp. No particular harm was done by their fire, but the Sub-Collector's party, which consisted of 39 police of all ranks with 32 carbines, was now cut off. They had no difficulty in holding out at Chódavaram until reinforcements came up, and by the 17th the force in the village amounted to 149 men. Some 400 officers and men of the 39th Native Infantry had also been landed at Cocanada on the 16th and were moving up the country. Meanwhile, however, at Rampa two captured constables were solemnly sacrificed before the chief shrine by the insurgents, the leaders of the latter announced that rebellion was their only hope, and the whole of the Rampa country was speedily ablaze.

In the next month (April) the disturbance spread to the Golgonda hills of Vizagapatam, and in July to the Rékapalle country in Bhadráchalam; but the causes of the disaffection there (which are mentioned in the accounts of Rékapalle and Dutcharti) were essentially different from those operating in Rampa itself.

The disturbed area now comprised over 5,000 square miles of wooded and hilly country. The operations of the troops were much hampered by the nature of the ground, and the malcontents took advantage of their superior knowledge of the country to maintain a harassing guerilla warfare, avoiding all direct encounters with the troops, but attacking isolated police-stations and burning or looting the villages of those who assisted the authorities. Troops were hastened up to the country, and by the end of 1879 the Government forces included, besides several hundred police drafted from neighbouring districts, as many as six regiments of Madras Infantry, two companies of Sappers and Miners, and a squadron of cavalry and a wing of infantry from the Hyderabad Contingent.

The chief leaders of the insurgents were four notorious characters named Chandrayya, Sirdar Jangam Pulicánta Sámbayya, Tamman Dora, and Ambul Reddi of Bodulúru. The second of these was arrested as early as April 29th, 1879. Chandrayya, however, scored many successes in the

Yellavaram division at the beginning of May, and succeeded in burning Addatígela police-station. He was nearly captured in the middle of that month, but in June he shut up a party of police under a European officer for some days in Addatígela. The spread of the disaffection to Rékapalle and Dutcharti, and the fear that the hill tribes of Pólavaram division might join the insurgents, led to strenuous efforts on the part of the authorities, and troops were moved up from all sides. The northern and eastern frontiers of the Rampa country were occupied by strong detachments of sepoys, and military posts were established along the banks of the Gódávari and Saveri. At the same time Mr. Sullivan, First Member of the Board of Revenue, was appointed (in July 1879) to visit the district and ascertain the real causes of the trouble and suggest remedies for it. The steps he took, which included the deposition of the mansabdar and a promise that the muttadars should thenceforth deal directly with Government, did much to allay the excitement, and before the end of August 1879 as many as 70 of Chandrayya's men had been captured, and Rampa was comparatively quiet.

Rékapalle was also pacified about the same time, and the apprehended rising in Pólavaram did not take place. The remaining rebels were now driven north to the hills of Golgonda and Jeypore. Ambul Reddi was captured in November 1879 and Chandrayya was killed in February 1880. Their removal broke the back of the trouble. Disturbances went on in a desultory fashion in the Vizagapatam district, and in October 1880 Tamman Dora made a brief incursion into that part of the country. But by November 1880 quiet was finally and everywhere restored.

The most deadly foe of the police and troops engaged in suppressing the outbreak had been the malaria which infests this part of the country. At the end of the March 1880, out of 2,400 men employed, no less than 590 were on the sick list. Many deaths occurred, and in many other cases those attacked were months before they completely recovered.

The mansabdar of Rampa, as has been said, was deposed. As the Government order put it, 'for gross misconduct and oppression the Government have cancelled absolutely and for ever the mansabdari tenure of Rampa and the mokhása tenure of the villages of the plain.' The mutta held by the mansabdar was also cancelled, and he himself was detained as a State prisoner at Berhampore. Most of the muttadars were either reappointed or replaced, and their position was defined. As early as September 1879 Mr. Sullivan had held a durbar at

CHAP. XV. CHÓDAVARAM.

which the new sanads were distributed. With four exceptions, the settlement was made with the muttadár actually in undisputed possession or, where the mutta had been annexed by the mansabdar, with the heir of the former muttadar. In arranging the terms of the tenure of each mutta, the loyalty or disloyalty of its owner in the recent disturbances was considered and the quit-rent was raised or reduced in accordance therewith Generally, however, the muttas were granted on the same terms as in 1848. The sanads contained two conditions; firstly, that a stipulated annual quit-rent, including an abkári tax and a local fund cess, should be paid annually to Government; and, secondly, that the muttadar should conduct himself loyally and peaceably, and should give every assistance to the Government in maintaining quiet and order. A warning was added that if the muttadar failed in his duties his mutta was liable to be resumed. The decision of Government as to the rights of the muttadars over the forests will be found in Chapter V.

The Rampa mutta had always been in the personal enjoyment of the mansabdar, and was resumed by Government. It had formerly consisted of thirteen villages. Ten of these, with the title of muttadar of Rampa, were given to the munsif of Chódavaram, who had given the greatest assistance to Government throughout the outbreak, had been their channel of communication with the muttadars, had obtained information regarding the movements of the rebels, and had got together a body of armed men to co-operate with the police and the troops. The grant was made free of quit-rent, and was conditional on the grantee's being of good behaviour, paying the local fund cess, and presenting to the Collector every year, in token of his allegiance, a bow and three arrows. The other three villages of the Rampa mutta were given to the muttadar of Marriváda, who had also shown his loyalty during the rebellion.

Sirigindalapádu.

Sirigindalapádu: One mile south-east of Chódavaram. Population 75. The village used to belong to the Bandapalli mutta; but at the settlement of 1879 it was given at the request of the muttadar to a relative of his, who was going to assist him in the management of the mutta, and who had shown himself loyal in the recent rebellion. It pays no quit-rent.

Tádapélli.

Tádapélli: Fourteen miles north-west by north of Chódavaram. Population 466. Chief village of a hill mutta containing nine villages. The quit-rent fixed in 1848 was Rs. 40, but it was illegally raised by the mansabdar to Rs. 100 in 1862. The muttadar did not take part in the insurrection of 1879 but many of his people did, and he himself not only assisted the insurgents with supplies but also concealed himself from the officers of Government and gave them no help whatever. In consideration of the fact however that his mutta is an isolated and rugged tract, right in the path taken by the rebels in their raids, it was considered at the settlement of 1879 that his conduct was more due to fear of the rebels than disloyalty to Government, and his quit-rent was only raised to Rs. 63.

Tunnúru: Ten miles north-west of Chódavaram. Population 80. Gives its name to a hill mutta containing 16 villages and paying a quit-rent of Rs. 35. This was returned as deserted at the settlement of Rampa in 1848, but by 1879 it had been reoccupied, and a sanad was accordingly given to a descendant of a former muttadar. Tunnúru.

Vádapalli: Twelve miles south-west of Chódavaram. Population 193. It was given to an ancestor of the present holder by Government in recognition of his services in the Rampa rebellion, on a quit-rent of Rs. 15. Vádapalli.

Velagapalli: Eight miles south-south-west of Chódavaram. Population 50. The chief place in a mutta containing six villages and paying a quit-rent of Rs. 21. In 1848 it also included the Pálem mutta; but at the settlement of 1879 it was found that these had been divided, and separate sanads were accordingly given to the respective owners in that year. Velagapalli.

Válamúru: Twenty miles west-north-west of Chódavaram. Population 35. Gives its name to a mutta containing 22 villages and paying a quit-rent of Rs. 42. This was one of the old Rampa muttas, but behaved well in the 1879 rebellion. At the settlement of that year there was a dispute about the succession which is described in Mr. Sullivan's report. Válamúru.

Vémulakonda: Ten miles north-west of Chódavaram. Population 95. Chief place in a mutta containing ten villages and paying a quit-rent of Rs. 26. The then muttadar joined in the rebellion of 1858, but the people took no part in the rising of 1879. Vémulakonda.

PÓLAVARAM DIVISION.

CHAP. XV. PÓLAVARAM.

THE Pólavaram division is the south-westernmost portion of the Gódavari Agency, and is the only part of the district which lies on the right bank of the river. The density of its population (103 to the square mile) is far above that of any of the other agency tracts. At the permanent settlement of 1802–03 it was all included in the Pólavaram estate. At present only 24 of its villages are zamindari land, of which twelve belong to the so-called Pólavaram and Pattisam estates, which are really one property in the possession of the present Pólavaram proprietor; five belong to the Gútála estate and four to the estate of Gangólu; and one village belongs to each of the muttas of Bayyanagúdem, Billumilli and Jangareddigúdem, which three form one estate. The fortunes of these various properties are referred to below.

Pólavaram is more fertile and more civilized than the other parts of the Agency. On the west and south it is as flat as the adjacent Yernagúdem taluk, though more covered with jungle. It possesses no industries worth mention. The attempts made to discover coal at Bedadanúru, the mica and plumbago of the division, and the chances of finding gold in its south-west corner, are referred to in Chapter I.

The Pattisam and Táduváyi temples are well known in the surrounding country.

Gangólu.

Gangólu: Eight miles west-south-west of Pólavaram. Population 1,784. Its hamlet Hukumpéta is the head-quarters of a zamindari which was acquired from the Gútála estate by purchase about 40 years ago, and is still held by the descendants of the purchasers. It comprises four villages and pays a peshkash of Rs. 1,240.

Gútála.

Gútála: Five miles south of Pólavaram. Population 3,300. Contains a vernacular lower secondary school for boys and a Sanskrit school. It was once the chief place of one of the 'pergunnas' of the ancient Pólavaram zamindari, and its history is sketched in the account of this latter below. In the circumstances there narrated, it was put up to auction in 1810. In 1812 and 1813 it was sold for arrears of revenue, and in 1827 it passed by private sale to one Maniyam Venkataratnam, an ancestor of the present holder. Since then various purchases and sales have much modified the extent of the estate. The most important of these were the purchase of 74 hamlets of the old Nágavaram mutta and the sale of the Gangólu mutta some 40 years ago. The estate now comprises five villages in the Pólavaram division (including Nágavaram and its hamlets) and five villages elsewhere. It pays a peshkash of Rs. 6,721.

Jangareddigúdem.

Jangareddigúdem: Thirty miles south-west of Pólavaram. Population 1,918. Head-quarters of a small estate consisting of this village, Billumilli and Bayyanagúdem, and paying a peshkash of Rs. 3,008. In 1832 Jangareddigúdem was subdivided from the Pólavaram estate in circumstances referred to in the account of that property below. It was subsequently bought (along with the other two villages) by the grandfather of the present holder some 50 years ago.

Páta Pattisam.

Páta Pattisam: A hamlet of this, called Pattisam Nidhi, forms a picturesque and rocky island in the Gódávari, three miles south of Pólavaram. The population of the whole village is 2,002. It is called Páta (old) Pattisam to distinguish it from Kotta (new) Pattisam, a hamlet of Gútála. A division of the old Pólavaram estate, containing five villages and paying a peshkash of Rs. 5,209, is called the Pattisam division, but this was never held separately from Pólavaram proper.

The village is the scene of a well attended festival at Sivarátri. The local *sthala puránam* says that the Pattisam hill went to the Himalayas to attend a conference of mountains, but, not being shown proper consideration, left the others and went and did penance by itself. By means of this penance it induced the Siva of the Himalayas to leave that range and come to Pattisam, where he now resides in the Vírabhadra temple. This temple also contains two stone images of women, called Aníswari and Puníswari, one of whom is represented as being in childbed. These are much worshipped by childless women desirous of offspring. The suppliant places her foot on a platform in front of the figures, and vows that if a child like a pearl or like coral is born to her, she will present a pearl or a piece of coral to the images. In another part of the same temple are figures of Durga and Mahishásuramardhani, the form adopted by the goddess Párvati when she killed the demon Mahishásura. Sheep and fowls are sacrificed before these idols, though they are inside the precincts of the temple. The spilling of blood is not as a rule permitted inside Bráhmanical shrines. The Vírabhadra temple has two villages attached to it, which bring in an annual income of about Rs. 2,000.

CHAP. XV. PÓLAVARAM.

Another sacred place on the Pattisam island is the Bhadrakáligundam, a pit in the bed of the river which is a favourite bathing-place. The Mahánandísvaram temple on another small island four miles up the river is also fairly well known. It is supposed to be the residence of the bull *(nandi)* which belongs to the Pattisam temple. It has one *agrahdram* village as an endowment, and this brings in Rs. 800 a year. On the island is a cave which is popularly supposed to be the entrance of an underground passage to Benares.

Pólavaram.

Pólavaram : Head-quarters of the Agency Deputy Collector (who, however, is temporarily located at Rajahmundry) and the deputy tahsildar. Population 4,455. It also contains the office of a sub-registrar, a local fund dispensary (established by Government in 1880), a police-station, a travellers' bungalow, a Government girls' school and an English lower secondary school for boys. It was formerly the chief place in the important zamindari of the same name, which formerly embraced the whole of this division and much of Yernagúdem and Rajahmundry taluks, but now comprises only twelve villages paying a peshkash of Rs. 6,713.

This estate was long under the independent rule of an ancient Hindu family who derived their authority from the Gajapati kings of Orissa, and are said to have been descended from that line. Little is known of the estate previous to the British occupation of the country, but the names of three of its zamindars, Venkatapati, Jagannátha, and Venkataráma, have been preserved. It was then divided into the three estates of Pólavaram, Gútála and Kottapalli, and subordinate to it was the small hill zamindari of Nágavaram.

In 1780 the zamindar, Lakshmináráyana Dévu, died leaving three sons named Mangapati Dévu, Narasimha Dévu and Vijayagópála Dévu, of whom the last was the only son of his second wife. Mangapati was the eldest of the three and succeeded to the zamindari. In 1781 Kottapalli, which had been temporarily in charge of another holder, was restored to the estate, and Mangapati was thus in possession of all three of the subdivisions of the property. As he was a minor, his díwán managed the estate for him. This man was the brother of Vijayagópála's mother, and he induced the Chief at Masulipatam to recommend (1782) that the estate should be divided into three so as to make a provision for each of the three brothers. This was done, and Pólavaram fell to Mangapati, Gútála to Vijayagópála, and Kottapalli to Narasimha.

In 1785 Dásu Reddi, the zamindar of Nágavaram, pretending that Vijayagópála's díwán was not managing the Gútála estate properly, captured that town and took the young Rája and his mother prisoners. He was perhaps egged on to do this by Mangapati, between whom and Vijayagópála's mother there was no love lost. A force of seven companies of sepoys marched up to liberate the prisoners and restore order. The Nágavaram zamindar then moved his prisoners to his own estate and the English force accordingly marched as far as Anantapalli. The zamindar then returned to Gútála, and the English force, supposing he would release the prisoners, retired. He still however refused to do so, and Gútála was accordingly captured. Two sepoys were wounded and about eighty peons killed and wounded on both sides during the attack. Dásu Reddi was sent to Masulipatam and Vijayagópála was restored to Gútála.

Similar disturbances took place in 1786-87, when the hill people, who were mostly adherents of Dásu Reddi's, were driven out of the Company's territory by a detachment of sepoys. In 1788 peace was for the time restored, and the jealousy between the branches of the Pólavaram family appeased, by placing the whole of the estate under one díwán.

This díwán managed the property efficiently till his death in 1790. A successor was then appointed with the apparent consent of the three brothers. The mother of Vijayagópála refused however to acquiesce in the new arrangement, and made herself supreme in Gútála. The Company's troops marched up to Gútála to bring her to order, and when they arrived she was discovered with her son in a room in the palace in which were two large open vessels of gunpowder. She threatened that if she was touched she would destroy herself and all that were near, and the Company's officer prudently retired. The lady was ultimately pacified, and surrendered quietly. She was taken to Masulipatam, Vijayagópála was detained at Rajahmundry, and Mangapati was recognized as zamindar of the united estates of Gútála and Pólavaram. Narasimha remained in charge of Kottapalli.

Thus far the disturbances in the estate had been due to private family feuds rather than to disloyalty to Government. The firmer revenue administration of the new Collectors appointed in 1794 however caused a real rebellion of the whole family. Mangapati gave a great deal of trouble to the authorities, failing to pay his peshkash and withholding the accounts which were necessary to ascertain how far he had suffered from the recent famine and what remissions should be granted him on that account. So obstinate was he, that the

CHAP. XV. — PÓLAVARAM.

Board of Revenue directed that he should be taken prisoner. He was accordingly seized and confined and his estate attached; but he was afterwards liberated on his agreeing to discharge the arrears in two years, to give security for the current revenue as it fell due, and to make an immediate payment of sixteen thousand pagodas.

At this juncture Vijayagópála escaped from Rajahmundry and took refuge with Linga Reddi, a hill chief whose estate lay on the east bank of the Gódávari above Pólavaram. He was induced by his host and a fugitive revenue defaulter (who had plundered Undi in 1798) to join them in a rebellion, and their combined parties commenced a *fitúri* by plundering two villages in the Pólavaram estate.

His brother's revolt encouraged Mangapati to give further trouble about his revenue. He claimed indulgence, which was refused. He promised to pay, but still delayed. His conduct became refractory and turbulent; and he made an exorbitant claim for a remission of over fifty thousand pagodas, and showed that he was prepared to back this up by force. Negotiations ensued while both the zamindar and the Government collected their forces for the expected struggle. The zamindar's demand was finally refused, and a military detachment moved rapidly up the country and captured Pólavaram. The zamindar however escaped, and the principal object of the officer in command, who had hoped to end the affair by seizing his person, was frustrated. A reward was offered for his apprehension and the country was placed under martial law. Mangapati first fled to the Nizam's Dominions, but returned when the coast was clear. A carefully planned attempt to capture him at Siruváka (21 miles north of Pólavaram) was unsuccessful, but he fled and was apparently never heard of again. It is supposed he took refuge in the Rampa country.

Meanwhile the outbreak started by Linga Reddi and Vijayagópála had been joined by the Rampa people, and sepoys had to be stationed both at Kottapalli and Indukúrpéta to keep them in check. In August 1800 they attacked Indukúrpéta, from which they were easily beaten back, and three days later a band of insurgents advanced as far as Purushóttapatnam opposite Pólavaram; and, within sight of the troops stationed there, seized the boats on that side of the river so as to cut off communication. Vijayagópála, whose heart had never apparently been in the rebellion, however surrendered; Narasimha, the zamindar of Kottapalli, who had also joined in the outbreak, was captured; and peace was gradually restored. The Pólavaram estate was given to a cousin named Lakshmináráyana Dévu, with whom the permanent settlement was made.[1]

Since that time subdivisions and revenue sales have played havoc with this ancient property. The first alteration in its limits occurred in 1808, when, in consequence of the accrual of large arrears of revenue, it was divided into the three muttas of Gútála, Pólavaram and Kottapalli, and the last of these (comprising 39 villages) was sold in auction. Gútála and Pólavaram remained under the old family, but next year the zamindar (Narasimha Dévu) broke into rebellion and they were both put up to auction, and the ancient line of the Pólavaram zamindars came to an end.

The Pólavaram mutta, of portions of which the present Pólavaram is made up, was purchased at this sale by one Bávàyamma. In 1812 it was sold again for arrears and was purchased by Báhu Baléndra Rázu, and in the following year it was sold yet once more and was bought by Kócharla Kóta Jaggayya, an ancestor of the present zamindar. On his death in 1832, the estate was subdivided by Government and given to different members of the family, and the only parts of it which remained to Rámachandra Venkatakrishna Rao, the son of Jaggayya and the grandfather of the present zamindar, were the two properties of Pólavaram and Pattisam which (with the addition of the Nallamillipádu estate purchased by the proprietrix who held the property from 1858 to 1888) from the present zamindari. Of the other portions which were subdivided off in 1832, the only village which has not since been purchased by Government is the Jangareddigúdem already referred to above. The Pólavaram estate was under the Court of Wards in the years 1832–35, 1846–54 and 1856–58.

Pólavaram village contains some tombs which are locally stated to be those of European soldiers who fell in the *fitúri* of Mangapati Dévu at the end of the eighteenth century. They bear no inscriptions. Another grim relic of the old disorders in these parts which existed here till recently was the gallows on which Subba Reddi and Kommi Reddi, the ringleaders of the *fitúri* of 1858, were hanged. This was carried away by the floods of 1900.

Táduváyi: Thirty-seven miles west by south of Pólavaram. Population 1,627. It is well known in this part of the country for its Siva temple, to which many pilgrims go at Sivarátri. The village contains a travellers' bungalow. Táduváyi.

[1] This account of these disturbances has been abridged from Mr. Morris' description in the original *District Manual*. The authorities on which he relied, which consist of MS. official records and printed reports, are quoted by him on p. 275 thereof.

YELLAVARAM DIVISION.

CHAP. XV. YELLAVARAM.

THE Yellavaram division of the Agency occupies the north-easternmost corner of the district. The whole of it is hilly, though considerable areas of level land lie among the hills, and, except for fifteen villages adjoining the plains, is covered by forest; it is also very malarious; the soil is poor and in the summer months water is always scarce; there are only 24 miles of metalled road in the whole of it; and the inhabitants are mostly Kóyas and hill Reddis. Consequently it is very backward and sparsely populated, and contains only 31 persons to the square mile. Some little irrigation is provided by a few tanks. The chief cereals are paddy, pulses and oil-seeds; but the hill men depend mostly on the produce of the tamarind trees, which grow to a great size. There are no industries worthy of the name in the division, except a very little basket making. There are five weekly markets.

Large areas which formerly belonged to the old Jaddangi estate are now Government land, but considerable tracts are held by the various hill muttadars referred to below. Round Jaddangi considerable tracts of forest have been reserved and the Forest department has opened up these with roads.

Addatígela.

Addatígela: Head-quarters of the division. Population 459. Contains a police-station, a travellers' bungalow, a local fund dispensary (established 1901) and one of the four weekly markets of the division. It is an insignificant place and little suited to be the head-quarters of a division, being unhealthy and surrounded with jungle.

The village was the scene of some stirring events during the Rampa rebellion referred to in the account of Rampa above. Almost the first act of the insurgent leader Chandrayya was to burn down the police-station there. This occurred at the end of April 1879. The station was rebuilt and re-garrisoned, but in June was again attacked by Chandrayya. On the twelfth of that month some police under a European officer were attacked by Chandrayya in this neighbourhood, kept under fire for four and a half hours, and finally driven to take refuge in the station. There they were attacked three days later. They had to unroof the thatched station buildings for fear of fire; a reinforcement of 20 men sent to their rescue was driven back by Chandrayya; and a sortie of theirs was also repulsed by him. Detachments were then hurried up from various quarters, and the station was relieved (without opposition) on the 25th of June.

Anigéru.

Anigéru: Two miles north-east of Addatígela. Population 211. Is the chief village of a mutta consisting of six villages and paying a quit-rent of Rs. 80. The muttadar's family is descended from the old mansabdar of Jaddangi who (see the account of that place below) was deposed in 1846. His infant son had in later years immense influence with hill people; and at the time of the Rampa rebellion he exerted it entirely in the favour of Government and materially to their advantage. It was decided to reward him by giving him the six villages of this mutta. They had formerly belonged to Dutcharti; but the holder of that mutta had not behaved well in the disturbances, and deserved no consideration. The grantee was succeeded by his son in 1887 and the latter was followed by his mother, who died in 1904.

Dutcharti.

Dutcharti: Ten miles nearly north of Addatígela; population 308. It is the chief village of the hill mutta of the same name which pays a quit-rent of Rs. 1,200. Till 1881 this was a part of the Golgonda taluk of Vizagapatam district. It was originally held on service tenure under the old Golgonda zamindar. His estate was sold for arrears and bought in by Government in 1837; and the muttadars under him thus became direct holders under Government on a service tenure.

This seriously lowered their status, as they were directly subject to the surveillance of the Collector's native *ámín*; and several disturbances followed.[1]

At the time of the outbreak of the Rampa rebellion of 1879 in this district the Golgonda muttadars had no such grievances against Government as existed in Rampa; but they still fretted against the restrictions which had been placed upon their powers, and the more daring spirits among them were moved by solicitations from across the border, by a hunger for loot, and by a desire to pay off old scores against the police.

The chief of the malcontents was Chekka Venkan Dora, muttadar of Dutcharti, whose grandfather had been manager of that mutta, and, on the death of his master without issue, had obtained a sanad for it himself. The first outbreak was caused by the action of one Dwárabandham Chandrayya, a man of some substance, who afterwards became one of the chief leaders of the rebellion. His house was searched,

[1] These are referred to in the account of Golgonda taluk in the *Vizagapatam Gazetteer*.

CHAP. XV. YELLAVARAM.

during his absence, by the police in connection with a dacoity. Furious that such a thing should have been done when only his womenfolk were present, he collected all the budmashes in the surrounding villages, descended into Dutcharti and burnt the police-station of Addatígela. This was at the end of April 1879. Numerous parties of insurgents who were beating up recruits, flying for shelter, or levying black-mail now resorted to this country; and, though no further open outrages were committed, troops had to be sent up into these hills.

Chekka Venkan Dora, muttadar of Dutcharti, had avoided any overt act of rebellion. But it was the belief of all the officers, civil and military, who served in those hills, that he had encouraged Chandrayya on the understanding that his own villages should be spared from plunder. It was beyond doubt both that his villages were not plundered and that he could, if he liked, have crushed the outbreak there and prevented the destruction of Addatígela. When, therefore, the rebellion was over, it was decided to remove Chekka Venkan Dora from his mutta. His brother, the present muttadar, was appointed in 1881. At the same time the six villages which now constitute the mutta of Anigéru (*q.v.*) were taken from Dutcharti to reward the loyalty of another influential hill chief. The muttas of Dutcharti and Guditéru, which were thought to be more accessible to the officers of this district, were also transferred from the Vizagapatam to the Gódávari Agency in the same year.[1]

Gurtédu.

Gurtédu, or Guditéru, is a village of 300 inhabitants and containing a travellers' bungalow, which gives its name to a mutta in the extreme north-east of the division. Like Dutcharti, it formed till 1881 a part of the Golgonda taluk of the Vizagapatam district. It pays Rs. 70 quit-rent. It is quite isolated from the rest of the Yellavaram division by the Dumkonda hill and can only be reached by the Yeduvampula pass through the Vizagapatam district or from Chódavaram *viâ* Bódulúru. Horses cannot get across this pass, and elephants have to be lightly laden. Along it may be seen the remains of the sangars built by the hill men during the Rampa rebellion.

Jaddangi.

Jaddangi: Nine miles east by north of Addatígela; population 537; contains a travellers' bungalow. Was once the head-quarters of a mansab which was formerly held on service

[1] Notification No. 217, Judicial, dated 29th June 1881. For these troubles in Golgonda, see the minute, dated November 1st, 1881, of Mr. D. F. Carmichael, Member of Council, who was appointed as Special Commissioner to arrange a settlement.

tenure under the old zamindár of Peddápuram. When that zamindari fell into the hands of Government, the muttadar held on the same tenure directly under the new owners. He rebelled in 1845 and the mutta was accordingly resumed. It contained 80 villages.

At Jaddangi is held one of the few markets in Yellavaram. Near the village is a cave containing the image of the well-known Bráhman saint Mándavya Mahámuni, who is supposed by the local people to have lived in the cave. The river Mádéru is said to have been called after him.

Kóta.

Kóta : Twelve miles north-north-west of Addatígela. Population 105. Contains a police-station, and is the chief village of the hill mutta of the same name, but is a petty collection of huts. It is said to have originally formed a part of the Rampa mansabdar's estate, under which it was properly held on service tenure. Under the muttadar there are five sub-muttas; namely, those of Yerragonda, Yarlagedda, Pasaraginri, Nulakamaddi, and Samagedda. Of these the first named pays a *kattubadi* to the muttadar of Rs. 80 a year, and the others each Rs. 50. The muttadar himself pays Government an annual quit-rent of Rs. 210.

The police-station seems to have been taken by the insurgents at the commencement of the Rampa rebellion, and an attempt made on March 17th 1879 by a force of police to reach and hold it was unsuccessful. It was however soon re-occupied, and resisted several attacks during April. It is now the most unpopular station in the district.

Móhanapuram.

Móhanapuram : Seven miles north-west of Addatígela. Population 138. It is the chief village of a hill mutta which was formerly under the mansabdar of Rampa, and since 1879 has been held on service tenure direct from Government. The quit-rent is Rs. 25.

Nellipúdi.

Nellipúdi : Twenty miles south-south-west of Addatígela. Population 835. Contains a travellers' bungalow and a weekly market. The village is held on mokhása tenure. It was given to the father of the late mokhásadar, who died in 1906, in recognition of his services to Government. The village was formerly part of the Rampa mansabdar's property. The quit-rent is Rs. 350.

Pandrapóle.

Pandrapóle : Eight miles north-west of Addatígela. Population 87. Another of the old Rampa muttas. The father of the present muttadar, who is also the muttadar of Kóta, was confirmed in possession in 1879 on a quit-rent of Rs. 70.

Rámavaram.

Rámavaram : Seventeen miles north-west of Addatígela and included in the Kóta mutta. Contains a travellers' bungalow. On a hill near this village is a small cave in which are four

CHAP. XV. YELLAVARAM.

idols. From the rock above hang stalactites from which water drips on to the figures below. The temple of Visvanátha in this village is worshipped by the Saivites in the neighbouring hills every Sivarátri. The god is considered especially potent in granting prayers for children.

Vírabhadrapurám.

Vírabhadrapurám : Three and a half miles east by south of Addatígela; population 225. On the Dévudu Pinjari hill close by is a small cave in which is an idol called Vírabhadrasvámi. This is worshipped every Sivarátri by the neighbouring hill people.

INDEX.

A

B

D

H

I

N

O

Q

R

S

V

W

MADRAS DISTRICT GAZETTEERS

GODAVARI
DISTRICT GAZETTEER

MADRAS DISTRICT GAZETTEERS

GODAVARI
DISTRICT GAZETTEER

STATISTICAL APPENDIX

F. R. HEMINGWAY

IN TWO VOLUMES

VOL. II

ISBN : 978-93-5324-407-1 (Set)
ISBN : 978-93-5324-409-5 (HB)
First Published, Madras, 1915
Published, 2020
Published by
Facsimile Publisher
12 Pragati Market
Ashok Vihar, Ph-2
Delhi-110052
E-mail: books@facsimilepublisher.com
Printed at: G. Print Process, Delhi.

Godavari District Gazetteer
Author: F. R. HEMINGWAY

MADRAS DISTRICT GAZETTEERS.

GŌDĀVARI.

VOLUME II.

PRICE, 1 *rupee*.] [1 *shilling* 6 *pence*

MADRAS DISTRICT GAZETTEERS.

STATISTICAL APPENDIX

FOR

GŌDĀVARI DISTRICT.

MADRAS:
PRINTED BY THE SUPERINTENDENT, GOVERNMENT PRESS.

1915.

TABLE OF CONTENTS.

* This table is *nil*.

I.—Area, Population, etc., in 1911.

Locality.	Area in square miles.	Number of			Population, 1911.			Population (both sexes) in 1901.	Percentage of variation (of population.)		Density of population per square mile, 1911.
		Towns.	Villages.	Occupied houses.	Total.	Males.	Females.		1891-1901.	1901-1911.	
(1)	(2)	(3)	(4)	(5)	(6)	(7)	(8)	(9)	(10)	(11)	(12)
Rajahmundry Division.											
Rajahmundry	376	2	88	35,638	189,260	94,434	94,826	161,070	+ 14·1	+ 17·5	503
Amalapuram	367	1	117	39,370	215,710	104,066	111,644	189,105	+ 7·7	+ 14·1	588
Razole	291	...	104	39,404	217,919	104,240	113,679	194,543	+ 9·2	+ 12·0	749
Bhadrachalam Agency Division.											
Bhadrachalam	911	...	328	10,587	55,952	28,244	27,708	48,658	+ 14·9	+ 15	61
Nugur	593	...	123	3,421	19,958	9,982	9,976	20,218	+ 44·5	− 1·3	34
Polavaram Agency Division.											
Polavaram	543	..	78	13,209	65,727	33,262	32,465	58,274		+ 12·8	121
Chodavaram	710	...	244	5,865	28,610	14,389	14,221	23,229	+ 14·6	+ 23·2	40
Yellavaram	919	...	329	7,633	36,655	18,619	18,036	29,681		+ 23·5	40
Peddapuram Division.											
Peddapuram	604	1	200	40,150	188,346	92,873	95,473	167,020	+ 3·2	+ 12·7	312
Ramachandrapuram	291	1	116	44,783	238,774	117,541	121,233	217,772	+ 10·8	+ 9·6	821
Cocanada Division.											
Cocanada	297	2	101	43,375	228,388	111,760	116,628	213,758	+ 16·5	+ 6·8	769
Pithapuram	193	1	49	19,247	96,824	47,986	48,838	84,089	+ 0·3	+ 15·1	502
Tuni	126	1	49	14,992	70,736	34,802	35,934	58,762	+ 2·3	+ 20·4	561
District Total ...	6,221	9	1,926	317,674	1,652,859	812,198	840,661	1,466,179	+ 10·10	+ 12·8	266

II.—Variation in Population since 1891.

Towns.	Population.			Percentage of variation of population.	
	1911.	1901.	1891.	1891—1901.	1901—1911.
(1)	(2)	(3)	(4)	(5)	(6)
The whole District ...	1,652,859	1,466,179	1,331,350	10·1	12·8
Amalapuram Taluk.					
Amalapuram	12,615	9,510	9,254	2·8	32·6
Cocanada Taluk.					
Cocanada *	54,110	48,096	40,553	18·6	12·5
Samalkota	15,483	16,015	13,409	19·4	— 3·3
PEDDAPURAM TALUK.					
Peddapuram	15,436	12,609	13,658	— 7·7	22·4
PITHAPURAM DIVISION.					
Pithapuram	15,316	13,220	13,731	— 3·7	15·9
Rajahmundry Taluk.					
Rajahmundry * ...	48,417	36,408	28,397	28·2	33
Dowlaishwaram ..	10,347	10,304	10,492	— 1·8	0·4
Ramachandrapuram Taluk.					
Mandapeta ...	9,546	8,380	7,650	9·5	13·9
TUNI DIVISION.					
Tuni	9,268	8,842	7,733	14·3	4·8

* Represents a municipal town.

III.—Roads.

Year.	Mileage of roads maintained.		
	Total.	Metalled.	Unmetalled.
(1)	(2)	(3)	(4)
	M.	M.	M.
1871–72	} *		
1876–77			
1881–82			
1886–87	437	357	80
1891–92	498	385	113
1896–97	499	421	78
1901–02	524	478	46
1906–07	676	555	141
1911–12	851	620	231

* Information for these years is not available.

IV.—List of Travellers' Bungalows.

Serial number.	Taluks and stations.	By whom maintained.	Nearest railway station, if any, and the distance from it.	Nature of accommodation.
(1)	(2)	(3)	(4)	(5)
	RAJAHMUNDRY DIVISION.			
	Rajahmundry Taluk.			
1	Burugapudi *	L.F.D.	Rajahmundry, 12 miles.	Two main rooms, two bath rooms, kitchen, and stables.
2	Gokavaram * ...	Do.	Rajahmundry, 21 miles.	One main room, bath room, store room, stable, and kitchen.
3	Rajanagaram * ...	Do.	Rajahmundry, 10 miles.	One central hall, two bed rooms, store room, stable, and kitchen.
4	Dowleishwaram.*	P.W.D.	Rajahmundry, 4 miles.	Two rooms, two verandahs, two bath rooms, two store rooms, stable and kitchen.
	Amalāpuram Taluk.			
5	Amalāpuram † ...	L.F.D.	Rajahmundry, 36 miles.	Two main rooms, two bath rooms, two verandahs, stable and kitchen.
6	Annampalli * ...	P.W.D.	Rajahmundry, 45 miles.	One main room, two bath rooms, two dressing rooms, one kitchen, stable and outhouse.
7	Bendamurlanka *.	Do.	Cocanada, 42 miles.	One central hall, one bath room, one store house, and kitchen.
8	Katrenikona † ...	L.F.D.	Rajahmundry, 48 miles.	Six rooms including bath rooms, two verandahs, stable and kitchen.
9	Mummidivaram †.	Do.	Rajahmundry, 44 miles.	Four rooms including bath rooms, two verandahs, stable and kitchen.
10	Rangapuram * ...	P.W.D.	Cocanada, 32 miles.	One central hall, two bath rooms, two dressing rooms, stable and kitchen.
11	Uppalaguptam †	L.F.D.	Rajahmundry, 48 miles.	Three rooms, two verandahs, stable and kitchen.
	Razole Taluk.			
12	Kottapeta * ...	L.F.D.	Rajahmundry, 26 miles.	One bed room, hall, kitchen, stable, and two bath rooms.
13	Tatipaka * ...	Do.	Rajahmundry, 39 miles.	Do. do.

* Annas 8 for a singl person and Annas 12 for a married couple.
† No charges.

IV.—List of Travellers' Bungalows—*cont.*

Serial number.	Taluks and stations.	By whom maintained.	Nearest railway station, if any, and the distance from it.	Nature of accommodation.
(1)	(2)	(3)	(4)	(5)
	RAJAHMUNDRY DIVISION—*cont.*			
	Razole Taluk—cont.			
14	Gannavaram * ...	L.F.D.	Rajahmundry, 32 miles.	One bed room, hall, kitchen, stable, and two bath rooms.
15	Do. * ...	P.W.D.	Do.	One main room, one dressing room and one bath room.
16	Sivakodu * ...	Do.	Rajahmundry, 42 miles.	One main room; two dressing rooms, two bath rooms, one store room, kitchen and stable.
17	Mulikapalli * ...	Do.	Rajahmundry, 43 miles.	Two halls, two bath rooms, one store room, kitchen, stable (under construction).
18	Lolla *	Do.	Rajahmundry, 12 miles.	One main room, two side rooms, two bath rooms, one store room, kitchen and stable for three horses.
	BHADRACHALAM (AGENCY DIVISION).			
	Bhadrachalam Taluk.			
19	Parnasala †	Rev. Dept.	Yellandu, 76 miles.	Thatched building; sufficient accommodation for one officer.
20	Dummagudem ‡ ..	Do.	Yellandu, 71 miles.	Tiled roof; sufficient for two officers.
21	Narasapuram § ...	Do.	Yellandu, 64 miles.	Thatched roof; sufficient for one officer.
22	Gouridevipeta §...	Do.	Yellandu, 71 miles.	Do. do.
23	Kundalur § ...	Do.	Rajahmundry, 77 miles.	Do. do.
24	Lakkavaram § ...	Do.	Yellandu, 89 miles	Do. do.
25	Devarapalli § ...	Do.	Yellandu, 65 miles	Do. do.
26	Sitarampuram §	Do.	Rajahmundry, 79 miles.	Do. do.
27	Singaram § ...	Forest Dept.	Yellandu, 62 miles.	Forest Rest-house.
28	Bhadrachalam §...	Do.	Yellandu, 52 miles.	Do.

* Annas 8 for a single person and Annas 12 for a married couple.
† 4 annas for a single person.
‡ Rent payable per diem is Re. 1 for a single person and Rs. 1-8-0 for married couple.
§ No charges.

IV.—List of Travellers' Bungalows—*cont.*

Serial number. (1)	Taluks and stations. (2)	By whom maintained. (3)	Nearest railway station, if any, and the distance from it. (4)	Nature of accommodation. (5)
	BHADRACHALAM (AGENCY DIVISION) —*cont.*			
	Bhadrachalam Taluk —cont.			
29	Boddegudem *	Forest Dept.	Godavari, 90 miles.	Forest Rest-house.
30	Madhavarowpeta *	Do.	Yellandu, 68 miles.	Do.
31	Edugurallapalli. *	Do.	Yellandu, 85 miles.	Do.
32	Jeediguppa * ...	Do.	Yellandu, 60 miles.	Do.
33	Sukkamamidi * ...	Do.	Godavari, 98 miles.	Do.
34	Kondepudi * ...	Do.	Godavari, 44 miles.	Do.
35	Pulusumamidi *	Do.	Godavari, 67 miles.	Do.
36	Tammileru * ...	Do.	Godavari, 48 miles.	Do.
37	Tatilanka * ...	Do.	Yellandu, 80 miles.	Do.
38	Somanamalla * ...	Do.	Godavari, 72 miles.	Do.
39	Pedakonda * ...	Do.	Godavari, 63 miles.	Do.
40	Murumur † ...	Do.	Godavari, 83 miles.	Do.
41	Kunavaram † ...	Do.	Godavari, 70 miles.	Do.
42	Narisingapeta * ...	Do.	...	Forest Range sheds.
43	Arkuri * ...	Do.	...	Do.
44	Educherlapalli * ...	Do.	...	Do.
45	Sarvella* ...	Do.	...	Do.
46	Seetarampuram. *	Do.	Rajahmundry, 79 miles.	Do.
47	Maddigudem * ..	Do.	...	Do.
48	Gollaguppa * ...	Do.	...	Do.
49	Tatlanka * ..	Do.	...	Do.
50	Ramaram * ...	Do.	...	Do.
51	Kundulur * ...	Do.	Rajahmundry, 77 miles.	Do.
52	Pulusumamidi *	Do.	Godavari, 67 miles.	Do.
53	Pothampalli * ...	Do.	...	Do.

* No charge.
† Rate per diem is Re 1 for a single person and Rs. 1-8-0 for a married couple.

IV.—List of Travellers' Bungalows—*cont.*

Serial number.	Taluks and stations.	By whom maintained.	Nearest Railway station, if any, and the distance from it.	Nature of accommodation
(1)	(2)	(3)	(4)	(5)
	BHADRACHALAM (AGENCY DIVISION).—*cont.*			
	Bhadrachalam Taluk—cont.			
54	Posaram *	Forest Dept.	...	Forest Range sheds.
55	Lakkavaram * ...	Do.	Rajahmundry, 89 miles.	Do.
56	Kalleru * ..	Do.	...	Do.
57	Sukumamidi * ...	Do.	...	Do.
58	Chintur * ..	Do.	Rajahmundry, 89 miles.	Do.
59	Kothur * ...	Do.	...	Do.
60	Enkur *	Do.	...	Do.
61	Kottapalli * ...	Do.	...	Do.
62	Jeedigupppa or Eswaragudem.*	Do.	...	Do.
63	Paidigudem * ...	Do.	...	Do.
64	Somanamallu * ...	Do.	...	Do.
	Nugur Taluk.			
65	Chandrapatla* ...	Rev. Dept.	Yellandu, 128 miles.	Thatched building, main hall, bath room, private room, front verandah, with out-houses for kitchen and stables.
66	Chakkupalli * ...	Do.	Yellandu, 116 miles.	Do. do.
67	Venkatapuram *	Do.	Yellandu, 100 miles.	Do. do.
68	Albaka * ...	Do.	Yellandu, 110 miles.	Do. do.
69	Edirada * ..	Do.	Yellandu, 101 miles.	Do. do.
70	Tegada * ...	Do.	Yellandu, 89 miles.	Do. do.
71	Uyyalamadugu *	Forest Dept.	Warangal, 70 miles.	Forest Range shed.
72	Pusuguppa * ...	Do.	Warangal, 78 miles	Do.

* No charge.

IV.—List of Travellers' Bungalows—*cont.*

Serial number. (1)	Taluks and stations. (2)	By whom maintained. (3)	Nearest railway station, if any, and the distance from it. (4)	Nature of accommodation. (5)
	BHADRACHALAM (AGENCY DIVISION) —*cont.*			
	Nugur Taluk—cont.			
73	Edira * ..	Forest Dept.	.arangal, 70 miles.	Forest Range shed.
74	Doli * ..	Do.	Warangal, 65 miles.	Do.
75	Pamunuru * ...	Do.	Warangal, 60 miles.	Do.
76	Pedamedisileru *	Do.	Warangal, 65 miles.	Do.
77	Cheekupalli * ...	Do.	Do.	Do.
78	Pengole * ...	Do.	Do.	Do.
79	Chelamala * ...	Do.	Warangal, 54 miles.	Do.
	POLAVARAM (AGENCY DIVISION).			
	Polavaram Division.			
80	Puliramudugudem (Rest-house). †	Forest Dept.	Kovvur, 38 miles.	Two rooms, two bath rooms, a verandah in front, two kitchen rooms and two stables.
81	Mulagalampalli (Rest-house). ‡	Do.	Ellore, 40 miles.	Two rooms, two bed rooms with a bath room, verandahs, in front and rear, two kitchen rooms and two stables.
82	Polavaram §	L.F.D.	Kovvur, 18 miles.	One main room, two bath rooms two dressing rooms, tiled verandahs, kitchen and stables (thatched).
83	Dandupudy ‡ ...	Do.	Kovvur, 26 miles.	One main room, two bath rooms, two dressing rooms, tiled verandahs, kitchen and stables (thatched).
84	Taduvayi ‡ ...	Do.	Ellore, 35 miles.	One main room, one bath room, one dressing room, front and side verandahs, kitchen and stables (tiled).
85	Puchikapadu ‡ ..	Do.	Ellore, 48 miles.	One main room, one bath room, one store room, front and side verandahs and combined stables and kitchen.

* No charge.
† Rupee 1 for a single person and Rs. 1-8-0 for a married couple.
‡ Annas 8 for a single person and annas 12 for married couple.
§ Annas 6 for a single man and annas 9 for a married couple.

IV.—List of Travellers' Bungalows—*cont.*

Serial number.	Taluks and stations.	By whom maintained.	Nearest Railway station, if any, and the distance from it.	Nature of accommodation
(1)	(2)	(3)	(4)	(5)
	POLAVARAM (AGENCY DIVISION) —*cont.*			
	Polavaram Division—cont.			
86	Kannapuram * ...	L.F.D.	Kovvur, 32 miles.	Two main rooms, two bath rooms, two dressing rooms two side verandahs, combined stables and kitchen.
87	Koyyalagudem. *	Do.	Kovvur, 28 miles.	Two main rooms, two bath rooms, two dressing rooms, tiled verandahs, stables and kitchen (thatched).
88	Jeelugumilli * ...	Do.	Ellore, 46 miles.	One main room, one bath room, one dressing room, verandah, kitchen and stables (tiled).
89	Buttayagudem. *	Do.	Ellore, 38 miles.	One main room with front and rear verandahs, two bath rooms, combined kitchen and stables.
90	Jangareddigudem.*	Do.	Ellore, 32 miles.	Two main rooms, two dressing rooms, two bath rooms, tiled kitchen and thatched stables.
	Chodavaram Division.			
91	Bodalur † ...	L.F.D.	Rajahmundry, 62 miles	Thatched roof, one big room, one bath room, one kitchen and one stable.
92	Chavala †... ...	Do.	Rajahmundry, 74 miles.	Do. do.
93	Maredumilli * ...	Do.	Rajahmundry, 52 miles.	Thatched roof, one big room, side room, one kitchen and stables.
94	Devarapalli * ...	Do.	Rajahmundry, 44 miles.	Do. do.
95	Gangugudem † ...	Do.	Rajahmundry, 43 miles.	Do. do.
96	Musurumalli † ...	Do.	Rajahmundry, 38 miles.	Do. do.

* Annas 8 for a single person and annas 12 for a married couple.
† Annas 4 for a single person and annas 6 for a married couple.

IV.—List of Travellers' Bungalows—*cont.*

Serial number.	Taluks and stations.	By whom maintained.	Nearest railway station, if any, and the distance from it.	Nature of accommodation.
(1)	(2)	(3)	(4)	(5)
	POLAVARAM (AGENCY DIVISION) —*cont.*			
	Chodavaram Division—cont.			
97	Chodavaram † ...	L.F.D.	Rajahmundry, 34 miles.	Pucca building with tiled roof, one big room with two side rooms for bathing, one front verandah.
98	Devipatnam ‡ ...	Do.	Rajahmundry, 27 miles.	Thatched roof building already in existence having become ruined, a pucca building with tiled roof is under construction.
	Yellavaram Division.			
99	Tummapuram ‡...	L F.D.	Samalkota, 30 miles.	Tiled building under construction.
100	Jaddangi ‡ ...	Do.	Samalkota, 38 miles.	Do. do.
101	Nillipudi ‡ ...	Do.	Rajahmundry, 26 miles.	Thatched roof, one room, one bath room, front verandah and kitchen.
102	Addatigala ‡ ...	Do.	Samalkota, 38 miles.	Tiled roof, one room, bath room, kitchen and stables.
103	Rayapalli ‡ ...	Do.	Samalkota, 45 miles.	Thatched roof, one room, bath rooms and kitchen.
104	Ramavaram ‡ ...	Do.	Samalkota, 55 miles.	Do. do.
105	Gurtedu ‡ ...	Do.	Samalkota, 77 miles.	Do. do.
	PEDDAPURAM DIVISION.			
	Peddapuram Taluk.			
106	Jaggampeta (for Europeans). ‡	L.F.D.	Samalkota, 13 miles.	Has got provision for cooking and halting.
107	Do. (for Indians). *	Do.	Do.	Do. do.
108	Yelesvaram ‡ ...	Do.	Samalkota, 24 miles.	Do. do.
109	Prattipadu * ...	Do.	Samalkota, 13 miles.	Provision for halting alone.

* Annas 4 for a single person and annas 6 for a married couple.
† Annas 6 for a single person and annas 9 for a married couple.
‡ Annas 8 for a single person and annas 12 for a married couple.

IV.—List of Travellers' Bungalows—*cont.*

Serial number. (1)	Taluks and stations. (2)	By whom maintained. (3)	Nearest railway station, if any, and the distance from it. (4)	Nature of accommodation. (5)
	PEDDAPURAM DIVISION—*cont.*			
	Peddapuram Taluk—cont.			
110	Kattipudi (for Europeans).†	L.F.D.	Durgada, 3 miles.	There is also an unendowed choultry for travellers. Has got provision for cooking and halting.
111	Do. (for Indians).*	Do.	Do.	Do. do.
112	Arempudi Annavaram.†	Do.	Kotapalli, 3 miles.	Do. do.
113	Nallachernvu (for Europeans).†	Do.	Samalkota, 13 miles.	There is also an unendowed choultry for the use of travellers.
114	Peddapuram ‡ ...	Do.	Samalkota, 3 miles.	Also an unendowed choultry for travellers.
115	Ramesampota ‡ ...	Do.	Samalkota, 9 miles.	Do. do.
116	Divily (Rest house).‡	Do.	Samalkota, 6 miles.	Has got provision for cooking and halting.
	Ramachandrapuram Taluk.			
117	Bikkavole ‡ ...	L.F.D.	Bikkavole, 2 miles.	One room, verandah, no kitchen room; there is also one unendowed choultry under the Taluk Board for travellers.
118	Anaparti ‡ ...	Do.	Anaparti, 1 mile.	Two rooms and two verandahs; there is also one unendowed choultry maintained by Taluk Board for travellers.
119	Dwarapudi ‡ ...	Do.	Dwarapudi, 1 mile.	Three rooms, two verandahs, one bath room and one kitchen shed.
120	Balabhadrapuram.†	P.W.D.	Bikkavole, 2 miles.	One hall, one verandah, two rooms, stable.
121	Do. (Rest house).†	L.F.D.	Do.	Dismantled; only sheds existing.
122	Kotipalli † ...	P.W.D.	Cocanada, 23 miles.	One room, verandah, kitchen and stable.

* Annas 4 for a single person and annas 6 for married couple.
† Annas 8 for a single person and annas 12 for married couple.
‡ No charges.

IV.—List of Travellers' Bungalows—*cont.*

Serial number. (1)	Taluks and stations. (2)	By whom maintained. (3)	Nearest railway station, if any, and the distance from it. (4)	Nature of accommodation. (5)
	PEDDAPURAM DIVISION—*cont.*			
	Ramachandrapuram Taluk—cont.			
123	Ramachandrapuram.*	P.W.D.	Dwarapudi, 11 miles.	One hall, two verandahs, two rooms, one kitchen shed, stable-shed. There is also one unendowed choultry maintained by the Taluk Board for the use of travellers.
124	Alamur †	L.F.D.	Dwarapudi, 12 miles.	One unendowed choultry for the use of travellers.
125	Dwarapudi † ...	Do.	Dwarapudi, below 1 mile.	Do. do.
126	Mandapeta (Rest house).†	Do.	Dwarapudi, 6 miles.	Dismantled, only sheds existing.
	COCANADA DIVISION.			
	Cocanada Taluk.			
127	Jagannathagiri.*	P.W.D.	Cocanada, 12 miles.	One main room, two side rooms, three bath rooms, kitchen and stables for two horses; tiled roof; furnished.
128	Do.	L.F.D.	Do.	Two parallel rows of tiled buildings, each consisting of four rooms with halls (Rest house).
129	Cocanada ‡ ...	P.W.D.	Cocanada, 1 mile.	Two complete sets of rooms two main rooms, two dressing rooms, two bath rooms, two store rooms, kitchen and godown, stables for four horses; equipped with furniture.
130	Cocanada (Rest house) otherwise called Brahmananda Mandiram (for Indians).†	L.F.D.	Do.	One big hall, two verandah rooms; tiled roof.
131	Rama Raopeta Rest house (for Indians).†	Do.	Do.	Tiled roof; accommodation for 3 families; big compound.

* Annas 8 for a single person and annas 12 for married couple.
† No charges.
‡ Rupee 1 for a single person and Rs. 1-8-0 for married couple.

IV.—List of Travellers' Bungalows—*cont.*

Serial number.	Taluks and stations.	By whom maintained.	Nearest railway station, if any, and the distance from it.	Nature of accommodation.
(1)	(2)	(3)	(4)	(5)
	COCANADA DIVISION—*cont.*			
	Cocanada Taluk. —cont.			
132	Chintapalli * ...	P.W.D.	Bikkavole, 5 miles.	One main room, roof tiled except central hall, thatched side rooms, one bath room.
133	Hope Island † ...	Forest Dept.	Cocanada, 12 miles.	Old Light House Superintendent's quarters, four godowns for lascars, one store room, one oil godown.
134	Samalkota * ...	L.F.D.	Samalkota, 2 miles.	Thatched roof, two midde rooms, two dressing rooms, two bath rooms, two store rooms, kitchen.
135	Coringa Rest house (for Indians).†	Do.	Cocanada, 12 miles.	Tiled roof. four rooms, one central hall with verandahs.
	PITHAPURAM DIVISION.			
136	Pithapuram (Padagaya).†	L.F.D.	Pithapuram, 1 mile.	This is a choultry for Indians; tiled roof, sufficient accommodation for eight families.
137	Uppada (Rest house).*	Do.	Pithapuram, 7 miles.	Sufficient to accommodate two officers at a time; no cooking rooms; tiled roof, two big rooms, two verandah rooms.
	TUNI DIVISION.			
138	Tuni *	L.F.D.	Tuni, 1 mile.	Two rooms, two bath rooms with verandah round, a kitchen, and stable, tiled roof.

* Annas 8 for a single person and annas 12 for married couple.
† No charges.

V.—Religions in 1911.

Taluks.	Hindus.			Musalmans.			Christians.			Others		
	Total.	Males.	Females.	Total.	Males.	Females.	Total.	Males.	Females.	Total.	Males.	Females.
(1)	(2)	(3)	(4)	(5)	(6)	(7)	(8)	(9)	(10)	(11)	(12)	(13)
RAJAHMUNDRY DIVISION.												
Rajahmundry	182,048	90,712	91,336	4,651	2,430	2,221	2,473	1,240	1,233	88	52	36
Amalapuram	212,319	102,465	109,854	2,842	1,328	1,514	449	219	230	100	54	46
Razole	214,420	102,662	111,758	3,194	1,419	1,775	305	159	146	...	...	...
BHADRACHALAM AGENCY DIVISION.												
Bhadrachalam	50,420	25,421	24,999	592	308	284	966	463	503	3,974	2,052	1,922
Nugur	19,577	9,788	9,789	296	155	141	85	39	46	...	...	...
POLAVARAM AGENCY DIVISION.												
Polavaram	50,422	25,630	24,792	1,450	703	747	179	96	83	13,676	6,833	6,843
Chodavaram	25,727	12,983	12,744	136	82	54	142	82	60	2,605	1,242	1,363
Yellavaram	36,305	18,433	17,872	106	66	40	244	120	124	...	...	...
PEDDAPURAM DIVISION.												
Peddapuram	184,628	90,990	93,638	2,468	1,237	1,231	1,154	605	549	96	41	55
Ramachandrapuram ...	233,662	115,027	118,635	3,614	1,762	1,852	1,498	752	746	...	...	...
COCANADA DIVISION.												
Cocanada	221,747	108,355	113,392	4,788	2,459	2,329	1,781	898	883	72	48	24
Pithapuram	94,524	46,874	47,650	1,220	925	995	331	164	167	49	23	26
Tuni	69,513	34,182	35,331	970	498	472	249	120	129	4	2	2
District Total ...	1,595,312	783,522	811,790	27,027	13,372	13,655	9,856	4,957	4,899	20,664	10,347	10,317

VI.—Vital Statistics.

Taluks.	Ratio per 1,000 of population of																			
	Births.										Deaths.									
	1903.	1904.	1905.	1906.	1907.	1908.	1909.	1910.	1911.	1912.	1903.	1904.	1905.	1906.	1907.	1908.	1909.	1910.	1911.	1912.
(1)	(2)	(3)	(4)	(5)	(6)	(7)	(8)	(9)	(10)	(11)	(12)	(13)	(14)	(15)	(16)	(17)	(18)	(19)	(20)	(21)
Rajahmundry Division.																				
Rajahmundry	26	27	26	29	27	28	29	28	32	33	22	15	21	20	19	27	28	19	25	25
Amalapuram	24	24	27	18	28	21	32	38	28	33	20	24	21	20	20	24	23	30	29	28
Razole	...	...	...	...	...	...	...	33	27	35	...	...	...	...	...	...	...	25	18	22
Bhadrachalam Division.																				
Bhadrachalam	20	19	21	23	20	25	30	32	31	38	17	19	18	19	17	30	27	35	30	25
Nugur	...	...	...	...	...	...	25	28	26	39	...	...	...	...	...	...	20	23	24	30
Polavaram Division.																				
Polavaram	23	21	22	21	27	26	30	31	29	33	22	20	23	19	21	25	26	32	21	24
Chodavaram	23	16	21	20	22	21	17	20	18	33	20	15	20	18	19	22	14	23	15	34
Yellavaram	18	14	17	17	20	18	25	21	18	26	17	15	16	15	16	22	15	15	12	25
Peddapuram Division.																				
Peddapuram	26	22	33	31	34	20	23	35	26	30	16	13	20	42	20	16	25	27	19	31
Ramachandrapuram	33	33	36	36	33	38	30	37	34	34	24	22	24	37	31	28	27	30	25	29
Cocanada Division.																				
Cocanada	18	20	23	22	18	20	21	23	22	18	15	13	17	18	12	16	16	18	17	17
Pithapuram	23	17	25	19	15	24	21	30	28	25	20	16	15	16	14	19	18	23	21	24
Tuni	36	35	36	36	36	35	36	38	35	39	25	28	28	25	26	22	21	22	29	26

Town Circles.																				
Rajahmundry	33	32	35	36	33	32	33	37	30	28	22	25	24	42	35	42	29	33	23	26
Cocanada	35	35	38	40	40	41	41	41	36	34	25	26	29	40	30	33	32	31	35	28
Amalapuram	40	35	39	43	14	47	52	38	33	35	21	20	25	33	10	33	34	26	29	26
Peddapuram	40	39	45	40	35	36	44	37	24	27	23	28	31	42	34	34	31	36	24	30
Mandapeta	34	35	44	36	31	39	38	34	35	32	26	30	29	26	35	22	23	25	27	26
Pithapuram	29	27	18	20	22	13	18	21	17	18	20	23	15	29	10	21	18	13	19	18
Tuni	39	40	34	31	29	26	29	31	25	23	28	29	26	39	23	23	21	26	27	23
Samalkota	25	20	21	26	13	22	28	35	30	36	21	18	22	23	19	20	20	31	32	34
Dowlaishwaram	24	25	28	24	30	35	31	40	35	29	20	22	25	19	27	32	29	35	30	25
Total for the District ...	28	30	33	29	30	33	32	33	29	31	21	18	20	23	24	24	23	27	21	26

N.B.—This table excludes the statistics relating to Europeans and Eurasians.

Average death rate is 23·9 per 1,000.

VII.—Causes of death.

(Average of the statistics for the five years ending 1912.)

Name of Talak or Division.	Ratio of deaths per 1,000 of population from						Total.
	Cholera.	Small-pox.	Plague.	Fever.	Dysentery and diarrhœa.	All other causes.	
(1)	(2)	(3)	(4)	(5)	(6)	(7)	(8)
RAJAHMUNDRY DIVISION.							
Rajahmundry	1	1	...	11	...	6	19
Amalapuram	2	1	...	6	1	10	20
Razole	2	1	...	9	1	15	28
BHADRACHALAM DIVISION.							
Bhadrachalam	1	1	...	13	1	14	30
Nugur	1	...		15	2	9	27
POLAVARAM DIVISION.							
Polavaram	1	1	...	19	1	5	27
Chodavaram	1	1	...	17	1	6	26
Yellavaram	1	1	...	14	2	4	22
PEDDAPURAM DIVISION.							
Peddapuram	1	...	..	15	...	9	25
Ramachandrapuram ...	2	...	...	8	1	15	26
COCANADA DIVISION.							
Cocanada	1	...	...	8	1	7	17
Pithapuram	2	...	...	15	...	5	22
Tuni	1	...	..	19	1	3	24
TOWN CIRCLES.							
Cocanada	...	1	...	6	4	18	29
Dowlaishwaram ...	3	2	...	5	...	13	23
Peddapuram	2	...	..	11	2	8	23
Pithapuram	...	...	...	4	1	4	9
Rajahmundry	2	...	...	9	4	19	34
Samalkota	1	...	...	7	1	4	13
Total for the District ...	2	5	...	11	1	10	29

VIII.—Castes, Tribes and Races in 1911.

Caste, Tribe or Race.	Strength.		
	Males.	Females.	Total.
(1)	(2)	(3)	(4)
I. HINDU AND ANIMIST CASTES.			
(a) *Tamil.*			
Chetti	1,785	1,873	3,658
Kaikolan	1,740	1,708	3,448
Palli	18,278	22,409	40,687
Yerukala	4,261	4,572	8,833
(b) *Telugu.*			
Balija	7,577	8,046	15,623
Bestha	656	595	1,251
Boya...	1,350	1,223	2,573
Brahman	30,112	30,767	60,879
Devanga	11,656	12,404	24,060
Gamalla	17,355	18,824	36,179
Gavara	3,259	3,302	6,561
Golla	27,980	32,113	60,093
Idiga	53,799	58,672	112,471
Indra	12,592	15,106	27,698
Kamma	27,605	29,473	57,078
Kamsala	18,360	18,668	37,028
Kapu	168,805	172,004	340,809
Komati	16,807	16,181	32,988
Konda Dora	2,524	2,756	5,280
Koyi	33,568	33,933	67,501
Kummara	5,992	6,007	11,999
Madiga	35,920	36,097	72,017
Mala	144,017	141,856	285,873
Mangala	8,621	8,856	17,477
Mutracha	527	483	1,010
Odde	3,988	4,123	8,111
Razu	11,218	11,480	22,698
Sāle	21,538	21,635	43,173
Satani	1,033	1,227	2,260
Segidi	102	109	211
Telaga	18,712	19,170	37,882
Tsakala	20,145	21,327	41,472
Uppara	3,802	4,188	7,990
Velama	16,570	16,806	33,376
(c) *Malayalam.*		*Nil.*	
(d) *Canarese.*			
Jangam	2,704	2,578	5,282
(e) *Oriya.*			
Karnam	1,177	1,196	2,373
Odiya	829	1,042	1,871

VIII.—Castes, Tribes and Races in 1911—*cont.*

Caste, Tribe or Race. (1)	Strength. Males. (2)	Females. (3)	Total. (4)
I. Hindu and Animist Castes—*cont.*			
(f) *Other Madras Languages.*			
Brahman	1,130	1,401	2,531
Kshatriya	9,708	10,072	19,780
Mahrati	120	111	231
II. Musalman.			
Dudekula	1,353	1,423	2,776
Pathan	110	103	218
Saiyad	1,524	1,558	3,082
Sheik	8,946	9,035	17,981
III. Christian.			
Indian Christian	4,545	4,473	9,018
IV. Others	27,798	29,676	57,474
Total	812,198	840,661	1,652,859

IX.—Classification of area and principal crops in Fasli 1322 (1912–13).

Items.	Rajahmundry Division.			Bhadrachalam Agency Division.		Polavaram Agency Division.			Peddapuram Division.		Cocanada Division.			District Total.
	Rajahmundry Taluk.	Amalapuram Taluk.	Razole (Nagaram) Taluk.	Bhadrachalam. Taluk.	Nugur Taluk.	Polavaram Division.	Chodavâram Division.	Yellavaram Division.	Peddapuram Taluk.	Ramachandrapuram Taluk.	Cocanada Taluk.	Pittapuram Division.	Tuni Division.	
(1)	(2)	(3)	(4)	(5)	(6)	(7)	(8)	(9)	(10)	(11)	(12)	(13)	(14)	(15)
	ACS.	ACS.	ACS.	ACS.	ACS.	ACS.	ACS.	ACS.	ACS.	ACS.	ACS.	ACS.	ACS.	ACS.
Government (Ryotwari land)	164,943	114,198	107,535	480,652	323,840	287,069	1,487	321,914	172,321	108,567	43,281	40	1	2,125,848
Minor inam	33,642	46,736	41,707	...	...	2 902	131	609	25,637	49,014	15,202	...	...	215,600
Whole inam	5,581	2,470	1,082		...	4,004		...	80,490	167	384	...	1,382	95,560
Zamindari	36,237	71,354	36,006	102,388	55,680	53,743	452,526	265,330	108.201	23,224	131,213	123,742	79,046	1,543,690
Total area by survey ...	240,403	234,758	186,330	583,040	379,520	347,718	454,144	587,853	386,669	185,972	190,080	123,782	80,429	3,980,698
Forests	21,681	8,432	...	275,182	61,747	69,557	...	105,938	46,030	...	54,955	...	...	643,522
Not available for cultivation	31,713	68,289	21,797	191,291	257,718	137,417	420,303	429,637	145,047	32,771	11,429	16,726	...	1,764,138
Culturable waste other than fallow	6,974	6,961	23,765	58,578	36,572	37,237	6,003	5,856	5,636	144	5,929	31,048	23,351	248,054
Current fallows... ...	70,544	31,366	23,789	441	5,963	46,922	6,789	22,487	55,171	17,946	12,811	18,122	11,291	323,642
Net area cropped ...	109,491	119,710	116,979	57,548	17,520	56,585	21,049	23,935	134,785	135,111	104,956	57,886	45,787	1,001,342
Area shown in village accounts ...	240,403	234,758	186,330	583,040	379,520	347,718	454,144	587,853	386,669	185,972	190,080	123,782	80,429	3,980,698

IX.—Classification of area and principle crops in Fasli 1322 (1912-13)—*cont.*

Items.	Rajahmundry Division.			Bhadrachalam Agency Division.		Polavaram Agency Division.			Peddapuram Division.		Cocanada Division.			District Total.
	Rajahmundry Taluk.	Amalapuram Taluk.	Razole (Nagaram) Taluk.	Bhadrachalam Taluk.	Nugur Taluk.	Polavaram Division.	Chodavaram Division.	Yellavaram Division.	Peddapuram Taluk.	Ramachandrapuram Taluk.	Cocanada Taluk.	Pittapuram Division.	Tuni Division.	
(1)	(2)	(3)	(4)	(5)	(6)	(7)	(8)	(9)	(10)	(11)	(12)	(13)	(14)	(15)
	ACS.	ACS.	ACS.	ACS.	ACS.	ACS.	ACS.	ACS.	ACS.	ACS.	ACS.	ACS.	ACS.	ACS.
Irrigated by Government canals... ...	5,445	104,749	84,880	25	...	...	...	...	8,202	111,943	88,360	...	...	403,604
Irrigated by private canals.	...	...	...	...	...	...	...	...	10,983	...	...	37,077	26,799	74,859
Do. tanks ...	29,368	...	...	919	358	10,346	6,013	4,074	33,239	2,192	1,096	13,208	11,710	112,523
Do. wells ...	...	...	...	...	...	...	...	...	32	35	...	5,000	2,037	7,104
Do. other sources.	854	...	...	659	...	248	...	419	111	...	...	2,601	5,242	10,134
Total area irrigated ...	35,667	104,749	84,880	1,603	358	10,594	6,013	4,493	52,567	114,170	89,456	57,886	45,788	608,224
Area under Cereals and pulses—														
Rice	46,008	111,021	81,867	7,325	5,136	14,965	5,233	4,151	55,873	132,508	107,379	34,090	20,782	626,338
Cholam	13,618	2,750	14,662	40,028	7,583	22,350	5,020	4,874	8,729	2,249	51	2,443	1,552	125,909
Cambu	2,696	57	194	...	...	2,825	599	3,646	13,783	45	312	920	8,550	33,627

Ragi	10,906	1,568	1,374	...	...	1,293	346	2,508	11,900	1,347	3,156	1,667	3,674	39,739
Others	28,676	18,560	18,565	5,862	1,824	6,078	2,323	11,254	43,052	35,188	10,192	13,073	14,106	208,753
Total ...	101,904	133,956	116,662	53,215	14,543	47,511	13,521	26,433	133,337	171,337	121,090	52,193	48,664	1,034,366
Oil seeds—														
Til or gingelly ...	16,517	1,260	6,086	2,245	1,741	3,927	8,840	2,854	9,615	13,182	1,901	382	5,860	69,410
Groundnut	1	11	2	...	...	...	...	...	...	...	...	...	...	14
Castors	1,912	630	177	658	33	5,923	1,551	134	752	199	9	69	30	12,077
Others...	.	...	...	...	...	...	...	...	...	216	...	..	...	216
Total ...	18,430	1,901	6,265	2,903	1,774	9,850	5,391	2,988	10,367	13,597	1,910	451	5,890	81,717
Condiments and spices.	858	4,106	6,573	179	50	135	153	86	939	4,799	975	4,044	660	23,557
Sugarcane, etc.	36	38	648	...	..	98	...	3	2,907	3,793	1,549	625	128	9,825
Cotton	1,203	5,891	11,316	692	504	61	250	272	8,759	234	46	5,272	751	35,251
Indigo, etc.	5	298	444	..	...	...	...	...	...	246	...	...	...	993
Drugs and narcotics—														
Tobacco	2,137	1,880	2,860	572	649	423	1,604	292	676	2 007	104	3	199	13,406
Others	...	49	4	...	...	...	...	...	...	41	...	...	...	94
Total ..	2,137	1,929	2,864	572	649	423	1,604	292	676	2,048	104	3	199	13,500
Fodder crops	14	6	172	...	...	...	...	...	...	13,383	2,530	...	60	16,165
Orchards and garden produce	4,686	26,197	23,630	27	...	303	350	56	3,891	2,767	2,496	684	783	65,870
Miscellaneous non-food crops	6	602	716	...	...	...	...	...	1	54	...	5	31	1,415
Total area cropped ...	129,279	174,924	169,290	57,588	17,520	58,381	21,269	30,130	160,877	212,258	130,700	63,277	57,166	1,282,659
Deduct area cropped more than once ...	19,788	55,214	52,311	40	...	1,796	220	6,195	26,092	77,147	25,744	5,391	11,379	281,317
Net area cropped ...	109,491	119,710	116,979	57,548	17,520	56,585	21,049	23,935	134,785	135,111	104,956	57,886	45,787	1,001,342

X.—Reserved forest and area proposed for reservation (in square miles) on 30th June 1913.

Taluks.	Reserved forest.	Area proposed for reservation.	Total of columns 2 and 3.	Area of taluk.	Percentage of column 4 to cultivated area.
(1)	(2)	(3)	(4)	(5)	(6)
Lower Godavari.					
Rajahmundry	23	...	23	376	13·51
Amalapuram ...	13	...	13	367	6·98
Polavaram	109	...	109	543	122·82
Yellavaram	186	...	186	919	34·74
Peddapuram	62	...	62	604	15·01
Cocanada	11	75	86	297	52·36
Upper Godavari.					
Bhadrachalam	427·73	8·91	436·64	911	485·15
Nugur		96·48	96·48	593	357·3
Total ...	831·73	180·39	1,012·12	4,610	64·68

Net revenue realized under forests during

1903-04.	1904-05.	1905-06.	1906-07.	1907-08.	1908-09.	1909-10.	1910-11.	1911-12.	1912-13.
(1)	(2)	(3)	(4)	(5)	(6)	(7)	(8)	(9)	(10)
Lower Godavari.									
RS. 1,36,270	RS. 1,33,156	RS. 1,13,025	RS. 70,413	RS. 1,18,641	RS. 1,05,903	RS. 1,32,190	RS. 1,13,972	RS. 1,30,353	RS. 1,03,525
Upper Godavari.									
...	...	...	46,504	41,956	40,162	65,698	33,781	44,849	59,796

NOTE.—With effect from the year 1906-07, the District was divided into Upper and Lowe Divisions.

XI.—Classification of area and money rates according to the last settlement.

(Part 1. Area under each money rate.)

Particulars.			Dry.						
			Rajahmundry Division.			Peddapuram Division.		Cocanada Division.	District Total.
Money-rates.			Rajahmundry Taluk.	Amalapuram Taluk.	Razole Taluk.	Peddapuram Taluk.	Rama-chandra-puram Taluk.	Cocanada Taluk.	
(1)			(2)	(3)	(4)	(5)	(6)	(7)	(8)
	RS.	A.	ACS.	ACS.	ACS.	ACS.	ACS.	ACS.	ACS.
Ordinary dry.	7	0	...	4,274	1,108	...	678	35	6,095
	5	8	...	...	...	145	...	...	145
	5	0	...	9,698	837	...	9,669	136	20,340
	4	8	1,752	...	..	12	...	...	1,764
	4	0	97	3,612	519	..	5,857	290	10,375
	3	12	7	...	...	21	...	...	28
	3	4	187	...	...	...	43	...	230
	3	0	64	1,253	304	...	1,144	643	3,408
	2	12	2,142	...	...	43	57	...	2,242
	2	8	2,740	2,102	457	1,280	884	542	8,005
	2	4	244	...	...	61	27	...	332
	2	0	...	3,442	643	..	35	808	4,928
	1	12	5,296	...	...	3,176	61	...	8,533
	1	10	1,793	...	...	1,005	...	...	2,798
	1	8		5,387	673	..	...	1,308	7,368
	1	4	8,049	2,015	2,242	11,211	801	989	25,307
	1	0	27,802	5,688	6,623	22,310	2,188	738	65,849
	0	12	...	5,315	6,356	...	..	...	11,671
	0	10	22,562		...	22,367	848	1,181	46,958
	0	8	14,034	283	2,979	16,659	961	146	35,064
	0	5	9,895	...	...	21,117	2,482	...	33,494
	0	4	...	...	669	...	...	...	669
Lanka.	11	0	...	1,331	40	...	175	...	1,546
	9	0	...	1,763	7	...	735	26	2,531
	7	0	...	456	140	..	391	73	1,060
	5	0	...	81	27	..	355	369	822
	4	0	56	18	...	...	35	153	262
	3	0	...	12	...	...	..	...	12
Padugai.	9	0	...	1,477	1,560	...	144	...	3,181
	7	0	26	1,125	998	...	497	23	2,669
	5	0	33	505	1,914	...	422	27	2,901
	4	0	167	79	779	...	75	46	1,146
	3	0	23	17	281	...	...	38	359
	2	8	...	12	269	...	...	...	281
Special rates.	4	8	3	...	..	...	...	...	3
	3	12	...	...	...	10	4	...	14
	3	4	14	...	...	48	3	...	65
	2	12	..	...	...	4	...	...	4
	2	8	4	...	...	268	...	23	295
	2	4	36	...		45	1	...	82
	1	12	3	...	...	...	...	..	3
	1	4	...	...	...	14	1	...	15
	1	0	...	...	...	5	1	...	6
Total ...			87,029	49,945	29,425	99,801	28,574	7,586	312,360

XI.—Classification of area and money rates according to the last settlement—*cont.*

(Part 1. Area under each money rate)—*cont.*

Particulars.			Wet.						
Money rates.			Rajahmundry Division.			Peddapuram Division.		Cocanada Division.	District Total.
			Rajahmundry Taluk.	Amalapuram Taluk.	Razole Taluk.	Peddapuram Taluk.	Ramachandrapuram Taluk.	Cocanada Taluk	
(1)			(2)	(3)	(4)	(5)	(6)	(7)	(8)
	RS.	A.	ACS.	ACS.	ACS.	ACS.	ACS.	ACS.	ACS.
Special rates under Eleru river.	12	0	...	...	...	3,366	...	...	3,366
	7	12	...	...	.	1,321	..	...	1,321
	12	0	...	470	970	...	6,492	812	8,744
	10	0	...	4,539	2,288	...	18,935	5,189	30,951
	9	0	...	6,430	3,998	...	16,092	8,400	35,520
	8	8	893	...	...	264	...	5	1,162
	8	0	341	6,179	3,595	...	3,490	7,768	21,373
	7	12	2,699	...	...	307	101	..	3,107
	7	0	573	6,066	3,187	124	360	4,866	15,176
	6	8	1,783	...	...	579	20	...	2,382
	6	0	...	4,086	2,061	...	...	2,222	8,369
	5	12	2,392	...	...	2,328	688	80	5,488
	5	4	453	...	...	547	2	...	1,002
	5	0	...	3,413	2,485	...	...	1,111	7,009
	4	8	2,816	1,735	1,508	4,322	270	496	11,147
	4	0	...	726	467	...	...	...	1,193
	3	12	1,367	...	...	2,147	84	...	3,598
	3	8	...	2,491	169	...	...	...	2,660
	3	4	1,655	...	...	2,361	78	333	4,427
	2	8	1,999	...	...	2,841	8	4	4,852
	2	4	2	...	...	212	...	20	234
	2	0	319	...	...	774	17	...	1,110
	1	10	29	...	...	28	...	...	57
Total ...			17,321	36,135	20,728	21,521	47,237	31,306	174,248

NOTE.—The figures given under Razole taluk represent those for the old Nagaram taluk. Razole taluk was formed in 1910 and the territorial limits of Amalapuram taluk were also changed in that year. Figures for the revised areas are not available.

XI.--Classification of area and money rates according to the last settlement--*cont.*

(Part 2. Classes and sorts included under each money rate.)

(a) *Dry lands in the delta.*

I	II	III	IV	V	XII	XIII	XIV	First Group.		Second Group.	
								Taram.	Rate.	Taram.	Rate.
									RS. A.		RS. A.
1-A	...	...	...	...	...	...	...	3	7 0	4	5 0
1	1-A	...	...	...	...	...	...	4	5 0	5	4 0
2	1	...	...	...	...	...	...	5	4 0	6	3 0
3	2	1	...	...	...	...	...	6	3 0	7	2 8
4	3	2	1	...	...	...	...	7	2 8	8	2 0
5	4	3	2	...	...	...	...	8	2 0	9	1 8
...	5	4	3	1	1	...	...	9	1 8	10	1 4
...	...	5	4	2	2	1	...	10	1 4	11	1 0
...	...	...	5	3	3	2	1	11	1 0	12	0 12
...	...	...	...	4	...	3	2	12	0 12	13	0 8
...	...	...	...	5	...	...	3	13	0 8	14	0 4

(b) *Wet lands in the delta.*

I	II	III	IV	V	XII	XIII	XIV	First class.		Second class.		Third class.		Fourth class.	
								Taram.	Rate.	Taram.	Rate.	Taram.	Rate.	Taram.	Rate.
									RS. A.		RS. A.		RS. A.		RS. A.
I-A	1	...	...	..	...		..	1	12 0	2	10 0	3	9 0	4	8 0
1	2			...	...	...	...	2	10 0	3	9 0	4	8 0	5	7 0
2	3	...	1	...	...	...	...	3	9 0	4	8 0	5	7 0	6	6 0
3	4	1	2	...	...	...	...	4	8 0	5	7 0	6	6 0	7	5 0
4	5	2	3	1	1	...	...	5	7 0	6	6 0	7	5 0	8	4 8
5	...	3	4	2	2	1	...	6	6 0	7	5 0	8	4 8	9	4 0
...	...	4	5	3	3	2	1	7	5 0	8	4 8	9	4 0	10	3 8
..	...	5	...	4	...	3	2	8	4 8	9	4 0	10	3 8	11	3 0
...	..	...	...	5	...	...	3	9	4 0	10	3 8	11	3 0	12	2 8

XI.—Classification of area and money rates according to the last settlement—*cont.*

(Part 2. Classes and sorts included under each money rate)—*cont.*

(c) *Dry and Wet lands in the Upland taluks.*

Class and sort of soil.	Dry.								Wet.					
	First Group.		Second Group.		Third Group.		Fourth Group.		First Class.		Second Class.		Third Class.	
	Taram.	Rate.	Taram.	Rate.	Taram.	Rate.	Taram.	Rate.	Taram.	Rate.	Taram.	Rate.	Taram.	Rate.
		RS. A.		RS. A.		RS. A.		RS. A.		RS. A.		RS. A.		RS. A.
I 1 ..	...	...	...	...	...	...	...	...	1	12 0	Special rates for the lands under the Eleru river.			
I 2 ...	...	...	..	...	...	...	...	...	4	7 12				
II 1 ...	1	5 8	2	4 8	3	3 12	4	3 4	2	9 0	4	7 12	6	6 8
II 2	2	4 8	4	3 4	8	1 12	8	1 12	5	7 0	8	5 4	10	3 12
III 1 ...	2	4 8	5	2 12	8	1 12	9	1 10	5	7 0	6	6 8	8	5 4
III 2 ..	6	2 8	8	1 12	10	1 4	11	1 0	8	5 4	9	4 8	11	3 4
III 3 ...	10	1 4	12	0 10	13	0 8	14	0 5	11	3 4	12	2 8	14	2 0
IV 1 ..	4	3 4	6	2 8	9	1 10	10	1 4	3	8 8	4	7 12	6	6 8
IV 2 ...	7	2 4	9	1 10	10	1 4	11	1 0	5	7 0	7	5 12	9	4 8
IV 3 ...	10	1 4	12	0 10	13	0 8	14	0 5	8	5 4	10	3 12	11	3 4
V 1 ...	6	2 8	8	1 12	10	1 4	11	1 0	6	6 8	9	4 8	11	3 4
V 2 ..	8	1 12	11	1 0	12	0 10	13	0 8	9	4 8	11	3 4	12	2 8
V 3 ..	...	...	...	...	...	...	...	...	12	2 8	14	2 0	14	2 0
VI 1 ...	4	3 4	4	3 4	6	2 8	7	2 4	6	6 8	8	5 4	10	3 12
VI 2 ...	7	2 4	7	2 4	9	1 10	10	4	9	4 8	11	3 4	13	2 4
VII 1 ...	6	2 8	6	2 8	8	1 12	9	1 10	4	7 12	7	5 12	10	3 12
VII 2 ...	10	1 4	10	1 4	11	1 0	12	0 10	7	5 12	9	4 8	12	2 8
VII 3 ...	13	0 8	13	0 8	14	0 5	14	0 5	9	4 8	12	2 8	14	2 0
VIII 1 ...	11	1 0	11	1 0	12	0 10	13	0 8	7	5 12	9	4 8	11	3 4
VIII 2 ..	12	0 10	13	0 8	14	0 5	14	0 5	9	4 8	11	3 4	14	2 0
VIII 3 ...	13	0 8	14	0 5	14	0 5	14	0 5	11	3 4	13	2 4	15	1 10

XI.—Classification of area and money rates according to the last settlement—*cont.*

(Part 2. Classes and sorts included under each money rate)—*cont.*

(d) *Dry lands in the rented villages and portions of villages in the Upland and Agency tracts.*

Class and sort of soil.	First group. Taram.	First group. Rate.	Second group. Taram.	Second group. Rate.	Third group. Taram.	Third group. Rate.	Fourth group. Taram.	Fourth group. Rate.
		RS. A.		RS. A.		RS. A.		RS. A.
III 1	1	4 8	3	2 12	6	1 12	7	1 10
III 2	2	3 4	5	2 4	8	1 4	8	1 4
III 3	4	2 8	6	1 12	9	1 0	9	1 0
III 4	6	1 12	8	1 4	10	0 10	10	0 10
III 5	9	1 0	10	0 10	11	0 8	12	0 5
IV 1	2	3 4	4	2 8	7	1 10	8	1 4
IV 2	3	2 12	5	2 4	8	1 4	9	1 0
IV 3	5	2 4	7	1 10	9	1 0	10	0 10
IV 4	7	1 10	8	1 4	10	0 10	11	0 8
IV 5	9	1 0	10	0 10	11	0 8	12	0 5
V 1	4	2 8	6	1 12	8	1 4	9	1 0
V 2	6	1 12	8	1 4	9	1 0	10	0 10
V 3	8	1 4	9	1 0	10	0 10	11	0 8
V 4	9	1 0	10	0 10	11	0 8	12	0 5
V 5	10	0 10	11	0 8	12	0 5	12	0 5
VI 1	2	3 4	2	3 4	4	2 8	5	2 4
VI 2	3	2 12	3	2 12	5	2 4	6	1 12
VI 3	5	2 4	5	2 4	7	1 10	8	1 4
VI 4	6	1 12	6	1 12	8	1 4	9	1 0
VI 5	8	1 4	8	1 4	9	1 0	10	0 10
VII 1	4	2 8	4	2 8	6	1 12	7	1 10
VII 2	6	1 12	6	1 12	8	1 4	9	1 0
VII 3	8	1 4	8	1 4	9	1 0	10	0 10
VII 4	9	1 0	9	1 0	10	0 10	11	0 8
VII 5	11	0 8	11	0 8	12	0 5	12	0 5
VIII 1	9	1 0	9	1 0	10	0 10	11	0 8
VIII 2	10	0 10	10	0 10	11	0 8	12	0 5
VIII 3	10	0 10	11	0 8	12	0 5	12	0 5
VIII 4	11	0 8	12	0 5	12	0 5	12	0 5
VIII 5	12	0 5	12	0 5	12	0 5	12	0 5

XI.—Classification of area and money rates according to the last settlement—*cont.*

(Part 2. Classes and sorts included under each money rate)—*cont.*

(e) *Wet lands in the rented villages and portions of villages in the Upland and Agency tracts.*

Class and sort of soil.		First class.		Second class.		Third class.	
		Taram.	Rate.	Taram.	Rate.	Taram.	Rate.
			RS. A.		RS. A.		RS. A.
III	1	3	7 0	4	6 8	6	5 4
	2	4	6 8	6	5 4	7	4 8
	3	6	5 4	7	4 8	9	3 4
	4	7	4 8	9	3 4	10	2 8
	5	9	3 4	10	2 8	12	2 0
IV	1	1	8 8	2	7 12	4	6 8
	2	2	7 12	3	7 0	6	5 4
	3	3	7 0	5	5 12	7	4 8
	4	4	6 8	7	4 8	8	3 12
	5	6	5 4	8	3 12	9	3 4
V	1	4	6 8	7	4 8	9	3 4
	2	6	5 4	8	3 12	10	2 8
	3	7	4 8	9	3 4	11	2 4
	4	9	3 4	10	2 8	12	2 0
	5	10	2 8	12	2 0	13	1 10
VI	1	4	6 8	6	5 4	8	3 12
	2	6	5 4	7	4 8	9	3 4
	3	7	4 8	9	3 4	11	2 4
	4	8	3 12	10	2 8	12	2 0
	5	9	3 4	12	2 0	13	1 10
VII	1	2	7 12	5	5 12	8	3 12
	2	3	7 0	6	5 4	9	3 4
	3	5	5 12	7	4 8	10	2 8
	4	6	5 4	9	3 4	11	2 4
	5	7	4 8	10	2 8	12	2 0
VIII	1	5	5 12	7	4 8	9	3 4
	2	6	5 4	8	3 12	10	2 8
	3	7	4 8	9	3 4	12	2 0
	4	8	3 12	10	2 8	13	1 10
	5	9	3 4	11	2 4	13	1 10

XI.—Classification of area and money rates according to the last settlement—*cont.*

(Part 2. Classes and sorts included under each money rate)—*cont.*

(f) ***Dry scale of Padugai and Lanka lands.***

I.	II.	Padugai.						Lanka.					
		Taram.	First group.		Taram.	Second group.		Taram.	First group.		Taram.	Second group.	
			RS.	A.		RS.	A.		RS.	A.		RS.	A.
I-A. ...	...	2	9	0	3	7	0	1	11	0	2	9	0
1 ...	I-A.	3	7	0	4	5	0	2	9	0	3	7	0
2 ...	1	4	5	0	5	4	0	3	7	0	4	5	0
3 ...	2	5	4	0	6	3	0	4	5	0	5	4	0
4 ...	3	6	3	0	7	2	8	5	4	0	6	3	0
5 ...	4	7	2	8	8	2	0	6	3	0	7	2	8
...	5	8	2	0	9	1	8	7	2	8	8	2	0

XII.—Rainfall.

Names of rain-gauge stations.	Average rainfall (1870–1909) in inches in												
	January.	February.	March.	April.	May.	June.	July.	August.	September.	October.	November.	December.	Whole year.
(1)	(2)	(3)	(4)	(5)	(6)	(7)	(8)	(9)	(10)	(11)	(12)	(13)	(14)
RAJAHMUNDRY TALUK.													
Rajahmundry	0·22	0·21	0·47	0·83	2·48	5·22	6·73	7·29	7·55	6·67	1·96	0·18	39·81
AMALAPURAM TALUK.													
Amalapuram	0·21	0·29	0·34	0·49	1·80	5·13	6·15	6·41	7·61	9·48	4·56	0·86	43·33
Mummidivaram *	0·08	0·67	0·76	0·86	1·17	5·68	4·22	7·90	6·51	6·86	3·69	9·93	39·33
RAZOLE TALUK.													
Kottapeta †	0·02	0·26	0·42	0·74	1·61	5·86	6·33	6·81	6·38	7·47	3·81	0·53	40·24
Razole	0·15	0·24	0·13	0·37	1·08	4·60	5·94	6·47	7·87	9·52	4·97	0·55	41·80
BHADRACHALAM TALUK.													
Bhadrachalam ‡	0·11	0·34	0·51	1·11	1·71	6·22	10·25	11·04	7·62	2·39	0·9	0·14	42·34
POLAVARAM DIVISION.													
Polavaram	0·23	0·34	0·51	1·43	2·40	5·60	8·03	7·70	7·26	5·30	2·00	0·23	41·03
CHODAVARAM DIVISION.													
Chodavaram	0·25	0·30	0·46	1·20	1·93	5·02	8·08	7·32	7·59	6·12	1·92	0·2	40·44

Yellavaram Division.													
Addatigala (Yellavaram) §	0·33	0·45	0·95	2·73	3·00	5·21	7·74	9·25	8·90	5·76	1·65	0·16	46.13
Peddapuram Taluk.													
Peddapuram	0·13	0·31	0·43	0·60	1·95	4·50	6·14	6·21	4·72	6·40	2·55	0·50	34·53
Prattipadu	0·14	0·37	0·48	1·02	2·13	4·70	6·10	5·46	7·19	6·54	1·68	0·46	36·27
Ramachandrapuram Taluk.													
Alamuru †	0·03	0·30	0·42	0·79	1·75	4·91	6·08	6·73	6·61	6·85	3·00	0·31	37·78
Ramachandrapuram	0·08	0·24	0·43	0·61	1·89	5·02	6·27	6·44	7·46	8·17	3·85	0·85	41·31
Cocanada Taluk.													
Cocanada	0·20	0·38	0·47	0·57	1·83	4·32	5·71	5·67	6·26	9·05	4·36	1·04	39·86
Coringa	0·21	0·29	0·34	0·57	1·60	4·78	5·22	5·25	6·39	11·00	5·27	0·38	41·80
Pithapuram Division.													
Pithapuram	0·18	0·22	0·30	0·66	1·74	4·00	5·27	5·59	6·29	7·09	2·33	0·59	34·26
Tuni Division.													
uui	0·23	0·35	0·44	0·81	2·14	4·22	4·98	4·98	7·79	6·64	2·14	1·01	35·68
District Average ...	0·17	0·41	1·87	6·38	0·28	6·78	4·78	6·46	7·15	2·95	7·28	0·56	39·07

* 1901—1909 † 1886—1909. —1909. § 1895—1909.

XIII.—Holdings, Cultivation and Demand in Fasli 1322 (1912-13).

Taluks.	Total holdings.						Cultivation including waste charged.				Miscellaneous revenue.	Total ryotwar demand.	Land cess.	Total demand of Land Revenue Ryotwar and Miscellaneous Cesses.
	Dry.		Wet.		Total.		Dry.		Wet.					
	Extent.	Assessment.	Extent.	Assessment.	Extent.	Assessment.	Extent.	Assessment including water-rate.	Extent.	Assessment including second crop charge.				
(1)	(2)	(3)	(4)	(5)	(6)	(7)	(8)	(9)	(10)	(11)	(12)	(13)	(14)	(15)
	ACS.	RS.	ACS.	RS.	ACS.	RS.	ACS.	RS.	ACS.	RS.	RS.	RS.	RS.	RS.
Rajahmundry Division.														
Rajahmundry	92,884	93,720	17,048	90,859	109,932	1,84,579	92,884	1,05,950	16,968	90,538	66,134	2,61,268	21,576	2,82,844
Amalapuram ...	30,390	1,15,734	32,846	2,39,549	63,236	3,55,283	30,390	1,40,985	32,846	2,91,265	2,90,059	7,19,534	59,961	7,79,495
Razole	34,727	1,26,707	22,098	1,69,671	56,825	2,96,378	34,727	1,54,461	22,098	2,08,893	3,34,060	6,94,619	55,704	7,50,323
Bhadrachalam Agency Division.														
Bhadrachalam ...	25,937	7,792	...	...	25,937	7,792	25,937	8,459	...	...	1,593	9,127	...	9,127
Nugur	8,768	3,031	...	...	8,768	3,031	8,768	3,031	...	...	1,937	4,023	...	4,023
Polavaram Agency Division.														
Polavaram	39,320	20,577	4,679	6,785	43,999	27,362	39,320	25,858	4,655	7,093	4,958	37,791	3,099	40,890
Chodavaram ...	1,010	1,200	166	657	1,176	1,857	1,010	1,249	166	693	700	2,702	317	3,019
Yellavaram	41,743	11,682	3,511	5,105	45,254	16,787	41,743	12,662	3,511	5,525	1,312	19,499	1,241	20,740

Peddapuram Division.														
Peddapuram ...	81,817	68,304	20,838	1,18,390	102,655	1,86,694	81,817	76,306	20,823	1,18,905	29,927	2,23,772	20,475	2,44,247
Ramachandrapuram.	28,390	1,08,093	47,551	4,57,879	75,941	5,65,972	28,390	1,74,358	47,546	5,17,442	4,38.338	11,24,286	83,171	12,07,457
Cocanada Division.														
Cocanada	7,085	15,056	31,908	2,59,701	38,993	2,74,757	7,085	23,018	31,908	2.88,929	1,99,924	5,10,509	39,214	5,49,723
Pithapuram	30	106	11	39	41	145	30	106	11	39	2,725	2,870	3,133	6,003
Tuni	...	...	1	4	1	4	...	...	1	4	1,363	1,367	1,512	2,879
Huzur Collections	...	...	...	...	...	...	...	...	...	...	10	10	...	10
Total ...	392,101	5,72,002	180,657	13,48,639	572,758	19,20,641	392,101	7,26,443	180,533	15,29,326	13,73,100	36,11,377	2,89,403	39,00,780

XIV.—Revenue payable by permanently settled estates in Fasli 1322 (1912–13).

Serial number.	Taluks and estates.	Peishcush.	Land cess.	Miscellaneous Revenue.	Total.
(1)	(2)	(3)	(4)	(5)	(6)
	RAJAMUNDRY DIVISION.				
	Rajamundry Taluk.	RS.	RS.	RS.	RS.
1	Bommuru	788	84	77	949
2	Buchampeta	739	152	122	1,013
3	Vundeswarapuram	630	93	50	773
4	Hukumpeta	1,297	78	116	1,491
5	Jalimudi	254	59	110	423
6	Katavaram	2,122	336	216	2,674
7	Muramanda I.A.	455	123	101	679
8	Do. I.B.	455	63	101	619
9	Vangalapudi	3,789	1,547	436	5,772
10	Muramanda II A. 2 B.	911	125	201	1,237
11	Vegayyammapeta	*	146	96	242
12	Pithapuram	†	7,089	2,872	9,961
	Total ...	11,440	9,895	4,498	25,833
	Amalapuram Taluk.				
1	Anatavaram	1,679	216	12,886	14,781
2	Bantumilli	200	78	1,541	1,819
3	Chinthanalanka and Viravallipalem.	3,534	3,359	501	7,394
4	Guttinadivi	651	520	12	1,183
5	Janupalli	218	31	1,799	2,048
6	Kesanakurru	11,333	1,800	5,548	18,681
7	Kotipallibhaga	‡	31	6	37
8	Krapa	2,362	236	3,031	5,629
9	Magam	1,732	156	8,650	10,538
10	Mukkamala	107	39	1,490	1,636
11	Nadavapalli	2,987	163	1,769	4,919
12	Pithapuram	§	1,446	31,510	32,956
13	Potukurru	908	107	4,959	5,974
14	Sirasavilli Savaram	300	69	1,396	1,765
15	Surasani yanam	529	246	533	1,308
16	Vilasa	1,440	298	10,008	11,746
	Total ...	27,980	8,795	85,639	1,22,414
	Razole Taluk.				
1	Palivela	18,592	2,784	3,793	25,169
2	Gopalpur	18,209	4,758	3,801	26,768
3	Mungondapalem	546	133	62	741
4	Pithapur	...	1,266	1,679	2,945
	Total ...	37,347	8,941	9,335	55,623

* Paid in Ramachandrapuram taluk.
† Paid in Pithapuram division.
‡ Paid in Vizagapatam.
§ Paid in Pithapuram division.

XIV.—Revenue payable by permanently settled estates in Fasli 1322 (1912-13)—*cont.*

Serial number.	Taluks and estates.	Peishcush.	Land cess.	Miscellaneous Revenue.	Total.
(1)	(2)	(3)	(4)	(5)	(6)
	POLAVARAM DIVISION.	RS.	RS.	RS.	RS.
1	Bayyanagudem	980	326	...	1,306
2	Jangamreddigudem	475	238	...	713
3	Billumilli	1,553	530	...	2,083
4	Gutala	6,721	1,157	...	7,878
5	Gangolu	1,240	924	...	2,164
6	Polavaram	6,714	1,092	...	7,806
7	Pattisam	5,211	904	...	6,115
	Total ...	22,894	5,171	...	28,065
	CHODAVARAM DIVISION.				
1	Veeravaram A or Pittapur Estate.	335	224	...	559
2	Veeravaram B or Toyyeru ...	220	265	...	485
3	Petah	546	247	...	793
4	Ravilanka	300	46	...	346
5	Dandangi	565	452	...	1,017
6	Gutala	...	56	...	56
7	Villages of the Polavaram Estate including Kondamodalu.	..	1,051	...	1,051
8	Bandapalli	42	23	...	65
9	Birampalli	42	23	..	65
10	Bodulur	60	5	...	65
11	Bolagonda	60	9	...	69
12	Chavila	50	2	...	52
13	Chidugumu	42	4	...	46
14	Choppagonda	21	4	...	25
15	Dorachintapalem	70	11	...	81
16	Geddada	21	11	...	32
17	Kundada	21	3	...	24
18	Kakur	40	3	..	43
19	Marivada	15	6	...	21
20	Maredumilli	42	2	...	44
21	Musurumilli	42	33	...	75
22	Nadunuru	42	3	...	45
23	Palam	21	20	...	41
24	Pamuleru	40	4	...	44
25	Tadepalli	63	7	...	70
26	Thammuru	35	5	...	40
27	Velagapalli	21	15	...	36
28	Vemulakonda	26	6	...	32
29	Votukuru	50	3	...	53
30	Valamuru	42	4	...	46
31	Vadapalli	15	4	...	19
32	Rampa	...	23	...	23
33	Pandirimamidi	..	7	...	7
34	Nimmalapalem	...	4	...	4
35	Angaluru	..	19	...	19
	Total ...	2,889	2,604	...	5,493

XIV.—Revenue payable by permanently settled estates in Fasli 1322 (1912-13)—*cont.*

Serial number. (1)	Taluks and estates. (2)	Peishcush. (3)	Land cess. (4)	Miscellaneous Revenue. (5)	Total. (6)
	YELLAVARAM DIVISION.	RS.	RS.	RS.	RS.
1	Anigeru Mutta	80	16	...	96
2	Dutcherti Mutta	1,200	168	...	1,368
3	Kota Mutta	210	127	...	337
4	Mohanapuram Mutta	25	22	...	47
5	Pandrapolu Mutta	70	58	...	128
6	Gurtedu Mutta	70	22	...	92
7	Nallipudi Mokhasa	350	65	...	415
	Total ...	2,005	478	...	2,483
	BHADRACHALAM DIVISION.				
	Bhadrachalam Taluk.				
1	Bhadrachalam	8,520	...	580	9,100
2	Rekapalli	4,998	...	212	5,210
	Total ...	13,518	..	792	14,310
	Nugur Taluk.				
1	Nugur	7,075	391	...	7,466
2	Albáka	1,445	80	...	1,525
3	Cherla	2,820	161	...	2,981
	Total ...	11,340	632	...	11,972
	PEDDAPURAM DIVISION.				
	Peddapuram Taluk.				
1	Dontamuru	3,267	1,465	853	5,585
2	Rayavaram	1,999	1,033	438	3,470
3	Kirlampudi Bit. No. II.	8,517	2,283	2,342	13,142
4	Jaggammapeta, A	29,051	7,323	4,778	41,152
5	Do. B	1,896	524	774	3,194
6	Do. C	2,162	586	302	3,050
7	Viravaram	26,759	6,903	3,423	37,085
8	Sirivada *	...	417	353	770
9	Kirlampudi Bit. No. I.	12,282	4,100	2,029	18,411
	Total ...	85,933	24,634	15,292	1,25,859
	Ramachandrapuram Taluk.				
1	Gudigalla Bhaga	58	98	89	245
2	Kotipalli	5,828	1,543	192	7,563
3	Kapilesvarapuram ...	8,533	1,958	921	11,412
4	Pithapuram	...	4,222	3,565	7,787
5	Parangipalli	607	244	321	1,172
6	Vegayammapeta	8,055	1,923	1,450	11,428
7	Vella	1,239	408	482	2,129
	Total ...	24,320	10,396	7,020	41,736

* This belongs to Pithapuram estate.

XIV.—Revenue payable by permanently settled estates in Fasli 1322 (1912-13)—*cont.*

Serial number. (1)	Taluks and estates. (2)	Peishcush. (3)	Land cess. (4)	Miscellaneous Revenue. (5)	Total. (6)
	COCANADA DIVISION.	RS.	RS.	RS.	RS.
	Cocanada Taluk.				
1	Injaram	2,936	989	252	4,177
2	Mallavaram	947	276	59	1,282
3	Nilapalli	480	198	12	690
4	Patavala	1,236	530	228	1,994
5	Nadavapalli	...	760	84	844
6	Pithapuram	...	17,423	19,625	37,048
7	Vegayammapeta	...	127	139	266
	Total ...	5,599	20,303	20,399	46,301
	PITHAPURAM DIVISION.				
1	Pithapuram	2,43,342	6,382	9,864	2,59,588
2	Kolanka	14,350	3,749	1,796	19,895
3	Gollaprolu	11,240	3,058	2,376	16,674
4	Uppada	666	168	149	983
5	Dharmavaram and Rachapalli ...	2,387	1,402	853	4,642
	Total ...	2,71,985	14,759	15,038	3,01,782
	TUNI DIVISION.				
1	Kotham estate	26,183	10,568	5,683	42,434
2	Pithapuram	...	3,139	3,673	6,812
	Total ...	26,183	13,707	9,356	49,246

XV.—Demand, Collection and Balance of Current

Taluks.	Demand.											
	Fasli 1313.	Fasli 1314.	Fasli 1315.	Fasli 1316.	Fasli 1317.	Fasli 1318.	Fasli 1319.	Fasli 1320.	Fasli 1321.	Fasli 1322.	Fasli 1313.	Fasli 1314.
(1)	(2)	(3)	(4)	(5)	(6)	(7)	(8)	(9)	(10)	(11)	(12)	(13)
Rajahmundry Division.												
Rajahmundry	320	269	280	298	277	305	313	321	321	310	320	269
Amalapuram	947	1,010	1,050	1,041	1,100	1 110	751	730	874	830	947	1,010
Razole	378	386	386	374	366	391	768	761	800	810	378	386
Bhadrachalam Division.												
Bhadrachalam	23	21	20	21	21	22	21	21	22	23	23	21
Nugur	...	...	...	...	...	...	16	15	15	15	...	...
Polavaram Division.												
Polavaram	64	59	61	66	69	69	72	75	75	71	64	59
Chodavaram	7	7	8	8	8	9	9	11	11	9	7	7
Yellavaram	21	18	22	21	20	21	22	3	22	23	21	18
Peddapuram Division.												
Peddapuram	389	364	404	414	401	407	414	419	407	397	389	364
Ramachandrapuram ...	1,160	1,269	1,263	1,205	1,238	1,226	1,253	263	1,301	1,249	1,160	1,269
Cocanada Division.												
Cocanada	522	584	600	574	600	607	594	591	615	597	522	584
Pithapuram	290	290	302	314	322	323	323	324	319	308	290	290
Tuni	41	41	52	59	62	63	65	65	62	52	41	41
District Total ...	4,162	4,318	4,448	4,305	4,484	4,553	4,621	4,619	4,844	4,694	4,162	4,318

Land Revenue and Cesses (in thousands of rupees).

Collected or written off.								Balance.									
Fasli 1315.	Fasli 1316.	Fasli 1317.	Fasli 1318.	Fasli 1319.	Fasli 1320.	Fasli 1321.	Fasli 1322.	Fasli 1313.	Fasli 1314.	Fasli 1315.	Fasli 1316.	Fasli 1317.	Fasli 1318.	Fasli 1319.	Fasli 1320.	Fasli 1321.	Fasli 1322.
(14)	(15)	(16)	(17)	(18)	(19)	(20)	(21)	(22)	(23)	(24)	(25)	(26)	(27)	(28)	(29)	(30)	(31)
280	298	277	305	313	321	321	310	...	...	...	...	...	...	...	...	...	...
1,044	1 041	1,100	1,169	747	730	798	823	...	...	6	..	...	1	4	...	76	7
386	374	366	391	768	761	797	810	...	...	...	...	...	...	...	...	3	...
20	21	21	22	21	21	22	23	...	...	...	...	...	...	...	...	...	...
...	...	...	...	16	15	15	15	...	...	...	...	...	...	...	...	...	...
61	66	69	69	72	75	75	71	...	...	...	...	...	...	...	...	...	...
8	8	8	9	9	11	11	9	...	...	...	...	...	...	...	...	...	...
22	21	20	21	22	23	22	23	...	...	...	...	...	...	...	...	...	...
404	414	401	407	414	419	407	397	...	...	...	...	...	...	...	...	...	...
1,263	1,205	1,238	1,226	1,253	1,250	1,301	1,242	...	...	...	...	...	...	...	13	...	7
600	574	600	607	594	591	615	597	...	...	...	..	...	..	...	...	...	...
302	314	322	323	323	324	319	308	...	...	...	...	...	...	...	...	...	...
52	59	62	63	65	65	61	52	...	...	...	...	...	...	...	...	1	...
4,442	4,395	4,484	4,552	4,617	4,606	4,764	4,680	...	...	6	...	...	1	4	13	80	14

XVI.—Remissions.

Taluks.	Waste remitted.																						Other Seasonal Remissions (excluding fixed remissions).										
	Wet.											Dry.																					
	Fasli 1313.	Fasli 1314.	Fasli 1315.	Fasli 1316.	Fasli 1317.	Fasli 1318.	Fasli 1319.	Fasli 1320.	Fasli 1321.	Fasli 1322.	Total.	Fasli 1313.	Fasli 1314.	Fasli 1315.	Fasli 1316.	Fasli 1317.	Fasli 1318.	Fasli 1319.	Fasli 1320.	Fasli 1321.	Fasli 1322.	Total.	Fasli 1313.	Fasli 1314.	Fasli 1315.	Fasli 1316.	Fasli 1317.	Fasli 1318.	Fasli 1319.	Fasli 1320.	Fasli 1321.	Fasli 1322.	Total.
(1)	(2)	(3)	(4)	(5)	(6)	(7)	(8)	(9)	(10)	(11)	(12)	(13)	(14)	(15)	(16)	(17)	(18)	(19)	(20)	(21)	(22)	(23)	(24)	(25)	(26)	(27)	(28)	(29)	(30)	(31)	(32)	(33)	(34)
Rajahmundry Division.																																	
Rajahmundry ...	...	32	2	...	...	2	1	1	2	1	41	...	...	...	...	...	...	...	...	...	...	...	1	22	22	1	31	3	3	1	3	1	88
Amalapuram ...	...	...	...	...	...	...	...	1	...	...	1	...	...	...	...	...	...	...	...	...	...	...	2	2	5	2	10	1	2	1	3	2	30
Nagaram (Razole) ...	...	...	...	...	...	...	...	...	...	...	...	...	...	...	...	...	...	...	...	...	...	...	1	...	...	1	4	1	...	1	2	3	13
Bhadrachalam Division.																																	
Bhadrachalam ...	...	...	...	...	...	...	...	...	...	...	...	...	...	...	...	...	...	...	...	...	...	...	...	...	...	...	...	...	...	...	...	...	...
Nugur ...	...	...	...	...	...	...	...	...	...	...	...	...	...	...	...	...	...	...	...	...	...	...	...	...	...	...	...	...	...	...	...	...	...
Peddapuram Division.																																	
Peddapuram ...	...	8	1	...	...	2	...	...	1	...	12	...	...	...	...	...	...	...	...	...	...	...	...	11	8	...	11	2	1	...	4	1	38
Ramachandrapuram.	...	2	...	...	...	1	...	...	...	...	3	...	...	...	...	...	...	...	...	...	...	...	...	1	7	...	4	3	2		...	4	21
Cocanada Division.																																	
Cocanada ...	...	1	...	...	...	...	...	...	...	...	1	...	...	...	...	...	...	...	...	...	...	...	1	2	6	...	2	5	...	...	...	1	17
Pithapuram ...	...	...	...	...	...	...	...	...	...	...	...	...	...	...	...	...	...	...	...	...	...	...	...	...	...	...	...	...	...	...	...	...	...

Tuni	...	...	...	...	...	...	...	...	...	...	...	...	...	...	...	...	...	...	...	...	...	...	...	...	...	...	...	...	...	...	...	...	...
POLAVARAM DIVISION.																																	
Polavaram	...	2	1	..	...	...	...	.	...	...	3	...	...	...	...	...	...	...	...	...	...	...	...	...	1	1	1	1	1	...	...	...	5
Chodavaram	...	...	...	...	...		...	...	...	...	...	...	...	...	...	...	...	...	...	...	...	...	...	...	...	...	...	...	...	...	...	...	...
Yellavaram	...	...	...	...	...	...	...	...	...	...	...	...	...	...	...	...	...	...	...	...	...	...	...	1	...	...	1	...	...	...	...	...	2
District Total ...	...	45	4	...	...	5	1	2	3	1	61	...	...	...	...	...	...	...	...	...	...	...	5	39	49	5	64	16	9	3	12	12	214

XVIII.—Prices in seers per rupee.

Fasli.	Rajahmundry Division.					Bhadrachalam Agency Division.		Polavaram Agency Division.		Peddapuram Division.					Cocanada Division.				
	Rajahmundry Taluk.	Amalapuram Taluk.		Razole Taluk.		Bhadrachalam Taluk.	Nugur Taluk	Polavaram Division.	Chodavaram Division.	Peddapuram Taluk.		Ramachandrapuram Taluk			Cocanada Taluk.		Pithapuram Division.	Tuni Division.	
	Rajahmundry.	Amalapuram.	Mummidivaram.	Kottapetta.	Sivakodu.	Bhadrachalam.	Venkatapuram.	Polavaram.	Chodavaram. (Gokavaram).	Peddapuram.	Prattipadu	Alamuru.	Ramachandrapuram.	Biccavole.	Cocanada.	Coringa.	Pithapuram.	Tuni.	District average.
(1)	(2)	(3)	(4)	(5)	(6)	(7)	(8)	(9)	(10)	(11)	(12)	(13)	(14)	(15)	(16)	(17)	(18)	(19)	(20)
									Rice (second sort).										
1313	14·8	14·4	..	13·2	13·0	12·0	...	13·5	13·4	13·2	15·3	15·1	15·0	...	12·8	15·1	14·5	16·0	14·9
1314	13·3	12·5	...	12·2	12·9	11·9	...	12·2	11·5	11·8	12·8	13·7	13·8	...	11·6	12·5	12·3	13·5	12·6
1315	11·08	10·25	...	10·07	10·01	9·75	...	10·14	9·88	9·89	11·0	11·58	11·10	...	9·92	9·34	10·08	10·43	10·30
1316	9·8	8·8	...	8·6	8·9	8·6	...	8·7	8·6	8·3	10·1	9·8	9·4	...	8·6	8·2	9·0	9·1	9·0
1317	9·0	8·3	...	7·9	8·5	8·0	...	7·6	8·3	8·1	8·6	9·2	8·8	...	7·8	7·8	8·3	8·6	8·3
1318	8·0	7·2	...	7·3	7·7	7·6	...	6·8	7·4	7·6	8·4	8·6	8·4	...	7·0	6·8	7·5	8·3	7·6
1319	9·8	9·7	...	9·1	9·4	9·1	8·2	8·3	8·7	9·9	10·7	10·4	10·7	..	10·0	9·3	9·8	9·2	9·5
1320	10·6	9·5	9·9	9·3	9·4	9·5	8·4	9·2	9·4	10·4	11·3	11·5	11·4	11·9	10·4	9·4	11·0	10·3	10·2
1321	8·6	7·8	8·7	7·5	7·9	8·7	8·6	7·8	7·9	7·8	8·5	9·8	8·7	9·2	8·3	7·8	8·4	8·4	8·3
1322	7·5	7·5	7·5	7·0	7·3	7·8	7·7	6·8	7·4	7·0	7·6	8·1	8·5	8·6	7·8	7·3	7·8	8·3	7·6

Paddy (first sort).

1313	22·8	...	...	...	...	...	...	...	...	...	24·5	22·2	21·8	...	19·5	...	22·0	25·4	22·6
1314	19·4	...	...	...	...	...	...	...	...	...	19·6	19·6	19·1	...	19·6	...	19·4	20·8	19·7
1315	16·08	...	...	...	...	...	...	...	...	...	15·62	17·23	16·70	...	15·07	...	15·64	16·22	16·08
1316	14·2	...	...	...	...	...	...	...	...	...	13·2	13·5	13·8	...	12·9	...	14·1	13·9	13·7
1317	14·1	...	...	...	...	...	...	...	...	...	12·6	12·6	13·3	...	12·2	13·1	12·9	13·1	13·0
1318	12·6	...	...	11·4	...	...	...	...	...	...	10·9	11·5	11·2	...	10·7	...	11·2	11·5	11·4
1319	16·8		...	...	...	...	...	...	...	...	14·1	13·4	15·9	...	15·0	...	15·1	14·2	14·8
1320	16·9	...	15·8	...	...	...	...	...	...	...	17·3	15·0	16·8	17·5	15·3	...	16·7	15·6	16·3
1321	14·5	...	12·6	...	...	...	13·2	14·4	...	...	12·7	12·9	13·1	12·9	12·8	...	13·0	14·0	13·3
1322	12·8		11·2	...	...	...	12·0	11·6	...	...	10·7	12·0	11·8	12·0	12·1	...	11·9	12·4	11·9

Paddy (second sort).

1313	24·8	22·8	...	20·1	21·1	...	...	24·0	...	22·4	25·3	27·7	23·7	...	22·2	25·3	23·4	26·3	23·8
1314	20·7	19·6	...	18·7	20·5	...	...	19·3	...	19·6	20·6	24·7	21·4	...	21·1	21·2	20·1	21·6	20·7
1315	17·69	16·44	...	16·09	16·13	...	...	16·62	...	16·91	17·46	20·20	18·12	...	16·24	15·86	16·51	17·16	17·03
1316	15·6	13·6	...	13·3	14·0	...	...	13·8	...	13·5	16·0	16·4	15·1	...	14·3	13·0	14·8	15·0	14·5
1317	14·9	13·5	...	11·8	13·3	...	.	12·6		12·4	13·6	14·4	14·2	...	13·1	12·4	13·7	13·9	13·4
1318	14·0	11·9	...	11·4	13·4	...		10·8	12·8	12·4	14·0	14·6	13·6	...	11·6	10·8	12·2	12·5	12·5
1319	17·4	14·7	...	14·0	16·0	...	13·8	13·1	...	15·9	18·3	16·9	17·3	...	16·2	15·0	15·7	15·5	15·7
1320	18·5	15·7	16·5	14·1	15·7	...	18·1	17·6	...	18·0	18·5	17·5	18·4	19·3	16·5	14·8	17·5	17·1	17·1
1321	15·3	13·3	15·6	11·5	13·2	...	16·4	13·3	...	12·6	14·4	17·0	15·0	14·1	13·7	13·5	13·5	14·6	14·2
1322	13·3	11·8	13·3	10·7	11·9	...	16·6	11·7	...	11·2	12·3	16·0	14·0	13·5	12·5	12·8	12·4	13·0	12·9

Horse gram.

1313	27·3	24·2	...	24·5	25·8	...	...	24·6	...	27·1	27·6	25·6	24·5	...	24·6	23·1	27·3	29·5	25·8
1314	23·6	24·9	...	22·8	25·1	...	...	24·2	...	23·2	24·3	22·9	20·6	...	21·8	20·2	22·4	24·3	23·1
1315	13·72	14·22	...	15·20	13·28	15·71	...	13·49	...	14·14	15·19	15·14	13·34	...	12·96	12·90	14·12	15·07	14·11
1316	14·8	13·8	...	14·1	12·7	...	...	11·9	...	15·0	15·2	14·4	13·5	..	14·3	12·4	14·3	15·7	14·0
1317	16·6	15·7	...	14·7	14·7	...	...	13·6		16·1	16·8	15·8	15·4	...	15·3	13·8	15·8	18·4	15·6
1318	13·5	12·5	...	13·2	12·9	...	...	12·4	14·8	12·8	13·5	14·0	12·7	...	12·7	13·8	12·7	14·1	13·2
1319	11·5	11·0	...	11·4	11·0	10·6	12·7	12·0	11·9	11·4	12·7	12·7	11·1	...	12·0	11·2	11·6	11·8	11·7
1320	14·3	14·6	13·3	14·7	13·6	9·5	...	12·7	20·4	15·5	16·3	14·3	14·3	16·3	15·0	13·1	15·5	17·9	14·8
1321	17·0	16·2	15·8	16·3	14·9	18·9	21·2	...	...	17·1	18·2	16·7	16·0	17·5	16·4	15·8	17·7	17·5	17·1
1322	14·9	15·0	15·8	15·6	14·5	...	18·7	12·7	17·0	16·1	16·1	14·8	14·7	15·7	15·7	15·9	16·5	15·2	15·6

XVIII.—Prices in seers per rupee—*cont.*

Fasli.	Rajahmundry Division.					Bhadrachalam Agency Division.		Polavaram Agency Division.		Peddapuram Division.					Cocanada Division.				
	Rajahmundry Taluk.	Amalapuram Taluk.		Razole Taluk.		Bhadrachalam Taluk.	Nugur Taluk.	Polavaram Division.	Chodavaram Division.	Peddapuram Taluk.		Ramachandrapuram Taluk.			Cocanada Taluk.		Pithapuram Division.	Tuni Division.	
	Rajahmundry.	Amalapuram.	Mummidivaram.	Kottapetta.	Sivakodu.	Bhadrachalam.	Venkatapuram.	Polavaram.	Chodavaram (Gokavaram).	Peddapuram.	Prattipadu.	Alamuru.	Ramachandrapuram.	Bicoacole.	Cocanada.	Coringa.	Pithapuram.	Tuni.	District Average.
(1)	(2)	(3)	(4)	(5)	(6)	(7)	(8)	(9)	(10)	(11)	(12)	(13)	(14)	(15)	(16)	(17)	(18)	(19)	(20)
									Cholam.										
1313	31·8	26·7	...	24·4	28·6	39·0	...	34·3	32·0	29·8	32·0	28·0	27·6	...	27·3	...	29·0	34·0	30·3
1314	23·0	22·8	...	19·6	27·2	27·1	...	25·4	27·5	21·6	22·7	28·5	18·4	...	21·9	...	19·8	24·2	23·1
1315	17·70	16·36	...	18·28	18·12	16·74	...	18·33	19·38	16·89	17·00	...	15·12	...	16·19	...	16·01	16·18	17·07
1316	17·1	15·6	...	15·9	13·7	18·3	...	15·6	13·2	15·6	15·7	...	12·8	...	14·7	...	14·3	15·7	15·4
1317	14·8	14·0	...	14·0	13·9	13·0	...	12·9	15·8	13·6	14·1	...	13·1	...	12·7	14·0	13·5	14·0	13·7
1318	18·7	12·9	...	12·5	11·9	10·2	...	11·3	12·6	11·5	12·1	...	11·6	...	11·4	...	11·3	12·2	11·9
1319	16·2	15·7	...	16·2	16·5	13·7	12·1	12·6	15·0	15·4	16·8	...	...	...	14·6	...	15·3	16·6	15·2
1320	17·8	16·2	16·1	16·5	17·3	15·2	14·6	15·4	18·2	17·0	17·9	18·0	16·3	16·3	14·4	...	15·4	18·8	16·5
1321	15·7	13·9	14·9	13·6	14·8	17·7	17·5	11·9	15·3	13·3	14·6	15·0	15·5	12·5	13·1	...	13·5	10·4	14·3
1322	13·0	12·7	13·9	12·6	13·1	13·7	15·7	12·3	11·4	12·5	13·0	15·2	13·8	10·9	12·0	...	12·0	13·7	13·0

Cumbu.

1313	...	...	...	...	...	...	...	...	...	35·5	35·0	...	...	...	...	...	...	33·4	34·6
1314	...	...	...	...	...	...	...	...	...	22·7	26·1	...	...	...	...	...	20·7	24·0	24·2
1315	17·80	...	...	...	...	...	...	...	...	18·52	19·32	...	...	...	...	...	...	17·39	18·39
1316	...	...	...	...	...	...	...	...	...	17·7	18·9	...	...	...	...	...	...	18·0	18·2
1317	...	...	...	...	...	...	...	...	17·8	14·5	15·8	...	12·9	...	...	...	...	14·0	14·7
1318	...	...	...	...	...	...	...	...	...	14·4	15·4	...	...	...	...	...	...	14·1	14·6
1319	21·4	...	...	...	...	...	...	...	...	19·0	21·4	...	...	...	17·0	...	18·6	17·9	19·2
1320	19·5	...	...	...	...	...	...	12·0	...	21·8	24·5	...	...	24·9	18·6	...	21·0	18·8	20·2
1321	15·6	...	...	...		...	...	10·7	21·1	14·8	14·9	...	...	17·3	14·1	...	14·1	15·3	14·8
1322	14·7	...	...	...	9·8	...	...	11·0	16·2	15·8	17·0	...	...	16·0	13·1	...	15·3	17·4	14·4

Ragi.

1313	31·0	27·1	...	23·0	23·6	...	...	26·1	31·0	35·4	33·5	26·4	28·2	...	28·6	28·5	31·9	35·7	29·3
1314	22·8	20·6	...	20·7	23·1	...	...	23·3	21·3	24·2	22·4	22·2	19·6	...	20·9	21·4	23·6	24·7	22·2
1315	18·52	16·12	...	17·55	16·14	...	...	19·08	16·87	17·88	17·32	18·67	13·50	...	16·03	14·40	17·22	17·44	16·86
1316	18·0	15·2	...	15·1	13·5	...	...	...	15·6	17·1	16·2	13·9	13·5	...	14·4	14·7	16·5	16·5	15·4
1317	14·6	12·7	...	12·3	13·2	...	...	...	13·9	14·0	13·2	13·6	12·4	...	12·8	13·3	13·6	13·7	13·3
1318	13·9	11·9	...	11·2	11·3	...	...	...	14·4	13·7	13·2	12·7	12·1	...	12·1	10·8	13·4	13·8	12·6
1319	18·1	15·5	...	12·6	16·0	.	...	...	15·2	17·8	17·8	13·8	15·4	...	16·7	13·2	18·5	17·2	16·0
1320	22·2	17·1	15·2	14·5	17·3	...	10·7	13·1	20·4	21·3	19·1	14·6	21·7	23·3	19·0	14·5	20·0	18·5	17·8
1321	14·2	13·2	13·7	12·2	12·8	...	14·6	13·4	14·9	15·0	13·8	14·1	15·6	15·9	12·5	11·5	15·2	15·0	14·0
1322	12·7	12·3	12·1	11·9	12·2	...	...	13·2	10·2	14·3	12·7	13·6	13·1	13·0	12·1	12·0	13·8	15·9	12·8

Salt.

1313	14·6	14·8	...	13·9	14·0	14·4	...	14·9	12·6	15·0	14·2	13·9	13·3	...	14·7	13·7	14·8	14·8	14·2
1314	15·1	16·0	...	17·1	16·5	14·5	...	17·4	13·0	17·3	16·1	16·3	16·7	...	16·8	15·3	16·7	17·1	16·2
1315	17·97	17·27	...	19·27	17·60	15·49	..	16·26	17·11	19·93	16·93	15·93	16·37	...	19·93	19·10	19·20	19·89	18·15
1316	19·4	20·0	...	20·4	20·4	18·1	...	16·8	15·9	20·4	18·0	20·2	17·9	...	20·5	20·4	20·4	21·2	19·3
1317	21·9	24·0	...	24·0	23·6	19·7	...	19·2	18·9	22·2	19·4	24·3	18·6	...	24·0	24·0	24·0	23·8	22·2
1318	22·7	24·0	...	24·0	20·3	22·1	...	19·2	18·8	24·0	20·7	24·6	19·0	...	24·0	23·8	24·0	25·6	22·5
1319	23·0	24·0	...	24·0	21·0	20·9	16·4	19·2	17·9	24·0	21·5	25·0	22·0	...	24·0	24·0	24·0	24·6	22·2
1320	23·1	24·0	24·0	24·1	21·6	18·4	12·9	19·2	15·9	24·0	21·5	25·0	22·0	22·0	24·0	24·0	24·0	24·0	21·8
1321	24·0	23·8	23·8	24·0	21·0	19·8	16·9	18·9	16·5	24·0	22·2	24·9	22·3	21·7	24·0	23·8	23·8	24·0	22·2
1322	24·0	24·0	24·0	24·0	21·0	19·0	15·9	19·2	15·8	24·0	22·0	25·0	21·9	22·0	24·0	24·0	24·0	24·0	22·1

XIX.—Income-tax.

(Part IV.—Other sources only.)

Taluks.	Rs. 1,000 to 1,500.		Rs. 1,500 to 2,000.		Above Rs. 2,000.		Total.		Incidence of taxation.		Objection petitions.	
	Number of assessees.	Amount of tax.	Number of assessees.	Amount of tax.	Number of assessees.	Amount of tax.	Number of assessees.	Amount of tax.	Per head of assessees.	Per head of population.	Number.	Percentage of these wholly or partially successful.
(1)	(2)	(3)	(4)	(5)	(6)	(7)	(8)	(9)	(10)	(11)	(12)	(13)
RAJAHMUNDRY DIVISION.		RS.		RS.		RS.		RS.	RS. A. P.	RS. A. P.		
Rajahmundry ... 1908–09	69	1,644	57	2,055	100	15,819	226	19,518	86 5 10	0 2 0	98	11·0
1909–10	72	1,688	64	2,506	98	15,295	234	19,469	83 4 7	0 1 11	98	19·4
1910–11	80	1,864	71	2,828	102	16,922	253	21,614	85 6 10	0 2 2	91	4·3
1911–12	91	1,108	69	3,723	99	16,882	259	21,713	83 13 4	0 1 10	76	23·7
1912–13	109	2,524	68	2,660	105	19,248	282	24,432	86 10 3	0 2 1	101	21·0
Amalapuram ... 1908–09	86	1,976	60	2,317	54	7,131	200	11,424	57 1 9	0 1 0	87	13·8
1909–10	97	2,220	58	2,233	52	6,460	207	10,913	52 11 6	0 0 11	104	15·4
1910–11	72	1,587	31	1,222	49	5,392	152	8,201	53 15 2	0 0 8	79	21·5
1911–12	67	1,468	34	1,302	53	6,111	154	8,881	57 10 8	0 0 8	76	13·2
1912–13	67	1,445	38	1,456	54	6,668	159	9,569	60 2 11	0 0 9	67	4·5
Razole 1908–09	48	1,138	18	686	27	3,417	93	5,241	56 5 8	0 0 5	54	22·2
1909–10	51	1,148	22	833	29	3,596	102	5,577	54 10 9	0 0 6	47	6·4
1910–11	91	2,068	37	1,407	43	5,510	171	8,985	52 8 8	0 0 9	72	18·0
1911–12	85	1,956	39	1,477	42	5,485	166	8,918	56 11 6	0 0 7	70	18·6
1912–13	87	1,980	43	1,638	49	6,307	179	9,925	55 7 2	0 0 9	85	17·7

Peddapuram Division.													
Peddapuram ...	1908–09	50	1,184	20	798	28	3,490	98	5,472	55 13 5	0 0 6	65	33·8
	1909–10	56	1,296	22	882	25	3,200	103	5,378	52 3 5	0 0 6	48	4·2
	1910–11	52	1,200	24	931	28	3,757	104	5,888	56 9 10	0 0 7	48	6·25
	1911–12	56	1,280	23	889	31	3,994	110	6,163	56 0 5	0 0 6	56	16·0
	1912–13	47	1,100	30	1,148	31	4,029	108	6,277	58 1 11	0 0 6	59	25·4
Ramachen-drapuram.	1908–09	69	1,604	51	1,988	34	3,479	154	7,071	45 14 8	0 0 6	49	20·4
	1909–10	78	1,864	50	1,932	36	4,224	164	8,020	48 14 5	0 0 7	53	4·0
	1910–11	88	2,080	59	2,303	36	4,696	183	9,079	49 9 9	0 0 8	90	12·2
	1911–12	85	2,020	67	2,590	35	5,779	187	10,389	55 8 10	0 0 8	65	7·7
	1912–13	76	1,784	73	2,828	35	6,055	184	10,667	57 15 7	0 0 9	61	21·3
Cocanada Division.													
Cocanada ...	1908–09	101	2,292	84	3,311	98	20,592	283	26.195	92 9 0	0 2 0	98	23·5
	1909–10	92	2,088	88	3,444	98	18,769	278	24,301	87 6 7	0 1 10	100	31·0
	1910–11	97	2,212	84	3,304	106	19,487	287	25,003	87 2 0	0 1 10	115	23·5
	1911–12	88	2,000	95	3,745	111	20,426	294	26,171	89 0 3	0 1 10	139	29·5
	1912–13	80	1,936	93	3,661	115	16,492	288	22,089	76 11 2	0 1 7	155	34·8
Dy. Tahsildars' Divisions.													
Pittapuram ...	1908–09	44	1,000	6	224	17	3,525	67	4,749	70 14 1	0 0 11	43	35·0
	1909–10	39	900	4	154	12	2,436	55	3,499	63 7 3	0 0 8	27	22·2
	1910–11	44	1,016	10	364	12	2,672	66	4,052	61 6 3	0 0 9	40	27·5
	1911–12	45	1,004	18	658	12	1,983	75	3,645	48 9 7	0 0 7	48	31·25
	1912–13	35	804	19	700	14	3,582	68	5,086	74 12 8	0 0 10	32	28·0
Tuni	1908–09	56	1,232	17	672	26	14,517	99	16,421	165 13 10	0 4 6	37	13·5
	1909–10	46	1,008	16	623	28	3,681	90	5,312	59 0 0	0 1 5	28	14·3
	1910–11	50	1,110	12	463	31	3,336	93	4,909	52 12 7	0 1 4	26	23·0
	1911–12	55	1,204	12	476	33	3,586	100	5,266	52 10 6	0 1 2	35	23·0
	1912–13	53	1,140	13	511	32	3,457	98	5,108	52 2 0	0 1 2	25	12·0
District total ...	1908–09	523	12,070	313	12,051	384	71,970	1,220	96,091	78 12 3	0 0 1	531	20·7
	1909–10	531	12,212	324	12,607	378	57,561	1,233	82,480	78 14 4	0 0 1	505	16·4
	1910–11	574	13,137	328	12,822	407	61,772	1,309	87,731	67 0 4	0 0 1	561	16·4
	1911–12	572	12,040	357	14,866	416	64,246	1,345	91,146	67 12 3	0 0 1	565	21·1
	1912–13	554	12,713	377	14,602	435	65,838	1,366	93,153	68 3 1	0 0 1	585	22·7

XX.—Abkāri and Opium.

— (1)	1903-04. (2)	1904-05. (3)	1905-06. (4)	1906-07. (5)	1907-08. (6)	1908-09. (7)	1909-10. (8)	1910-11. (9)	1911-12. (10)	1912-13. (11)
Country Spirits.										
Number of retail shops licensed	862	409	429	599	603	602	568	553	540	516
Issues in imperial proof gallons	56,614	32,940	37,138	32,671	60,555	61,169	51,972	53,831	54,745	54,612
Number of persons per retail shop	2,485	3,145	2,998	2,414	2,398	2,402	2,581	2,986	3,061	3,203
Gross receipts from duty ... . Rs.	2,55,109	1,52,533	1,65,422	2,36,204	3,09,710	3,07,605	2,98,856	3,10,375	2,97,275	3,22,661
Do. do. rentals ... . ,,	1,15,314	89,192	89,896	94,616	1,07,348	1,65,185	1,74,459	1,71,918	1,75,344	1,76,191
Toddy.										
Number of retail shops licensed	1,341	775	780	775	776	729	762	685	669	629
Number of persons per shop	1,597	1,660	1,649	1,660	1,657	1,802	1,751	2,157	2,244	2,387
Gross receipts from tree-tax ... ... Rs.	4,86,968	2,42,551	2,69,987	2,65,270	2,89,382	3,53,160	3,73,305	3,57,377	3,68,444	3,58,794
Do. do. rentals ... ... ,,	2,90,300	1,23,613	1,23,630	1,21,398	1,49,381	1,76,769	1,91,691	2,14,851	2,13,951	2,03,215
Ganja, Bhang.										
Number of retail shops licensed	39	29	30	30	30	30	30	32	30	24
Quantity sold in seers	1,668	1,251	1,284	1,225	1,394	1,197	1,106	1,166	1,228	1,473
Number of persons per shop	54,921	44,349	42,871	42,871	42,871	43,798	43,798	51,609	55,095	68,869
Gross receipts from duty ... ... Rs.	7,227	6,832	6,450	8,409	8,571	8,244	6,750	7,297	11,730	12,090
Do. do. rentals ... ... ,,	8,340	5,247	6,257	5,887	5,801	7,836	9,336	11,961	7,627	8,347
Opium.										
Number of retail shops licensed	467	344	346	345	344	344	319	302	289	228
Quantity sold in seers	17,823	11,718	11,847	11,741	12,228	14,903	14,107	12,598	12,036	12,064
Number of persons per shop	4,929	4,203	4,179	4,191	4,203	4,203	4,596	5,469	5,739	7,249
Gross receipts from duty ... ... Rs.	3,25,472	3,05,778	3,13,562	3,17,571	3,26,441	4,16,503	2,85,042	2,46,707	2,60,942	3,00,180
Do. do. rentals ... ... ,,	86,652	56,515	59,987	55,721	56,027	72,963	74,945	79,890	80,673	96,408

XXI.—Revenue Receipts.

— (1)	1904–05. (2)	1905–06. (3)	1906–07. (4)	1907–08. (5)	1908–09. (6)
	RS.	RS.	RS.	RS.	RS.
Land Revenue and rates (a).	44,67,088	41,09,448	41,05,320	42,88,095	38,97,055
Stamps	5,18,448	4,29,462	4,32,916	4,27,739	4,40,828
Excise	6,45,254	6,78,067	7,46,636	8,93,260	10,41,357
Income-tax including penalties.	94,727	94,338	94,531	1,00,983	1,07,921
Forests (b) ...	1,92,302	1,71,540	1,69,629	2,22,725	2,05,659
Registration (c) ...	55,071	52,601	57,699	64,567	67,371
Opium	3,62,563	3,73,759	3,73,502	3,82,678	4,89,661
Salt (d)	11,36,389	13,17,041	12,13,830	7,39,548	5,83,426
Customs	1,82,670	1,75,060	5,43,410	7,41,018	4,88,204

—	1909–10. (7)	1910–11. (8)	1911–12. (9)	1912–13. (10)
	RS.	RS.	RS.	RS.
Land revenue and rates (a).	40,34,011	40,15,628	39,70,198	43,06,604
Stamps	4,95,101	4,95,343	5,20,606	5,67,485
Excise	10,87,588	10,85,308	10,90,389	10,97,880
Income-tax including penalties.	1,08,385	94,136	1,08,459	1,14,832
Forests (b) ...	2,60,605	1,95,448	2,29,247	2,44,487
Registration (c) ...	72,958	68,465	71,040	77,854
Opium	3,59,987	3,26,597	3,41,615	3,96,588
Salt (d)	6,42,325	6,42,323	6,53,440	7,35,321
Customs	3,61,537	3,33,250	3,50,769	3,69,813

(a) The figures for the years 1908–09 onwards do not include rates.
(b) Figures under Forests are for the fasli years.
(c) Figures under Registration are for the calendar years only.
(d) The figures are for Cocanada Sub-division.

NOTE.—The Guntúr district was formed in October 1904 out of Gódávari, Kistná and Nellore districts. Figures for the revised Gódávari district are not available for 1903–04.

XXII.—Sea-borne trade.

(Total trade in each port.)

Name of port.	Imports.				
	1908-09.	1909-10.	1910-11.	1911-12.	1912-13.
(1)	(2)	(3)	(4)	(5)	(6)
COCANADA.	RS.	RS.	RS.	RS	RS.
Merchandise.	53,90,143	54,27,804	59,50,748	46,35,681	48,42,671
Treasure ...	...	...	...	...	...
Total ...	53,90,143	54,27,804	59,50,748	46,35,681	48,42,671

Name of port.	Exports.				
	1908-09.	1909-10.	1910-11.	1911-12.	1912-13.
	(7)	(8)	(9)	(10)	(11)
COCANADA.	RS.	RS.	RS.	RS.	RS.
Merchandise.	2,69,68,369	1,99,78,759	1,95,15,870	2,49,50,371	2,73,74,286
Treasure ...	...	19,94,000	...	...	...
Total ...	2,69,68,369	2,19,72,759	1,95,15,870	2,49,50,371	2,73,74,286

XXII-A.—Sea-borne Trade : Chief Imports and Exports in selected ports.

(Average of five years ending 1912–13.)

Imports.

Name of port. (1)	Articles. (2)		Quantity. (3)	Value. (4)
				RS.
Cocanada *cum* Coringa.	Carriages and carts including cycles and motor cars and cycles	val.	...	69,891
	Grain and Pulse—			
	Pulse	cwt.	8,894	53,043
	Rice in the husk	„	47,217	1,88,786
	Rice not in the husk	„	54,941	3,26,838
	Other sorts	„	7,492	48,129
	Machinery and Millwork ...	val.	...	40,189
	Metals—			
	Copper	cwt.	956	47,451
	Iron and steel	tone.	1,072	1,72,610
	Other metals (mainly Aluminium)	„	498	1,89,835
	Oils—			
	Mineral, Kerosene ...	gall.	4,309,149	15,71,821
	„ Other sorts	„	83,203	73,863
	Vegetable not essential—			
	Coconut	„	52,032	81,423
	Groundnut	„	254,661	3,78,485
	Other sorts	„	78	169

Exports.

Name of port. (1)	Articles. (2)		Quantity. (3)	Value. (4)
	Coir—			RS.
Cocanada *cum* Coringa.	Manufactures	cwt.	14,510	63,137
	Drugs and medicines (mainly nux-vomica)	val.	...	63,840
	Dyeing and Tanning substances—			
	Myrabolams	cwt.	26,065	76,089
	Other sorts	„	2,203	20,996
	Fibre for brushes and brooms (palmyra fibre)	„	25,840	3,73,651
	Grain and Pulse—			
	Pulse	cwt.	77,741	3,87,001
	Rice in the husk	„	98,020	3,18,375
	Rice not in the husk	„	1,060,160	64,36,375
	Other sorts	„	36,291	1,34,103
	Horns and hornmeal	„	2,588	71,880
	Manures—			
	Bones	tons.	996	44,638
	Other kinds	„	311	28,053
	Oils—			
	Castor	gall.	575,721	6,94,461
	Groundnut	„	61,703	94,441
	Other sorts	„	29,329	45,402

XXII-A.—Sea-borne Trade : Chief Imports and Exports in selected ports—*cont.*

(Average of five years ending 1912–13.)

Imports.

Name of port. (1)	Articles. (2)		Quantity. (3)	Value. (4)
Cocanada *cum* Coringa.	Spices—			Rs.
	Betelnuts	lb.	718,671	69,692
	Sugar—			
	16 Dutch standard and above.	cwt.	9,192	93,113
	Other sorts of sugar	,,	38,344	1,00,466
	Textiles—			
	Cotton—			
	Twist and yarn	lb.	486,039	2,36,078
	Piece-goods	yds.	680,794	1,27,134
	Jute, gunny bags	No.	1,929,517	4,92,497
	,, Other kinds	val.	...	29,813
	Wood and Timber—			
	Teakwood	cub. tons	2,989	2,61,227
	Other kinds	val.	...	42,917
	All other articles	,,	...	5,65,752
	Total ...		...	52,61,222

Exports.

Name of port. (1)	Articles. (2)		Quantity. (3)	Value. (4)
Cocanada *cum* Coringa.				Rs.
	Oil cakes	cwt.	121,240	3,86,328
	Provisions and oilman's stores—			
	Ghee	lb.	557,455	2,71,522
	Other sorts	val.	...	2,36,131
	Seeds—			
	Coriander	cwt.	9,925	76,571
	Castor	,,	253,093	18,09,943
	Cotton	,,	165,954	5,62,258
	Sesamum (Til or gingelly) ...	,,	122,016	11,22,566
	Sugar—			
	Sugar 15 Dutch standard and below	cwt.	19,540	1,20,359
	Textiles—			
	Cotton, raw	,,	258,020	76,74,415
	Hemp, raw	,,	25,545	3,43,669
	Jute, raw	tons.	281	52,854
	Tobacco—			
	Unmanufactured	lb.	5,756,769	14,25,818
	Manufactured	,,	34,075	27,273
	All other articles	val.	...	11,94,182
	Total ...		...	2,41,56,331

XXIII.—Income and Expenditure of Local Boards in 1912-13.

—	District Board.	Taluk Boards including Unions in them.				Total.
		Rajahmundry.	Polavaram.	Peddapuram.	Cocanada.	
(1)	(2)	(3)	(4)	(5)	(6)	(7)
REVENUE AND RECEIPTS.	RS.	RS.	RS.	RS.	RS.	RS.
Land Revenue—						
House-tax	..	6,827	...	15,037	10,795	32,659
Rents, etc., of fisheries	...	97	...	175	383	655
Miscellaneous ...	15	805	38	857	764	2,479
Local rates—						
Cess on land ...	1,46,822	67,376	12,630	34,572	44,874	3,06,274
Railway cess ...	...	...	...	...	...	...
Interest—On Government Securities, etc.	73	101	...	1,219	35	1,428
Law and Justice—Courts of Law—						
Fines under Police and other Acts.	...	553	...	564	403	1,520
Education—						
School fees	..	29,024	1,604	3,492	1,773	35,893
Contributions ...	9,400	30,028	4,979	16 263	12,274	72,944
Other receipts ...	...	21	10	...	...	31
Medical—						
Hospital receipts—						
Contributions ...	6,344	1,393	210	648	210	8,805
Other receipts ...	14	485	11	1,029	959	2,498
Minor Departments—						
Veterinary, etc., receipts.	842	...	...	...	...	842
Miscellaneous—						
Choultry receipts ..	...	8,772	..	18,776	235	27,783
Market and slaughter house receipts.	...	11,595	203	7,809	10,511	30,118
Contributions ...	...	...	...	...	...	...
Other receipts ...	658	828	42	793	2,501	4,822
Railways—Net receipts.	...	...	...	...	...	...
Civil Works—						
Ferry receipts ...	20,765	...	...	...	...	20,765
Tolls	12,579	...	...	...	..	12,579
Contributions—						
Contribution from Government.	2,60,738	15,962	9,215	20,917	20,966	3,27,793
Other contributions...	6,064	3,635	176	2,708	706	13,289
Debt, deposit and advances.	94,891	522	20	369	2,516	98,318
Total Receipts ...	5,58,700	1,78,024	29,138	1,25,228	1,09,905	10,00,995
EXPENDITURE.						
Refunds—Land revenue and local rates.	20	12	...	15	15	62
Interest on loans, etc.	...	...	...	...	...	...
General administration—						
General establishment of Local Funds.	3,017	4,484	976	4,451	3,906	16,834
Other expenditure ...	7,104	3,396	1,710	2,449	2,579	17,238

XXIII.—Income and Expenditure of Local Boards in 1912-13—*cont.*

—	District Board.	Taluk Boards including Unions in them.				Total.
		Rajahmundry.	Polavaram.	Peddapurum.	Cocanada.	
(1)	(2)	(3)	(4)	(5)	(6)	(7)
EXPENDITURE—*cont.*	RS.	RS.	RS.	RS.	RS.	RS.
Education—						
Secondary schools ...	...	19,613	1,871	...	...	21,484
Elementary schools .		50,122	11,304	28,825	27,202	1,17,453
Other schools	3,178	46	..	85	99	3,408
Other expenditure ..	119	...	10	287	256	672
Medical—						
Hospitals and Dispensaries.	9,574	14,871	4,876	14,482	6,378	50,181
Vaccination	— 7	2,137	1,660	2,140	1,579	7,509
Sanitation	3,616	5,127	454	11,610	7,084	27,891
Plague	463	...	...	...	...	463
Other epidemics ...	393	261	105	182	326	1,267
Other expenditure ...	4,047	...	...	...	...	4,047
Minor Departments—						
Public exhibition and Fairs.	1,598	...	...	...	...	1,598
Veterinary and other charges.	...	...	...	...	...	...
Superannuation, etc.—						
Pensions,gratuities, etc.	7,044	761	89	553	278	8,725
Stationery and Printing—						
Stationery supplied from Central stores	...	...	...	...	...	...
Printing work at Government and private presses.	573	334	85	435	345	1,772
Miscellaneous—						
Markets and slaughter-houses.	...	14	108	363	359	844
Choultries	...	5,772	...	15,488	419	21,679
Lighting	..	1,044	...	1,409	1,206	3,659
Other expenditure ...	...	256	54	617	349	1,276
Railways—						
Construction of railways.	...	...	...	...	...	...
Other expenditure ...	...	...	...	...	...	...
Civil Works—						
Civil buildings ...	14,920	12,805	2,081	13,573	4,971	48,350
Communications ...	2,98,885	36,209	3,436	62,379	31,965	4,32,874
Sanitary works and other works of public improvements.	47,086	16,589	3,722	22,933	19,190	1,09,520
Establishment, tools and plant.	52,124	8,248	763	13,318	4,877	79,330
Contributions ...	603	...	...	...	...	603
Other expenditure ...	5,024	762	472	126	116	6,500
Debt, deposit and advances.	39,660	15,509	15	6,748	1,644	63,576
Total Expenditure	4,99,041	1,98,372	33,791	2,02,468	1,15,143	10,48,815

XXIV.—Income and Expenditure of Municipalities in 1912–13.

— (1)	Rajahmundry. (2)	Cocanada. (3)
	RS.	RS.
Opening balance ...	36,454	37,164
RECEIPTS.		
Tax on buildings and lands	28,011	30,491
Water and drainage tax on buildings and lands ...		24,124
Tax on vehicles with springs, animals and carts ...	5,708	7,289
Tax on arts	5,652	7,251
Tolls	14,999	15,946
Tax on private, menial and domestic servants	...	...
Realization under special Acts	132	513
Rent of lands, buildings, etc., and sale-proceeds of lands, etc.	5,330	3,641
Conservancy receipts	407	146
Fees and revenue from—		
Educational Institutions	3,358	548
Medical do.	367	492
Markets and slaughter-houses	7,680	12,279
License fees	1,093	3,777
Other fees	640	1,461
Fines under Municipal and other Acts	658	1,644
Interest on investments and premium on loans ...	206	400
Grants and contributions from—		
Government	32,745	75,524
Local Boards	3,166	4,000
Other sources	..	1,004
Recoveries for services rendered to private individuals.	4,403	10,667
Miscellaneous	517	6,722
Sale-proceeds of Government securities and realizations of sinking fund.	...	...
Loans	...	2,860
Advances recovered	470	*Nil.*
Total Receipts ...	1,16,442	2,10,779
Total including balance ...	1,52,896	2,47,943
EXPENDITURE.		
Grant 1—		
Communications	11,421	16,894
Buildings	3,631	24,062
Miscellaneous public improvements	2,319	592

XXIV.—Income and Expenditure of Municipalities in 1912-13—*cont.*

(1)	Rajahmundry. (2)	Cocanada. (3)
EXPENDITURE—*cont.*	RS.	RS.
Grant 1—*cont.*		
Drainage		1,437
Water-supply	621	20,287
Establishment	1,446	1,641
Tools and plant and other stores	13	77
Contributions for public works	...	6,043
Grant 2—Education	9,065	9,057
Grant 3—		
Hospitals and dispensaries	8,127	12,396
Vaccination	412	678
Registration of Births and Deaths	392	378
Conservancy, road-cleaning and road-watering ...	24,356	26,802
Contributions	437	145
Plague charges	2,106	795
Veterinary charges	...	100
Grant 4—		
Lighting	4,391	7,830
Markets and slaughter-houses	961	1,432
Choultries and travellers' bungalows	1,220	144
Avenues	8	137
Public garden, survey of land, fire, pounds and other charges.	4,161	11,703
Grant 5—		
Supervision and management	4,382	9,430
Repayment of debt	5,994	7,316
Interest on debt	4,120	5,678
Discount on investment	...	...
Advances	1,243	88
Refunds	73	164
Investments	..	...
Total Expenditure ..	90,899	1,65,315
Closing balance ...	61,997	82,628
Total including balance ...	1,52,896	2,47,943

XXV.—Education in 1911

Taluks.	Number of literates.		Literates per thousand of population.		Literates in English.	
	Males.	Females.	Males.	Females.	Males.	Females.
(1)	(2)	(3)	(4)	(5)	(6)	(7)
Rajahmundry Division.						
Rajahmundry	11,962	2,467	127	26	2,725	193
Amalapuram	10,516	871	101	8	938	15
Razole	10,463	1,586	100	14	580	44
Bhadrachalam Agency Division.						
Bhadrachalam ...	1,126	218	40	8	163	11
Nugur	331	22	33	2	30	1
Polavaram Agency Division.						
Polavaram	1,748	196	53	6	206	1
Chodavaram	354	41	25	3	46	2
Yellavaram	405	40	22	2	19	1
Peddapuram Division.						
Peddapuram	7,078	924	76	10	671	15
Ramachandrapuram ...	11,579	1,472	99	12	760	8
Cocanada Division.						
Cocanada	15,356	2,947	137	25	3,006	337
Pithapuram	4,739	761	99	16	765	39
Tuni	2,560	248	74	7	269	2
District Total ...	78,217	11,793	96	14	10,178	669
Hindus	73,456	10,052	94	12	8,894	190
Mussalmans	2,971	398	222	29	450	4
Christians	1,721	1,331	347	272	817	473
Others	69	12	7	1	17	2

XXVI.—Schools and Scholars on the 31st March 1913.

Class of institutions.	Number of institutions.							Number of scholars.		
	Government.	Municipal.	Local Fund.	Native States.	Aided.	Unaided.	Total.	Males.	Females.	Total.
(1)	(2)	(3)	(4)	(5)	(6)	(7)	(8)	(9)	(10)	(11)
PUBLIC.										
Arts Colleges	1	...	...	...	...	1	2	345	...	345
Professional Colleges ...	...	...	...	...	...	...	...	...	...	...
a Secondary schools for boys	2	1	5	...	7	3	18	5,586	33	5,619
a Secondary schools for girls	...	...	...	...	2	...	2	40	85	125
b Higher Elementary schools for boys ...	...	...	1	..	1	1	3	214	46	260
b Higher Elementary schools for girls ...	8	...	..	...	1	1	10	6	1,744	1,750
c Lower Elementary schools for boys ...	29	25	395	...	429	169	1,047	37,597	10,109	47,706
c Lower Elementary schools for girls ...	20	...	4	..	33	10	67	132	3,456	3,588
Training schools for masters	1	...	1	...	1	1	4	337	3	340
Training schools for mistresses	1	...	...	...	1	...	2	...	41	41
Other special schools	...	...	...	...	...	...	...	...	...	...
Total ...	62	26	406	...	475	186	1,155	44,257	15,517	59,774
PRIVATE.										
Advanced	...	...	...	...	...	...	4	261	36	297
Elementary	...	...	...	...	...	...	110	1,706	270	1,976
Total ...	...	...	...	...	...	...	114	1,967	306	2,273
Grand Total ..	62	26	406	...	475	186	1,269	46,224	15,823	62,047

(*a*) Includes European High and Middle schools.
(*b*) Relates to Elementary schools with standards above the fourth.
(*c*) Relates to Elementary schools with standards up to and including the fourth Elementary schools with standards below the fourth and European Primary schools.

XXVII.—Expenditure on Schools in 1912–13.

Nature of schools.	Expenditure on all classes of schools.		Colleges.		Secondary schools.		Higher Elementary schools.		Lower Elementary schools.		Training schools.		Technical and Industrial schools.	
	Total.	Net.	Total expenditure.	Net expenditure.	Total expenditure.	Net expenditure.	Total expenditure.	Net expenditure.	Total expenditure.	Net expenditure.	Total expenditure.	Net expenditure.	Total expenditure.	Net expenditure.
(1)	(2)	(3)	(4)	(5)	(6)	(7)	(8)	(9)	(10)	(11)	(12)	(13)	(14)	(15)
	RS.	RS.	RS.	RS.	RS.	RS.	RS.	RS.	RS.	RS.	RS.	RS.	RS.	RS.
Government ...	1,34,645	98,636	53,203	33,582	16,457	2,229	12,264	12,127	20,911	20,883	31,810	29,815	...	...
Local Board ...	1,40,593	1,03,923	...	...	21,483	— 3,078	714	642	1,17,535	1,05,498	861	861	...	...
Municipal ...	18,121	14,015	...	...	3,482	— 50	...	...	14,639	14,065	...	...	...	...
Aided	1,33,203	22,078	...	...	63,393	7,144	3,168	1,413	57,594	11,775	9,048	1,746	...	...
Unaided	87,272	27,339	18,726	224	49,540	12,397	5,303	5,303	11,386	7,098	2,317	2,317	...	...
Private	8,779	2,431	...	...	3,826	911	...	...	4,953	1,520	...	...	...	...
District Total ...	5,22,613	2,68,422	71,929	33,806	1,58,181	19,553	21,449	19,485	2,27,018	1,60,839	44,036	34,739	...	...
Receipts (taken in abatement of charges in working out net expenditure) from—														
Provincial Funds.	...	54,775	...	...	...	13,825	...	653	...	33,500	...	6,797	...	...
Local Funds ...	...	2,099	...	...	...	...	...	...	...	26	...	2,073	...	...
Municipal Funds.	...	110	...	...	...	...	...	...	...	...	...	110	...	...
School fees ...	...	1,74,292	...	29,396	...	1,18,567	...	402	...	25,907	...	20	...	...
Subscriptions ...	...	8,946	...	...	...	3,799	...	909	...	4,032	...	206	...	...
Endowments ...	...	13,106	...	8,000	...	2,392	...	...	...	2,714	...	...	...	...
Other sources ...	...	863	...	727	...	45	...	...	...	...	...	91	...	...

XXVIII.—Hospitals and dispensaries in 1912.

Name of hospital or dispensary.	Whether Government Local Fund, Municipal or private.	In-patients.						Out-patients.				Tatal number of patients treated both in-door and out-door.	Total expenditure during the year.
		Number of beds available for		Daily average number treated.				Average daily attendance.					
		Men.	Women.	Men.	Women.	Children.	Total.	Men.	Women.	Children.	Total.		
(1)	(2)	(3)	(4)	(5)	(6)	(7)	(8)	(9)	(10)	(11)	(12)	(13)	(14)
													RS.
Addatigala	Local Fund.	...	...	...	...	...	...	13.18	3.97	3.93	21.08	3,826	1,562
Amalapuram	Do.	4	4	2.11	0.65	0.04	2.80	54.14	20.25	19.85	94.24	18,608	3,205
Bendamurlanka	Do.	...	...	...	...	...	...	32.77	9.97	8.73	51.47	9,529	1,540
Bhadrachalam	State Public.	10	6	3.14	0.34	...	3.48	44.12	19.93	16.73	80.78	11,376	3,570
Biccavole	Local Fund.	...	...	...	...	...	...	29.77	10.34	10.38	50.49	9,091	1,461
Chodavaram	Do.	...	...	...	...	...	...	12.16	3.15	2.53	17.84	3,407	1,201
Cocanada	Municipal.	40	14	30.43	12.45	0.97	43.85	85.62	30.78	22.43	138.83	23,521	8,336
Cocanada (Women and Children's Dispensary).	Local Fund.	...	8	...	5.62	0.54	6.16	...	72.28	34.04	106.32	11,911	3,582
Cocanada Branch	Municipal.	...	...	...	...	...	...	96.13	33.26	34.85	164.24	27,860	3,277
Coringa	Local Fund.	...	...	...	...	...	...	31.66	9.89	8.64	50.19	7,711	1,499
Coonavaram	State Public.	...	...	...	...	...	...	18.31	4.50	5.49	28.30	4,835	1,405
Dowlaishwaram	Local Fund.	...	...	...	...	...	...	42.43	17.93	23.33	83.69	14,967	1,582
Gokavaram	Do.	...	...	...	...	...	...	22.68	6.85	6.50	36.03	6,588	1,136
Kothapeta	Do.	...	...	...	...	...	...	33.06	7.44	5.27	45.77	12,747	1,808
Mandapeta	Do.	...	...	...	...	...	...	47.19	28.94	20.25	96.38	16,080	1,387
Mummidivaram	Do.	...	...	...	...	...	...	20.85	10.51	13.63	44.99	7,220	1,790
Peddapuram	Do.	4	4	3.22	0.75	0.02	3.99	49.00	19.63	16.51	85.14	15,440	2,498
Pithapuram	Do.	4	4	3.25	1.45	0.02	4.72	52.74	25.91	19.60	98.25	15,497	2,643

Polavaram	Do	...	...	...	...	...	...	39·40	8·40	10·40	58·20	10,222	1,899
Prattipadu	Do.	...	...	...	...	...	...	17·49	5·67	6·38	29·54	5,120	1,428
Rajahmundry	Municipal.	20	20	17·23	5 68	1·31	24·22	124·64	43·28	45·00	212 92	35,044	6,355
Rajahmundry Branch ...	Do. ...	...	...	...	...	...	...	50·96	21·68	22·52	95·16	11,140	1,055
Ramachandrapuram	Local Fund.	4	3	2·59	1·28	0·34	4·21	49·51	19·07	13·41	81·99	14,112	3,564
Razole	Do.	...	...	...	...	..	...	22·41	4·02	6·26	32·69	7,823	1,305
Tuni	Do.	3	2	2 09	0·85	...	2·94	49·84	18·60	21·37	89·81	16,993	2,200
Venkatapuram	State Public.	..	...	...	...	...	...	16·04	3·63	4·44	21·11	4 526	1,743
Yeleswaram	Local Fund.	...	...	...	...	..	...	15·95	14·95	15·01	45·91	8,517	1,309
District Total ...		89	65	64·06	29·07	3·24	96·37	1,072·05	474·83	417·48	1,964·36	333,711	64,340

XXIX.—Vaccination.

Taluks and Municipalities.	Number of persons successfully vaccinated.			Registered birth-rate per 1,000 of population.			Average number of successful cases of vaccination on children under one year during the three years ending 1912-13.
	1910-11.	1911-12.	1912-13.	1910.	1911.	1912.	
(1)	(2)	(3)	(4)	(5)	(6)	(7)	(8)
Rajahmundry Division.							
Rajahmundry	3,271	3,564	3,149	28	32	33	823
Amalapur	6,408	6,374	8,681	38	28	33	1,310
Razole	4,279	6,688	5,635	33	27	35	1,305
Bhadrachalam (Agency) Division.							
Bhadrachalam ...	1,459	1,730	1,658	32	31	38	469
Nugur	1,363	1,077	473	28	26	39	181
Polavaram (Agency) Division.							
Polavaram	2,424	1,889	2,276	31	29	33	809
Chodavaram ...	1,186	993	1,179	20	18	33	286
Yellavaram ...	1,484	1,356	1,303	21	18	25	359
Peddapuram Division.							
Peddapuram ...	5,808	6,580	7,321	35	26	30	3,844
Ramachandrapuram.	5,237	7,127	7,764	37	34	34	3,080
Cocanada Division.							
Cocanada	4,297	4,992	5,017	23	22	18	1,751
Pittapuram ...	2,256	2,675	3,054	30	28	25	973
Tuni	1,585	1,998	2,200	38	35	39	712
Municipalities.							
Cocanada	3,668	3,202	2,978	41	36	34	1,238
Rajahmundry ...	2,462	2,397	2,810	37	30	28	1,278
Total for the district.	47,187	52,642	55,498	33	29	31	18,418

XXX.—Civil Justice.

(Average of the Statistics for the years 1903–12.)

Class of Court.	Number of all original suits disposed of.	Average value of suits of which value was estimable in money.	Number of appealable decrees passed in disposed of cases.	Appeals preferred.	Appeals decided.	Decisions confirmed.	Percentage of decisions confirmed to total disposals.
(1)	(2)	(3)	(4)	(5)	(6)	(7)	(8)
Plains.							
Village Courts	15,027	11	...	1	1	1	100
Revenue Courts	376	105	243	32	29	14	48
District Munsifs' Courts ...	3,315	331	2,308	349	301	171	57
Subordinate Judges' Courts.*	71	10,285	47	9	6	3	50
District Judge's Court* ...	38	10,739	25	...	...	...	...
Agency.							
Village Courts	...	..	...	...	.	...	...
Revenue Courts	13	52	6	3	3	2	67
District Munsifs' Court ..	361	43	186	12	12	5	41
Assistant Agent's Court † ...	40	442	22	4	4	2	50
Government Agent's Court.	1	10,500	1	...	..	...	...

* Information regarding appeals preferred to High Court is not included in these figures as it is not available in the Local Courts.

Note.—As the territorial jurisdiction of the District Court and the Subordinate Courts has been revised at the time of the trifurcation of the Godavari and Kistna districts in 1905, the statistics from 1906 only have been given.

† The Assistant Agents' Court, Bhadrachalam, came into existence in 1905 and the Agency Munsif's Court, Nugur, in 1908.

XXXI.—Criminal Justice.

(Number of persons convicted of certain offences in each of the ten years 1903–12.)

Offence.	1903	1904	1905	1906	1907	1908	1909	1910	1911	1912
(1)	(2)	(3	(4)	(5)	(6)	(7)	(8)	(9)	(10)	(11)
Murder	1	...	2	1	1	1	...	1	...	1
Culpable homicide	..	.	...	...	1		1	2	1	1
Hurts and assaults	260	337	212	313	205	374	305	450	516	491
Other offences against the person	48	71	43	39	52	71	112	120	92	76
Dacoity		...	...	...	...	...	2	...	...	1
Robbery	4	7	10	5	2	4	8	7	7	6
House-breaking	47	52	62	66	33	56	29	35	20	17
Cattle theft	27	27	32	34	24	45	36	70	58	50
Other theft	311	380	384	365	304	388	393	393	429	425
Other offences against property	108	133	80	70	141	146	116	147	189	243
Offences against public tranquillity (Chapter VIII)	157	43	83	111	80	140	122	71	86	102
Other offences against the Penal Code	261	272	462	463	359	358	316	566	561	726
Total ..	1,224	1,322	1,100	1,472	1,202	1,583	1,440	1,862	1,959	2,139
Security for keeping the peace and for good behaviour	15	16	21	38	23	53	79	77	32	34
Offences under the Madras Salt Act (IV of 1889)	75	58	13	24	10	3	8	7	17	14
Offences under the Madras Abkari Act (I of 1886)	286	451	378	630	861	508	753	703	815	134
Offences under the Madras Forest Act (V of 1882)	312	208	279	280	88	189	119	127	103	193
Offences under the Madras District Municipalities Act (IV of 1884).	659	679	1,033	1,197	1,085	1,306	763	951	719	883
Other offences against special and local laws	2,183	1,716	829	1,324	2,058	2,384	2,905	3,274	3,095	3,202
Grand Total ...	4,754	4,450	3,953	[illegible]	5,327	6,026	6,067	7,004	6,710	6,899

XXXII.—Work of Criminal Courts.

(Average of the statistics for the ten years 1903–12.)

Class of Courts. (1)	Number of original cases instituted. (2)	Number of appeals received. (3)
Village Magistrates	676	...
Bench do.	4,132	...
Special do. *	136	...
Stipendiary Sub-Magistrates	7,984·6	..
Deputy, Assistant and Joint Magistrates ...	378·6	335
District Magistrate	6	21
Court of Sessions (Plains) †	47	62
Do. (Agency)	4	4

* The Special Magistrates' Courts at Draksharam and Samalkota were opened in 1907 and 1909, respectively.

† The territorial jurisdiction of the Sessions Judge was curtailed in 1905 by the transfer of Tanuku, Ellore, Bheemavaram and Kovvur Taluks and a portion of Narasapur Taluk to the Kistna District.

N.B.—Sub-Magistrates' offices were newly opened at Mummidivaram and Biccavole in 1910 and Kottapeta Division was transferred to Razole Taluk from Amalapur in 1910. Divisional Magistrates' Courts at Peddapuram and Bhadrachalam were opened in 1904 and 1905 respectively. Nugur Taluk was included in the Bhadrachalam Division in 1909. The jurisdiction of the District Magistrate was curtailed by the transfer of Tanuku, Ellore, Narasapur, Bhimavaram and Yernagudem Taluks to the Kistna District in 1904 and enlarged by the addition of Nugur Taluk in 1909. The whole of Kovvur, Bhimavaram, Ellore and Tanuku were transferred to Kistna and part of Narasapur, Nagram Island being left here.

XXXIII.—Police and Jails in 1912.

Taluks.	Number of Police.		Police Force.					Revenue Talaiyaris.	Number of known depredators	Number of Subjails.	Total accommodation in them.
	Stations.	Outposts.	Inspectors.	Sub-Inspectors.	Head Constables.	Constables.	Police Talaiyaris.				
(1)	(2)	(3)	(4)	(5)	(6)	(7)	(8)	(9)	(10)	(11)	(12)
RAJAHMUNDRY DIVISION.											
Rajahmundry ...	3	3	1	6	17	126	118	129	58	1	30
Amalapuram ...	2	...	1	4	6	55	188	259	30	1	22
Razole ...	2	1	..	4	7	60	186	256	58	2	18
BHADRACHALAM DIVISION.											
Bhadrāchalam ...	4	...	1	4	9	78	83	...	4	1	12
Nugur ...	3	...	1	3	7	33	50	...	6	1	3
POLAVARAM DIVISION.											
Polavaram ...	4	1	1	4	12	55	95	23	11	1	12
Chodavaram ...	2	...	1	2	7	63	31	2	...	..	...
Yellavaram ...	1	...	..	1	2	34	21	19	2	...	
PEDDAPURAM DIVISION.											
Peddapuram ...	3	1	1	3	8	74	211	131	38	2	28
Ramachandra-puram.	3	2	1	6	11	86	199	370	59	3	44
COCANADA DIVISION.											
Cocanada ...	5		*2	6	24	160	179	194	92	1	30
Pithāpuram ...	1	...	1	2	3	29	83	..	23	1	12
Tuni ...	2	..	...	2	4	38	84	.	9	1	16
Total ...	35	8	†16	58	129	1,156	1,528	1,383	390	15	227

* Includes one Sergeant.

† The totals include the reserve force of one Inspector, three Sergeants, eight Sub-Inspectors, 12 head constables and 265 constables the prosecuting staff of one Inspector and one Sub-Inspector and two Sub-Inspectors appointed as readers to Superintendent and Assistant Superintendent of Police.

SUPPLEMENT TO THE "A" VOLUME OF THE DISTRICT GAZETTEER, GODAVARI.

Chapter I, "Physical Description," page 1, *paragraph* 2.—*Add* the following note:—

"The territorial limits of the district have been recently revised by the "transfer to it of the Nugur taluk from the Central Provinces. A readjustment "of the areas of the old taluks of Amalapuram and Nagaram has also been "made, resulting in the formation of the Razole taluk in place of the Nagaram "taluk. As at present constituted, the district consists of eight taluks and "five Deputy Tahsildars' divisions."

Chapter IV, "Agriculture and Irrigation," page 91, *end.*—*Add* the following as a fresh paragraph :—

"A Deputy Director of Agriculture is located at Rajah-"mundry to give advice to the ryots in agricultural matters "free of charge. There are Veterinary Hospitals in charge of "Veterinary assistants at Rajahmundry, Cocanada and Pitta-"puram and a fourth will shortly be started at Amalapuram. "There are also three touring Veterinary assistants in the district "who visit the several taluks and villages. A Government "breeding bull is supplied to the Rajahmundry taluk."

Chapter V, "Forests," page 96.—After line 6 *insert* the following as a fresh paragraph :—

"The scheme for the reservation of Rampa forests has "been finally sanctioned in G.O. No. 140, Revenue, Forests, "No. 7, dated 15th January 1914. An area of about 300 square "miles of "inaccessible" forest which is at present subject neither "to exploitation nor to "podu" will be surveyed and demarcated "and all felling and "podu" in that area will be prohibited. In "the remaining area of "accessible" forest in which podu is not "to be interfered with, fellings will be restricted and brought "under control by localising them every year, by raising the "seigniorage rates on timber by 50 per cent. by employing "a special land revenue establishment to mark the trees selected "for felling, and by paying the Muttadars concerned two "annas for each tree felled as a reward for preventing the "felling of unmarked trees."

Chapter VI, "Occupations and Trade," page 103, *first paragraph.*—*Add* the following note to this paragraph :—

"There are two cotton presses in Rajahmundry where cotton is ginned "and the lint is exported to England."

Page 105.—*Add* the following paragraphs at the end of the page under the head " Metal work."

" Consequent on the location of a D.P.W. Workshop at " Dowlaishwaram, many of the local people are receiving training " in improved methods of iron work; and as a result, iron safes " are being made in Dowlaishwaram and Rajahmundry.

" The manufacture of aluminium vessels has become one " of the flourishing industries of the district. Aluminium sheets " are imported from England and vessels are made out of " these. Rajahmundry is the place where this industry is carried " on on a fairly large scale and the vessels prepared there are, " besides being sold throughout the district, exported to the " neighbouring districts and also to the Nizam's dominions. " The people finding these vessels much cheaper than those of " other kinds of metal, are using them to a great extent. Small " waste pieces of this metal are melted and converted into bars " and ornaments for the legs are made out of them. As these " ornaments look more or less like silver ones, they are largely " worn by women of the poorer classes."

Page 112.—*Insert* the following note at the end of paragraph 1:—

" The workers have since increased, their number being about 700 now. " The weekly output of lace is valued at between two and three thousand " rupees."

Page 114.—*Substitute* the following *for* lines 1 to 17 on this page:—

" being 3,966 yards on the north and 4,400 yards on the " south side. Of this extent 2,700 yards of revetment and 87 " yards of groin on the north and 2,500 and 260 yards of " revetment and groin respectively on the south, had been " erected as early as 1855, and the groins were extended con- " siderably in 1887 and very largely in 1893. The north groin " was further extended by 600 yards since 1905. To remove " the difficulty experienced from the mud creek mentioned " above, the main channel was diverted into the former, thereby " forming an entirely new channel which was designated the " 'Hammick channel.' This was opened by Sir Murray Hammick, " the then Governor of Madras, in August 1912. A portion of " the south groin was demolished, and the stone thereof utilised " for the bund, put across the old channel connecting the old " north and south groins. The latest extension of the old north " groin thus became the south groin and a new north groin 500 " yards long, was erected from the eastern extremity of the " Hammick channel. Further extension of both the groins into " seven feet of water is now under consideration. But in view " of the heavy outlay involved in the scheme and of the present

" financial condition of the Cocanada Landing and Shipping " Fund, it is more than doubtful whether the scheme can be " carried into effect in the near future. Since the new channel " was brought into existence, communication between the shore " and the shifting in the anchorage has been far more satisfac- " tory than it had been for some years past, loaded boats " proceeding out of the new channel at all times of tides, except " in the months of March and April when the tides are very " low."

Chapter VII, " Means of communication," pages 127 *and* 128—*Water carriage—the rivers—last paragraph of page* 127.—*For* the fourth sentence *substitute* the following :—

" One of the two steam ferry boats working in the " Gōdāvari at Rajahmundry having gone out of order, the right " of plying the two steamers was leased out by the District " Board in 1909 to contractors for a period of 15 years on " condition of having the necessary repairs executed at their " own cost. The lessees accordingly got the necessary repairs " done at considerable expense and both the steamers are " now in good working condition. The crew are paid by the " lessees."

And *substitute* the words "these steamers" *for* the word "they" occurring in the third line at page 128 of the "A" Volume.

Chapter IX, " Public Health."—*Add* the following note to supplement information in regard to the medical institutions in the district :—

" The Lady Havelock Hospital for women and children at Cocanada has " now a maternity ward called 'Sri Raja Ravu Mangayyamma Rao Bahadur " Memorial Lying in wards' attached to it. It is well-equipped and accommo- " dates six patients. The Raja of Pittapuram has generously defrayed the cost " of its construction."

Chapter XI, " Land Revenue Administration," page 180, *line* 13.—*Add* the following paragraph :—

" In 1908, the village establishments in Government " villages were again revised. Madras Act II of 1894 has been " extended to all the proprietary and whole inam villages in the " district."

Chapter XIII, " Administration of Justice," page 191.—*Insert* the following note to supplement the information relating to Registration in the "A" Volume :—

" The District Registrar's jurisdiction has, since 1st January 1913, been " extended to the Revenue district of Vizagapatam. He is assisted by a Joint " Registrar attached to his office. He is stationed at Cocanada. The Sub- " Registrars' offices at Cocanada and Coringa have been abolished and a new " Sub-Registrar's office opened at Samalkota. The District Registrar and all " the Sub-Re istrars are also Registrars of births and deaths under Act VI of

"1886. The District Registrar and the Sub-Registrars at Amalapuram, Rajah-
"mundry and Ramachandrapuram are *notaries public*. The Sub-Registrars of
"Draksharamam and Samalkota are Special Magistrates.

"The Registration Act was extended to the Nugur taluk in 1909 and the
"Taluk Head Clerk is the ex-officio Sub-Registrar."

Page 193.—*Insert* the following after paragraph 1 :—

"*Crime.*—"Polavaram taluk is no longer the chief place "for dacoities.

"*Yanadis or Nakkalas.*—The registration as criminal "gangs of these people was discontinued in 1910. There are "at present 236 male Nakkalas known to the police and they are "scattered over the Rajahmundry, Peddapuram, Ramachandra-"puram, Cocanada and Pittapuram taluks and are formed into "19 gangs. Four of these gangs residing at Ramachandra-"puram, Peddapuram, Alamur and Mamidikuduru, who were "found to have been habitually addicted to crime have been "ordered by Government to be registered as criminal tribes "under section 3 of the Criminal Tribes Act III of 1911. The "question of restricting their movements to a settlement is under "consideration."

Page 194.—*Insert* the following at the end of line 3 on this page :—

"*Other Criminal classes.*—Of the criminal classes mentioned "in this paragraph, only Pachappas and Yerukulas were regis-"tered as C.I.D gangs in 1910. There were 130 registered "members with 119 females and 171 children. These two "gangs were registered as criminal tribes under the Act and "sent to the settlement at Kalichedu (Nellore district) and "Seethanagaram (Guntur district)."

Police—The existing force.—*Substitute* the following *for* the existing paragraph :—

"The existing police force is in charge of a District Super-"intendent of Police stationed at Rajahmundry, aided by two "Assistant Superintendents one at Cocanada and the other at "Bhadrachalam. The head-quarters of the District Superintend-"ent of Police will be removed to Cocanada as soon as the "required buildings are constructed there. The three taluks, "viz., Nugur, Albaka and Cherla of the Central Provinces were "transferred to this district in 1909 and were formed into a "Circle in charge of an Inspector.

"The reorganisation of the police force recommended by the "Police Commission of 1905 has been introduced in the district. "According to this scheme, the old divisions were formed into "circles. All the police stations are in charge of English-"knowing Sub-Inspectors. The force has also been consider-"ably increased. There are at present 35 police stations and "8 out-posts. A separate patrol police consisting of one Sub-"Inspector (European), one head constable and two constables "was sanctioned in 1911 to prevent the pilfering of cargo "between ship and shore at the port of Cocanada.

"Two armed reserves are maintained, one at Rajahmundry "and the other at Rampa-chodavaram. The strength of the "former is one Inspector, three sergeants, 11 head constables "and 129 constables. A portion of this will be retained at "Rajahmundry with a sergeant in charge when the head-quarters "is removed to Cocanada. The strength of the Rampa reserve "is 5 head constables and 54 constables. This reserve is in "charge of a circle Inspector and performs the ordinary duties "of the station.

"An emergency force of 5 head constables and 60 constables "is kept at Rajahmundry and another force of 2 head constables "and 24 constables at Rampa-Chodavaram."

Chapter XIV, Local Self-Government, page 198, *last paragraph.—Insert* the following with reference to this paragraph :—

"It is under contemplation to introduce a proper supply by "the construction of water-works and investigation to this end is "now going on. It is also under contemplation to improve the "drainage system."

Page 199, *last paragraph.—Add* the following :—

"The bund has since been constructed."

Chapter XV.—" Gazetteer " " Nugur taluk."

This taluk is a long narrow strip of land lying on the left bank of the Gōdāvari river from the end of the Bhadrachalam taluk for a distance of about 66 miles; it nowhere exceeds 16 miles in width. On one side the deep water channel of the Gōdāvari forms its boundary with H.H. the Nizam's territory, on the east and north it marches with Bastar state and its south, and abuts for a distance of 6 miles on Bhadrachalam taluk. It comprises a narrow belt of alluvial land along the river and range of hills ending in a scarp near the Taliperu and marking with its highest points the boundary with Bastar. This range is in fact a plateau with precipitous slopes on the western side, down which in the wet weather fall several beautiful cascades; on the eastern side the land falls away gradually to the Bastar territory.

The only river of importance besides the Gōdāvari is the Taliperu, a broad stream running down, from Bastar and intersecting the taluk, but there are many 'vagus'—hill streams—which, having a short precipitous course to run from the hills to the river, have cut out through the alluvial land deep channels which form a serious impediment to travelling by road.

The cultivation is almost entirely confined to the fertile land along the river margin. There are however a few isolated patches in enclosures in the forests which occupy the greater part of the taluk. Even on the river bank the cultivation is not continuous but is interrupted by forest extending to the water edge. The cultivation is in the main identical with that of Bhadrachalam taluk, the only notable difference being that the 'Podu' cultivation countenanced in Bhadrachalam is strictly prohibited in Nugur. Cholam is the staple crop but there is also a fair amount of paddy, while the cultivation of tobacco in the rich lankas is rapidly extending mainly through the efforts of the ryots from the lower district.

There are no indigenous industries. Older accounts of the taluk make mention of silk culture but there is now no trace of this, although it is still carried on to some extent on H.H. the Nizam's side of the river.

A considerable amount of fish is taken from the Gōdāvari and its affluents, chiefly the Taliperu, but the manner of their capture cannot be commended. The main kinds taken—labco, mahseer, carnatic and other carp are caught by driving them into a bay with a large net, and then either catching them with a circular cast net or hitting them on the head with sticks. At other places traps of sticks and bamboos are erected while a common trick is, where a suitable place can be found, to enclose the river with small bunds and then poison all the fish with a certain bark. Such methods are extremely destructive particularly as fish of all sizes are taken but the small fry are never of course put back.

The revenue administration is similar in almost all respects to that of Bhadrachalam, although the taluk is still governed by the rules and regulations developed in the Central Provinces, involving the use of terms largely foreign to Nugur. The Koyas of the hills are however more restricted than their brethren of Bhadrachalam. Their "podu" cultivation has long been prohibited and they are not, as their relatives of Bhadrachalam are, allowed to distil as much arrack as they can drink. They must obtain it at the recognised arrack shops. The taluk is divided into two Revenue Inspectors' firkas; there are five patwaris' ranges and a patel and kotwal to each village.

There is at present one superior proprietor of Yelama family over the whole taluk. He resides at Naspur in H.H. the Nizam's territory near Sironcha, and never sets foot in Nugur, for there is a family tradition that he will die, if he crosses a stream a few miles to the north of Venkatapuram. His father and grandfather are both reputed to have perished there.

At about the end of the seventeenth century, the ancestors of the present zamindar obtained possession of the estates which through various vicissitudes have been retained by the family. The major portion of the property is on the Hyderabad side but in the territory handed over to the British, they held the

Surdeshmooks of Sironcha, Nugur, Albaka and Cherla and are now recognised as the superior proprietors of these lands. The estates are in the hands of a Naib under whom in Nugur taluk are three Kamdars, petty ill-paid officials of considerable affluence.

At the time of the settlement by Captain Glasfurd, the local managing agents in Nugur, Albaka and Cherla were recognised as inferior proprietors. They were in effect minor independent chiefs whose main occupation appears to have consisted in raiding the surrounding country, so that in the case of Cherla and Albaka they became the curse of all their neighbours. The family of the Cherla Rajas however died out and no trace remains of them but an evil memory and a few earthen mounds pointed out as the remnant of their fort at Cherla. The superior proprietor bought in the rights of the Albaka Dhorwa and now only the Nugur inferior proprietor remains. This family also was in danger of expiring but the heiress married a Kshatriya from the plains and the disaster was averted. The present inferior proprietor manages the estate in a careful business-like manner and has shown commendable public spirit in the development of Venkatapuram, the head-quarters of the taluk and of his estate.

Venkatapuram.—Situated close to the Gōdāvari is now the taluk head-quarters. The taluk office is in course of construction together with a hospital, a rest-house, a police station and quarters for officers, clerks, constables and peons. The village is being carefully laid out, particularly the new suburb Elwinpeta. A weekly market has been instituted and the village is in a prosperous condition. There is also a Sub-Registrar's office, the head clerk of the taluk being the ex-officio Sub-Registrar.

Cherla.—Once the head-quarters of the inferior proprietor, includes a police station and a post office. Here is also a decayed Saivite temple, the only temple in the taluk, but it is hoped that the institution of a weekly shandy at Glassonpet, a mile from the main village, will restore a little of the faded lustre of this ancient village.